Ashe County: A History

A New Edition

CONTRIBUTIONS TO SOUTHERN APPALACHIAN STUDIES

1. *Memoirs of Grassy Creek: Growing Up in the Mountains on the Virginia–North Carolina Line.* Zetta Barker Hamby. 1998

2. *The Pond Mountain Chronicle: Self-Portrait of a Southern Appalachian Community.* Edited by Leland R. Cooper and Mary Lee Cooper. 1998

3. *Traditional Musicians of the Central Blue Ridge: Old Time, Early Country, Folk and Bluegrass Label Recording Artists, with Discographies.* Marty McGee. 2000

4. *W.R. Trivett, Appalachian Pictureman: Photographs of a Bygone Time.* Ralph E. Lentz II. 2001

5. *The People of the New River: Oral Histories from the Ashe, Alleghany and Watauga Counties of North Carolina.* Edited by Leland R. Cooper and Mary Lee Cooper. 2001

6. *John Fox, Jr., Appalachian Author.* Bill York. 2003

7. *The Thistle and the Brier: Historical Links and Cultural Parallels Between Scotland and Appalachia.* Richard Blaustein. 2003

8. *Tales from Sacred Wind: Coming of Age in Appalachia. The Cratis Williams Chronicles.* Cratis D. Williams. Edited by David Cratis Williams and Patricia D. Beaver. 2003

9. *Willard Gayheart, Appalachian Artist.* Willard Gayheart and Donia S. Eley. 2003

10. *The Forest City Lynching of 1900: Populism, Racism, and White Supremacy in Rutherford County, North Carolina.* J. Timothy Cole. 2003

11. *The Brevard Rosenwald School: Black Education and Community Building in a Southern Appalachian Town, 1920–1966.* Betty J. Reed. 2004

12. *The Bristol Sessions: Writings About the Big Bang of Country Music.* Edited by Charles K. Wolfe and Ted Olson. 2005

13. *Community and Change in the North Carolina Mountains: Oral Histories and Profiles of People from Western Watauga County.* Compiled by Nannie Greene and Catherine Stokes Sheppard. 2006

14. *Ashe County: A History; A New Edition.* Arthur Lloyd Fletcher. 2009 [2006]

15. *The New River Controversy; A New Edition.* Thomas J. Schoenbaum. Epilogue by R. Seth Woodard. 2007

16. *The Blue Ridge Parkway by Foot: A Park Ranger's Memoir.* Tim Pegram. 2007

17. *James Still: Critical Essays on the Dean of Appalachian Literature.* Edited by Ted Olson and Kathy H. Olson. 2008

18. *Owsley County, Kentucky, and the Perpetuation of Poverty.* John R. Burch, Jr. 2008

19. *Asheville: A History.* Nan K. Chase. 2007

20. *Southern Appalachian Poetry: An Anthology of Works by 37 Poets.* Edited by Marita Garin. 2008

21. *Ball, Bat and Bitumen: A History of Coalfield Baseball in the Appalachian South.* L.M. Sutter. 2009

22. *The Frontier Nursing Service: America's First Rural Nurse-Midwife Service and School.* Marie Bartlett. 2009

23. *James Still in Interviews, Oral Histories and Memoirs.* Edited by Ted Olson. 2009

24. *The Millstone Quarries of Powell County, Kentucky.* Charles D. Hockensmith. 2009

25. *The Bibliography of Appalachia: More Than 4,700 Books, Articles, Monographs and Dissertations, Topically Arranged and Indexed.* Compiled by John R. Burch, Jr. 2009

26. *Appalachian Children's Literature: An Annotated Bibliography* Compiled by Roberta T. Herrin and Sheila Quinn Oliver. 2009

Ashe County: A History

A New Edition

ARTHUR LLOYD FLETCHER

CONTRIBUTIONS TO SOUTHERN APPALACHIAN STUDIES, 14

McFarland & Company, Inc., Publishers
Jefferson, North Carolina, and London

The present work is a reprint of the library bound edition of Ashe County: A History, *published in 2006 by McFarland. (The first edition was published in 1963 by the Ashe County Research Association.)*

LIBRARY OF CONGRESS CATALOGUING-IN-PUBLICATION DATA

Fletcher, Arthur Lloyd, b. 1881.
Ashe County : a history / Arthur Lloyd Fletcher.— New ed.
p. cm. — (Contributions to southern Appalachian studies ; 14)
Includes index.

ISBN 978-0-7864-4329-1
softcover : 50# and 70# alkaline paper ∞

1. Ashe County (N.C.)— History. I. Title.
F262.A7F5 2009
975.6'835— dc22 2006029045

British Library cataloguing data are available

On the cover: Background— Jefferson, county seat of Ashe (*Skyland Post* photograph); Sheriff's deputies Walter Phillips (left), Wiley Burgess and Bob Watson with a confiscated whiskey still; Graybeal's Drug Store; original Ashe County cheese plant; inset at top ©2009 Shutterstock.

Manufactured in the United States of America

McFarland & Company, Inc., Publishers
Box 611, Jefferson, North Carolina 28640
www.mcfarlandpub.com

Preface to the New Edition

All of us who have an interest in Ashe County history are indebted to Arthur Fletcher, and to members of the Ashe County Research Association — the sponsor when this book was created. Much has changed for the county since the book was published more than forty years ago, yet much endures. Copies of the book are prized for the wealth of information about people and events which are of interest to us today.

In this re-publication, we have assembled an expanded index of the main text as well as names of those veterans of military service who were listed in Appendices 1, 2 and 3, along with the Appendix 4 names of grantors and grantees for land conveyances from 1778 through 1794. Our team members for this project were Gene Hafer, Don Long and Carol Williams, who diligently reviewed, entered and checked the thousands of additional names added to the index. It will be easier now to use this book to research for names of the people who have been a part of this unique and treasured place.

We are grateful to McFarland & Company, Inc. for undertaking to provide this improved resource for students of our history.

Ashe County Historical Society
September, 2006

Contents

List of Illustrations

(All illustrations appear between pages 32 and 33)

Preface to the Original Edition (1963)

The writing of this book has not been an easy task. The men and women now comprising the Ashe County Research Association, Inc., first started the movement for writing a history of Ashe in 1953 and organized the Ashe County Historical Society in that year. It flourished for a time and then disappeared. The matter, however, was not forgotten and out of it came the organization, backed by some of Ashe County's leading men and women, at home and abroad. Their names appear elsewhere in the book.

Seeking a person who would undertake the research and writing involved, they remembered that the writer had been active in the 1953 venture, had long been interested in the matter, and might be willing to undertake it. Rightly or wrongly, the writer agreed to try to do the job, without pay, and the Association placed the project in his hands without restrictions. He was elected historian and was directed to do it in his own way and with no time limit.

As one of his first steps the writer sought help from Wade E. Eller, honor graduate of Trinity College (now Duke University), a leading educator in Ashe and an outstanding civic leader. He had been one of the leaders in forming the first Ashe County Historical Society. For thirty years or more he had made a careful study of Ashe County genealogies. It had been an absorbing hobby to which he had given much time, and in steel files at his home near Warrensville he had a card index of 50,000 or more Ashe County citizens who had come and gone. In addition, he had much valuable source material about Ashe county history.

It was my idea that to save on expenses, I should confine my part of the history to official records in the North Carolina Department of Archives and History, at Raleigh; the records in the Library of the University of North Carolina, Chapel Hill; Duke University Library, Durham; the Library of North Carolina State College, Raleigh; the North Carolina State Library, Raleigh; and the records of the State Departments of Public Instruction, Public Welfare, Health, Labor, Conservation and Development, Agriculture, Employment Security Commission, State Extension Service, and other state agencies. Mr. Eller was to be in on this, attending to county records at the courthouse in Jefferson and the various county agencies, but his particular and most important contribution was to be a comprehensive study of Ashe County genealogy. He approved of this approach to the problem.

But, as it turned out, both of us were too late, or nearly so. The writer is still going, after three periods of hospitalization from heart attacks, one major surgical operation, and other ills that flesh is heir to, while Wade E. Eller, to everybody's regret, has been completely disabled and is presently in the U.S. Veterans Hospital at Johnson City, Tennessee. As a consequence, there is no genealogical study of Ashe.

Dr. Archibald Henderson in the foreword to his two-volume *History of North Carolina* inveighs against histories that he describes as "genealogical dictionaries," "skeletal studies of dry statistics," "museums of stuffed shirts," and the like.

Those who read the pages that follow will find in Chapters 5 to 19 plenty of statistics. To the writer these statistics are not dry and uninteresting. They tell stories of industry, skill, resourcefulness, and hardihood. As to stuffed shirts, an expression Dr. Henderson borrows from modern slang, the reader will find in every chapter a host of shirts and with the material available can do his own stuffing. They will turn out to be stuffed with dynamic personalities who helped to make Ashe County what it is today.

On his own, the writer decided to write a history for the general reader and not for the historian, or for the genealogist. Uncertain about the wisdom of this, he found comfort in Dr. Henderson's foreword in which he states flatly that the reader will not find a single footnote in the two big volumes of his book, and no bibliography.

In this book it will be found that source records are referred to generally in the text, but if it happens that interest about any movement, or about any one of the hundreds named, more or less casually, justifies further exploration, there is nothing to keep the reader from becoming an amateur researcher and looking things up for himself.

This book is not intended to be a textbook for use in the public schools, although Chapters 1 to 4, which deal with the historical and geographical backgrounds of the county might be useful in the schools. The writer has found few school boys and girls who knew anything about the matters covered by these chapters and, also, precious few adults.

The succeeding chapters take up one activity of the county at a time, carrying through on every chapter from the beginning to the present. They are designed to give the adult reader an understanding of how Ashe County grew from 947 square miles of wilderness, lost behind vast mountains, to what it is today.

There will be critics who will find errors of omission and commission, including alleged errors as to historical facts and myriads of smaller slips, such as misspelled names, incorrect initials, etc. These criticisms I will take regretfully because I was brought up in a hard school. Many years ago, as a young reporter, I was warned by a wise old managing editor to be careful about names. Said he: "Names make news. Get them right."

In my opinion, names make history, and I have tried earnestly to get them right. Where I have failed I respectfully refer the critics to the ancient records I have had to work with, in many cases dimmed by time, and hand-written. They were hard to read but not as bad as those records that had been photostated or microfilmed in the modern way.

Looking back over the finished work I find phrases here and there that I might change if I were writing it over but I do not find reason to apologize to anybody for anything. I did the best I could under the circumstances, which was all I promised the Association in the beginning, and I respectfully invite those who do not like it to write their own.

I wish to express appreciation for the courteous and efficient help that I received from the North Carolina Department of Archives and History; the North Carolina State Library; the Library of the University of North Carolina; the Library of Duke University; the Olivia Raney Library of Raleigh; the Library of North Carolina State College; the county officials of Ashe, and the officials of the various State Departments at Raleigh, including the Departments of Public Instruction, Agriculture, Public Welfare, Health, Labor, Conservation and Development, Mines and Mining, the State Extension Service, the Employment Security Commission, the office of the Secretary of State, and other State Agencies.

To many individuals I am indebted for help and encouragement, among them these:

Fred N. Colvard, R. G. Lassiter, Charles S. Neal, Roland H. Koontz, C. E. Gardner, William B. Austin, Mrs. Ruth Cox Hurt (and her husband, the late A. B. Hurt, for more than eighteen years county superintendent of schools), Ira Thomas Johnston, Dr. James L. Ballou, Dr. Dean C. Jones, Dr. Mary Michal, Miss Frances Tucker, Gwyn B. Price, Hugh Crigler, John H. McGuire, Larry P. Colvard, Bernard B. Graybeal, Rev. Charles R. Stafford, Urcle Sheets, Rev. Rexford Campbell, Dr. John W. Luke, Dr. R. H. Stone, Huber P. Hanes, Jr., L. Polk Denmark, Dr. Dean Colvard, and others.

Arthur L. Fletcher
Raleigh, N.C.
March 1963

ASHE COUNTY: A HISTORY

CHAPTER ONE

BISHOP SPANGENBERG DISCOVERS ASHE—EARLY SETTLERS—DANIEL BOONE, PIONEER—EARLY RECORDS

I

Bishop Spangenberg

There has been controversy about who discovered Ashe County. There can be no doubt, however, that the first comers to this area were Indians. The Cherokees, the Creeks, and the Shawnees hunted over it and waged war with one another over hunting rights and over possession of desirable portions of it, but they left little evidence of their possession. At Old Fields and a few other points in Ashe, a few artifacts have been found, including such things as stone axes, broken pieces of pottery, arrowheads and the like, but nowhere is there evidence of long occupancy by the Indians.

There is doubt about the first white men to visit Ashe County, but there is no doubt that the first to visit the area and to leave a written record of it were Bishop Augustus Gottlieb Spangenberg, head of the Moravian Church in America, and his associates, Timothy Horsefield, Joseph Mueller, Henry Antes, Johan Merck, and Herman Loesch, the last-named being the only member of the Bishop's party to become a permanent citizen of North Carolina. Bishop Spangenberg's diary, carefully preserved over the years by the Moravian Church, tells in detail of their explorations in North Carolina.

Back of the Bishop's expedition into North Carolina lies an interesting story involving the "Unitas Fratrum" (Unity of the Brethren), now known as the Moravian Church. It got this name from a small German province named Moravia, which literally was their last stand in Europe. They had been persecuted almost to extinction. By good fortune, long delayed, they found protectors in Moravia, chief among them being the famous Count Nicolaus Ludwig Zinzendorf. Convinced that the church would find no peace in Europe and its members no economic security and no religious freedom, Count Zinzendorf and the church leaders set about exploring the possibility of transporting the Moravians to America and establishing colonies of Moravians where men would be free to worship God according to the dictates of their own consciences. Their first venture was a colony at Bethlehem, Pennsylvania, which prospered. Spangenberg, who had been made a bishop in 1744, was assigned as Moravian Bishop for America and when the Moravian settlement at Bethlehem began to be crowded, he was given the task of locating suitable lands for a larger settlement.

In locating such lands, Count Zinzendorf and the elders of the church decided that their best hopes lay in lands under the British flag and they approached various landowners in England. In the Earl of Granville, a descendant of one of the original Lords Proprietors, who at one time owned all of North Carolina, they found a landowner to their liking. Of the original Lords Proprietors only Granville's ancestors had held on to their share of North Carolina originally granted by the King, and he held title to all of North Carolina from the Atlantic to the Southern Sea (Pacific Ocean), lying south of the Colony of Virginia and north of a straight line crossing the State of North Carolina at 35 degrees, 34 minutes north latitude, which is close to the southern boundary lines of Iredell, Rowan, Davidson, Randolph and Chatham Counties of today.

The Earl of Granville, eager to colonize his vast acreage and to secure colonists of the right kind, made careful investigations of the Moravians. Count Zinzendorf, Bishop Spangenberg, and other leaders of the church were able to convince the Earl of Granville that the Moravians were the kind of people he wanted; that they were deeply religious, frugal, and thrifty. Their colony could be depended upon to become swiftly self-sustaining as they had done in Pennsylvania. The Moravians, in the main, were brick and stonemasons, potters, carpenters, blacksmiths, millwrights, cobblers, tanners, tailors, gunsmiths, and farmers, with a sufficient number of trained ministers and teachers to look after the educational and spiritual needs of every community that they established.

Granville was pleased with what he heard about the Moravians and entered into an agreement to let them have 100,000 acres of land on a quitrent basis, this being an established rent of freeholders in that day by which the tenant came into full possession of the land quit and free of all other services, upon payment of an annual "quitrent," the amount of which was fixed by agreement. Under this his title was absolute and so remained as long as he, or his successors, paid the quitrent.

With this contract completed, Bishop Spangenberg was directed to go to the lands of the Earl of Granville in the province of North Carolina and choose a suitable tract of 100,000 acres for the establishment of a Moravian settlement. In those days it was a hazardous undertaking to explore the wilderness. He might have assigned the task to one of his assistants at Bethlehem but it is indicative of his sturdy character and the physical fitness evident from his portraits preserved by the Moravian Church, that he took upon himself the difficult task of finding a suitable place for his people in the wilds. To accompany him he chose five of the brethren at Bethlehem, all of them skilled in various occupations and fully capable of appraising the advantages and disadvantages of any area they visited.

On August 25, 1752, the little party left Bethlehem on horseback. On August 27 they arrived at Philadelphia and on September 4, 1752, the Bishop notes in his diary that they arrived in Virginia, "which swarmed with Negroes." On September 18, 1752, they finally made contact at Edenton with the surveyor, Francis Corbin, representing the Earl of Granville, and set out for the west.

While at Edenton Bishop Spangenberg was approached by several persons with lands to dispose of and one very attractive area in Virginia, with 100,000 acres or more in it, was offered. It had the advantage of water transportation. In fairness, he reported this to his superiors but he showed his awareness of international intrigue by placing this query at the bottom of the page describing this land:

"Do not the French lay claim to the above-mentioned land?"

Bishop Spangenberg was not impressed by the country around

Edenton. In his diary he tells of high water on the Roanoke, a flood height of twenty-eight feet, and flooded lands and farms, and vast swamp areas where mosquitoes abounded and chills and fever beset the people who tried to live there. He resolutely set his course for the west, stating that in his judgment their hope of finding suitable land lay "in Anson County." At that time there was no Wilkes or Rowan or Surry, and Anson extended from Orange to the west indefinitely and from the southern boundary of Granville's possessions to Virginia.

The trail which the Bishop and his party followed was well marked and led them through what is now Guilford County and thence southwest to its end at the Catawba River. Along this trail homes had been established and small farms laid out. Writing of the province of North Carolina as he was preparing to enter Anson County, Bishop Spangenberg said that "after having travelled 153 miles and about to enter Anson, the last county on the west, I have seen nothing of the handicrafts. Almost nobody has a trade. In 140 miles I saw not one wagon, nor any sign of one."

From the end of this trail there was nowhere to go except, as he said in his diary, "into the bush." It is related that they went up Little River from the Catawba and in what is now Alexander County they looked over various areas and made some preliminary surveys, but nowhere found 100,000 acres in one tract that they considered suitable. They spent some time surveying the area around the headwaters of the Catawba and they finally decided to cross the Brushy Mountains and strike the headwaters of the Atkin (Yadkin).

At the time this decision was made (November 29, 1752) they were in camp on the upper fork of the second, or middle Little River (now Wilson's Creek, branch of John's River) flowing into the Catawba not far from Quaker Meadows. The Bishop's diary relates that they were seventy to eighty miles from any house, had seen no wagon or other farm equipment or utensils, and had met wandering bands of Cherokees who were on hunting expeditions and were friendly. There were plenty of "Indian signs" everywhere and the country was wild. These are his words describing it:

We are in a region that has perhaps been seldom visited since the creation of the world. We are some 70 to 80 miles from the last settlement in North Carolina and have come over terrible mountains and through dangerous ways.

At this point they encountered a lone hunter who volunteered to guide them across the Brushy Mountains to the Yadkin. It developed that he did not know the way and instead of leading them across the lesser mountain range to the Yadkin, he led them in a frontal assault on the Blue Ridge at one of its most inaccessible places. They reached the top in what was to be Ashe, at Blowing Rock, or thereabouts. Under date of December 5, 1752, the Bishop wrote this in his diary:

We have reached here after a hard journey over very high, terrible mountains and cliffs. A hunter whom we had taken to show us the way and who once knew the path to the Atkin, missed the trail and led us into a place where there was no way out except by climbing an indescribably steep mountain. Part of the way we climbed on hands and knees, dragging after us the loads we had taken from the backs of the horses, for had we not unsaddled them they would have fallen backward down the mountain—indeed this did happen once; part of the way we led the horses which were trembling like a leaf. When we reached the top we saw mountains to the right, to the left, before and behind us, rising like great waves in a storm.

In another diary entry of the same date, the Bishop told of a typical Ashe County winter storm:

We put up our tent but had barely finished when there came such a windstorm that we could hardly stand against it. I think I have never felt a winter wind so strong and so cold. The ground was covered with snow; water froze by the fire. Then our men lost heart! What should we do? Our horses would die and we with them. For the hunters had about concluded that we were across the Blue Mountains and on the Mississippi water-shed.

Typical also of Ashe, the sun shone brightly on the following day and the temperature rose. They party had the good fortune to find wild hay for the horses, a hunter brought in a deer, and prospects brightened. Bearing in mind his original plan to get back on the Yadkin, Bishop Spangenberg set about following the stream that he found east of Boone, to determine if it doubled back to the south and in some way cut through what he called the "Blue Mountains" to the Atkin.

The party took note of much desirable acreage along what was found to be the South Fork of New River, but they found no tract of 100,000 acres. How much of what is now Ashe County was explored, is not certain. From his description of recognized landmarks, including White Top Mountain, which he called Meadow Mountain, because of the open land at the top of it, it is evident that the Bishop and his party covered the Old Fields area in Ashe and followed the stream down to Grassy Creek, or thereabouts. This was one of his conclusions about Ashe County land:

> The soil is suitable for raising corn, potatoes, etc. It is also admirably suited for cattle-raising, with an abundance of meadow land.

As the party went along they appraised the land through which they traveled, noting the groves of crab apples, which the Bishop thought might be useful for making vinegar; the abundant water power, which the millwright said could be utilized to operate grist mills; the frequent open fields and "balds," which the farmer said would furnish abundant hay for many cattle, sheep, and horses; the clear, sparkling streams and wonderful springs of pure, sweet water, conducive to good health.

If any Ashe County citizen doubts that Bishop Spangenberg traveled over a goodly portion of Ashe, he has only to read the Bishop's account of his travels in the area which he wrote on December 14, 1752, at his camp on the Yadkin where Lewis Fork enters the main stream. He had made up his mind to determine if they were on the Mississippi watershed and he had finally decided that they were, and that the river he was following did not flow into the Yadkin. This meant that he was in fact on land claimed by the French, who relied on treaty rights to all lands drained into the Mississippi, and he wanted no entanglement with international land disputes. His entry in his diary at his Lewis Fork camp furnishes a description of the twists and bends and turnings of New River which travelers today recognize and appreciate. He wrote:

> Here we are at last, after a difficult journey across the mountains.

We were completely lost and whichever way we turned we were walled in. Not one of our company had ever been there before and path and trail were unknown—though how can one speak of path or trail where none existed? We crossed only dry mountains and dry valleys and when for several days we followed the river [New River] in the hope that it would lead us out, we found ourselves only deeper in the wilderness, for the river ran now north, now south, now east, now west, in short to all points of the compass! Finally we decided to leave the river and take a course between east and south, crossing the mountains as best we could. One height rose behind the other and we travelled between hope and fear, distressed for our horses which had nothing to eat.

Their course "between east and south" took them across the Blue Ridge and down Lewis Fork to the Yadkin. Here ends Bishop Spangenberg's connection with the early history of Ashe County. His diary contains further reference to Ashe's scenery, natural resources, and its many springs of sweet water, which he found far superior to the water on the eastern slopes of the Blue Mountains. He had seen no more beautiful land anywhere.

Following the Yadkin down, the party surveyed two tracts in what is now Wilkes County. The first covered 5,000 acres and the second, a much larger tract, embraced the land where Wilkesboro stands. Here the Bishop learned of an available tract of 100,000 acres in the three forks of the Yadkin, near what is now Winston-Salem, and it was there that new "Wachau," named for Count Zinzendorf's estate in Germany, was established. By January 13, 1753, the survey of the tract had been completed and Bishop Spangenberg and his party started back to Bethlehem, Pa. The last entry in his diary, dated February 12, 1753, is: "Arrived at Bethlehem, well and happy."

While he apparently forgot about his explorations beyond the "Blue Mountains," he made note in his diary of certain developments in the western part of North Carolina that were noteworthy and significant.

As stated elsewhere, his diary does not disclose any liking for the general run of settlers that he encountered in the lowlands of eastern North Carolina. He found many of them to be "lazy and shiftless, others refugees from debt, deserters of wives and children, or persons who had fled to escape punishment for evil deeds."

He had no desire to establish his Moravian colony among neighbors such as he found in the east and he was delighted to find among the families that had settled along the Yadkin and had pushed on up into the foothills of the Blue Mountains, a thrifty, hardworking, religious group of people. He wrote:

> Having crossed the length and breadth of North Carolina, we have found toward the west, nearer the mountains, that many families are moving in from Virginia, Maryland, Jersey and even New England. In this year alone [1752] more than 400 families have come with horse and wagon and cattle. Among these are sturdy farmers and skilled men and we can hope they will greatly help Carolina.

II

Early Settlers and Where They Came From

While none of the people who impressed Bishop Spangenberg so much had found their way into Ashe at the time of his explorations, there was mounting evidence all along the Yadkin and up into the foothills of the Blue Ridge that the immigrants from the colonies named and from piedmont and eastern North Carolina, all seeking new lands, would eventually find their way in and this they did in increasing numbers. They came from the north and east by two main roads, or trails, following river valleys that run northeast and southwest. These were the "Great Wagon Road" through the Shenandoah Valley and on into North Carolina, and the "Upper Pennsylvania Road." These immigrants were mainly English, German, and Scotch. As will be related elsewhere, political disturbances uprooted many settlers in North Carolina and sent them into the wilderness seeking new homesteads. They came into the country west of the Blue Ridge by trails that may have been longer, though not as difficult as the one followed by Bishop Spangenberg. Others came in from the south by way of the river valleys.

No one knows who was first to establish a real home in what is now Ashe County. Wheeler's *History of North Carolina*, published in 1850, says that the first settlers came in 1755. It is doubtful that there was a permanent settler in Ashe that early. There is evidence that David Helton, William Walling, and William McLain, all of Montgomery County, Virginia, came to this area in 1770 on a hunting expedition. On the banks of Helton Creek, named for David, they built a hunter's cabin. A creek nearby running into Helton, is known to this day as Walling Creek.

These men apparently had no idea when they set out on their hunting trip, of establishing permanent residence in Ashe, but they liked the country so much they decided to return to it and build homes. This they did in 1771 and so far as the records show, theirs were the first homes in Ashe. What happened to these pioneers is not known. There is a tradition that they were tories, loyal to the British King, as were many sturdy mountaineers of that day, and they so remained until after the Revolutionary War. In the period following the war they found themselves unpopular and subject to persecution. In addition, their land titles were insecure. In the face of this situation they moved west with the tide of immigration that was flowing into Kentucky, either with Daniel Boone or following a trail which he had blazed.

III

Daniel Boone, Pioneer

There is much of legend and tradition about Daniel Boone and his connection with the mountain area that constituted the northwestern corner of North Carolina and that became Ashe County in 1799. The "Daniel Boone Trail" has been marked across what was Ashe in Daniel Boone's day but is now Watauga County, the trail entering the county at Cook's Gap, six miles east of Boone, the county seat of Watauga, appropriately named for the great explorer. There is a marker at Cook's Gap, another at Three Forks Baptist Church, and a third on the courthouse lawn in Boone. A fourth is at Hodges' Gap, west of Boone, a fifth at Straddle Gap, and a sixth at Zionville, near the Tennessee line. These markers were erected by the Daughters of the American Revolution and there is no reason to doubt that Boone traveled this trail many times.

There is reason to believe also that Boone spent considerable time in other parts of the territory that later became Ashe. He brought members of his family into the area and aided them in establishing homes on the South Fork of New River, near Obids. In Ashe County Book of Deeds No. 5, page 509, it is recorded that Jonathan Boone, brother of Daniel, sold 245 acres of land on the north side of New River to one John Hardin for $600. In Ashe County Deed Book "F," page 170, it is recorded that Jesse Boone, another close relative of Daniel, entered 100 acres of land.

Boone married into the Bryan family and members of that family joined in his explorations. Some of them settled in the area close to Obids on the New River and it is said that at one time Boone planned to establish a permanent home there. In the old cemetery at Obids there is a slender granite stone, six feet or more in length, which Boone is said to have selected as his own tombstone. He moved on and the marker was placed over the grave of one Thomas Calloway, where it may be seen today.

From available records it is certain that Boone was a man of great courage, resourcefulness, and daring. He was a skilled hunter and woodsman and a great leader of men. Withal he had simple, unswerving faith in God and he sought to bring into the new land he was helping to open up, men of his own type. In his own words he stated his creed:

> ... for my part I am as ignorant as a child all the Religion I have to love and fear God believe in Jesus Christ Do all the good to my neighbors and myself that I can and do as little harm as I can help and trust on God's mercy for the rest and I believe God never made a man of my principle to be lost.

If the men who followed him to the west, many of whom dropped out of his parties and settled along the way, believed as he did, the area acquired at least a nucleus of desirable settlers and Ashe County has reason to bless his memory and be thankful for his leadership in the dim and troubled years between 1769 and 1790.

For all of Boone's demonstrated ability as a leader of men, his skill as a fighter, and his record as one of the all-time great pioneers of America, he was as helpless as a baby when it came to dealing with the land grabbers of his day, a vicious crew who saw opportunity for quick profits under the rapidly expanding economy of the times. Boone entered into a contract with a syndicate composed of North Carolina and Virginia politicians to open up large areas in Kentucky for settlement and in their service he underwent peril and hardship for several years. He had absolute faith in them, believing that their announced plans for settling desirable families in the wilderness that was then southwest Virginia and Kentucky, were sound and honest and best for the new land and its people. He was disillusioned when he found that deeds to valuable lands given him for his services by these promoters were entirely worthless. To his dismay, he found that he was one of many who were defrauded.

Boone could have instituted suit against the land thieves in court and might have received some remuneration for the labors he had performed and the dangers and risks that he had undergone in their service, but typical of the man that he was, he shouldered his rifle and headed west again. This time he left the United States and settled in Missouri, on the banks of the Missouri River. Missouri did not become a part of the United States until 1803. He died in Missouri in 1820 at the age of 85.

IV

Early Records—Thomas McGimsey—Dr. Elisha Mitchell

While others, in steady stream, were coming into Ashe and discovering its advantages, few took time to write anything about what they found in the county. The next written record is an original letter in the files of the North Carolina Department of Archives and History, from Thomas McGimsey, himself a citizen of Ashe and at one time Clerk of Court in Ashe, written under date of May 3, 1811, to Thomas Henderson, editor of the Raleigh *Star* (Thomas Henderson papers, 1810, 1811, file 341, North Carolina Department of Archives and History). Mr. McGimsey wrote:

> That tract of country called Ashe County was first settled in the year 1755. Captain John Cox informs me that he recollects when there were but 2 or 3 hunters' cabins from the lead mines to the head of the

Watauga. It is about 120 miles long and from 5 miles to 45 miles wide. Great part of Ashe County is mountainous and hilly, yet the soil is extremely rich, yielding an abundance of wheat, rye, oats, barley and buckwheat and other vegetables equal to any cold country on earth.

This is a fine county for pasture and meadows, from which great numbers of cattle and sheep are raised, which bring much wealth to the farmer. The air is pure and the water is good, if not superior to any on earth. People live long in Ashe County.

The face of the country is clothed with large and lofty timber of black walnut, sugar tree maple, buckeye, hickory, chestnut, and spruce pine. Clover, strawberries and blue grapes are natural to grow everywhere. Cranberries also in great plenty.

As that country has always had plenty of game, the first settlers who lived there for the purpose of hunting, were much opposed by the Indians, in particular by the Shawnees and the Cherokees, until the end of the late war. Since they have made no incursions into these settlements.

The main water courses are the New River, or head of the Great Kanawha, and its auxiliary branches flowing from the Blue Ridge, Iron and Stone Mountains.

The country abounds with mines and minerals. There are at present five sites of good iron works within the County of Ashe. Great store of minerals has lately been found which is thought to contain great quantities of silver and gold.

The people of Ashe County send to market cattle, sheep, butter, cheese, lard, beeswax, venison hams, deer-skins and ginseng to the amount of upwards of thirty thousand dollars yearly.

People in this County improve more in Religion than in the study of arts and sciences but it is hoped that more pains will be taken to improve the youth in the one as well as the other.

Mr. McGimsey added the following postscript:

The lands in Ashe County sell for five dollars to five cents per acre.

The next written record of Ashe is from the pen of Dr. Elisha Mitchell, who came south from his native state, Connecticut, in 1817 to become professor of mathematics at the University of North Carolina. He became profesor of chemistry in 1825 and was picked to head a geological and agricultural survey. He made a journey into Ashe in 1827 and came back to Ashe in 1828. Like his distinguished predecessor, Bishop Spangenberg, he kept a diary. In it he wrote frankly that he found the citizens of Ashe to be lazy. He said:

> Many parts of the County are as fine as the best in New England but the old habits of depending on little cleared patches of land and hunting, persisted after the game was all gone.
>
> It is a favorite theory of mine that Ashe has greater facilities for maintaining its soil in a state of productiveness (by means of clover) than any other part of North Carolina; that all of the forests will hereafter be cut down and converted into extensive pastures on which will be fed vast herds of cattle and flocks of sheep; that it will be hereafter abundantly more populous than at present and even sought as an agreeable place of residence.

Leaving Ashe after his second journey in 1828, in the month of July, he set down this word picture of the County that had impressed him so much:

> Rode down to Jefferson. They were making hay by the wayside. The pleasant smell of hay, the sight of rows of cocks in the beautiful green meadows, such as I had been accustomed to in my childhood, the delicious coolness of the air, the shadows of the mountains and the luxuriant foliage and the blocks of chesnuts extending up their sides, made the ride delightful.

Dr. Mitchell made detailed reports of his geological findings in Ashe that will be covered under the heading "Mining," but if he came back to Ashe again there appears to be no record of it. He loved mountains and spent many happy summers exploring the mountains of Western North Carolina. He was of the opinion that Mount Mitchell, which was named for him, was the highest mountain in America east of the Rockies and it was in trying to establish this that he met his death in a fall while climbing the mountain alone on June 27, 1857.

CHAPTER TWO

WAR OF THE REGULATION–REVOLUTIONARY WAR –STATE OF FRANKLIN

I

War of the Regulation

What happened in eastern and piedmont North Carolina between 1768 and 1771 would not be important in any account of the development of Ashe County and other western North Carolina counties but for the fact that the turmoil and strife of that period gave impetus to a new tide of population movement that flowed west and found trails, or made new trails, that enabled hundreds of North Carolina families to cross the Blue Ridge and establish homes in the wilderness that later became Tennessee. No one knew it at the time, but this turmoil and strife that lasted three years and ended in the Battle of the Alamance in May, 1771, was the forerunner of the Revolutionary War. The seeds of the Revolution were sown here.

William Tryon, who took oath of office as the British Governor of North Carolina on April 3, 1765, found a bad situation confronting him. The British government, just at the point of becoming an empire, had decided in 1763 that the colonies would have to bear a substantial part of the cost of government and its Parliament had passed a law providing for a heavy stamp tax. This covered all commercial transactions, legal documents, imports and exports–in fact there was a stamp tax for almost every transaction. In all, no less than fifty-four kinds of documents and papers were included in the taxed list, running from marriage licenses to ship clearance papers. No legal document was valid without the proper stamp.

It was noted that the sheriffs, clerks of court, and other officials representing the government apparently neglected no opportunity to add to the oppressiveness of the tax levy and they increased the tax burden by the infliction of various penalties. The British government finally, in 1766, repealed the controversial stamp tax law, to the great delight of the so-called "maritime" counties, where import and export and general mercantile and business activities were concentrated. Trouble, however, continued in the so-called "border" counties. They got litttle relief and there was continual turmoil and confusion, especially in Anson, Orange, and Granville counties. Their leaders looked upon the British change of face on the issue of stamp taxes as only a temporary palliative. As a matter of fact, for them oppression still came from "courthouse rings" of the day. Since no man was strong enough to stand up against these corrupt officials alone, they quite naturally sought union, one with another.

In an organized band of men along the border, known among themselves as the Regulators, the disgruntled freemen found an organization to their liking. It had been established to deal with border ruffians. These settlers, so far removed from law enforcement officers, had been so greatly harassed by horse thieves, cattle thieves, killers, robbers, and highwaymen they found it necessary to band together for the protection of lives and property. From fighting bandits and murderers it was but a step to opposing oppression by the government and its local officers. The organization increased in numbers and from regulating border conditions, undertook the "regulating" of public officials. It had grown to such importance that Governor Tryon took notice of the Regulators in a proclamation issued on June 21, 1768, denouncing them as traitors and outlaws. He was soon thereafter to undertake to stamp out by military force the general insurrection the organization had brought about in the border counties, these being Mecklenburg, Anson, Rowan, Orange, and Granville, commonly known as the Granville District, and all of them covering greater areas than they do today.

The end of the War of the Regulation came on May 15, 1771, when Governor Tryon with his army of 1,068 well-armed militiamen from the eastern North Carolina counties met the Regulators, numbering more than 2,000 men, on the banks of the Alamance

River. The Regulators were not an army but a mob. Less than half of them had arms of any kind and they had no trained officers. The battle lasted about two hours and ended with the complete defeat of the Regulators. Six prisoners who had taken part in the insurrection were hanged. Governor Tryon, with his own pistol, killed one prisoner. One Benjamin Merrill, described as "a pious man with a large family," who had captained a militia unit in Rowan county, of which the Ashe county area was at that time a part, had this terrible sentence pronounced against him:

> That you be hanged ——; that you be cut down while yet alive; that your Bowels be taken out and burnt before your Face; that your Head be cut off, your Body to be divided into four quarters, this to be at his majesty's Disposal.

In his official report to the King Governor Tryon boasted that the insurrection was completely crushed and the rebels who had not complied with his proclamation ordering them in to take an oath of allegiance to the King, had been deprived of their homes and driven out of the province. In many cases their homes were burned, their barns destroyed, their crops ruined and their livestock confiscated. For this great achievement Governor Tryon was highly praised by his King and the King's counselors in London.

Governor Tryon was a soldier by profession and an exceedingly stern one. He demanded that every citizen who had been connected with the Regulators appear at the county courthouse and take an oath of allegiance to the King, and in six weeks following the battle of Alamance, six thousand citizens of the border counties named above had complied with his order, many of them hopeful of better government but undoubtedly many of them with mental reservations.

Though granted amnesty by the Royal Governor, it was soon evident that all was not well with the freedom-loving citizens who had been labeled outlaws. They found that the same corrupt officials held the county offices and the same bands of lawyers, whose exorbitant fees had helped to cause the insurrection, still surrounded the courthouses. Many hundreds found flaws in their land titles, or so the lawyers said, and hundreds of them gave up the hopeless battle, packed their scanty belongings, and went west. Those Regulators who had not sought amnesty, but had refused to take the oath of allegiance, had moved out soon after their crushing defeat at Alamance and many others who had apparently bowed to tyranny followed them.

For example, in the "Jersey Settlement," now in Davidson County, but at that time in Rowan County, was the Jersey Baptist Church, probably the largest rural church in the State at that time. This church saw its membership decrease in less than two years from 160 to fewer than 60. A Baptist historian, writing in 1772, is quoted by Dr. Archibald Henderson in his *History of North Carolina* (p. 253) as reporting "the heavy depletion in the membership of churches of that denomination, [estimating] that 1,500 Baptist families had moved away since Alamance. Some part of this exodus turned toward the Watauga country." The exodus was by no means confined to the Baptists.

In the Watauga country that Dr. Henderson refers to, the uprooted and dispossessed homeseekers found the Watauga, Holston, and Nolichucky settlements.

In these settlements, particularly that of the Watauga Association, they found warm welcome and conditions to their liking. The people of these settlements believed that they were in Virginia and so held until later surveys revealed that they were in North Carolina. At any rate, they knew they were far from the seat of any organized government, and being desirous of living under law, the Watauga Association came into existence, with a written constitution and a duly established form of government.

The people of the Watauga area found the newcomers from the Granville District of North Carolina to be desirable citizens, eager for participation in organized government and law abiding by preference.

Tyrannical Governor Tryon, who had left North Carolina immediately after the Battle of the Alamance, had denounced them bitterly in public proclamation, portraying them as "unruly, rebellious traitors, disloyal to the King," and he gloried in having defeated them in battle, hanging many of them and in seeing to it that (in his own words) "the houses and plantations of the outlaws were laid waste and destroyed as the owners fled out of the province."

Their new neighbors in the mountains did not find them to be the kind of people Governor Tryon had said they were. It should be noted here that Joshua Martin, who succeeded Tryon as governor and was himself a stern and cruel leader who did little, if anything, to make life easier for the people, in a letter to Lord Dartmouth said this about the Regulators:

> Notwithstanding evidences of the most licentious, gross and criminal violences on the part of this wretched people, yet a residence among them last summer afforded me a full conviction of their having been grievously oppressed by the sheriffs, clerks and other subordinates of government.

The record discloses, however, that Governor Martin did nothing to correct these abuses. Not a sheriff, clerk or other corrupt official was removed from office or even reprimanded. For example, Colonel Edmund Fanning, chief of the oppressors, Clerk of the Court of Orange, Colonel of the County, attorney and legislator, was convicted on half a dozen charges of corruption. He was fined a penny in each case, and continued in office. Others were dealt with in similar fashion.

Such conditions were not to be long endured by free men and they moved to do something about it. They were not aware of the significance of it at the time, but their action started the movement for independence in America. George Bancroft, the noted historian, found that the survivors of the Battle of the Alamance were not "cowed" by their defeat, but came out of the conflict with as much zest and courage as ever. To find a place where royal officials would not oppress them, they headed into the trackless west.

In the Watauga, Holston, and Nolichucky settlements, all in the fringe area and uncertain as to the colony that claimed jurisdiction over their lands, the Regulators found settlers exercising what Dr. Henderson calls "squatter rights" over homesteads set up far from oppressive tax collectors and other corrupt officials of government.

They were warmly welcomed and, based upon the three settlements, they fanned out over the area west of the Blue Ridge and north to the Virginia line, accepting without reservation the government already established.

Commenting on it, Dr. Henderson described the Watauga Association and its form of government as "an experiment in squatters' sovereignty beyond the pale of either provincial or royal authority. This drive across the Alleghany frontier had progressed to a point where, during Governor Martin's administration, notable beginnings of a frontier commonwealth were set up within North Carolina's nominal jurisdiction to the west."

John H. Wheeler, who wrote and published his *History of North Carolina* in 1850, had this to say about the Regulators:

> From their first assembly at Maddock's Mill [October, 1766] to the final catastrophe on the banks of the Alamance [May, 1771], the great principle laid down was that they should pay no tax but what was lawful and imposed by their representatives in Assembly. This was the great germ of American liberty.

An additional tribute to the Regulators, that should make their descendants proud—and there are many of them in Ashe County—is found in Vol. VIII, *North Carolina State and Colonial Records*, where Col. W. L. Saunders has written:

> Of the forty-seven sections of the State Constitution adopted in 1776, thirteen, more than one-fourth, are the embodiment of reforms sought for by the Regulators.

Evidently they were not the kind of people described by Governor William Tryon or by his successor, Governor Joshua Martin.

There is no way of determining from the records available today how many of the defeated and dispossessed Regulators found their way up into the high foothills of the Blue Ridge and across its crest, but a study of the genealogical records of scores of families presently in the area will disclose that many of them came from Granville, Orange, and Rowan Counties and elsewhere in the Granville District between 1771 and 1776.

II

The Revolutionary War

As the dispossessed citizens of piedmont and central North Carolina and other land-hungry immigrants from the north came into the area west of the Blue Ridge, they found themselves in Indian territory. The first to invade this area were received kindly because ostensibly they came to trade, or on hunting expeditions. As the white man began to set up trading posts settlements sprang up around them and the Indians awoke to the realization that the whites were taking possession of their lands. There were armed clashes, bloody murders, and Indian massacres.

There were efforts to settle matters by treaty between the Indians and the invading white men. Some treaties were effective and lasting. Others were not. A disturbing factor was the French and Indian War, part of the Seven Years War in Europe, which was in fact the first world war, involving as it did Great Britain, France, and Spain. The French had aroused the Indians, promised them protection from the British invaders, and set them to killing and burning along the borders. This war ended in 1763 with the complete defeat of France, but the enmity of the Indians against the whites had been intensified and it in no way decreased.

Consequently, the early settlers west of the crest of the Blue Ridge found themselves beset by savage Indians, including the Iroquois, the Cherokees, the Creeks, and the Shawnees. All the settlers had gotten out of the triumph of British arms was the end of French claims to the lands lying west of the Blue Ridge and draining into the Mississippi. The Indian claims to the same territory were more vigorously asserted and Indian hatred of all whites became even more bitter.

With France out of the way, Great Britain undertook to set apart most of the territory that had been claimed by France for the Indians. By a restrictive order known as the "Proclamation Line of 1763" the British government sought to establish a line along the crests of the mountains, dividing the lands drained by the streams that flowed into the Mississippi from those lands draining into the Atlantic Ocean. The lands west of this line were to be reserved for the Indians and permanent settlement of whites should not be made.

While the acquisition of lands after this order of the British Crown had become effective was no longer easy, there was no way of holding back the tide of immigration that was spreading over the fertile valleys of the mountainous areas of North Carolina, Virginia, and what is now Kentucky. The hardy settlers disregarded the Proclamation Line of 1763, took what they wanted, and in the face of peril held it by force and arms.

By the time the people of the eastern seaboard, from the New

England States to Georgia, were ready to declare their independence and to wage war against Great Britain, they found ready for service in the mountains a band of fighting men, skilled in border warfare and ready to aid their brothers of the east. It developed rather quickly that there would be need of them to guard the western frontier. The British, led by officers trained in warfare, were quick to form alliances with the Iroquois, the Cherokees, and other great Indian tribes, and to promise them protection from white settlers. They furnished the red men with arms and ammunition, trained them, and set them on the war-path. Thereafter, for the duration of the war, no man's home was safe in this mountain region.

There is a scarcity of records about the participation of the men of the mountains in the Revolutionary War. While every man in the region was under arms and on the alert constantly to prevent raids on the colonies from the west, they did not find themselves regimented with the Colonial armies. Under their own leaders they provided defense of their homes and the western frontiers but they also found time to aid the Colonial armies. Colonel John Sevier, Colonel Benjamin Cleveland, Edward Moody, William J. Braswell, William Davis, Benjamin Bingham, John Adams, George Smith, Moses Yarber, Captain Robert Love, Daniel Cutbirth, Joseph Calloway, Berry Toney, David Witherspoon, Samuel Johnston, Aaron Johnston, Daniel Boone, Jesse Duncan, John Shirley, William Calloway, Samuel McQueen, John Witherspoon, Robert Cleveland, Benjamin Greer, and many others served faithfully in the fight for freedom.

In addition to hostile Indians attacking from the west and north, the Colonial armies had to contend with foes from within. Not every settler sympathized with the fight for freedom. There were tories all over North Carolina and they were particularly troublesome in the area that is now Ashe. There was constant battle with them. Colonel Ben Cleveland, often criticised for his severity, fought them relentlessly, shooting them on sight and hanging most of those that he captured. Tory groups were equally merciless. The only battle of the Revolution to be fought in Ashe County was the Battle of the Big Glades fought between a force of Americans led by Captain Robert Love, and a force of 150 tories on their way to Charlotte to join Lord Cornwallis in July, 1780. Historians are generally agreed that the "Big Glades" was another name for Old Fields, presently in Ashe County and which was owned at the time by Colonel Ben Cleveland. Captain Love defeated the tories and greatly aided the movement to form a regiment of mountain men to help check Cornwallis in his triumphant sweep northward through North Carolina. His victory enabled men to join in the undertaking who could not have done so with the tory menace threatening their homes.

While their firm defense of the western border and their control of tories was important to the cause, the most spectacular service by the mountain men came at the Battle of Kings Mountain which marked the beginning of the end for the British in the original thirteen colonies and in all of America south of Canada. In September, 1780, word came to Colonel John Sevier that American forces in the South were in a bad way. Lord Cornwallis, commanding the British armies in the South, was winning one battle after another, and was set for a sweep through North Carolina and on into Virginia that would end resistance to British arms. It was his plan to drive through the state with three columns of British regulars, reinforced by several thousand tories. He would lead the center column. On his right would be a column commanded by Colonel Banastre Tarleton. On his left and close to the mountains would be Colonel Patrick Ferguson, who had tangled with detachments of mountaineers in South Carolina and had a sort of vendetta against them. In fact, before the columns started to move, he had issued a proclamation on his own. He paroled one Samuel Phillips, a relative of Colonel Isaac Shelby, and sent him to deliver a message to Colonel Shelby and the officers of the militia on the waters of the Holston, Watauga, and Nolichucky, which was as follows:

> If they did not desist from their opposition to the British arms he would march his army over the mountains, hang their leaders and lay their country waste with fire and sword. (Summers' *Southwest Virginia.*)

Colonel Shelby was not dismayed. He had already been in conference with Colonel Sevier and the two immediately set about the raising of a force to deal with Ferguson. Colonel Shelby hastened to Abingdon, Virginia, to counsel with Colonel William Campbell, commanding the Virginia militia in that district. Campbell was more than sympathetic. He responded quickly and with the aid of his brother, Colonel Arthur Campbell, assembled 400 riflemen and marched them to Jonesborough, North Carolina (now Tennessee). Colonel Shelby mustered 240 from Sullivan County, North Carolina, and Colonel Sevier brought in 240 more from Washington County, North Carolina. Burke and Rutherford counties, North Carolina, sent 160 men under Colonel Charles McDowell and Colonel Andrew Hampton. From Wilkes and Surry counties, North Carolina, Colonel Ben Cleveland and Major John Winston brought 350 fighting men. When they headed south to find the enemy, the force numbered something over 1,000 men and they were joined on their way by 300 men from South Carolina under Colonel James Williams, bringing their total strength up to approximately 1,600 men.

By modern standards they were poorly equipped, but for their day and time they were a formidable force. Theodore Roosevelt, in his *Winning of the West*, paid high tribute to the spirit and daring of this little army. He describes their equipment for combat as follows: "Every man carried a small-bore rifle, a tomahawk and a scalping-knife. A very few of the officers had swords and there was not a bayonet nor a tent in the army."

The assembled colonels, all of equal rank, showed no trace of jealousy. L. P. Summer, in his *History of Southwest Virginia*, credits Colonel Shelby of North Carolina with the suggestion that Colonel William Campbell of Virginia be placed in command of the expedition. It met with unanimous approval. Mindful of military proprieties, they sent a message to General Gates, commanding the American armies in the South, acquainting him with the situation. Summers quotes the official report in this regard as follows:

> No officer having properly a right to command in chief, on the first day of October, 1780, we dispatched an express to Major General Gates, informing him of our situation, and requested him to send a gen-

eral officer to take command of the whole. In the meantime Colonel Campbell was chosen to act as commandant till such general officer should arrive.

What followed is history. The situation did not permit delay. The men of the mountains did not wait for General Gates to send a general officer to lead them, nor did they wait for Colonel Ferguson to come and find them. They set out as quickly as possible to find him and his army. Ferguson's army consisted of 1,125 men, a large part of them British regulars and all of them well trained and well armed.

Colonel Campbell commandeered every horse in his army. There were only 910 serviceable horses available and those men who could not be mounted trudged toward the enemy afoot. By forced marches, by day and night, the mounted contingent came upon the enemy in the afternoon of October 7, 1780.

On the long hard march over rough and rugged terrain the mountaineers had subsisted almost entirely on parched corn. Stops for resting men and horses were few and far between, and during the night preceding their attack they had marched forty-five miles under cover of darkness.

From all accounts, Colonel Ferguson was surprised. He had been apprised of their coming by two deserters from the American army, but he had not expected them to get there so quickly. He had taken position on the top of Kings Mountain, about at the line between North Carolina and South Carolina. To his mind the level area on top of the mountain, hedged about by rock cliffs and trees, was ideally suited for defense. He is reported to have made this sacrilegious boast:

"I am on Kings Mountain. I am the king of this mountain and God Almighty could not drive me from it."

If the backwoodsmen had fought as the British regulars had been taught to fight, the outcome might have been different. In the long years of establishing homes in the wilderness and defending them against the Indians they had learned to fight like Indians. Approaching the enemy with great caution, they dismounted and faded into the trees. Colonel Campbell and his staff of colonels divided their forces into three battle groups and placed them so that Colonel

Ferguson and his army was completely surrounded. No avenue of escape was left to them. As the American forces had planned it, it was to be a battle to the death.

And that was exactly what it turned out to be. The battle lasted barely two hours. When it ended, Colonel Ferguson was dead with six bullets in his body. Of his force of 1,125 men, 119 were dead, 123 were wounded, and 664 were prisoners. Twelve tories in Ferguson's forces were hanged. A few escaped. The American loss was 28 killed and 62 wounded.

Some forty miles away Lord Cornwallis, the British commander-in-chief, got the bad news and in a matter of hours his army and the force under Tarleton were being withdrawn to bases in South Carolina. The immediate effect was the disbanding of tory groups, which had been flocking to the British colors, and an increase of activity by the American forces. There was a general uplift of American morale everywhere the story of the Battle of Kings Mountain was told.

Cleaning up after battle, the American forces found themselves in posession of a great store of arms and ammunition. Colonel Campbell knew how badly the American army needed these supplies. He organized a supply train, and with prisoners of war pressed into service to carry supplies and equipment the train headed for Hillsboro to turn the spoils over to the American army, at that time commanded by General Gates.

Military experts, and historians following their lead, do not rate Kings Mountain as a decisive battle, but it marked the turning point in the war. The war was to continue another year or more. Of all the historians, George Bancroft had the clearest conception of its importance. He said that this battle "was the fatal blow which utterly disconcerted the plans of Cornwallis, and forced him into that change of policy which had its end at Yorktown."

With this victory behind them, the men from the back of the Blue Ridge saw no further pressing need of their service in the American Army. As they saw it there was vastly more need of their services at home, where tories were still active and where Indians were continually raiding white settlements at the instigation of the British. There were only old men and young boys at home to protect their women, children, and property. As a consequence, these fighting men headed back to their homes in ever increasing numbers and when time came to turn the wagon train of supplies and prisoners over to the American army at Hillsboro, there were more prisoners to deliver than there were soldiers to make the delivery. It is certain that a considerable number of them remained to serve under General Greene and General Gates at Camden, Cowpens, Sherrill's Ford, Ramseur's Mill, Guilford Courthouse, and Yorktown, but the majority of them headed back to their own battlefields in the west. Colonel William Campbell, it may be noted, promoted to general, died at Yorktown.

III

The State of Franklin

There is ignorance in North Carolina and Tennessee about the State of Franklin which came into existence on December 14, 1784, and after five tumultuous years ceased to exist in 1789. During that period the new state functioned under a constitution drawn up by duly elected representatives of the people, fashioned after the Constitution of the State of North Carolina. If other states and other portions of North Carolina and Tennessee forget Franklin, the people of northwestern North Carolina and of east Tennessee should not. Franklin embraced the three counties of Washington, Greene, and Sullivan and the independent colonies on the Watauga and the Holston. It extended west from the crest of the Blue Ridge and must have included most of the area that is now Ashe County. That some of the inhabitants of this area must have been uncertain about their state, or were playing it safe, is shown by the fact that some ancient deeds to lands in Ashe were found to have been registered at Jonesborough, the capital of Franklin.

The new state had a population in excess of twenty-five thousand people. They were led by a wise, bold and patriotic group, including John Sevier, Landon Carter, Samuel Doak, Charles Carter, William Cocke, Evan Shelby, Samuel Houston, and others.

These men did not counsel or seek separation from the State of

North Carolina by violence. It is true that there had been sentiment for years for the formation of a new state in that part of North Carolina lying west of the Blue Ridge. Colonel Arthur Campbell of Virginia, who had assisted in raising the little army that went to Kings Mountain with John Sevier, Benjamin Cleveland, and their fighting men, proposed a new state to be made up of parts of North Carolina and southwest Virginia. These sections, so far from the seats of government in both states, got little benefit from association with counties on the eastern seaboard.

Colonel Campbell and Colonel Sevier, speaking for the people of the mountains in Virginia and in North Carolina, pointed out that contact over trackless mountains with the seats of government in both state was well-nigh impossible. A local emergency might wipe out an entire settlement before the state could move to help, no matter how desirous of helping the state might be. They pointed out that the Revolutionary War which the men of the mountains had helped to win at Kings Mountain, had been over for ten years but apparently the British had failed to notify their Indian allies. The Indians had continued their raids and there had been no help from the states in dealing with them. The settlers had had to fight their own battles.

So, when Congress passed the Resolution of Cession in 1783, calling on all of the states to cede to the federal government their undeveloped western lands, with the idea of setting up new states to the west, there was great interest on the part of Colonel John Sevier and his associates. Their representatives in the General Assembly of North Carolina were alerted. That body, meeting in special session in April, 1784, passed a resolution approving cession, provided that the Congress accept cession within twelve months.

This resolution had not passed without opposition. Thirty-seven votes had been cast against it and when the General Assembly met in regular session in October, 1784, the ranks of the opposition had been increased and the resolution of cession was repealed.

However, much had happened in the meantime. Following the April, 1784, meeting of the General Assembly, Colonel Sevier and his forces got busy. They called a meeting of freeholders at Jonesborough in August, 1784, to make plans for statehood. Little was done and the meeting adjourned to reconvene on September 16, 1784. Because the North Carolina General Assembly was to meet soon after this date there was further adjournment, to November, 1784, to see what the Assembly would do.

The so-called "separatists" were dismayed by the action of the North Carolina General Assembly in repealing its resolution of cession. With all due respect to the mother state, they held that she had no right to repeal the resolution until after the year was up. And believing that their cause was just, they proceeded with their plans for separation. As the record shows, the North Carolina separatists did not follow the outlines of the new state that Colonel Campbell proposed, but confined their operations to territory recognized as part of North Carolina. This included most of what is now Ashe, Alleghany, and Watauga counties of North Carolina, and Washington, Hawkins, Sullivan, and Greene counties of Tennessee.

It is significant that the separatists at no time desired to be governed except by law. Following their meeting in November, 1784, they called a constitutional convention to meet at Jonesborough on December 14, 1784. Their first action was to adopt a resolution providing for separation of Washington District, then embracing all of what is now Ashe, Alleghany, and Watauga counties in North Carolina, and Washington, Sullivan, Hawkins and Green counties, Tennessee. This action was not unanimous. The vote was twenty-eight for separation and fifteen against. Representing Washington District, the largest unit in the proposed "State of Franklin," which included the area that was later Ashe, were Colonel John Sevier, Colonel John Tipton, Thomas Stewart, the Reverend Samuel Houston, William Cocke, Charles Robertson, William Murphey, Joseph Wilson, John Irwin, William Trimble, William Cox, Landon Carter, John Chisholm, Samuel Doak, John Bean, Samuel Williams, and Richard White. Of these, only Colonel Tipton is recorded as voting No.

The convention voted to be governed by the laws of North Carolina until a new government could be set up, and adopted a constitution based upon the Constiution of the State of North Carolina.

The years that followed were tumultuous, with no little feuding and fighting and considerable shedding of blood. Colonel John Sevier was elected governor in March, 1785, when the Franklin General Assembly met at Jonesborough.

There is not space here to tell of the ups and downs, the successes and the failures, the victories and defeats that attended the short-lived State of Franklin. It is a story of enthralling interest and those who would read it all are referred to Judge Samuel Cole Williams' book, *History of the Lost State of Franklin.* Judge Williams, a former Justice of the Supreme Court of Tennessee and a historian of unusual ability, published his book in 1933.

From available records, it is evident that Governor Sevier was a wise leader. He kept disorders at a minimum within the borders of Franklin and administered the laws with fairness. He finally became convinced that the best interests of his people lay in being reunited with North Carolina and with the consent of his General Assembly he began negotiations for such reunion. He secured assurance that back taxes, not paid to the State of North Carolina for five years, would not be assessed against property owners and that no man would be deprived of his homestead without due process of law.

At the February term of the Superior Court of Greene County (Tennessee), 1789, (to quote Judge Williams' *History*):

> ...John Sevier, Joseph Hardin, Henry Conway and Hugh Wear, came into court and took the oath of allegiance, agreeable to the Act of the Assembly in such cases made and provided. Then truly the State of Franklin had come to an end.

Throughout the life of the State of Franklin there had been doubt about its eastern boundary line. It is of record that citizens in parts of the state were given the privilege of paying taxes to the State of Franklin or to the State of North Carolina and were free to choose the state. Gradually Washington District, later to be Washington County, Tennessee, had extended a loose and uncertain jurisdiction to the crest of the Blue Ridge. When the Second Act of Cession was passed by the North Carolina General Assembly of 1789 it established North Carolina's boundary line along the crest of the Stone Mountains, a low range west of the Blue Ridge. This left the people living in what later became Ashe County, completely without county affiliation. They did not desire to be without the benefits of county government and in the General Assembly of 1792 (Chapter 32, Public Laws of 1792) they secured the enactment of a law annexing their area to Wilkes County, North Carolina. The preamble to this Act states their position with regard to what was, in reality, "re-annexation" to Wilkes, and defines the boundaries of the area so re-annexed, as follows:

> Whereas a part of Washington County was by the Cession Act retained in the State and although remaining in the said State the inhabitants thereof are deprived of the benefit of the laws and government of the same for the want of being annexed to some other county:
>
> . . . Beginning at the most southwardly part of Wilkes County line on the Burke County line, and running due west to the dividing ridge between the waters of the Watauga and Doe rivers, thence along the extreme height of said ridge to the line of the ceded territory, then along the said line to the Virginia line to the old line of Wilkes County; and that all of the land north and east of the aforesaid line, shall be and the same is hereby annexed to the said County of Wilkes.

This action was not taken without argument. The Franklinites, who had lost out in their own efforts toward statehood, sensed that statehood on a grander scale was imminent and it was part of their strategy to hold on to every foot of territory to which they had laid claim. The inhabitants of this area who chose annexation to North Carolina rather than taking their chances with a nebulous state in the west found their course ably supported by legislators in the east. Probably the most influential of these was Memucan Hunt of Granville County, a powerful political leader of his day who served as State Treasurer from 1776 to 1778. He had acquired a large tract of land on Helton Creek and he wanted it to be and remain North Carolina territory. General William Lenoir, and many others interested in land in this area, joined in the battle.

The creation of the new State of Tennessee followed, as foreseen and predicted by John Sevier, when the Congress of the United States, on June 1, 1796, admitted the State of Tennessee into the Union, the first state to be erected out of a territory of the United States.

In the new state, as had been the case in the State of Franklin, John Sevier was first and foremost. He became Tennessee's first governor and he served six two-year terms, an all-time record for his State.

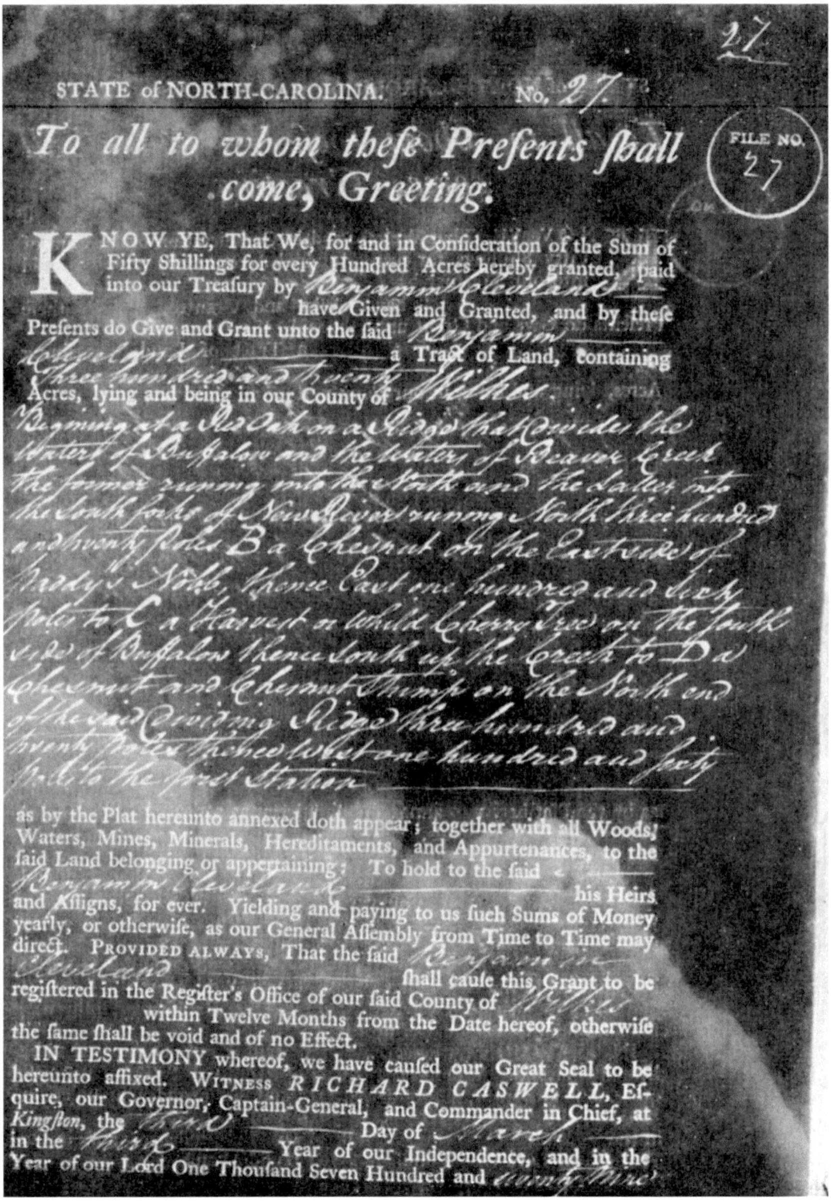

27

STATE of NORTH-CAROLINA. No. 27.

FILE NO. 27

To all to whom these Presents shall come, Greeting.

KNOW YE, That We, for and in Consideration of the Sum of Fifty Shillings for every Hundred Acres hereby granted, paid into our Treasury by Benjamin Cleveland have Given and Granted, and by these Presents do Give and Grant unto the said Benjamin Cleveland a Tract of Land, containing Three hundred and twenty Acres, lying and being in our County of Wilkes. Beginning at a Red Oak on a Ridge that divides the Waters of Buffalow and the Waters of Beaver Creek the former running into the North and the latter into the South forks of New River running North three hundred and twenty poles B a Chesnut on the East side of Paddy's Nobb, thence East one hundred and sixty poles to C a Harvest or White Cherry Tree on the South side of Buffalow thence South up the Creek to D a Chesnut and Chesnut Stump on the North end of the said dividing Ridge three hundred and twenty poles thence West one hundred and sixty poles to the first Station

as by the Plat hereunto annexed doth appear; together with all Woods, Waters, Mines, Minerals, Hereditaments, and Appurtenances, to the said Land belonging or appertaining: To hold to the said Benjamin Cleveland his Heirs and Assigns, for ever. Yielding and paying to us such Sums of Money yearly, or otherwise, as our General Assembly from Time to Time may direct. PROVIDED ALWAYS, That the said Benjamin Cleveland shall cause this Grant to be registered in the Register's Office of our said County of Wilkes within Twelve Months from the Date hereof, otherwise the same shall be void and of no Effect.

IN TESTIMONY whereof, we have caused our Great Seal to be hereunto affixed. WITNESS *RICHARD CASWELL*, Esquire, our Governor, Captain-General, and Commander in Chief, at *Kingston*, the Third Day of March in the Third Year of our Independence, and in the Year of our Lord One Thousand Seven Hundred and seventy-nine

This grant conveyed to Colonel Benjamin Cleveland, hero of the Battle of Kings Mountain, the land upon which the town of West Jefferson now stands. The instrument was signed by Governor Richard Caswell and dated March 3, 1779.

Top: A typical mountain home of the early days. Originally built more than 100 years ago near the present site of Glendale Springs Hotel, this cabin was moved by its owner, J. Baxter Miller, to a spot on Highway 16. *Bottom:* This grist mill, built by Absalom Bowers in 1825, is still in operation on the Colvard Farm near Jefferson. Owner Fred N. Colvard appears in the photograph.

World War I touched Ashe County homes. The first draftees in 1917 are shown, *top*, in a photograph belonging to R. W. Barr of West Jefferson, as they arrived in West Jefferson, having marched with their luggage from the courthouse, led by a makeshift band. When Ashe County returned from the war they were welcomed home by speeches and picnics such as this one served in a field near Healing Springs High School. (Photograph courtesy M. F. Denny, Crumpler.)

Typical of Ashe County scenery are these two views made by photographers of the North Carolina News Bureau. *Above:* Mount Jefferson as seen from north of the town of Jefferson. *Below:* The Blue Ridge Parkway near Milepost 261 sweeps past Mount Jefferson, left, and Little Phoenix Mountain. There are 28 miles of this famed highway in Ashe County.

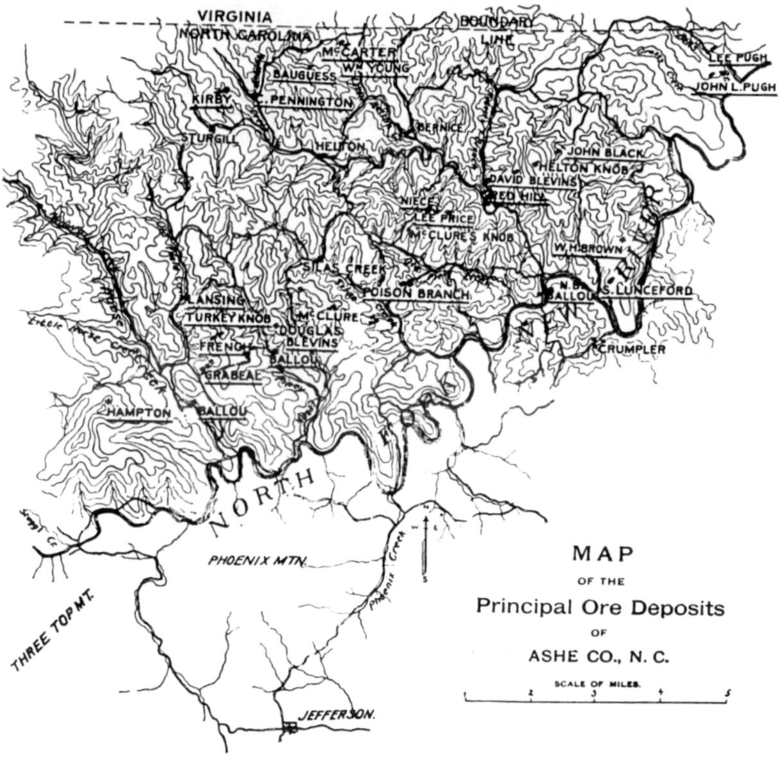

Top: Will Banks (on gallows, right) was hanged before this crowd in 1906. (Photograph courtesy R. W. Barr, West Jefferson.) *Bottom:* This N.C. Geological Survey map shows the distribution of Ashe County's abundant mineral deposits.

Top: Bethany Methodist Church at Baldwin is widely regarded as one of the most beautiful rural churches in America. *Bottom:* The First Baptist Church, West Jefferson.

Consolidated schools have brought modern educational facilities to rural counties such as Ashe, replacing one- or two-teacher community schools. Shown here are, *top,* Ashe Central High School at Jefferson and Beaver Creek High School in West Jefferson.

Jefferson, county seat of Ashe, nestles in a beautiful valley at the foot of Big Phoenix Mountain. (*Skyland Post* photo.) West Jefferson in 1917 presented the appearance in the lower picture, loaned by R. W. Barr.

Top: Plant of the Sprague Electric Company on North Fork of New River near Warrensville. (Photograph courtesy Urcle Sheets, plant manager.) *Bottom:* Phoenix Chair Company occupies this plant in West Jefferson. (Photograph courtesy R. W. Barr.)

Two views of the plant of the P. H. Hanes Knitting Company at Jefferson show the exterior and the busy interior. (Photograph courtesy P. Huber Hanes, Jr.)

Contemporary trends in architecture are apparent in the Ashe County Office Building at Jefferson, *top,* and the First National Bank Building, West Jefferson.

The original Ashe County cheese plant became a county landmark. Milk was brought in from local dairy farms in large cans to begin the process.

Top: The pipe factory in West Jefferson used primarily native laurel to make its products. *Bottom:* The tobacco auction was an active place. It was attended by buyers as well as by folks who came to enjoy the show.

Top: Graybeal's Drug Store with Dr. J.K. Hunter's dental office upstairs. *Bottom:* Tucker Hotel is shown in the lower picture with Mr. and Mrs. Tucker on the porch to welcome their guests.

Top: Downtown West Jefferson, about 1938. *Bottom:* Three armed deputies—Walter Phillips (left), Wiley Burgess and Bob Watson—with a confiscated whiskey still.

Colonel Arthur L. Fletcher, Ashe County native who moved to Raleigh and served for many years as North Carolina Commissioner of Labor, is author of this history of his home county.

CHAPTER THREE

ASHE CREATED—BOUNDARY CHANGES—WHO CAME FIRST—THE U. S. CENSUS REPORTS

I

Ashe Created

Miss Adelaide Fries, late of Winston-Salem, who did such an excellent job of collecting, translating from the German language, and editing the old records of the Moravians for publication by the North Carolina Historical Commission, wrote a county history, *Forsyth, A County on the March.* Her first paragraph notes the curious fact that those who settled in the area that is now Forsyth County selected their land in Anson County, settled in Rowan, went through the Revolutionary War in Surry, through the War of 1812 and the Mexican War in Stokes, and volunteered for service in the War Between the States from Forsyth—"and yet the location never changed!"

It was even so with Ashe. When Bishop Spangenberg found it by accident, his hunter-guide having lost his way, it was in Anson County, according to the English, but if you paid heed to the treaty claims of the French, its waters drained into the Mississippi and it was, therefore, a possession of France. Later the area was to be claimed by Rowan County (1753), by Surry County (1771), and by Wilkes (1777). The State of Franklin, which was in existence from 1784 to 1789, claimed most of the area. Following the end of the State of Franklin, it was claimed by Washington District, later to become Washington County, North Carolina, and still later Washington County, Tennessee, but it was re-annexed to Wilkes County by the North Carolina General Assembly in Chapter 32,

Public Laws of 1792, where it remained until "erected as a separate and distinct county" by the General Assembly of 1799 (Ch. 36, Public Laws of 1799). Without moving from their homesteads the hardy pioneers of Ashe had been citizens of four counties, two states, and one foreign country—"and yet the location had never changed!"

The Act of the General Assembly of North Carolina of 1799, creating Ashe Conty, is probably the shortest ever passed setting up a county in North Carolina.

The county was named for Samuel Ashe, Revolutionary War patriot, who had served as Superior Court Judge for three terms and had been elected Governor in 1795 and re-elected in 1796 and 1797.

The Act reads as follows:

> The General Assembly Do Enact,
>
> That all of that part of the County of Wilkes, lying west of the extreme height of the Appalachian Mountains, shall be and the same is hereby erected into a separate and distinct county by the name of Ashe.

Ashe County today covers 427 square miles of territory. When created its territory was 977 square miles, including, as it did, all of what is now Ashe, Alleghany, and Watauga Counties.

II

Boundary Changes

During the years Ashe County has suffered many changes of boundary lines, the majority of them due to local disputes and disagreements. The first of these came in 1807 when the General Assembly enacted Chapter 70, Public Laws of that year, authorizing a commission to re-survey and re-establish the dividing line between Ashe and Burke Counties. For some obscure reason action was delayed and the survey was finally made in time for the General Assembly of 1814 to act on it. The Commission surveyed the boundary set up in the Act of 1807, which was as follows:

> Beginning at Blowing Rock on the Blue Ridge, near Yadkin Spring, running thence a due west course, crossing some of the head-waters of

Watauga River to the top of the ridge dividing the head-waters of Watauga River and Elk Creek, then along the extreme height of the ridge to the Grandfather Mountain, thence along the extreme height of the ridge that divides the waters of Toe River from those of Watauga and Elk Creek, to the Tennessee line, leaving all of the waters of Toe River, and the head-waters of Watauga south of said due west line, in Burke, and all of the waters of Elk and waters of Watauga north of said line, in the County of Ashe . . . the commissioners to extend and mark the line from Blowing Rock west to the top of the ridge between Watauga waters and Elk waters, and no further.

The official survey was finally completed and the General Assembly of 1814 confirmed it in an act that may be found in Chapter 72, Public Laws of 1814. The Act fixed the boundary line as follows:

That the following, towit: beginning at the Yadkin Spring, thence along the extreme height of the Blue Ridge to the head spring of Flat Top fork of Elk Creek, thence down the meanders of said creek to the Tennessee State Line, shall be and the same is hereby declared the permanent dividing line between the Counties of Burke and Ashe.

A goodly slice of Wilkes County was annexed to Ashe by the General Assembly of 1835 (Ch. 81, Public Laws of 1835). The Act transferred to Ashe County

. . . all of that part of the County of Wilkes, lying north and northwest of a line to be drawn from the extreme height of a Nob called Dockery Nob, running so as to include all of the inhabitants, lying north of a direct line from said Nob to a point running northeast, so as to strike the now dividing line at 5½ miles distance from Dockery Nob, running a northeastwardly course until it strikes the Ashe County line.

What may well be described as a major operation on the County of Ashe was performed in 1849 when Ashe's State Senator, George Bowers of Jefferson, and one of Ashe County's representatives in the House, Reuben Mast of Valle Crucis, headed a movement to slice off the western end of Ashe and set it up as a separate county to be known as Watauga. There was opposition to the movement, but by making common cause with interests seeking at the same session to establish new counties to be known as Forsyth and Alamance, the partitioners won. They were aided materially by one

Jordan Councill, Jr., a brother-in-law of Senator Bowers, living at Councill's Store post office, now Boone.

While slices of territory were taken from Wilkes, Caldwell and Yancey, the big cut was from Ashe, which lost 320 square miles of territory and 3,348 people. There were 129 slaves, 29 free Negroes, and the remainder whites. As stated in the Public Laws of 1848-1849 (Ch. 25) the new county was established as follows:

> That a county be and is hereby laid off and established by the name of Watauga, to be composed of parts of the counties of Ashe, Wilkes, Caldwell, and Yancey, beginning at the State line in Lemuel Wilson's plantation, and running with the State line in a northern direction two miles; thence running as near as may be, in a direct line (so as to leave Thomas Sutherland in the County of Ashe) to the top of Big Bald Mountain; thence to the mouth of Elk Creek on the south fork of New River; thence down the river to the mouth of a creek that runs down through Samuel Cooper's plantation; thence to the Deep Gap of the Blue Ridge; thence along the dividing ridge between the waters of Stony Fork and Lewis's Fork waters of the Yadkin River, to where the road leading from Wilkesboro to Deep Gap, crosses the top of the Laurel Spur; thence to Elk Creek at the Widow Hampton's; thence to the top of the White Rock Mountain; thence to the top of the Blue Ridge at the nearest point to the Yadkin Springs; thence along the extreme height of the Blue Ridge to the top of Grandmother Mountain; thence with the line of Burke County to the corner of McDowell County; thence to the State line where it crosses the Yellow Mountain; thence with the State line to the beginning.

The next legislative action affecting the territory of Ashe came in the General Assembly of 1858-1859 (Ch. 3 Public Laws of 1858-59). Like the Act of 1849, this Act was also a "major operation." It sliced 230 square miles off the eastern end of Ashe for a new county to be called Alleghany. The boundaries of the new county were fixed as follows:

> Beginning in the Wilkes County line on the top of the Blue Ridge at the Mulberry Gap, running with the public road to Flint Hill; thence a direct line to the top of Frank's Knob; thence to the South Fork of New River, at the mouth of Prather's Creek; thence down the meanders of said river to the junction with the North Fork of said river; thence north to the Virginia line; thence east with the Virginia line to the Surry County line; thence with the Surry County line to the Wilkes County line; thence with the Wilkes line to the beginning....

Beginning in 1872 and running on down through the years there were acts of the General Assembly making changes affecting the boundary lines of Ashe. In 1872 a strip of land between the farms of Joshua Long and Henry Bare was annexed to Alleghany (Ch. 109, Public Laws of 1871-72).

By Act of the General Assembly (Ch. 153, Public Laws of 1876-77) the line between Wilkes and Ashe was changed so as to include James Burgess and Rufus Calloway in Ashe County.

In 1877 parts of Ashe and Wilkes were annexed to Watauga (Ch. 167, Public Laws of 1876-77) and the boundary lines between Ashe and Wilkes were changed in 1879 (Ch. 295, Public Laws of 1879). In 1885 a slight shift in the dividing line between Ashe and Wilkes was authorized (Ch. 109, Public Laws of 1885) but this Act was repealed by the General Assembly at the next session (Ch. 177, Public Laws of 1887).

Part of Ashe was annexed to Alleghany in 1899 (Ch. 256, Public Laws of 1889) and another part to Alleghany in 1891 (Ch. 236, Public Laws of 1891). Ashe gained territory from Wilkes in 1891, when a considerable area that had been in Wilkes was transferred to Obids township, in Ashe (Ch. 57, Public Laws of 1891).

The record discloses considerable unrest and dissatisfaction with boundary lines. In many cases the legislative acts cited herein contain the names of some of the leading citizens who were not pleased with their citizenship in Ashe, or Wilkes, or Alleghany, or Watauga, and who sought relief at the hands of the Legislature. The records show that lines were so run as to "include R. M. Miller, Thomas Griffin and H. L. Burgess, Jr., in the County of Ashe" (Ch. 57, Public Laws of 1891). By act of the 1893 Legislature, the county line between Ashe and Alleghany was changed "so as to include William Rose in Alleghany County" (Ch. 234, Public Laws of 1893).

To settle small disagreements as to county jurisdictions, the Legislature ordered re-survey and relocation of the Ashe-Wilkes line in 1895 (Ch. 341, Public Laws of 1895). For the same reason, the Legislature in 1899 authorized the changing of the Ashe-Alleghany line in the neighborhood of Laurel Springs and Cranberry Creek. Among the citizens mentioned in this Act (Ch. 105, Public Laws of 1899) are Levi Cox, R. L. Doughton, and Henry M. Key. Key, the Act stated, "lives on said line and may remain a citizen of Alleghany County."

An Act was passed in 1901 (Ch. 714, Public Laws of 1901) to restore the old boundary line between Wilkes and Ashe, "to the top of the Blue Ridge." Six years later, the Wilkes-Ashe boundary line was again changed (Ch. 987, Public Laws of 1907) and part of the Act was changed at the next session (Ch. 222, Public Laws of 1909) so as to "include the present lands of Charles and T. F. Miller in Ashe County."

In 1911 an Act (Ch. 77, Public Laws of 1911) transferred all of the lands of James Calloway "now lying in Ashe County" to the County of Wilkes. In 1913 (Ch. 82, Public Laws of 1913) the General Assembly changed the line between Ashe and Wilkes so as to annex the farms of James Bowlin to the County of Wilkes.

The changes brought about by Chapter 22 of the Public Laws of 1909 and by Chapter 132 of the Public Laws of 1911, evidently did not satisfy the citizens affected and the General Assembly repealed them (Ch. 16, Public Laws of 1913).

The line between Watauga and Ashe was changed in the vicinity of Todd by Chapter 34, Public Laws of 1915.

The General Assembly was called upon to change the line between Ashe and Wilkes again and did so in Chapter 425, Public Local Laws of 1931, this time to include all of A. L. Miller's farm in Wilkes. The General Assembly of 1933 repealed this Act.

The General Assembly of 1957 (Ch. 876, Public Laws of 1957) repealed Chapter 82, Public Laws of 1913, transferring back to Ashe County the lands of James Bowlin and Samuel Miller which had been taken away from Ashe in 1913.

III

Who Came First

The question, "Who came first?" to Ashe County will probably never be answered to the satisfaction of anybody. Bill Sharpe in his *Geography of Ashe County* notes that Bishop Spangenberg and his explorers were there in 1752, but he also states that history records that Peter Jefferson and his surveying party, engaged in establishing the line between North Carolina and Virginia, were on Pond Mountain in 1749. Sharpe says that so far as his research goes, the first white man to acquire title to land in Ashe County was James Baker, in 1773.

When the new county came into existence in 1799 there was a rush in the office of the Register of Deeds. The first deed registered in Book 1 of the Register's office was dated October 3, 1799. It was executed by Aaron Marsh and it conveyed to Robert Nall two hundred acres of land at the fork of Buffalo Creek. The consideration was fifty dollars. It was probated in open court and filed for registration at the May term, 1800. John McMillan was Clerk of Court.

The second conveyance registered was a grant signed by Governor William R. Davie, conveying 100 acres of land to Peter Little. The fixed fee was fifty shillings for 100 acres. This grant was dated December 13, 1798.

It will not be possible to record here all of the names of the first landowners in Ashe County, but it is thought that space should be given those named below who appear in Book 1 in the office of the Register of Deeds of Ashe County and in the old volumes covering Ashe County deeds and grants now in the vaults of the North Carolina Department of Archives and History at Raleigh, these being Vol. A, 1778-1811; Vol. B, 1778-1805; Vol. –, 1778-1808; Vol. –, 1779-1804; and Vol. –, 1780-1820. It is not contended that the list contains the name of every person who acquired real estate in Ashe between 1778 and 1820. The records disclose that there were often delays of months and even years between the date of acquiring a deed or grant and the legal registration of it.

In checking over the list it should be remembered that available records are frequently illegible, or nearly so, and the researcher found a great variance in Christian names and surnames. For example, the name of Burkett is spelled four ways. Graybeal, as the name is spelled today, was Grable, Grabeal, Graybill, Grabil. Johnson and Johnston seemed to have been used interchangeably. And so it goes. All the researcher could do was to write the name as he was able to decipher it, and as it appeared in the records. The list follows:

A

William Adkins, George Anderson, Thomas Anderson, Daniel Ayers, John Allen, William Allison, Bartholomew Austin, John Adams, Present Atkins, James Ausborn, John Atkins, John Ayers, Richard Allen, John Ashley, George Adams, Henry Anderson, William Anderson, John Austin, James Ashley, Thomas Allen, Isaac Adkins.

B

Henry Brewer, John Baker, Ezekiel Baird, Andrew Baker, Stephen Baldwin, Robert Boyd, Christian Burkett, Elisha Baldwin, Daniel Bumgarner, William Baldwin, Morris Baker, Elizabeth Blackhand, Hiram Baird, Jonathan Baker, George Bower, William Boliver, Shumack Brown, Aaron Bowers, Louis Bonner, James Brown, John Bower, John Barton, John Brown, Benjamin Brown, Joseph Burkett, Zechariah Baker, Solomon Blackman, Francis Bogan, George Brooks, Majer Bowers, John Bumgard, Joseph Black, Richard Burton, William Byers, Allen Burton, Edmond Blackburn, Jonathan Boone, Thomas Bouchelle, Francis Bryan, Solomon Baker, Thomas Brooks, Jesse Boone, William Bayley, James Baker, Valentine Brown, Bedent Baird, Absolom Bower, Archibald Blankenship, Joseph Baldwin, Samuel Brooks, Alexander Brown, Christian Burkhard.

Zach Baker, David Burket, John Burton, Frederick Black, Wells Blevins, Elisha Baldwin, Adam Bowers, Lewis Bumgarner, Daniel Bates, Christian Burket, James B. Bumgard, Jacob Baker, Braxton Bryan, Jacob Brinegar, Joshua Badger, Lewis Barnes, James Blevins, David Burkhard, Shadrach Brown, Andrew Bolin, James Bradley, Frank Bryan, Meredith Ballou, Joseph Brooks, John Burkett, Samuel Baker, Blodgett Baird, Adam Brinegar, Benjamin Brown, Jacob Bare, Peter Brown, James Blevins, Morgan Briant, Joseph Blevins, Peter Bowers, Moses Baker, George Brown, William Bowers, Hardin Burton, Jonathan Buck, William Beard, Wilse Blevins, Theophilis Baldwin, Larkin Bumgard, Lewis Bonner, Joseph Burket, George B. Brooks, Samuel Burns, Jeremiah Baker, John Baldwin, Elizabeth Blackburn, William Baird, Andrew Baker.

C

Elisha Collins, Benjamin Cutbirth, Joseph Colwell, P. Craybill, Thomas Calloway, John Calloway, Windal Crouse, Samuel Castle, William Connelly, Joseph Couch, James Chappel, William Carrell, Coonrod Crup, Samuel Curtis, James Curtis, Elijah Curtis, Joshua Curtis, John Cox, Daniel Conner, Elijah Conley, David Cox, David Coltrane, Samuel Cox, David Cone, James Campbell, John Cornelius, William Connelly, Mathias Carpenter, Emanuel Custer, Enoch Chambers, David Coleman, Robert Cates, John Carrel, Adam Craws, Jacob Craws, Hodge Councill, Able Cook, James Chester, William Clawson, Thomas Connelly, Stephen Chappel, William Carrel, John Campbell, Joshua Cox, Michael Crider, Thomas Collins, John Colerain, William Cornett, John Conley, William Cunningham, Joseph Calloway, Devalt Coons.

Andrew Cox, Nathan Chaffin, James Chapman, Thomas Calloway, Ebexander Cox, Eli Cleveland, Col. Arthur Campbell, Henry Chambers, Jonathan Coleman, Samuel Cox, John Couch, Elijah Calloway, Drury Carrell, William Colvard, James Collins, Stephen Creech, Jacob Carpenter, Jesse Chapman, Isaac Chapman, William Cook, Jourdin Councill, Samuel Cassler, Joseph Couch, Samuel Carter, James Crawford, Joshua Carter, James Craford, George Chappell, Charles Calley, Joshua Coutch, James Cash, William Creech, Conrad Coldiron, Zachariah Campbell, Joseph Colwell, Edward Connelly, Rankin Cox, David Curtis, James Coldiron, William Cornett, Adam Crouse, Thomas Curtis, Sebert Choat, Risden Cuffer, Joseph Clark, Rasden Cooper, Phelp Curly, Zacheriah Cambill, Michael Cook, Jesse Cox, Joseph Couch, John Custer.

D

Joshuay Duncan, Peter Delp, James Dickson, Meshack Davis, John Dick, Joseph Doughton, Henry Dulhuer, Benjamin Duggs, George Davis, James Dotson, David Drigger, Daniel Doritey, William Devenport, Moses Dickson, Jacob A. Dyer, David Dickson, Daniel Dougherty, James Davis, Benjamin Drigger, William Davis, Benjamin Darnell, Thomas Dickson, Joseph Dowden, Abner Dunkin, Caleb Dyer, John Duglass, Reuben Debord, Benjamin Debord, John Dugger, Daniel Dickson, Joshua Duncan.

E

William Edwards, John Estep, John Elsbury, Jacob Eversal, David Edwards, John Eller, Landrine Eggers, Absalom Eaton, George Everby, David Eggers, Shadrach Estep, Henry Earnest, David Earnest, William Evans, Elijah Estep, Hugh Eggers, James Elliot, Daniel Eagers, Sterling Edwards, Jacob Eller, Peter Eller, William Ellison, Adolphus Earvin, Young Edwards, William Evins, David Engram, Abraham Eaton.

F

Andrew Forgerson, Peter Fouts, Nimrod Francis, David Fouts, John Fender, Nimrod Fender, David Fess, Jacob Faw, Gabriel Fender, Charles Francis, Enoch Fletcher, Jacob Fess, Ebenezer Fairchild, Andrew Fergerson, John Fletcher, Leonard Fouts, John Ford, James Fletcher, David Fees, Stephen Floyd, Maleath Fann, Elijah Francis, John Foster.

G

Peter Goodman, William Greer, Thomas Gibson, Richard Green, Martin Gambill, Samuel Griffith, Peter Graybill, Coonrod Grub, Jacob Graves, Jeremiah Green, John Green, William Griffith, Henry Graybill, John Graybill, David Griffith, William Gambill, Amos Green, John Gray, Jesse Gambill, William B. Gray, Samuel Griffith, Elijah Ginnings, Joel Gibson, Peter Goodman, John Gordon, Benjamin Greear, Peter Gross, Richard Greer, Martin Gambill, Richard Gest, John Griffitts, Lemuel Greear, Simon Grass, James Griffith Nathaniel Gordon, Benjamin Green, James Grimsley, Joseph Greer, Isaiah Green, Allen Grayham, Wyatt Griffith, Joseph Graves, William Greer, Thomas Gibson, Henry Grabell.

H

John Holeman, Mathias Harmon, Permenos Howard, Thomas Hoage, Nathan Horton, William Harris, David Hoppers, Joshua Hitchcock, Peter Hart, James Hurley, Henry Hardin, William Hart, Cutbirth Harmon, Joseph Hagarman, James Holsclaw, William Holmesworth, Samuel Hicks, John Holsclaw, Benjamin Hibbard, Vincon Hollandsworth, Peter Hurt, James Hunt, William

Hubbert, John Hull, Bletcher Hardin, Thomas Hubbard, William Holmes, Polly Howard, Moses Hately James Hathorn, Isaac Hire, Godfrey Harmon, William Hewton, John Hall, Daniel Hopper, George Houk, John Hardin, John Hollandsworth, Samuel Hathorn, Stephen Hart, Nathan Horton, Jesse Hall, Randal Hubbard, John Hash, John Holloway, John Henson, Nathan Hubbard, Benjamin Herndon, William Houck, Nathan Hanes, Isaac Hitchcock, Henry Heatley, Robert Hash, John Hopper, Anthony Harmon, William Hampton, Vincent Hollandsworth, Amos Halsey, Thomas Hagaman, George Hartzog, William Harbert, Josiah Harper, James Howell, A. Harmon, William Hill, Daniel Hopkins, James Henson, Jesse Hall, Josiah Hart, Reuben Hartley, Michael Houk, William Halsey, David Hant, Milly Humphreys, Memucan Hunt, Samuel Hicks, Able Hunt.

I

Richard Isaacs, Caleb Isaacs, Isaac Ingram.

J

Alexander Johnston, Rowland Judd, William Johnston, Elijah Jennings, William Jones, John Judd, Vinson Jones, Gabriel Jones, John Jones, Samuel James, Daniel Jones, Thomas Johnson, James Jackson, Elijah Jeans, George James, Levi Jones, William Johnson, John Jeans, Theophilus Johnson, Richard Henry Johnson, James Johnston, Archibald Jackaway, Edmond Jones, William Judd, Richard Johnston, Richard H. Johnson, Suzannah Jones, Daniel Jones, Samuel Johnson, William Jeans, Samuel Johnston, John Johnston.

K

Daniel Kesler, John Kesler, Robert King, George Koons, John Koons, Joseph Kesler, Edward Ketchum, Francis King, James King, John Koonts, Edward R. King, Michael Krider, Jacob Keller, John Kepler, Ulrich Kepler, Charles Kelly, Samuel Kesler, Elijah Kilbourn, Aaron Kennedy, Robert Knight George Koonse, Edward King, Joseph Kipps, Daniel Kissler, Edward Ketcham.

L

Peter Little, Gideon Lewis, Thomas Laston, William Lenoir, John Long, Alex Latham, James Lewis, John Landreth, Stephen Landreth, John Lile, Daniel Landreth, Isaac Lewis, Lemuel Lunsford, John Long, Thomas Landers, Jesse Lind, Zachariah Landers, John Lorance, Bary Lyal, Thomas Lenoir, Alexander Lyal, Charles Lewis, John Lipps, Richard Linville, Benjamin Long, Aaron Linville, Moses Landers, John Levitch, Thomas Linville.

M

George Miller, William Maxwell, Jacob May, James Maxwell, Joseph Moss, Henry Michel, John McMillan, Daniel Miller, James Miller, Christian Merriam, Spencer Mullins, Joseph Miller, John Miller, Abraham Mitchell, Daniel Mikel, Henry Mitchell, Joseph Mast, Demsey Massengill, Benjamin Mills, David Miller, William Morehead, William Moxley, William May, James Mulhey, Nathreldred Massengale, Sidney Maxwell, William Mullins, James Morris, Isaac Mills, John Miller, Jr., Daniel Morris, Henry Miller, Samuel Michael, Joseph Morphew, Archibald Mossman, James Massengill, William Manard, Isaac Mitchell, James Morphew, James Murphy, William Michael, Henry Michael, Abraham Michel, Jesse More, Adam Mast, Daniel Moxley, Abram Mitchell, Thomas Marshall, William Mink, David Mast, Edward Moody, John Morris, Gibson Maynard, John Maxwell, James Madan, Spencer Mullins, John Mikel, John Money, Abram May.

Mc

William McNell, William McGaha, Dan McCann, John McBride, Moses McDaniel, James McCaleb, John McMillan.

N

Gilbert Norris, Ephraim Norris, John Northern, John Norris, Robert Nall.

O

Elias Osborn, Lawrence Owens, Seth Osborn, Robert Osborn, Zack Osborn, Barnet Owen, Stephen Osborn, John Orear, Ephraim Osborn, Edmond Jay Osborn.

P

Elijah Pope, Timothy Perkins, Micoyah Pennington, Henry Poe, William Perkins, Johnnie Phipps, John Poe, William Philpott, William Pennington, William Phipps, Jesse Phipps, John Perry, Julian Pugh, William Poe, Mary Powell, Luther Perkins, Robert Persons, Benjamin Pennington, Joseph Perkins, Theophilas Petty, Levi Pennington, John Pumphrey, Ephraim Pennington, Lomay

Powers, Richard Perry, Nathan Pope, Joseph Plumer, William Price, Solomon Parsons, Lemuel Powers, Ambrose Parks, William Phips, John Patton, Aaron Pierce, Daniel Pouts, Stephen Perkins, Elijah Powal, Jacob Peterson, Jonathan Phillips, Thomas Porter, William Pevy, William Powers, Joab Patterson, Thomas Patton, Samuel Pitman, Larkin Pumphrey, Nealey Patton, Augustine Passmore, William Peery, Nathaniel Pew, Robert Perceval, William B. Purkins, John Phips, Nathan Poe, James Profit, James Parsons, Julian Pew, Micajah Pennington, Jesse Plumer, Joseph Plummer, Samuel Parsons, Ezra Phillips, Lester Perkins, Robert Parsons, Benijah Pennington, Samuel Phipps, Meshac Plummer, Micajah Pennington, Lewther Perkins, Henry Poe, John Peery, Julien Pugh, Daniel Pepple.

Q

Robert Quincey.

R

James Reed, Daniel Richardson, Abraham Rowland, David Richardson, James Richardson, Thomas Rutherford, Nathan Roysden, Jacob Roop, William Right, Benjamin Right, Samuel Robinet, John Reece, Eli Regin, David Ratin, Jesse Royd, Stephen Reid, Jacob Rees, Malachi Roberts, Jesse Reeves, William Richardson, William Ray, Joseph Rowland, Easter Roten, Hiram Rees, Connally Richardson, John Reslar, Joseph Ray, Ruben Ross, John Richardson, Michel Ritter, James Roten, George Reves, William Reves, Stephen Read, Charles Roark, Thomas Rutherford, David Roughton, Antony Reves, Jesse Ray, John Rees, Valentine Rese, David Roten, Silas Reynolds, Andrew Roland, Martin Right, Anthony Rees, Josiah Roughton, Joseph Roten, Rhuban Ross, Westley Renalds, William Reed, Elijah Roark, Jacob Reepe, Eli Ragan.

S

William Smith, John Scritch, Harry Smith, William Surgener, Stephen Scritch, Francis Sturgill, Moses Smith, Joseph Stoneycipher, Christian Shares, A. Smith, William Spencer, Simon Shull, Henry Smith, Henry Sheets, John Stuts, Zechariah Spurlin, Daniel Stump, Ale Smith, John Singil, George Smith, James Sturgill, Frank Shull, Isra Stoneycipher, William Snow, David Scritch, Levi Stafford, Henry Snider, John Sheets, William Stamper, Delia Spurling,

Absalom Smith, Samuel Stedman, More Stamper, David Smith, Thomas Swift, Joel Stoggil, Andrew Sheets, John Stongal, Salome Sherer, Burlette Ship, Robert Sherer, William Strunk, Lewis Sheppard, Mary Shull, Frederick Shull, Isaac Selsbury, Paul Summers.

Zachariah Summers, Christian Sherer, John Siglar, Michael Stocken, Christian Share, Samuel Stoneycipher, James Stephens, Francis Stogil, Jacob Scholt, Alexander Smith, David Smith, Elexander Smith, Andrew Sheets, William Snow, James Stoggel, Horace B. Satterwhite, David Sands, Robert Stitt, Alex Smith, Joseph Sands, William Stoggill, George Soiles, Ephraim Sandaford, Andrus Stritt, John Sheets, Jonathan Smith, Milton Stocker, Lewis Shepperd, Michael Strucker, Montford Stokes, Daniel Strunk, Jacob Surgerer, Ephraim Stonaford, Alexander Sutterland, Reuben Stringer, John Stanly, Robert Shearer, Isaac Spencer, Samuel Scott, Owen Sizemore, Ezra Stoneycipher, Thomas Snow, Solomon Stamper, Michal Stuckard, George Sizemore, Pleasant Smith, Joel Sturgill, John Sturgill, William Sikes.

T

Thomas Testerman, George Terry, John Toliver, Charles Toliver, Moses Toliver, William Tired, Thomas Torplett, Thomas Triplett, Jesse Taylor, Isaac Taylor, James Tatum, Jesse Toliver, Thomas Tatum, Jacob Torgerson, Thomas Type, James Toliver, James Thompson, Gosham Thompkins, Welborn Thomas, Christopher Thomas, Joshua Toliver, Andrew Turner, John Trout, John Taylor, Joseph Toliver, George Tyre, Graham Tomkins, William Thomas, William Taylor, William Tyrie, George Tyney, Thomas Tyrie, Robert Thompson, Robert Tredway, William Turman, George Tirey, Thomas Testament, James Thomkins, Thomas Testerman.

V

Samuel Vanderpool, Abraham Vanderpool, James Vanwinkle, Nathaniel Vannoy, Richard Vanover, John Vaught.

W

William Waters, William Weaver, Richard Williams, Joseph Williams, William Walters, Lazarus Whitener, David Wagoner, Samuel Wilcoxson, Squire Wilcoxson, John A. Woodruff, Moses Woodruff, Joshua Weaver, James Williams, Benjamin Webb,

Gideon Welborn, Allen Watson, Isaac Weaver, William Wallen, Isaac White, Joshua Weathers, Abram Walker, Andrew Williams, Luke White, James Woody, Benjamin Ward, Adam Wilkes, Joshua Weatherspoon, Adam Wagoner, Phillip Workman, John Williams, Gideon Wilburn, Isaac Wilborn, Mark Weaver, Jesse Weaver, David Witherspoon, William Weaver, John Wagg, Henry Waggoner, William Wyatt, Lazarus Whitehead, Josiah Wallis, Peter Whitaker, William Whitaker, Joseph Wyatt, William Waller, Phillip Williams, William Whittington, Richard Ward, Benjamin Wright, Henry Williams, Richard Willis, Jonathan Wilson, Duke Ward, Carter Whittington, Richard P. Williams, John Wason, Adam Wilkes, William Wiat, Samuel Wilcox, Elijah Wilcoxson, Samuel Wilcocks, Loggins Woody, Jacob Willson, Allen Woodruff, Charles Williams, John Webb, Joseph Weaver, Vernon Williams, William Watt, Thomas Wood, David Waggoner, Robert Whit, William Walders, Phillip Wortman, William Wells, Samuel Wilcoxson, Joseph Williams, Squire Wilcoxson, John Whittington.

Y

John Younce, William Yates, William Young, Joshua Yeates, French Younce, Frederick Younce, Lorance Younce, John Yount.

The majority of the documents registered in Book No. 1 and in the old record books referred to earlier, were fee simple deeds to tracts of land to the citizens named. How the grantors got their titles to the lands they sold, and from whom, is not recorded here. The other conveyances were grants, impressively signed and sealed by "Our Governor, Captain General, and Commander-in-Chief at Raleigh." These grants usually conveyed much larger tracts of land than the deeds, the grants running from 30 to 3,000 acres or more. There are grants of record signed by Governor Richard Caswell, in 1784; by Governor Richard Dobbs Speight, in 1792; by Governor Samuel Ashe, in 1797; by Governor William R. Davie, in 1798; by Governor Benjamin Williams, in 1799; by Governor James Turner, in 1802; and by Governor Nathaniel Alexander, in 1805.

It is interesting to note that real estate dealers were active. The land speculators were everywhere and they found plenty of eager buyers. For those who had money and could show good character, there were thousands of acres of unclaimed state land subject to grants at a fee of 50 shillings for each 100 acres. That many availed themselves of this opportunity, there is abundant evidence in the record. For example, General William Lenoir, Revolutionary War hero, is said to have received grants for 41,000 acres in Ashe County. In Book 1, referred to above, sixty-six of his grants are registered, totaling 8,217 acres. It is nowhere recorded that General Lenoir or his fellow real estate dealers of that day resorted to fraud or that they fixed exorbitant prices on the lands they acquired so cheaply.

Judging by the number of deeds on record for the period ending about 1820, the following deserve to be listed as big real estate men of the day:

General William Lenoir, Robert Nall, Timothy Perkins, Meredith Ballou, Jesse Ray, David Miller, William Snow, Jesse Reeves, Andrew Baker, Elisha Baldwin, Gideon Lewis, Nathan Horton, Martin Gambill, Joseph Doughton, William Maxwell, Sidney Maxwell, Charles Toliver, Samuel Robinett, John Koontz, John Bower, George Bowers, Daniel Eggers, George Koontz, Thomas Sutherland, Thomas Calloway, John Cox, Luther White, Luther Perkins, David Earnest, Eli Cleveland, and probably many others.

IV

U. S. Bureau of the Census Reports

The new nation wasted no time in getting its Census Bureau started. Its first, dated 1790, found Ashe County a part of Wilkes and the area embracing what became Ashe in 1799 was listed in the Census Report as "Eighth Company, Wilkes County." The names of the free whites sixteen years of age and older, including heads of families, were:

Jess Council, Jurdean Council, Aaron Ingland, Ezek Ingland, Jacob Moss, Joseph Moss, Ben Greer, Richard Green, Nat Hinton, Henry Chambers, James Ayer, Thomas Elison, Mary Murphy,

Sarah Colman, William Miller, Falle Reece, John Brown, Andrew Wood, Jo Stonycipher, Daniel Egers, Josh Duncan, Mary Baker, Casper Cabel, James Tomkins, Ben Bailey, Joseph Sewell, Thomas Hampton, Ben Culberth, Dan Culbert, Sam Wilson, James Sheppard, Jake Calliway, Elijah Calliway, Robert Judd, Jeremiah Bloomer, William Vannoy, Richard Calliway, Champion Givin, Thomas Linville, William Whitenton, Shad Estepp, John Whittenton, Thomas Linvill, Baker King, Jesse Green, John Hanes, Ezekiel Beard, Sam Beard, James Haselan, Sam Hicks, John Haselan, Ben Ward, Lewis Stephen, John Ward, Bashiba Smith, Frederick Severs.

In this Census of 1790, under the heading "Eighth Company, Wilkes County," which is known to have included all, or nearly all, of the area that was to become Ashe nine years later, the enumerators reported a total of free white males sixteen years of age and older, including heads of families, of 77. Free white males under sixteen totalled 107. Women and girls, with the exception of three listed as heads of families, were not counted. In the area there were ten Negro slaves.

There is no other official record of the population of the area, comprising 947 square miles, which was taken from Wilkes to form Ashe County in 1799, and this would tend to support the guess of various historians that there were not more than fifty families in the area at the close of the Revolution. Following the war, with the hostile Indians pushed back, settlers came thick and fast.

In *History of Watauga County* by Dr. Daniel J. Whitener, head of the Department of History, Appalachian State Teachers College, Boone, North Carolina, Dr. J. E. Hodges gives a brief account of those who came first to the area. According to Dr. Hodges, the first to raise their cabins in that part of Ashe that became Watauga in 1849 were Samuel Hix and James Holtsclaw, on land near Valle Crucis, in 1780. They were followed by Thomas Hodges in 1781 and in 1783, through Cook's Gap, came William Miller, Nathan Horton, and Ebenezer Fairchild, all from the Jersey Settlement in Rowan County.

Dr. Hodges notes that in the names set down by the Census enumerators for the Census of 1790 there were many names common to Ashe, Watauga and Alleghany today as reference to the list in Chapter Three will show. It is true that some of the names have disappeared, but that does not mean that the blood of the pioneers is not still there. As Dr. Hodges indicates, the pioneers were too much occupied with establishing homesteads in a trackless wilderness to waste any time setting up records of their undertakings and that is what makes the way of the researcher and the historian of today difficult.

John P. Arthur, respected historian, who wrote *History of Western North Carolina* and followed it with *History of Watauga County*, found no records of the few pioneers who braved the dangers and hardships of the area that became Ashe in 1799 and settled there prior to the Revolution. He states that the "white occupation of North Carolina had extended only to the Blue Ridge when the Revolution began."

He is authority for the statement that in those days there were no settlers at all in that part of Ashe which became Alleghany in 1859. It had been visited frequently by hunters from Virginia and central North Carolina, but no one had settled there until after the War. He tells the amusing story of three brothers named Maynard who came from Surry County in 1786 and built cabins along Glade Creek. They lived there in peace for six years and then Francis Bryan, of Orange County, settled five miles away, followed soon thereafter by Joel Simmons, William Woodruff, and a man named Crouse. This brought the total of families in the area to seven, making it entirely too crowded for the Maynard brothers, who moved on to Kentucky.

Arthur mentions among the first settlers in this part of Ashe, William Taylor, David Edwards, William Edwards, and Joseph Doughton, and he adds that the Cox, Gambill, and Reeves families probably lived in 1799 in the borders of what became Ashe. Another interesting character to make his appearance here after the Revolution, was John McMillan born in Scotland, who became Ashe County's first Clerk of Court.

The official United States Census of 1800, listing males above sixteen years of age and heads of families, is as follows:

A

Elijah Arm, William Allison, William Adkinson, George Anderson, John Adams, William Agers, Daniel Agers, Sandrin Agers, Hugh Allison, Jonathan Allen, John Airs, Bartholomew Austin.

B

Morris Baker, Elisha Baldwin, James Baker, Meredith Ballou, James Bumgard, Francis Bryan, Christian Burkett, Jonathan Baker, Thomas Brooks, Stephen Baldwin, William Baldwin, Solomon Barker, John Baldwin, John Burton, Justice Bolons, Joseph Burkett, Samuel Bumgarner, Henry Bare, George Bower, Frederick Black, Will Blevins, Henry Brewer, Tagle Brooks, John Bower, Daniel Bumgarner, Joseph Brown, John Brown, Samuel Baker, Blodgett Biard, Ezekiel Biard, Shadrach Brown, Benjamin Blackburn, William Brown, Samuel Barnes.

C

Henry Conley, Thomas Calloway, James Cash, John Calloway, Joshua Cox, Thomas Collins, James Chepser, Koonrod Colerain, Adam Crowell, William Conley, Thomas Conley, John Conley, Sam Conley, Stephen Chappell, John Cox, Elijah Calloway, John Cornelius, James Calloway, Phillip Church, Vindery Collins, Michael Cride, Mathias Carpenter, Henry Crouse, John Carrel, John Cox, Koonrod Croup, William Carrel, John Carrel, Sr., Jacob Crouse, Windle Crouse, Valentine Collins, John Collins, James Carrel, Joseph Caldwell, Daniel Conner, Ambrose Collins, Joseph Couch, Sarah Coleman, Jonathan Coleman, Hodge Council, Jonathan Council, James Campbell, Elijah Curtis, Samuel Curtis, Joshua Curtis, Abel Cox, David Curtis, Enoch Chambers, Casper Cable, Henry Chambers, David Coleman, James Chambers, Phillip Church.

D

William Davis, George Davis, John Davidson, John Denny, James Davis, William Davis, Charles Daniel, Caleb Dyer, Peter Delph, Thomas Dickson, John Dirk, James Dickson, Thomas Davis, William Davis.

E

John Eller, Sterling Everrath, William Everrath, John Ellisberg,

Elizabeth Eller, Jacob Everson, John Estip, Young Edwards, David Edwards, Barnabas Evans, Elijah Estip, Henry Earnest.

F

Charles Francis, William Filpot, Andrew Fouts, Peter Fouts, Gabriel Fender, John Fender, Nimrod Fender, John Ford, Ben Fairchild, Charles Francis, Abineser Fairchilds, Cyrus Fairchilds.

G

Arch Gibson, Ezekiel Gibson, Joel Gibson, Koonrod Green, Benjamin Grimes, Peter Grabeal, Henry Grabeal, Church Gilley, Peter Goodman, Martin Gambill, William Gambill, Samuel Griffith, Andrew Gibson, Richard Green, Jeremiah Green, William Green, Benjamin Green, Jeremiah Green, Jr., Benjamin Green, Jr., John Green, Equilla Green.

H

William Hart, Peter Hart, William Hill, Jacob Huntsinger, Parmensies Howard, William Hilliams, Moses Hubbard, William Harris, James Hildreth, Jesse Hall, Marshall Hall, William Henson, Stokes Hubbard, James Hubbard, Thomas Hubbard, William Hubbard, Samuel Henson, James Henson, Thomas Hubbard, Sr., John Henson, William Henson, Benjamin Hubbard, Daniel Hopkins, John Hitchcock, Francis Hurley, Isaac Hitchcok, James Hitchcock, Joshua Hitchcock, Alex Hutchison, William Hollandsworth, Henry Hardin, Johnson Hampton, Samuel Hicks, Cutliff Harmon, Thomas Hodge, Nathan Harmon, Jeremiah Hamilton, Joseph Hagerman, Samuel Hicks, John Holman, Isaiah Holman.

J

Alexander Johnson, Galbert Jones, Elijah Jimson, Henry Jacock, V. Jones, Jonathan Jones, John Jones, James Jackson, William Johnson, Samuel Jackson, Thomas Jackson.

K

William Kepler, George Koons, Daniel Kepler, Joseph Kepler, John Kepler, Woodrick Kepler, Robert King.

L

Gideon Lewis, Sr., Joseph Loggins, Charles Little, Gideon Lewis, Jr., Lamish Lunsford, Alexander Latham, John Lunsford, James Lewis, Stephan Landreth, William Landreth, John Long, James Lewis, Jr., Abraham Linville.

M

William Maxwell, Jacob May, Jr., Joseph McMillan, Henry Michael, William May, William Moxley, Joseph Miller, William McGahah, John Maxwell, Sidney Maxwell, Jacob May, Kathy Miller, George Miller, Darwin Mainor, Abraham Mitchell, David May, James Mutley, John McBride, Henry Michael, James Maxwell, William Miller, Arch Mackleroy, Jacob Moss, Joseph Mass, Thomas Mardey, William McNeill, James McNeill, James McCaleb.

N

Joseph Nichols, Shippe Nowlin, Robert Nall, Gilbert Norris, George Nome, Ephraim Norris, John Northron, Francis A. Norris.

O

John Osborn, John Overton, Jeremiah Osborn, Lawrence Owen, Robert Osborn, Barnett Owens.

P

William Poe, Micajah Pennington, William Pennington, Edmond Poe, Henry Poe, Benjamin Pennington, William Pennington, Jr., John Pearris, Theophilis Petty, Timothy Perkins, Elijah Pope, Nathan Pope, Walls Pennington, Ephraim Pennington, Ephraim Pennington, Jr., Reuben Pennington, Levi Pennington, Micajah Pennington, John Pew, Samuel Phipps, William Perry, Abraham Potter, Samuel Pittman, William Perry, Ezra Phillips, James Proffit.

R

Cannaday Richardson, Samuel Robinett, James Richardson, Jesse Ray, Joseph Roland, Eli Ragan, Jesse Reeves, Daniel Reynolds, Andrew Roland, Abraham Roland, Stephen Reid, Bodge Rimer, James Rippey, Thomas Rutherford, James Reid, William Reeves, Daniel Richardson, Valentine Rease, Nathan, Ragsdon, John Rease, Jacob Reece, Anthony Rease, Martin Russell, Charles Regan.

S

Jonathan Stamper, John Stamper, George Sizemore, Owen Sizemore, Michael Stucker, Christian Shearer, Phillip Seigler, Zechariah Spurlin, Mark Strowd, William Stamper, Jacob Seabolt, Richard Stringer, David Smith, Harrison Smith, Andrew Sheets, Henry

Shutt, William Smith, Sarah Shearer, Solomon Scott, Alexander Smith, Levi Stafford, Samuel Steadham, Jeremiah Steadham, John Stugel, William Shepherd, Charles Smith, Adam Seabolt, Robert Shievers, John Shaver, Joseph Stonycipher, Abram Smith, George Smith, Elizabeth Striss, Frederick Shell, Simon Shell, Edmond Stogsdell.

T

Thomas Tyre, John Tyre, Nathan Taylor, David Thompson, John Taylor, Isaac Taylor, Moses Toliver, Alexander Thomson, William Tyne, Jesse Toliver, John Toliver, Thomas Testament, Charles Toliver, Thomas Triplett, Graham Tompkins, Benjamin Tompkins.

V

Benjamin Van Winkle, James Van Winkle, John Vanderpool, Anthony Vanderpool, Samuel Vanderpool, Abraham Vanderpool, Winen Vanderpool.

W

Talton Woody, William Walters, Isaac Weaver,Mark Weaver, John Williams, John A. Woodruff, John Williams, Jr., Richard Williams, Isaiah Whitaker, Samuel Wilson, William Wyatt, Henry Wagoner, Moses Woodruff, Luke White, James Wooten, Joshua Weaver, William Weill, James Williams, Gideon Welborn, William Weaver, Benjamin Webb, Isaac White, John Whittenton, Benjamin Ward, Duke Ward, George West, Thomas Ward, William Whittenton.

Y

John Younce, Frederick Younce, Benjamin Yates.

In the homes of the citizens listed above, the U. S. Census enumerators found a total of 2,783 people in Ashe County. Because there were few roads and extremely difficult trails over the entire terrain that was Ashe in 1800, the census-takers doubtless missed many householders. The spelling of names may be confusing, but they appear as they are spelled in the official reports.

It is not possible to give here the names of heads of families reported by the census takers at subsequent census takings. The information given above is designed to answer the question, "Who

Came First?" The list of the first landowners and the list of the citizens found by the census takers should contain the name of the man who came first but they may not.

At this point it may be as well to give other U. S. Census statistics as to Ashe County's population, down to the present:

The Census of 1810 showed 3,694 people in Ashe County. In 1820 there were 4,335; in 1830, 6,987; in 1840, 7,467; in 1850, 8,777; in 1860, 7,956; in 1870, 9,573; in 1880, 14,437; in 1890, 15,628; in 1900, 19,581; in 1910, 19,074; in 1920, 21,001; in 1930, 21,019; in 1940, 22,664; in 1950, 21,878; in 1960, 19,768.

As these figures indicate, Ashe lost 2,110 in population between 1950 and 1960, bringing the population back to about what it was in 1900.

From the beginning Ashe has had stability of population. The old families whose names appear in the lists above, with few exceptions, are still in Ashe. Ashe County's birth rate has always been high but as the young grew up they went away, seeking opportunity and adventure as their fathers and grandfathers had done before them. Until late years, improved agricultural processes and industrial development did not come to Ashe. There was little to offer in the way of a satisfactory future and many ambitious boys and girls went to other areas. Always the families adjusted and always there were enough left to keep the home fires burning. As one commentator put it, "Ashe County land, after the first few decades, was rarely for sale."

This made for solidarity and a close-knit citizenship of high quality that every Ashe County man and woman, at home or abroad, is immensely proud of, and they are not concerned that the population figures do not climb from census to census. They are not like the general run of folk who clamor for more people, anybody from anywhere. They agree wholeheartedly with the late William Allen White, famous editor of the Emporia (Kansas) *Gazette*, who said: "The editor who hollers for more population without regard to the kind of population is a fool who doesn't know his own business."

Consequently, they are not disturbed by Census figures showing small gains or even losses in population and are quite content to let people in the rest of the country go their ways, leading more or less happy bumper-to-bumper lives. Not that Ashe County has not joined the modern tread toward automobiles, radios, televisions, and the like. Handsome cars are parked alongside homes and around the new industrial enterprises that are springing up and radio and television aerials sprout from nearly every rooftop. But the fact remains that there is a hard-rock variety of citizenship in Ashe that loves the county, its people, its customs, its green fields, its quiet secluded valleys, its towering mountains, and is happy to stay there.

Someone said of Ashe County citizens recently that they are like the Irish who love their country most and leave it the quickest. The explanation is that the Irish leave to make enough money to come back and stay, and that is true in Ashe. The exigencies of living are such these days that not all who plan to come back are able to do so, no matter how strong may be their desire. But the records show that many do return and their number is increasing from year to year.

As the census statistics indicate, the decrease between 1950 and 1960 in Ashe was in the wholly rural townships. Two townships, Jefferson and West Jefferson, showed small gains. The record for all the townships is as follows:

Chestnut Hill, 583, a decrease of 168; Clifton, 1,619, a decrease of 230; Creston, 596, a decrease of 284; Elk, 555, a decrease of 150; Grassy Creek, 524, a decrease of 180; Helton, 868, a decrease of 61; Horse Creek, 745, a decrease of 303; Hurricane, 722, a gain of 83; Jefferson, 2,660, a gain of 427; Laurel, 505, a decrease of 50; North Fork, 879, a decrease of 415; Obids, 798, a decrease of 109; Old Fields, 922, a decrease of 209; Peak Creek, 1,024, a decrease of 224; Pine Swamp, 1,039, a decrease of 201; Piney Creek, 1,034, a decrease of 236; Pond Mountain, 379, a decrease of 147; Walnut Hill, 1,006, a decrease of 118; West Jefferson, 3,310, an increase of 472.

The towns in the County had populations in 1960 as follows:

West Jefferson, 1,000, an increase over 1950 of 129; Jefferson, 814, an increase of 455; Warrensville, 116, a decrease of 4; Lansing, 278; Todd, 32, a decrease of 20.

As figured by the Bureau of the Census, Ashe County's decrease in population in 1960, from the 1950 figure, was 9.6 per cent. It is interesting to note that Alleghany County lost 5.2 per cent, while Watauga lost 9.9 per cent.

Ashe County showed 46.3 persons per square mile, while Alleghany showed 33.6 persons per square mile, and Watauga, 54.8 persons.

Few persons of alien birth have lived in Ashe County. Lumbering and mining operations at various times brought citizens of other states to Ashe but these generally moved on after mining ceased and after the timber was gone.

Negroes have never been numerous in Ashe. Gradually, as farms were developed and farm acreage increased, prosperous farmers began to acquire slaves. The number had grown to 492 in 1830. In 1840 there were 497. In 1850 there were 595 slaves and 86 free Negroes. In 1860 there were 533 listed as "non-white."

Thus the Negro count stood when the War Between the States began and after it was over there were 582 free Negroes in Ashe, listed under the heading "non-white" in the Census of 1870. The Negro population reached its peak in 1880 when it numbered 963. It has been decreasing from census to census since. In 1950, the Negro population was 279 and in 1960, out of a total of 19,768, non-whites constituted one per cent of the population.

The 1960 Census reports show 5,242 households in Ashe County, with an average population per household of 3.75. This was a decrease of households of one per cent. The percentage of population under eighteen years of age was 38.1 per cent; eighteen to sixty-four years of age, 51.7 per cent; sixty-five years of age and older, 10.2 per cent; married males over fourteen were 69.2 per cent and married females over fourteen were 67.2 per cent. Married males eighteen years old and older were 49.4 per cent.

Under the heading, "population in group quarters" Ashe is credited with 136 persons. This group is defined as including inmates of institutions and nurses' homes, and similar groups. Another Census item of interest is headed "fertility ratio," which, being interpreted, is the ratio of children under five years old per 1,000 women fifteen to forty-nine years old. The 1960 Ashe County ratio of fertility was 433. The Alleghany ratio was 397, the Watauga ratio was 350, and the Wilkes ratio was 462.

CHAPTER FOUR

PERILS AND HARDSHIPS–THE GEOGRAPHY OF ASHE–CLIMATE AND SOILS

I

Perils and Hardships

Mention has been made of the perils and hardships that the first comers to Ashe County faced and endured. At the risk of dwelling too much on these things it is considered worth while to make a few comparisons between then and now, in order that their descendants of today in Ashe and those scattered to the far ends of the earth may have proper appreciation of the courage, resourcefulness, and steadfastness of their ancestors.

Much has been said in recent years about "underdeveloped countries" and about "distressed areas." The people of the United States, North Carolina and Ashe County along with the rest, have approved the pouring out of billions of dollars in tax money for the relief of foreign countries suffering from their own mistakes and bad management and threatened with hunger, disease, and anarchy.

On the domestic front, the nation today is mindful of the plaint of any "distressed area" and the government, flanked by the American Red Cross, comes swiftly to the rescue if there is unemployment, or if there are high winds, or deep snows, or rampaging flash floods. The new land that the forefathers of Ashe came to occupy was truly an "underdeveloped country" and there was no compassionate government to come to their aid and help them with their problems. No matter how great the distress of an individual or of the people of an area, there was nobody to help. They had to stand on their own feet and fight their own battles, conquer the wilderness without outside aid, and solve their own problems.

True, there was a government behind them after the Revolution. Because the Indians had been pushed back, the perils lessened somewhat but the hardships did not. This government, which they had helped materially in establishing, was an experiment in government, called a "republic" and no one knew whether it would live or die. It consisted of thirteen quarrelsome, loosely knit states, stretched along 1,200 miles of Atlantic seaboard. It was demoralized by seven years of war and its affairs were in chaotic condition. Its currency was of doubtful value and was accepted with reluctance. The new nation was woefully weak and the state in which they found themselves was in even worse condition.

It is to be wondered how Ashe County citizens of today would stand up under conditions like those faced by their ancestors 160 years ago! With the comforts, conveniences, utensils, machines, equipment, and improvements that everybody takes for granted, it is true that those classed as most needy in Ashe County today are infinitely better off than were the most fortunate in those hard days.

Try to imagine establishing a home and making a living in a land where there were no railroads; where there was little transportation even in the eastern part of the struggling new republic and almost none in the mountains; where there were no roads except streaks of clay or sand in the east and nothing resembling a road in the mountains; no telephone or telegraph; no electric service; no markets; no mercantile establishments–not even a country store; no industry; infrequent and undependable mail service in the east and none at all in the west; few doctors and hospitals in the east and none in the mountains; few and very crude agricultural implements in the east and none available in the mountains.

Admittedly, the new lands they gazed upon were beautiful. There were lovely wooded hills, sparkling streams, and majestic mountains, but living on scenery is not to be recommended. There was obviously fertile soil, but lacking farming equipment, work animals, and other necessities, their chances of survival as farmers seemed slim. But survive they did!

With courage and physical stamina that people marvel at today, they gained a foothold in the wilderness and they were never displaced. How they brought this about will never be known, for there was no one to take note of their deeds and set them down for succeeding generations to ponder over and to profit by.

It would be interesting to know how the first settlers came into the wild country that lay west of the crest of the Blue Ridge. As related in another chapter a large number of families displaced by the War of the Regulation sought refuge in the west, but they found that a frontal assault on the Blue Ridge was well-nigh hopeless. Many stopped in the foothills of the Blue Ridge, in what is now Wilkes, Caldwell, and Surry counties.

Somehow word reached the refugees that west of the crest of the Blue Ridge, on the waters of the Watauga, Nolichucky, and Holston rivers, pioneers from Virginia and points north and northeast had established settlements and in ever-increasing numbers those oppressed people began moving west.

The only written account of this movement is found in the records of the Moravian Church at Salem telling of the groups of tight-lipped men and women passing through Salem in 1771, 1772, and 1773. They were reluctant to tell anyone where they came from or where they were going. It was noted, however, that they headed north from Salem and the indications are that they crossed the Blue Ridge and into Virginia at Fancy Gap, or thereabouts. Once over the Ridge, which was easier to cross here, they probably did not find it difficult to locate what was called the "Old Warriors' Trail," a well defined and much used Indian trail leading southwest along the western side of the Appalachian range and into what is now Tennessee.

Following this trail the refugees from eastern North Carolina came upon the so-called Watauga settlements along the Watauga, Nolichucky, and Holston rivers. These settlers had come over the same trail from Virginia and points north and east and believed they were in Virginia, a belief which the newcomers accepted without question.

It is highly probable that some of the displaced and persecuted North Carolinians found other trails over the Blue Ridge and may have approached these same settlements from the south but there is no record of it.

To add to the hardships of the period following the Revolution came the problem of securing valid title to desirable lands. The Federal and State governments had adopted the policy of giving grants of land to honorably discharged veterans of the Revolutionary War. Then, as in the aftermath of other wars, many discharged soldiers were ready to qualify for the land grants but were not interested in farming. Consequently there were lands to be had for very little which could be sold at tidy profits and a horde of land sharks moved in. Many hundreds of homesteaders fell for the sales talk of the land grabbers of the day and literally "lost their shirts." In many cases the lands they bought and paid for were unfit for farming and, therefore, useless for a population that had to depend on farming. In hundreds of cases, particularly in the new lands of Tennessee and Kentucky, there had been fraud in procuring the lands the promoters were offering and the homesteaders found their land titles defective, were dispossessed and were forced to move on. Many of them went to Kentucky and farther west into what is now Ohio, Indiana, Illinois, and Missouri.

II

Geography of Ashe

Between 1783 and 1799 a veritable flood of settlers came into the area that became Ashe. Many hundreds more passed through it on the way to Kentucky and lands farther west. By dint of intensive exploration they had discovered gaps in the formidable Blue Ridge and when they reached the crest at Cook's Gap, Phillips' Gap, Deep Gap, Flat Gap, Daniel's Gap, Reddies River Gap, or Mulberry Gap, they found to their surprise that the Blue Ridge was a ridge on the eastern side but no ridge at all on the west. They found themselves standing on the edge of a vast plateau, stretching west, southwest and northwest as far as their eyes could see. Rolling woodlands of fairly uniform height lay before them and from these woodlands rose here and there lofty mountains, four thousand to five thousand feet above sea level. Later day geodetic surveyors were to determine these altitudes and to find that the tableland from which these mountains rose had an average elevation of close to three thousand feet. The pioneers as they traveled over it found, even as travelers do today, that they were never out of sight of one or more of Ashe's great mountains. Moreover, they found that there were numerous streams running through this plateau, ranging from New River, with its two forks, North and South, to scores of creeks and branches. The beds of these streams determined the way the present highway system developed. The first trails were along streams and these trails grew into roads. Dr. Elisha Mitchell, whose explorations in Ashe are mentioned elsewhere, reported in his diary that in going to the Meredith Ballou iron mines in 1827 he crossed Helton Creek thirty-two times in ten miles.

The county is blessed with creeks, among them being Grassy, Helton, Silas, Piney, Horse, Stag, Mill, Copeland, Big Laurel, Roundabout, Rock, Brushy Fork, Long Shore Branch, Phoenix, Buffalo, Three Top, Hoskin Fork, Nathan's, Dog, Naked, Beaver, Old Fields, Rocky Shoal Branch, Little, Elk, Peak, Mulberry, Cranberry, Roan, Bear, Obids, Pine Swamp, and many others, all of them draining into New River. This river's two branches, the North and South forks, originate in Ashe near the boundary line between Ashe and Watauga and unite in the eastern edge of Ashe, a few miles from the Virginia line, to form part of the boundary between Ashe and Alleghany. All of the waters of Ashe and Alleghany drain into New River.

New River is a stream of rare beauty, eye catching and soul satisfying in its loveliness, and it must have so appeared to the pioneers who came first. The plow had not turned over the sod and the New and its tributaries did not run red when rain fell. Even today, the red flood of yesterday is forgotten quickly because the rapid flow of water carries away evidences of soil erosion quickly and the waters of Ashe sparkle again.

Geologists, those men of science who read the history of countries in their rocks and soils, agree that countless thousands of years ago the area that is 'round about Grandfather Mountain and Blowing Rock was the first part of North Carolina to emerge from the primeval ooze, when "the earth was without form and void." No part of America is older. They rate New River as North Carolina's oldest river and it is the only large river in North Carolina to flow north. As the mountains emerged from the sea, as fortune would have it, the land tilted to the west and northwest and the escaping waters began the work of erosion that resulted in present day valleys and water courses.

What few people know is that back in the dim and distant ages the New River of Ashe County which flows north into Virginia and cuts across the Appalachian chain, was part of the mighty Teays River. The comparatively small basin of the New, comprising about 760 square miles, most of it in North Carolina, held the headwaters of the Teays.

It is difficult to visualize what the Teays must have been in its heyday. Today the Ohio is looked upon as a truly great river and the Mississippi as the greatest of all in America. Both of these, according to scientists, were tributaries of the Teays. Dr. Raymond E. Janssen, professor of geology at Marshall College, Huntington, West Virginia, in a scholarly account of extensive research and study published in the *Scientific American* of June, 1952, traces the Teays from its beginning in the southwestern edge of Ashe County to Gauley Bridge, West Virginia, along the present bed of New River, to where New River unites with Gauley River to form the Kanawha. The Teays followed the bed of the Kanawha to Charleston, West Virginia, and ran thence in a northwesterly direction to a point beyond Fort Wayne, Indiana, thence almost due west to Lincoln, Illinois, where it was joined by the Mississippi. At this point the Teays turned south to empty into an embayment of the Gulf of Mexico, which at that time extended to a point near St. Louis, Missouri, where the Illinois River now meets the Mississippi.

New River as it was when the first settlers came across the Blue Ridge and found it and New River as it is today is about what it was when it was part of this ancient river. It acquired the name of Wood's River when exploring surveyors, probing west into the wilderness from Virginia about 1740, discovered a river running north that no one had ever heard of. Major Abraham Wood, variously referred to as Colonel Wood and Major General Wood, headed the exploring group that found the stream and it was named in his honor. Later, for reasons not disclosed in the record, it was renamed New River. There is no indication of changes in its channel for many ages and today, as it did ages ago when it was the Teays, it flows around the bases of the mountains and the rolling hills, through the lush meadows of Ashe and on into Virginia.

Ashe County is today a county of numberless unnamed mountains. Mountains that would stand out, attract attention and acquire names and prestige elsewhere, get no attention. An Ashe County legislator was asked if there was a beautiful view from his home. He replied:

"Just so-so. You can see the roof of Zeke Blevin's house but outside of that there ain't nothing but a mess of mountains."

Some of the "mess of mountains" acquired names. Probably the most spectacular is the mountain which Ashe County citizens of today are struggling to rename Mount Jefferson, but which most of the first settlers called the Nigger and others the Negro. No one knows who first gave it the name Nigger, or Negro, but anyone who has seen this great mountain in winter can understand how it got its name. Its trees for the most part are stunted because of the elevation, and when their foliage is off, the bare black rocks are all you see. It is a solid black mountain.

There is a tradition that it got its name because runaway slaves hid there and also that at one time it was a "station" of the so-called "underground railroad," the famous organization backed by the Quakers to help fugitive slaves get across the Ohio and to freedom in the North. That the organization did operate through Ashe County is fairly certain, but Dr. Elisha Mitchell in his famous diary was describing the view from Negro Mountain in 1827 and identifying the great black rock at the top as gneissoid granite. Earlier than this, back in 1809, one William Walter registered a deed conveying to him a tract of land "on the west side of Negro Mountain." All of this was before the underground railroad was even dreamed of.

North of the Negro, with the North Fork of New River curling around its northern base, was a beautiful mountain that someone named the Phoenix. This someone might have been Michael Eller, who came to Rowan County when Rowan included what is now Ashe. The ship in which he came from Germany was named the "Phoenix." The Ellers to this day are among the leading citizens of Ashe.

East of the Phoenix is Little Phoenix, the two separated by a deep gap. To the west is Paddy Mountain and who named it and why is not known. Farther west is Bluff Mountain, with its beautiful waterfall, and west of that is majestic Three-Top Mountain.

Here and there over the plateau, the pioneers found "balds," lands already cleared and covered with blue grass. Some of these balds were on mountain tops and others on smaller hills.

Ashe is in the northwest corner of North Carolina. It is bounded on the north by the state of Virginia. On the east is Alleghany County. Wilkes County bounds it on the south and on the south and southwest is Watauga County. The state of Tennessee bounds it on the west. The Stone Mountains, a low range, form the county's western barrier and separate it from Johnson County, Tennessee.

Ashe is favored with twenty-eight miles of the world-famous Blue Ridge Parkway, which follows along the crest of the Blue Ridge from the Virginia line to the Watauga line and on southwest by way of Asheville into the Great Smoky Mountains National Park.

III

Climate and Soils

A noted writer, describing the first settlers of the area that is now western North Carolina and east Tennessee, of which Ashe is a part, said that the pioneer of that day came equipped with three essentials, a rifle, an axe, and a Bible. Those who could contrive ways and means of bringing more did so, but few there were who could.

The rifle furnished food and protection from hostile Indians and with the axe the settler felled trees, cleared away a spot for the erection of his cabin and by dint of hard labor provided an open space around his cabin for the growing of corn, potatoes, and other vegetables. With fish and game abundant, he felt no particular urge to do more farming than was necessary to supply the needs of his own family. As game became scarce and hard to find, established habits and customs were not easy to shake off and from explorers of the area came accounts that the inhabitants were inclined to laziness and shiftlessness. They still cultivated the little patches around their cabins, and as they accumulated cattle, hogs, and other livestock, they utilized the foods of the forest for their hogs and the blue grass that covered the "balds" for the pasturage of their cattle and sheep.

Eventually, the pioneer was to learn many things about the climate and soils of the country he was settling in. Bishop Spangenberg, who is mentioned elsewhere, came to what is now Ashe in midwinter. He was in Ashe in December, 1752, and January, 1753, and he records in his diary now in the archives of the Moravian Church at Winston-Salem facts about the soils of Ashe which those who followed him did not discover for a hundred years or longer.

He also gave an account of the first night he and his associates spent in Ashe (December 5, 1752) when water froze by the fire and men and horses could hardly stand against the storm. He made this statement: "I think I have never felt a winter wind so strong and cold."

Remembering that Spangenberg and his men came from Pennsylvania and that Spangenberg himself had been born and reared in the high mountains of Germany, it is safe to conclude that he had experienced cold weather and had sound basis for his evaluation of Ashe County's winter weather. The homesteaders, coming after the good Bishop, did not have his diary for information and guidance, and had to learn the hard way of the vicissitudes and discomforts that awaited them.

The average temperature in Ashe in January is 36 degrees Fahrenheit. The maximum is 60 degrees in December, 61 in January, and 63 in February. The absolute minimum is 7 degrees below zero in December, 15 below zero in January, and 15 below zero in February. The average date of the last killing frost in the spring is about April 30 and the first in the fall comes about September 30.

This gives a growing season varying from 150 to 160 days.

As a general thing, much snow falls in Ashe County. There is usually a total annual snowfall of 25 inches. Often snowfalls are light but occur frequently and keep the ground covered three to four inches deep for weeks. Occasionally the snowfalls are extremely heavy and cover the earth two to three feet deep. Such a snow fell in 1959 and there are legends about even heavier snowfalls in 1886 and 1888 and as far back as 1838. The "big snow of 1886" was deep enough to cover all fences and was on the ground so long that Ashe County's deer population, along with other game, was almost completely destroyed. The United States Weather Bureau states that while the average snowfall for North Carolina is less than eight inches, there are years when there is little or no snow outside the mountain region and "big snows" come along about one year out of four.

On the credit side, the records disclose that summer and fall temperatures are moderate. The most severe weather is experienced during January and February and the average July temperature in Ashe ranges from 68 to 70 degrees Fahrenheit. Under housing conditions that prevail in Ashe today, the climate is favorable for year-round living, but in the days when all houses were of logs, axe-hewn from the forest, winter living was difficult.

In the matter of rainfall, Ashe County was blessed with a bountiful supply, then and now. The average annual precipitation over a period of twenty-five years has ranged from 48 to 52 inches per year, according to the Weather Bureau of the Department of Commerce (see Tech. Bul. 115, N. C. Agricultural Experiment Station), which is authority for the preceding statistics about Ashe County climate. An earlier publication, *Soil Survey of Ashe County*, by R. B. Hardison and S. O. Perkins, working under the late Hugh H. Bennett of the United States Department of Agriculture, published in 1914, gives the annual precipitation as 60.2 inches and divides it as follows:

December, January, and February, 14.4 inches; March, April, and May, 14.4 inches; June, July, and August, 16.6 inches; September, October, and November, 14.8 inches.

Like the rest of the state, Ashe County is sunny. The total

amount of sunshine varies from about 53 per cent of the total possible in winter to about 70 per cent in the fall. The average for the year is close to 61 per cent. The record kept by the Weather Bureau shows that the fair day average is 165; partly cloudy, 100; and cloudy, 100. Important to the grower of all crops in Ashe, from tobacco and truck crops to household gardens, is the statement of the Bureau that over a period of twenty-five years, the average warm season precipitation in Ashe, from April to September, has been from 28 to 32 inches.

The relative humidity average is a trifle lower than the statewide average of 54 per cent.

While the early settler in Ashe had much to learn about the climate he was venturing into, he was equally ignorant of the soils that the area offered. As related elsewhere, the earliest comers, the Moravians, saw possibilities in the soils they found and pronounced them ideal for growing wheat, corn, rye, barley, potatoes, beans, flax, cabbage, and many other crops. They saw unbounded prospects for growing livestock of all kinds, to be fed on the fine grass that grew wild on the balds and cleared places, and they set all of this down in their records. Dr. Elisha Mitchell, coming later, bemoaned the fact that Ashe County was tied to an economy that depended upon hunting and fishing for meat and garden patches around log cabins for vegetables. This continued, said the worthy Doctor (in 1828), after the game was gone, but he prophesied that there would be an awakening and that Ashe County would eventually clear its fields and support great herds of cattle and sheep and hogs.

Ashe County finally arrived, but it took her sons a long time to get there. In a publication issued in 1913 by the United States Department of Agriculture and the North Carolina Department of Agriculture, appears this statement:

> It was not until about 1880 that Ashe began to make any considerable progress along agricultural lines. A few good plows had been introduced as early as 1872, but these were the exceptions. Before this time nearly all of the farm implements in the County were home-made, the iron being taken from mines in the county. The cutting and shocking of corn was practiced for the first time in 1882 and about the same time

wheat growing over the entire county began. The first grain drills were introduced in 1884. Scarcely any commercial fertilizers were used prior to 1891.

According to this publication corn growing had been started and had increased to a point where it was the county's leading crop. Hay was second in importance and so the record stood in 1913. There will be more to follow along this line in a chapter concerning Ashe County agriculture.

In the matter of soils, their virtues and their weaknesses, and the use the various soils in the county should be put to, it should be admitted that the hardy pioneer of the early days, equipped with his rifle, his axe and his Bible, was at marked disadvantage with his descendant of today who has only to call at the County Agricultural Agent's office, take a peek at the county soil map on the wall or turn over to the Agent samples of his soil for analysis and report, all without cost to him.

The official report of the United States Department of Agriculture and the North Carolina Department of Agriculture, reporting on the soils that the newcomers to Ashe entered upon, states that "Ashe County lies wholly within the Appalachian Mountain and Plateau province. Its soil is largely residual, having been derived from the underlying rocks through processes of weathering. Along the streams there are narrow strips of alluvial soils which are made up of materials washed from the uplands and deposited over the contiguous flood plains."

These residual soils have different characteristics because of the character of the parent rocks.

This report classifies 99,392 acres in Ashe as Chandler silt and stony loam, steep to very steep and moderate, very poor crop land, fair to poor as pasture.

Ashe loam comes next, with 69,696 acres. It is classified as too steep and stony for crop land, though many small areas are in cultivation. It is rated good for green beans, potatoes and cabbage, fair for hay and good for permanent pasture.

Talladega loam follows, with 36,828 acres. It is in two classifications, silty clay loam and stony silt loam. Both are rated as poorly suited for crops and very poor to fair for permanent pasture.

Porter's clay loam is next with 31,104 acres. It is steep and stony for crops, though many small areas are in cultivation. It is reported good for potatoes, green beans, cabbage, fair for burley tobacco and very good for pasture.

Toxaway loam, with 15,360 acres, is next. This is alluvial soil and must be drained for crops or pasture. It is rated very good for corn, green beans, cabbage, hay, and pasture.

Clifton clay loam, 11,136 acres, good general cropland, though susceptible to accelerated erosion. Good for corn, very good for wheat, good for green beans, cabbage, burley tobacco, very good for hay and pasture.

Various smaller tracts, classified as Porter's stony loam, Talladega stony loam, rock outcrop and Ashe stony loam, totalling 9,664 acres, are not rated as good croplands and generally are classified as very poor even for pasture.

The main relationships existing among the several series of soils listed above are briefly described in the publication above referred to as follows:

> The Porter's soils are characterized by the brown, or reddish brown to red color of the surface material, and the red color and brittle, or only moderately pliable structure of the sub-soil, which is usually a clay;
>
> The Talladega soils have about the same color characteristics as the Porter's, the most important differences being the decidedly greasy feel of the Talladega material resulting from the presence of a large quantity of mica flakes;
>
> The Ashe series is characterized by the brown, or yellowish brown color of the surface soils, and by the yellow color and moderately pliable structure of the subsoil, which is generally a clay;
>
> The Chandler soils in color features practically coincide with those of the Ashe series. They differ from the latter in having a decided greasy feel, particularly in the sub-soil, owing to a high content of mica flakes. The relation of the Chandler soils to the Ashe, is practically the same as that of the Talladega to the Porter's;
>
> The Clifton soils have a brownish color in the surface portion and an ocherous-yellow to a yellowish-brown color in the subsoil;
>
> The alluvial soil is represented by one type, the Toxaway loam, consisting of materials deposited by overflow and repeated additions of soil material in suspension carried by water coming from the uplands.

This is typically a brown to a dark-brown loam, underlain by yellowish clay loam.

Summing it up, it is established that the soils of Ashe County are formed from the rocks of three geological formations, (1) the Cranberry granite, (2) the Roan gneiss, and (3) the Carolina gneiss. There are small areas of other formations but they are not important. Ashe loam comes from Cranberry granite and the stony type of soils mainly from Roan gneiss. Talladega clay loam and Chandler loam, as well as the smaller areas referred to, come from Carolina gneiss.

The experts of the national and State departments of agriculture conclude their report of their research and study with these conclusions:

(1) The Toxaway loam is the most desirable land in the county and for corn and grass it is better than any of the other soils;

(2) The Clifton stony loam, generally occupying the crests of the highest mountains, is not well suited for corn and wheat but produces good rye and grass;

(3) The Ashe loam is well adapted to the production of the clovers and produces fair yields of corn, rye, and buckwheat;

(4) Porter's clay loam, and Porter's stony loam, where not too steep, are the best upland soils of the county, and are especially suited to produce the clovers, hay, corn, rye, oats, and buckwheat;

(5) Talladega clay loam and the smoothest parts of Talladega stony loam, are productive soils and grow corn, wheat, rye, oats, and buckwheat;

(6) Chandler loam produces light crop yields but is susceptible of improvement.

CHAPTER FIVE

COURT OF PLEAS AND QUARTER SESSIONS–BOARDS OF COUNTY COMMISSIONERS–LEGISLATORS AND COUNTY OFFICERS

I

Court of Pleas and Quarter Sessions

When Ashe County was "erected as a separate and distinct county" by the North Carolina General Assembly of 1799, the first institution to be set up was the Ashe County Court of Pleas and Quarter Sessions. Its personnel was to consist of the justices of the peace resident in the new county's area and their successors were to be chosen as provided by law.

The second body created by the State Legislature for Ashe was a commission, composed of Nathan Horton, John Bowers, and Jesse Taliaferro (Quoting the Act, Chapter 36, Public Laws 1799), "for fixing a proper and convenient place near the center of said county, whereon to erect public buildings for said county."

The Act further provided that "until the courthouse shall be erected, or some convenient place fixed on by the Commissioners aforesaid, the Court of Pleas and Quarter Sessions for the County of Ashe shall be held at the house of Jacob Huntsenger."

The Act went on to provide that courts should "be held on the second Monday in February, May, August, and November of each and every year."

As taxes necessarily go along with government, public taxes in Ashe were fixed at one shilling on every poll and four pence on every 100 acres of land.

With that done the General Assembly left the new county to its own devices. The new Ashe County Court of Pleas and Quarter Sessions, the predecessor of the present-day Board of County Commissioners, took over and the enormous task of creating a new county in the wilderness was under way. There were no State or Federal funds available to draw from and the issuance of bonds that would pass the financial burdens on to future generations had not been dreamed of. The only income was from the small tax levied by the General Assembly and the only available resources were those natural resources in the rough that lay about them. With these the county started to build.

It would be interesting to know exactly how the County Court went about the task. Unfortunately the record is fragmentary in some spots and nonexistent in others. The books containing the accounts of the proceedings of the Court from 1799 to 1806 are missing. During this period there was much confusion. Records were shifted from one place to another and there were frequent changes in record keepers. It is quite possible that the county officials of those days did not consider their records highly important, dealing as they did in large measure with matters more or less trivial and not seriously affecting the public interest. Consequently the records were carelessly lost, or they may have been deliberately destroyed because considered of no value.

Certain it is, however, that the County Court of Pleas and Quarter Sessions, as authorized by the General Assembly, proceeded to set up a county administrative organization to carry out the objectives of the General Assembly, provide for the welfare and safety of the county's citizens, and establish orderly processes under the law for mining, commerce, agriculture, and industry. It might be said that the new county needed everything, with the exception of natural resources, which were useless without skilled men to develop them.

The County Court, fully aware of this, set about licensing skilled men to build grist mills, sawmills, carding mills, and other establishments driven by water power; to encourage the setting up of iron forges, blacksmith shops, woodworking shops, and many other activities needed in a new land. There was special and critical need of iron, as all iron tools and implements had to come into the county by pack horse, or on two-wheeled carts. It was early discovered that Ashe had iron in abundance and skilled iron men were induced to come in by offering large grants of land to those who set up iron forges and actually produced iron suitable for plows, hoes, axes, horseshoes, wagon tires, and the like. As early as 1811 Thomas McGimsey reported five successful iron forges in operation in Ashe and many more were to come.

In its routine activities the County Court must have found plenty to do because there was feverish activity in the real estate field and there were hundreds of deeds, grants, mortgages, powers of attorney, and other legal documents, all of which had to be probated in open court by competent witnesses. In addition the Court had to attend to hundreds of other matters, large and small.

The special commission named by the General Assembly (Ch. 36, Public Laws of 1799) to select a "proper and convenient place near the center of said county, whereon to erect public buildings for said county," had been enjoined by the Act "to exercise the duties of their appointment as soon as possible after the passage of the Act." Apparently they proceeded with reasonable speed to select such a site.

If there was community rivalry over the location of the county courthouse and other public buildings, there is no record of it. The commissioners found what they wanted where the town of Jefferson now stands and it was part of the farm of Adam Bowers. For one hundred dollars they bought from Adam Bowers fifty acres of land. It was a rectangular tract, extending east and west 111 poles and north and south 72 poles. The deed was dated November 19, 1800, and it is recorded in Book A, page 80, in the office of the Register of Deeds of Ashe County.

Apparently the site selected was generally satisfactory. The County Court approved it and named a building committee to proceed with the construction of the necessary buildings. This committee was composed of George Koontz, Nathan Horton, and John Cox. Later records disclose that John Bowers became trustee of public buildings, presumably by appointment of the building committee, or of the county court. The records do not say.

Just who named the new county seat is not known. It happened that right at that time a great Virginian, Thomas Jefferson, was finishing a term as Vice-President of the United States and was headed for the presidency. He was immensely popular in North Carolina and it is not strange that his name was chosen for the new town. Jefferson became the first town in the nation to bear his name.

It is a courious fact that for many years the United States postal authorities called the town Jeffersonton. The Official U. S. Postal Guide issued April 1, 1831, so listed it. The next available guide, dated 1849, called it Jefferson. In his diary for 1827 and 1828, Dr. Elisha Mitchell called the town Jeffersonton once and Jeffersontown once. An act of the General Assembly (Ch. 40, Private Laws of 1825) concerning a road to be built with Jefferson as one terminus, referred to the town as Jeffersonton.

However, the General Assembly some twenty-two years prior to the act referred to, had officially confirmed the town's name as Jefferson. This may be found in Chapter 75, Private Laws of 1803, which reads:

> Be it enacted by the General Assembly of the State of North Carolina, and it is hereby enacted by authority of the same, that the town already laid off at the court-house in the County of Ashe, shall be and the same is hereby established as a town by the name of Jefferson.

This act, though not in the usual form for the incorporation of towns, may be considered as Jefferson's first charter. It provided for a government by a board of commissioners composed of three owners of lots in the town of Jefferson to be elected annually by lot owners. Nobody else could vote for commissioners. The board was authorized to make laws and regulations for the government of the town and these applied to everybody. The county sheriff was authorized and directed to hold the elections annually under pain of forfeiting ten pounds for failure to comply.

For reasons not stated the town of Jefferson asked the General Assembly to pass another act of incorporation and this was done by Chapter 254, Public Laws of 1854-55. That act did not change the limits of the town. It fixed a tax rate of 50 cents on the poll; 12½ cents on the $100 of property; $3 on every store, grocery, and tavern; $2 on exhibitors of native and artificial curiosities; $1 on sleight-of-hand performers and organ grinders; 50 cents on carriages of pleasure. The act named commissioners as follows:

Quincy F. Neal, James Wagg, E. C. Bartlett, Samuel C. Waugh, and James W. Gentry. No mayor was named in the act.

Again for reasons not stated, the town was incorporated again by Chapter 176, Private Laws of 1915, with no change except a different slate of officials, these being:

Walter H. Worth, Mayor; E. A. McNeil, Charlie Neal, and Dr. J. W. Colvard as aldermen, and J. E. Koontz as town constable.

This organization did not long exist and the General Assembly of 1917, by Chapter 74, Private Laws of 1917, incorporated the town again with W. T. Colvard, Mayor, and Eugene Wagg, W. E. Gentry, and W. E. McNeill as aldermen. B. F. May was named town constable.

At this point it would probably be wise to take a closer look at the legal entities called "Courts of Pleas and Quarter Sessions" which were set up in most of the states and which continued to function in North Carolina until the new Constitution of the State was adopted in 1868, after which boards of county commissioners took over. Because old institutions and old terminology linger long in memory, there are still people in Ashe who speak of the regular monthly meetings of the Board of Commissioners as "Commissioners' Courts."

The "County Courts of Pleas and Quarter Sessions" was lifted bodily from ancient English law and it was aimed at giving people the right to govern themselves, to deal with lawbreakers on their own, to insure justice to all, the high and the low, in full measure and without discrimination. In the Ashe County Court of Pleas and Quarter Sessions there was no looking to Raleigh or to Washington for help with any problem. The common citizens comprising the court pooled their wisdom, considered all pleas carefully, and rendered judgment. There is nothing of record to indicate that these courts ever lost favor with the people.

As constituted, the Ashe County Court was made up of the duly appointed justices of the peace. Usually three of the justices held the quarterly court and the personnel of the presiding group changed from term to term. In that way all of the justices of the peace in the county had opportunity to serve in the trial of cases, settling of disagreements, and all phases of the Court's routine business. There were occasions when all justices of the peace, except when excused for illness, were required to attend, among these being the terms set for the election of county officers.

In the beginning the Ashe County Court of Pleas and Quarter Sessions had jurisdiction in both civil and criminal cases. Every term of court was complete with a grand jury, this being a jury of inquiry similar to our grand juries of today, with the duty to receive complaints and accusations in criminal cases, examine state's evidence and issue bills of indictment where trial should be had, and a petit jury, this being the ordinary jury of twelve men for the trial of civil and certain criminal actions. There was provision, even in the beginning, for appeals to courts made up of special tribunals composed of Superior Court judges, but these courts were far away and there is no evidence that they were made use of in Ashe to any considerable extent. The State of North Carolina, because of the increase of litigation, found it necessary to extend its judicial system and between 1800 and 1806 there were many changes. Superior Courts were set up throughout the State and were given jurisdiction of civil actions, except in minor cases left to the courts of the justices of the peace. To these superior courts was given jurisdiction over all criminal actions where the offense was classed as felony. The County Court of Pleas and Quarter Sessions retained jurisdiction in misdemeanors.

To get an idea of the role that these county courts played in the development of the State, one should remember that among their duties were the following:

The election of county officers; the maintenance of law and order through the operation of their jury system; the bonding of county officials; responsibility for orderly conduct of office by county officials; the registration of markings and brands of cattle and hogs in a free range country; the probating of deeds, grants of land, mortgages, and other legal papers, and the proper registration of same; the laying off and construction of roads; the appointment of road overseers and the assignment of citizens to work the roads; the appointment of justices of the peace and constables; the construction of public buildings; the levying of poll and property taxes; the care of the poor; the maintenance of the county's faith and credit; the welfare of orphans; and many others, too numerous to mention.

That the General Assembly wisely recognized that the "County Courts of Pleas and Quarter Sessions" were close to the hearts of the people and highly regarded as safeguards of the people's liberty, is shown by the fact that the courts were never abolished. They continued to function without material changes, exercising in many cases concurrent jurisdiction with the Superior Courts, until 1868. After that date their successors, the "Boards of County Commissioners," were in many respects the same old "Courts of Pleas and Quarter Sessions." The boards are free today of a great burden of clerical work, and of litigation, civil and criminal, which burdened the County Courts of Pleas and Quarter Sessions, and county officers are elected by the people. In other respects the duties and responsibilities are about the same as those of the old county courts.

While there are no written records available to show how the affairs of Ashe County were being carried on for the first five years or more, there is every reason to believe that the County Court was carrying on effectively during this period. The first recorded session of the Court was held on May 12, 1806, when the May term convened with the following justices of the peace constituting the court:

Alexander Smith, John McBride, and Charles Toliver.

Some of the changes in court procedures, above referred to, had gone into effect in the piedmont and eastern parts of the State but they were a little slow in reaching Ashe. By legislative action, Ashe was placed in the Morgan Judicial District, with two terms of court per year, in March and September, and the first Ashe County Superior Court term of record was the March term of 1807.

The May term, 1806, of the Court of Pleas and Quarter Sessions, therefore, carried on as usual. It is worth noting that the first grand jury of record for this county court was composed of the following:

Sidnaiah Maxwell, foreman; James Sturgill, Allen Woodruff, Samuel Griffith, Seth Osborne, George Koons, John Green, James

Dickson, Levi Pennington, Benjamin Hubbard, Charles Kelly, James Mulkey, William Harris, Alex Latham, Cyrus Fairchild.

Edward King was appointed constable of the court.

One of the first pieces of business was the election of seven constables, each of whom was required to give acceptable bond for five hundred pounds, as follows:

William Ray, Adam Burton, Shadrack Calloway, Joshua Weaver, Jacob Pope, Jacob May, and Daniel Struck.

As will be noted here and elsewhere in the accounts of the early years, the citizens of Ashe had not gotten away from English currency. Bonds were fixed in pounds, taxes levied in pounds, shillings, and pence, and fees for official services collected in the same way. The same practice prevailed in business and commerce and it so continued for many years after the Revolutionary War.

At this term (May, 1806) the court performed one of its most important functions in the election of a sheriff. Under the law the justices of the peace of the county, constituting the group from which the presiding justices of the County Court were chosen from term to term, elected all county officers. The justices present were:

William Weaver, Micajah Pennington, John Calloway, John Koontz, William McNeil, Bedent Baird, William Reeves, Joseph Doughton, Alexander Smith, John McBride, Nathan Horton, James Bumgard, Thomas Testerman, Soloman Baker, Elijah Pope, Charles Toliver, and Joseph Roland.

They elected Martin Gambill sheriff and tax collector, requiring him to give bonds of two thousand pounds for each office. His bonds were signed by John Cox and Jesse Reeves.

Indicating a custom of the times and a proceeding that the county court went through frequently, there is this entry on May 12, 1806:

"William Lewis, an orphan, be bound to Gideon Lewis until he is 21 years old, who agrees to give him one year's schooling, a horse and saddle and bridle worth $50.00 and a freedom suit when free."

Gideon Lewis, a leading citizen of his day, was required to give bond to carry out the agreement.

Taking note of approaching state and congressional elections, the court named officials for three polling places as follows:

At William Maxwell's, with William Connelly and John Toliver as judges for the congressional election; William Harris and Samuel Phipps for the state election;

At the county courthouse, with William Weaver and James Bumgard, judges for the state election and Alex Smith and Jesse Ray, judges for the congressional election;

At Three Forks, David Miller and Captain John Brown, judges for the state election and James McCaleb and Henry Ernest, judges for the congressional election.

Three polling places for the immense area of 947 square miles that was Ashe County in those days!

At the next term of court, which was held in August, 1806, the grand jury was made up of Thomas Calloway, foreman; Benjamin Ward, David Bireley, Henry Graybeal, Andrew Sheets, John Estep, William May, Willie Pennington, J. L. Weaver, William Snow, Daniel Hopper, Carter Whittenton, Samuel Phipps, and James Lewis.

At the November term, 1806, the County Court directed the sheriff to ask for bids for the erection of a whipping post and stocks at the county jail.

At this session the court took steps to lay off a road north from Jefferson, across the Phoenix Mountain. Thereafter, at every meeting of the court of which there is record, road location and road building and maintenance appeared to have been of prime importance. There was constant laying off of new roads and improvement of the old. Scores of road overseers were appointed, assigned sections of road and "hands" to work them.

Under the law, every overseer was assigned a sufficient number of workers, generally designated as "road hands," to work his section of road. He was held to strict accountability by the County Court and was required to make regular reports on his operations. That system prevailed for a century or more in North Carolina. In fact there are Ashe County citizens living today who remember working as road hands. The service was required of every citizen, high and low, rich and poor. Only the aged and the infirm were excused from road duty and the Court was the only agency that could excuse. When "warned out," as the operation was named, the citizen reported at the place designated for assembly, with his own tools. Failure to report as directed brought severe punishment. The overseer was required to report the delinquent to the next session of the County Court, which meted out stiff punishment.

As a matter of fact, this road building and road maintenance was no light chore. In the case of some of the main roads across the county, citizens living within five miles of the roads were required by law to work the roads when, if, and as ordered by their overseers.

The first mention of a practicing attorney at law in the county appears in the minutes of the August, 1806, term, where it is recorded that Robert H. Burton presented his license to practice law and was admitted to the Ashe County bar. At the May term, 1807, Burton McQueen and Sanders Donaha presented their licenses and were admitted to the Ashe County bar. There is an entry in the minutes of this term that "Thomas McGimsey resigned as attorney-at-law." Saunders Donaha was elected county attorney, presumably to succeed McGimsey.

At this term, George Bower served as constable to the court. Jonathan Baker was elected sheriff and David Earnest was elected clerk of court. Earnest's bond for two thousand pounds was signed by James Bumgard and Alexander Smith. In the minutes of the same session is the statement that Samuel Cox was elected sheriff and there was no mention of what happened to Baker.

In the Superior Court records of the county, Thomas McGimsey is said to have been appointed Clerk of Court and Master at the March term, 1807, and to have resigned at the September term, 1807. As above stated the Superior Court was just beginning to function in Ashe in 1807 and McGimsey must have been connected with it. There is no mention of his connection with the County Court during that period.

J. P. Arthur, in his *History of Western North Carolina* (p. 159) states that the first term of Ashe County Superior Court was the March term, 1807. He said that Francis Locke was the presiding judge. Locke appointed John McMillan Clerk of Court and fixed his bond at two thousand pounds.

Exactly where the first session of Ashe County Superior Court was held, Mr. Arthur, after diligent research, was unable to determine. There were those who claimed that it was held in an old log church in what was known as McEwen's Meadow in front of where the present courthouse stands. Others contended that it was in an old Baptist Church about half a mile from Jefferson on the Beaver Creek Road. It is certain that Judge Locke did not hold court in the courthouse, as the courthouse, a log structure, had been slow in building. It is recorded that the courthouse was completed in time for the regular meeting of the County Court at the November term, 1809. It was presented at that session and accepted by the Court. The county jail, also a log structure, was accepted at the same time. John Bowers, who had been serving as trustee of public buildings during construction, resigned and was succeeded by Esquire Smith and Thomas Calloway.

The first county courthouse stood at the crossing of the Helton road and a road running east and west through Jefferson, now known as Main Street. It was replaced by a brick courthouse in 1832 or 1833 on the same site. The present courthouse was erected in 1904 on practically the same site except that it was set farther back from the road.

The first jail, according to Mr. Arthur *(History of Western North Carolina*, p. 161), was the second jail west of the Blue Ridge and served the county until 1833 when it was replaced by a brick structure. This jail was burned in the spring of 1865 by men wearing Yankee uniforms and was rebuilt on the same site.

It is worth recording that the first Superior Court grand jury for Ashe County, so far as the records go, was summoned for the March term, 1807. It was composed of the following:

Nathan Horton, foreman; James Bumgard, David Earnest, John Brown, Eli Cleveland, Joseph Couch, John Koontz, Jonathan Baker, Elijah Pope, Jesse Ray, Samuel C. Cox, John Holman, Joshua Cox, Elijah Calloway, John Judd, Alexander Johnson, Morris Baker, and William Weaver.

In the minutes of the County Court of Pleas and Quarter Sessions there is no mention of the drastic changes in court procedure that were taking place, but it is noticeable that after 1807 there was no further mention of grand juries being summoned and empaneled by the County Court. Superior courts took over jurisdiction in most of the civil and criminal actions, leaving to the County Court the other duties that it had been performing. Thereafter the principal service of the County Court to the Superior Court was the maintenance of jury lists and the drawing of grand juries and petit juries for the regular terms of Superior Court, at the same time maintaining its own petit jury system.

It is noteworthy that there was a dearth of legal talent in Ashe County in the early days. Between 1799 and 1807, and perhaps later, the County Court was authorized by law to admit licensed lawyers to the Ashe County bar. Thomas McGimsey, an Ashe County citizen, appears to have been the first resident attorney. He was active in county affairs but appears to have been more real estate dealer than attorney. He served Ashe as representative in the House in 1807, and again in 1808 and 1809.

In 1807 Henry Young Webb and Anderson Mitchell presented their licenses and were admitted to the Ashe County bar, but they, like Robert Burton, Burton McQueen, and Saunders Donaha mentioned above, were not residents of Ashe. They lived elsewhere and in accordance with the customs of the day they practiced their profession in Ashe and probably in several other counties.

After the establishment of the new Superior Court system and its extension to Ashe in 1807, Ashe County had two Superior Court sessions annually, in March and in September. Superior Court judges were chosen by the General Assembly. By law, the judges were required to "ride" the judicial districts. No judge could hold court in any county twice in succession. Consequently, there was call for much riding in those days and all of it difficult. The custom developed of lawyers meeting at specified points and riding the districts with the presiding judge. This afforded, generally speaking, a congenial, if saddle sore, cavalcade and assured plenty of attorneys at every court, ready and willing to accept employment.

Among the traveling lawyers of the day there were many who later attained fame. Many noted judges developed from the hardy young lawyers who rode the rough and rugged trails that passed for roads and earned meager fees for their labors. Even the judges in those days drew annual salaries of only $1,950. Among these judges, all of whom served in Ashe one or more times, were Leonard Henderson, who was later to become Chief Justice of the North Carolina Supreme Court; Thomas Ruffin, who also was to rise to the Supreme Court of North Carolina; John Hall; Francis Locke; Samuel Lowrie; Robert H. Burton; Duncan Cameron; John Louis Taylor, later to be Chief Justice of the Supreme Court; Frederick Nash; Richmond Pearson, later Chief Justice; Spruce McCay; and Anderson Mitchell.

Justice was stern in those days, and strictly impartial. There is record that Judge Spruce McCay fined six jurors, all prominent citizens, ten pounds each for being delinquent. Peter Hart, prominent citizen, paid forty shillings and spent a night in jail for making a noise in court. John Northern and Gideon Lewis, also leading citizens, paid fines of twenty shillings each for not answering when their names were called.

The whipping post, pillory, and stocks ordered by the County Court of Pleas and Quarter Sessions at their November term, 1806, were accepted and paid for at the August term, 1807, and put to use in dealing with misdemeanants of all kinds. For minor offenses the offenders stood for specified periods in the stocks or were subjected to a specified number of blows from a whip wielded by a strong armed deputy sheriff.

For more serious offenses there were more serious punishments. For instance, there is the record of the punishment meted out by the presiding judge at the March term of Ashe County Superior Court in 1809 in the case of a prominent citizen convicted of perjury:

> Fined ten pounds and said Carter Whittington to stand in the pillory for one hour, at the expiration of which time both of his ears to be cut off and entirely severed from his head, and his ears so cut off be nailed to the pillory by the officers and there to remain to the setting of the sun, and the sheriff of this county carry this judgment immediately into execution and that said Carter Whittington be confined until fine and fees are paid.

Official records show that this citizen had served the county as a member of the Court of Pleas and Quarter Sessions and in other positions of trust and responsibility.

Penologists of this day and time would pronounce such sentence for any crime whatsoever a relic of the dark ages and the world would be shocked at its execution. It was, however, in accordance with the law at that time. The stern forefathers of Ashe, who had axed their way into a trackless wilderness, enduring fearful hardships, found nothing amiss in the punishment inflicted. To them crime was crime and called for real and drastic punishment.

So, with strict laws, based upon the old English common law, with but little of the ancient severity eliminated, the people of Ashe had little crime to contend with and they went forward building their own unit of government on a sound foundation.

They early set about using their representatives in the General Assembly, whose names and years of service are recorded elsewhere. Apparently they did not ask the General Assembly to do anything for them that they could do for themselves.

Farmers and livestock growers were finding it hard to keep wolves from destroying their cattle, hogs, and sheep, and asked authority to levy a tax to start wolf hunting on a large scale. There were plenty of them in Ashe. Bishop Spangenberg, in his diary, had reported that he had never heard anything to equal their howling at night.

In Chapter 85, Public Laws of 1801, the General Assembly authorized the County Court to levy a tax of six pence on every poll and two pence on every $100 worth of land for the purpose of exterminating wolves. Ashe County was blessed with hunters and there followed great activity in hunting and trapping wolves. According to tradition, the greatest hunter of them all was Wilburn Waters. J. A. Testerman of Jefferson has written a very interesting book about this famous hunter, who was not only a successful exterminator of wolves but a great bear hunter. He was born in Wilkes County but came to Ashe when just a boy. He established his home in the northwestern corner of the county, in the Pond mountain-White Top area, and died there in his sixty-seventh year. He was buried near Union Church. An impressive monument has been erected over his grave. Gradually he and his associates cleared the forests of wolves and reduced the bear population until it was no longer a menace.

Following the books of minutes of the proceedings of the Court of Pleas and Quarter Sessions one finds that not all verdicts of the court were as severe as the one above referred to. For instance:

> Abner Duncan, brought into court in an action for slander, for having accused James Campbell of stealing a hog, signed a certified statement that if he ever made such charge, it was while he was in a state of intoxication or otherwise deranged.

The charge was thereupon dismissed.

John McMillan, first clerk of court and a large landowner, registered his hog mark, "viz, a crop off the left ear and two slits in the right ear." This is only one of many similar entries which consumed much time of the court.

At the November term, 1806, John Bowers, John Kesler, and Joseph Kesler were appointed to assess town lots in Jefferson for taxation.

At the February term, 1807, Luke White was authorized to build a mill on his own land at the mouth of Phoenix Creek. At this session, taxes for the next year were set at "6 shillings 3 pence on the poll and 2 shillings and one pence on the 100 acres of land, state tax and poor tax included."

At the August term, 1807, the first account of the granting of land for setting up an iron forge appeared. The County Court was acting under Chapter 293, Public Laws of 1788, which authorized a land grant up to 3,000 acres to any person who set up a forge and produced 5,000 pounds of iron. The grant so entered had to be to land duly certified by the County Court as unfit for agricultural uses. The entry was to Daniel Dougherty, "for the use of the Iron Works that the said Daniel Dougherty built on the Bigg Helton."

At the November term, 1807 another grant of 3,000 acres went to Thomas Calloway for setting up an iron forge with required production. (Book of Deeds D, p. 88, Office of Register of Deeds of Ashe County.)

That there were similar grants to Meredith Ballou, William Harbard, and others is certain, but the only other grant appearing in the County Court records was to Jesse Ray at the November term, 1827, covering 3,000 acres in the Three Top section certified by the court as unfit for cultivation.

There are no entries of particular importance for the remainder of 1807 and the year 1808. At the May term, 1809, Samuel Cox was elected sheriff and, as already stated, the courthouse was accepted at the November term, 1809.

At the February term, 1810, it is recorded that the taxable property in Ashe for 1809 was: 176,900 acres of land; 460 polls; 7 stud horses; two taverns; one store.

At the May term, 1812, taxable property was listed as follows: 173,797 acres of land; 449 polls; 6 stud horses; 3 taverns; 3 stores.

At this term Adolphus L. Eulin was admitted to the Ashe County bar and elected solicitor for the Court.

At the May term, 1818, taxables for 1817 were listed as follows: 197,588 acres of land, valued at $197,128; 528 polls; 4 stores; 1 toll gate; 7 stud horses.

At the May term, 1819, it is recorded that David Earnest resigned as Clerk of Court, George Bowers was licensed to "retail spiritous liquors in the town of Jeffersonton," John Bowers was elected county trustee.

At the August term, 1821, James Mawell was appointed prosecuting attorney "in the room of Thomas McGimsey, resigned."

At the May term, 1826, the value of all town property for taxation was $9,668, and the total town tax collected was $38.37½. The number of acres of land on the tax books was 209,997, valued at $219,960. The number of taxable polls was 676.

At the November term, 1826, Meredith Ballou was excused from jury duty because of deafness.

At the February term, 1827, Thomas Calloway is reported as having renewed his bond as Clerk of Court, with Meredith Ballou as surety, and Meredith Ballou renewed his own bond as county surveyor.

The May term, 1820, elected John Ray sheriff, and fixed taxes at $1.00 on the poll and 33 1/3 cents on every $100 worth of land and town property.

At the May term, 1828, W. W. Alexander was elected county solicitor, John Gambill was elected sheriff, John Bowers was re-elected county trustee and taxes were levied at 16 cents on the $100 worth of land or town property and 40 cents on each poll. The court appointed a committee consisting of Jonathan Faw, George Bowers, and Anderson Mitchell to select a suitable place for a new whipping post and stocks.

At the August term, 1828, the court licensed Robert Gentry and D. E. Moore to "sell spiritous liquors by the small measure."

At the May session, 1829, John Gambill was reelected sheriff. John Bowers resigned as county trustee and was succeeded by Drewery Senter. County tax was levied at 80 cents on each poll and 25 cents on each $100 of property; 5 cents on each poll and 22 cents on each $100 of property for poor tax.

Minute books of the County Court are missing for several years after 1830 and there is nothing of record to indicate anything other than peaceful, sound, and uneventful rural life for Ashe.

Dr. Elisha Mitchell, University of North Carolina professor of chemistry who was also a geologist, had visited Ashe in 1827 and 1828 and, as his diary indicates, he had found much to please him. There was commendable agricultural activity. While waiting in Jefferson for Attorney Anderson Mitchell, who was away "electioneering," he induced a Mr. Faw to climb Negro Mountain with him. Says he:

"And a rugged ascent it was! Some of the plantations in view presented a noble appearance, but oh, what an ocean of mountains!"

"Jeffersontown," he said, "has six or eight dwelling houses, rather shabby."

He went on to relate that in all of his travels over Ashe he found only log cabins.

What took place after 1828 is not a matter of record, but between that date and 1850 Jefferson went forward in the building of homes, store buildings and other needed structures. During that period the imposing brick house of George Bowers, still standing on Main Street, presently owned by Wert Neal, and other brick and frame residences were erected. As will be related elsewhere, George Bowers was not only an outstanding legislator but he was a successful business man and farmer. He was a large slaveowner. It was while pursuing a runaway slave that he was drowned in the Yadkin River on October 7, 1861.

George Bowers used his big brick home as a residence, a post office, a store, and a hotel. During this same period there was much building activity as Jefferson grew. Among those who put up homes well out of the log cabin class were Henry Rollins, Sheriff E. C. Bartlett, J. E. Foster, N. A. Foster, William P. Waugh, Nathan

Waugh, John M. Carson, Colonel R. Murchison (of the mercantile firm of Waugh, Poe, and Murchison), Wiley P. Thomas, Dr. James Wagg, Dr. L. C. Gentry, and many others. In fact, Jefferson was the largest town in the mountains in the early 1800's.

While Jefferson was expanding, other parts of the county were growing also. Noted physician and writer Dr. Aras B. Cox, taking time off for politics, became Clerk of the Superior Court in 1849 and was reelected in 1853. He lived in the eastern part of the county when elected but later bought a farm seven miles from Jefferson. Stephen Thomas, of Creston, established a store and tavern at Creston, which prospered. David Worth, also at Creston, was a tanner by trade and became one of the county's leading citizens. Zachariah Baker, at Creston, was a successful farmer and livestock man. The Graybeal family, of Dutch ancestry, came to the area before it was a county and contributed much to building a sound foundation for the new county. So did the Ellers, who came to Ashe from the Jersey Settlement, now in Davidson County, and settled on the North Fork of New River.

John P. Arthur in his *History of Western North Carolina* (page 166) lists these and many others among the men who were developing all parts of Ashe County in the early days. He pays tribute particularly to Henry Poe, Martin Gambill, Thomas Sutherland, Timothy Perkins, John Cox, Henry Hardin, Canada Richardson, James Douglas, Daniel Dickerson, Elijah Calloway, Meredith Ballou, and Thomas Harbard.

Mr. Arthur goes on to say:

> Besides these there were many others whose names awaken much unwritten history: Miller, Blevins, Ham, Reeves, Woodie, Barr, Goodman, Ray, Burkett, Thomas, Houck, Kilby, Ashley, Jones, Gentry, Smith, Plummer, Lewis, McMillan, Colvard, Barker, Senter, Maxwell, Calhoun, Sapp, and Oliver.

To this list he might have added Price, Vannoy, Neal, Garvey, Weaver, Ward, Calloway, Lewis, Estep, Cox, Pennington, McCaleb, Bumgard, James, Seagraves, Sheets, Earnest, May, Snow, Phipps, Johnson, Johnston, Campbell, Todd, Austin, Doughton, Duncan, Dickerson, Osborne, Hamilton, and others.

Mr. Arthur does not mention in the pages devoted to Ashe the fine pioneers of Watauga, who in the early hard days between

1799 and 1849 were citizens of Ashe County, but in the section devoted to Watauga he pays tribute to Joseph Brown, who came to what was Ashe in the early days; the sturdy Mast family, which settled at Valle Crucis; William Farthing, Baptist minister, and his family; Simon Shull and his descendants; John Moretz and his family; and Benjamin Howard, whose daughter married Jordan Council, Sr., who established a store and trading post where the town of Boone now stands. Here was located the first post office in what is now Watauga, known as "Council's Store," a name which it retained until after the new county was sliced off of Ashe and named Watauga in 1849. Thereafter Council's Store post office became Boone. As prominent persons among the first settlers of this part of Ashe, Arthur mentions Amos and Edward Green, Jackson, Steven and Abner Farthing, James McCauless, Elisha Coffey, Lee Foster, Malden and Calvin Harmon, Seaton Mast, Lorenzo Whittington, George Moody, and Henry Taylor. These men and others like them had started thriving communities at Shulls Mill, Valle Crucis, Meat Camp, Cove Creek, Beaver Dam, and other places. Most of them arrived in the area prior to 1799, and the others in the early 1800's.

Written record of the activities of the Ashe Court of Pleas and Quarter sessions for the period of the War Between the States and the years immediately preceding the war is nonexistent. If records were set down, in the confusion of war times they were lost. It is safe to assume that the Court of Pleas and Quarter Sessions carried on until the new State Constitution became effective and the Ashe County Board of Commissioners took over in 1868.

II

The Board of County Commissioners

The story of what the Ashe County Court of Pleas and Quarter Sessions did between 1799 and 1868 has been told in part in the preceding section of this chapter. Admittedly the record is not complete, but perhaps enough has been garnered from available records to give some idea of the large part the court played in the lives of the people. It was truly a busy agency of Government and it touched the life and activities of all of the people.

In other parts of this history will be information about road-building, which concerned every session of the court; progress in establishing and supporting schools; the founding and growth of churches of various denominations; the improvement of agriculture; the establishment of mills for the making of meal and flour; and the development of iron mines and the setting up of forges to produce iron for household, farming and commercial uses. In all of these areas and more, the Court of Pleas and Quarter Sessions labored faithfully from its begining in 1799 until its end in 1868.

What the Court of Pleas and Quarter Sessions did during the long War Between the States is nowhere recorded. Because Ashe County was cut off from the rest of the State by the Blue Ridge Mountains, it was not possible to keep up with what was going on outside of its boundaries. It is certain, however, that the court was staunchly and firmly loyal to the cause of the Confederacy and saw to it that the county's obligations to the State and its fighting men were duly fulfilled.

Not everybody in Ashe County was completely loyal to the South. The institution of slavery was never popular in Ashe County and when the War Between the States came on there was little enthusiasm for slavery. As a matter of fact, the census of 1860 showed only 391 slaves in Ashe and 142 free Negroes. Probably not more than a dozen families owned slaves, and there was no interest in perpetuating slave-holding. However, because the citizens of Ashe were strong for states' rights, they threw their support to the South and went along with the rest of the State when it finally seceded from the Union.

Besides furnishing its quota of fighting men for the Confederacy, Ashe County, well removed from the area where contending armed forces were fighting and destroying property, was called upon to furnish large quantities of agricultural products for the armed forces and its mines and forges operated day and night to produce the iron they needed. A lead mine in northwestern Ashe furnished lead for Confederate rifles. The agency directing these and related activities was the Court of Pleas and Quarter Sessions.

There was not an accurate selective service system in those days, but the Confederacy had to institute the draft system and the agency to see to its effective operation was the Court of Pleas and Quarter Sessions. It also set up a rationing system and saw to it that the available food supplies were equitably distributed to the wives and children of the men in the army, with special attention given to the widows and orphans of soldiers.

There were those who carried their hatred of slavery to the point where they enlisted and served in a Yankee regiment recruited in Ashe, Watauga and east Tennessee. Others took to the woods and were contemptuously referred to as "bushwhackers." They lived by thievery by day and by night, and the "Home Guard," made up of men too young or too old for the army, was kept busy. Because the maintenance of law and order was the particular province of the Court, it must have carried a tremendous load between 1861 and 1865.

Because there was no large ex-slave population to deal with, Ashe County was spared the turmoil and violent dissensions of Reconstruction and the new agency called the "Board of County Commissioners," doubtless found it easy to take over under the North Carolina Constitution of 1868. They found themselves relieved of the trials of misdemeanors and of many clerical duties. Probably the biggest burden lifted from their shoulders was the election of county officers. Thereafter, these officials were to be chosen by the people.

It is not possible to set down here in detail all that has happened to the county since the Board of County Commissioners took over but an effort will be made, as in the preceding section devoted to government by the Court of Pleas and Quarter Sessions, to give a general idea of the month-to-month activities of the county's governing body.

The Constitution of 1868 required all counties to have a Board of Commissioners of not more than five men. It was also required that each county have a treasurer, a register of deeds, a sheriff and a surveyor. Under the new Constitution the commissioners were to have supervision and control of penal and charitable institutions, schools, roads, bridges, taxation, and management of the finances of the county as prescribed by law.

As fortune would have it, the new board found itself saddled with debt and after struggling with it for ten or more years, they referred their troubles to the General Assembly of North Carolina, which in Chapter 259 of the Public Laws of 1881 authorized the Commissioners to levy a property tax sufficient to produce enough revenue to pay $2,000 annually on the public debt.

This revenue was increased to $3,000 per year in 1885.

The first Board of County Commissioners, meeting on September 5, 1870, was composed of Chairman J. B. McMillan, Gideon Weaver, Wm. Maxwell, Poindexter Blevins, William H. Hamilton, and John H. Vannoy. It is interesting to note that Captain Joseph W. Todd, an eminent lawyer, was paid $18 for serving as examiner of teachers in 1869 and 1870. At the same board meeting Captain Todd was appointed head overseer of the public road from Jefferson to the mouth of Phoenix Creek.

Two years later, in 1872, the board was composed of Chairman E. C. Bartlett, David Worth, Amos Mitchell, John H. Carson and William Shepperd.

The 1874 board, made up of Chairman Poindexter Blevens, E. C. Bartlett, Gideon Weaver, John Osborne, and J. B. Miller, asked the North Carolina General Assembly to approve the levying of a special tax to build a new jail and met the problem of uniform listing of taxes by appointing a special commission from the magistrates of the county to come up with a workable plan. This body was composed of the following: Absolam Roark, from North Fork Township; Laurel, John Pennington; Staggs Creek, Joshua Roark; Horse Creek, John Eldreth; Piney Creek, James Eller; Helton, David Dickerson; Chestnut Hill, J. C. Plummer; Peak Creek, William B. Carson; Pine Swamp, E. E. Phillips; Old Fields, R. T. Hardin; Jefferson, H. H. Ray.

The board reflected Ashe County's respect for churches by approving the incorporation of various churches in order to prevent and control disorder at church gatherings. Among those incorporated were Greenwood Methodist, Landmark, Mad Creek, Apple Grove, Maple Springs Baptist and many others.

In succeeding sessions of the board there was more pressure for road improvements. Every section of the county was clamoring for road improvement. Many toll roads were proposed and some were laid out and constructed by private subscriptions. No citizen living along the toll roads so constructed was relieved of his regular road duty, but in most cases he was relieved of paying tolls on the new roads.

There was particular interest in the construction of a good road south to Wilkesboro, as this was the best North Carolina outlet to markets. Colonel Nathan Horton, leading citizen of his time in the days of the Court of Pleas and Quarter Sessions, was prime mover in the construction of a toll road from Wilkes through Ashe to Jefferson and on to the Tennessee line. A goodly portion of his personal fortune went into the construction of that part of the road which lies between his home and the Tennessee line. Because he found it too heavy a burden, Colonel Horton had offered the so-called "Horton Turnpike" to the State without charge. Typical of the tolls levied on this and other toll roads in the county, were these: For each 4-wheel carriage, 50 cents; each 2-wheel vehicle, 20 cents; each passenger on horse, 10 cents; each foot passenger 5 cents, mules and horses 5 cents per head, cattle 2½ cents per head; hogs and sheep, 1 cent per head.

From the written accounts of the meetings of the board it is evident that they were always mindful of the need of transportation and paid special attention to "roads that went somewhere and served useful purposes."

Human nature being what it is, not every citizen took kindly to the working of the roads. From time to time the board had to "get tough" with those who feigned illness and were excused from duty by their overseers. There was much controversy about this action. For lack of workers roads deteriorated into almost impassable trails. The board, despairing of getting action from the overseers, finally set up a regulation requiring every citizen who claimed to be physically unable to work the roads to secure a physician's certificate of illness before being excused. Dr. J. O. Wilcox and Dr. L. C. Gentry were appointed examiners and the applicant had to pay a fee of one dollar for each examination. Thereafter, it is related, the "road hands" reported for duty as directed.

The idea of getting state aid in the construction of better roads appealed to the board and in 1887 they took steps to secure state convicts to construct a road from Jefferson north toward Marion,

Virginia "by way of the Mineral Springs, commonly called Healing, or Thompson's Springs, to the Virginia line, nearest and most practicable route toward Marion, Virginia."

Apparently the board decided that a road to market by way of Wilkesboro was a hopeless proposition and they turned their attention to reaching Marion, Virginia, the closest railroad connection. This resulted in trade relations with Virginia and the subsequent designation of Ashe, Alleghany and Watauga as the "Lost Provinces." They were in North Carolina, but their principal trade and business connections were out of the state.

It is worth noting that in its earliest days the Ashe County Court was "welfare-minded." The poor were never forgotten even in the county's first days, and from those first days down to recent years there was always a tax levied to take care of the poor. From the beginning, the county maintained a county home, or "poor house," as it was called. Always, when a new board of commissioners came into office, the first act was to select a "keeper of the poor-house," and his compensation was fixed on a per head basis.

Among the earlier records it appears that compensation for caring for the poor was fixed at approximately $4.00 per person per month. For this amount the keeper was to furnish food and lodging and "clothing in accordance with their station in life."

In the minutes for the meeting of October, 1876 appears this entry:

"Ordered by the Board that the paupers of Ashe county be sold out to the lowest responsible bidder on the 16th day of October, 1876 by sealed bids." It is recorded that contract for one year was awarded to Alfred Barker "at $40 for each pauper for 12 months."

The county had acquired land and had built and furnished a county home. The first county home was on Phoenix Creek and had very little tillable land with it. By modern day standards, furnishings of the home were scanty. An inventory was reported in the minutes of the board meeting for June, 1877 as follows:

"Five feather-beds, 5 bed-steads, 46 bed covers, 9 pillows, 3 pots, 5 milk crocks, 1 tea-kettle, 1 beaker, 2 jars, 12 teacups, 11 saucers, 18 plates, 2 work pans, 1 cupboard, 1 table, 8 knives, 8 forks, 5 tablespoons, 6 teaspoons."

As of June 5, 1877, there were seven paupers in the poor-house.

The poor-house was later moved to the Beaver Creek section on very fine land, and the new establishment richly deserved the title of "Ashe County Home." Succeeding "superintendents" operated the farm connected with the home on a share basis, substantially reducing the cash outlay per inmate of the home.

The justices of the peace in Ashe carried on after the adoption of the new Constitution in 1868 about as they did before, but they came to the conclusion that the governing body was too large for economical administration. At their regular meeting on August 5, 1878 they took steps to stream-line the administrative set-up. They reduced the number of county commissioners for the term from five to three and abolished the office of county treasurer. In the matter of the number of county commissioners the board decreed that future boards might consist of five members, if desired, but a board of three was recommended. The justices of the peace making this decision were:

Jacob Graybeal, James P. Waugh, R. T. Hardin, T. S. Bouchelle, A. D. Cowles, E. E. Phillips, W. B. Carson, E. H. Fairfax, G. W. Woodie, J. C. Plummer, Poindexter Blevins, S. Pennington, Pat Graham, James Eller, J. M. Grimsley, Isham Goss, John Horn, J. P. Ashley, Gideon Weaver, and Joseph L. Johnson.

The justices selected George H. Hamilton, David Worth, and James Eller as county commissioners and their first recorded act was the levying of a tax of 90 cents on the $100 for property and $2 on each poll.

The board, finding it difficult to collect taxes due from the shifting population of the town of Ore Knob, Ashe County's copper mine, authorized James E. Clayton, one of the operator-owners of the mine, to collect the taxes from the workers in the mine. The assessment of the Ore Knob property was reduced from $40,000 to $30,000. Later, in 1903 this tax valuation was to be reduced to $8,000.

This board was succeeded in 1878 by one consisting of James Eller, J. S. Howell, Andrew Reeves, and Chart Phipps.

On May 3, 1880, the board ordered a special election on the sale of liquor in Pine Swamp township. The result was thirty against the sale of liquor and twenty for.

The board took a step forward in the welfare field by employing Dr. James Wagg as county physician.

A new board consisting of N. H. Waugh, J. B. McMillan, T. S. Bouchelle, Stephen Pennington and James Eller went into office on August 2, 1880. This board was still holding on through 1881, when Dr. L. C. Gentry was elected county physician. In 1882 it is noted that they made a prominent lawyer, George W. Bower, superintendent of streets in Jefferson.

In 1885 the Board of County Commissioners adopted a new policy with regard to paupers, ordering that no pauper be accepted at the county home in the future unless approved by a majority of the magistrates of the pauper's township.

On January 7, 1886, a new board came into office headed by Capt. John Dent. Other members were Mack Absher and Isham Goss.

At its regular meeting on March 4, 1889, the board called up six prominent citizens of the county for failure to report to their road supervisor for working the roads. These were R. A. Hamilton, George H. Hamilton, W. B. Burkett, Alex Bullis, Lee Horton and George Anderson. They were found guilty as charged, and the board's verdict was that they be given until April 1, 1889 to pay the proper amount in cash to their overseer, Lee W. Duvall, to cover the time lost, or "to make their time on the Jefferson-Healing Springs road."

At its June meeting in 1891 the board levied a general tax of 66 2/3 cents on the $100 and a special county tax of 16 2/3 cents. At this session a county board of education was announced, consisting of A. Weaver, William Blevins and J. B. Houck.

The board, faced with unpaid bills, set about getting an accurate inventory of all unpaid accounts, and ordered that all persons with claims against the county have said claims duly certified and present them to the board on or before the first Monday in September, 1891, or their claims would be invalidated. Subsequent accounts of board meetings have no reference to the results of this effort.

On October 5, 1896, the board consisted of Chairman E. E. Phillips, L. S. Jones and D. A. Martin. On March 1, 1897, W. S.

Eastridge was chairman and J. S. Miller and W. H. Graybeal were the other members. It is interesting to note that this particular board in 1898 dropped the opprobrious name "poor-house" and thereafter for a time referred to that institution as "alms-house."

In January of 1901 the board consisted of Chairman H. G. Phipps, D. M. Graybeal and B. V. Idol. They elected Robert H. McNeill county attorney at a salary of $50 per year and Dr. Manly Blevins was made county physician. He was later, after two years of service, succeeded by Dr. J. W. Colvard. The tax levy for 1901 was 66 2/3 cents on the $100 and $2 poll; special levy, 20 cents on the $100 and 20 cents on the poll; 10 cents on the $100 for roads and 30 cents on the poll. The general road law was adopted for Ashe County, as was the state law requiring "lawful fences." At its May meeting in 1901, the board made the North Fork of New River a lawful fence from the mouth of Silas Creek to the mouth of Piney Creek and from the mouth of Silas Creek up the river to the falls near Zackary Parsons' place.

At the June meeting of the board in 1902 there was an entry that George W. Bower and T. C. Bowie were paid $5 each for legal advice. The tax levy went up to 88 2/3 cents on the $100 and $2.66 on the poll. The board ordered the construction of a new bridge across the South Fork of New River at a cost of $500. W. W. Howell was appointed manager of the county home.

By 1904 the need of an adequate courthouse had become apparent and the board that was elected proceeded to initiate the county into the new world of high finance that was beginning to take over throughout the State. There was no cash available for the project and the board decided to issue $20,000 of six per cent bonds for the courthouse. The bonds were issued and sold to one J. M. Holmes of Chicago, Ill., at a premium of 2 per cent. The board at the time consisted of Chairman H. G. Phipps, John H. Mercer and D. M. Graybeal. T. C. Bowie was attorney for the board. The tax levy for 1905 was 66 2/3 cents on the $100 and $2 on the poll; 20 cents on the $100 and 60 cents on the poll for county institutions including interest on bonds; 10 cents on the $100 and 30 cents on the poll for roads. There was a special levy in Jefferson school district of 30 cents on the $100 and 90 cents on the poll. The keeping of the county home was let to J. M. Goodman, who entered into a contract "to keep, support and maintain the inmates, furnishing them with good, sufficient and wholesome food and the necessary apparel suitable to their condition and station in life." The consideration was to be $5.75 per inmate per month.

Under the next board, J. L. Thompson took over the county home at 19 cents per day per inmate.

The board which took over the county government on January 1, 1907 consisted of Chairman Joseph W. Calloway, Felix McGuire and Elihu Graybeal. This board, taking note of the need of suitable quarters for the newly organized First National Bank of Jefferson, leased one room in the courthouse to the new institution for 12 months at $40 for the year.

At its October meeting in 1907 the board levied a special tax to provide for a minimum school term in Ashe as required by state law for all of the counties.

In 1907 and 1908 agitation for a bond issue, or a stock subscription, to aid in the construction of a railroad from Virginia into North Carolina, engaged the attention of everybody in Ashe. The "Virginia Southern Railway Co.," which was said to have a line under construction to Mouth of Wilson, Virginia, proposed to extend the line to Jefferson if the county would subscribe to $100,000 of the company's capital stock. At its meeting on July 3, 1908, the board ordered an election on the issue and set September 14, 1908, as the date to vote on it. The election carried by a majority vote. The registration books showed 3,425 qualified voters and those voting for the purchase of stock numbered 2,101.

The project did not materialize. The promoters did not extend their line to Mouth of Wilson, but the railroad idea was not forgotten. The new board, coming in on January 1, 1909, took steps to provide funds for the building of a railroad into the county from Virginia or from Tennessee. This board was composed of Chairman H. A. Eller, W. H. Garvey and F. P. McGuire. A bond election, calling for the issuance of $250,000 in bonds toward the financing of the undertaking, was set for October 16, 1909. The issue did not carry, the vote being 476 for and 997 against.

This same board paid off the bonds issued to build the new

county courthouse and it sold the county home to J. M. Goodman for $1,000, keeping Goodman to his contract for the care of paupers.

The board of 1911, with Chairman H. A. Eller, J. M. Dickson and W. H. Garvey, faced badly needed road and bridge improvement and among other major operations agreed to repair the bridge over New River on the Jefferson-Wilkesboro turnpike, provided that Ashe County citizens would not be charged for using the turnpike.

This turnpike, a joint effort financed by the State, private subscription from citizens of Ashe and Wilkes counties and county appropriations, had been in the process of construction for several years, with the State furnishing convict labor and the counties food and lodging and guards to handle the convicts. The result was a sand-clay road, with improved grades, a great advancement over the old road. It gave every promise of becoming a financial success until the disastrous rainy season of 1916 swept it almost completely away. There was never any effort to rebuild and reestablish the toll road and it quickly reverted to the level of the old local dirt roads. Except for improvement in grades and a few bridges not washed away, the roads were about as before the floods of 1916.

The board in 1916, composed of Chairman I. H. Stuart, J. F. Scott and J. E. Walters, had caught a vision of what could be done with bond issues and started to rebuild county bridges with a bond issue of $20,000. Among the first projects completed was a bridge across North Fork of New River at Crumpler at a cost of $5,400. Their successors in 1917, Chairman Ambrose Shepherd, R. L. Dickson and J. T. Ready proposed the borrowing of $200,000 from the State for roads. Upon submission to voters on May 8, 1917 the bonds were defeated. There were 423 votes for and 1,841 against.

In November, 1917 the board voted to pay $10 for every $100 contributed to build a "rock road" from Jefferson to Smethport, or on any other road of equal length in the county. The following year the board voted to accept $9,200 of federal aid for road work to be done under regulations set up by federal and state highway authorities.

While good road sentiment appeared to be the main interest during this period, it was evident that the county was waking up in the field of public education as well. At its August 6, 1917 meeting the board levied a special tax of 15 cents on the $100 and 3 cents on the poll for schools. This was a general county tax and was in addition to the special taxes for schools already voted in seven school districts. Interest in special school district taxes was growing in the county. For example, a special school tax had been voted in June, 1917 with only seven votes against it, in Grassy Creek school district.

The board at its meeting in January, 1919 abolished the office of the county treasurer and appointed the Bank of Lansing, Lansing, North Carolina, as county financial agent under a bond of $55,000. The board took steps to modernize the courthouse and jail by installing plumbing and entering into contract with W. E. McNeill, owner of the Jefferson water system, to furnish water at a cost of $50 per year to be paid in equal installments every five years. The contract was to run for 20 years.

The 1918 board, composed of Chairman J. M. Tucker, S. A. Hartsoe and W. A. Weaver, decided to meet all federal requirements for United States aid in building roads. The county was asked to contribute a fourth of the cost and the board pledged the levying of a tax sufficient to pay the county's part.

The 1919 board ordered an election on the issuance of $200,000 of 5½ per cent road bonds. There were 1,268 votes for the bond issue and 1,198 against. There was provision that the bonds, if and when issued, should not exceed 15 per cent of the total tax valuation of the county.

At this juncture there entered upon the scene, by legislative enactment, the Ashe County Good Roads Commission, composed of Chairman S. G. Parsons, Secretary A. A. Price and Ambrose Shepherd. W. R. Bauguess was attorney for the commission.

Taking stock of the situation, the new commission found that the county had a bonded indebtedness of $29,000 and the total tax valuation for 1918 had been $4,592,552.

At the August 1919 meeting the County Board of Commissioners found that the special school tax districts had increased to eight.

To take care of the largely increased bonded indebtedness they levied a special tax of 30 cents on the $100 and 90 cents on the poll. Added to this was a state tax of 47 2/3 cents on the $100 and a general county tax of 37½ cents on the $100, with the usual poll taxes added. The general school tax was fixed at 13 cents on the $100 and 39 cents on the poll.

Road-building boomed. Everybody was excited about it. The $200,000 of 5½ per cent bonds sold readily and the money went rapidly. To keep itself in business the Good Roads Commission called for more money. The amount was set at $300,000. The bonds were to be offered at 5½ per cent, with the promise that the interest rate might be raised to 6 per cent if the bonds would not sell at 5½. The bonds were sold to Spitzer & Co. and Pruden & Co. of Toledo, Ohio in November, 1920 as 6 per cent bonds at par with accrued interest.

Ambrose Shepherd resigned from the Good Roads Commission and was succeeded by G. M. Donnelly.

The Board of County Commissioners going into office on January 1, 1921 was composed of Chairman J. W. Graybeal, J. M. Welborn and J. C. Crawford. This board faced an increasing demand for lower taxes and finally ordered a reduction of 33 1/3 per cent in tax valuations. A review board to work out details of this reduction was composed of J. W. Graybeal, J. M. Welborn, J. C. Crawford, G. W. Eller and W. T. Colvard.

On April 11, 1921, the board approved the borrowing of an additional $100,000 for roads, and levied a special road tax of 50 cents on the $100 and $1.50 on the poll. At the same time the general school tax was fixed at 30 cents on the $100 and 90 cents on the poll.

In October of 1921 the board put into effect a special act passed in 1911 to provide for working prisoners in the county jail on the roads. Labor arrangements were made for using prisoners from Alleghany and Watauga on Ashe County roads.

On June 3, 1922 Hurricane township was created in the northwest corner of Ashe.

In January, 1923, a new board came into office, consisting of Chairman J. E. Walters, W. P. Colvard and J. C. Crawford. On

May 1, 1925 this board authorized the issuance of $310,000 of serial bonds for roads. The tax levy for 1924 went up to 60 cents on the $100 and $1.80 on the poll for bonded debt, plus 10 cents for sinking fund, 15 cents for general county, 3 cents for township roads. Special school district taxes went up from 10 cents to 30 cents.

The 1925 board, consisting of Chairman Thomas K. Miller, H. G. Robinson and Oliver Ham faced the necessity of providing a new jail and let contract for same to Jenkins-Miller Construction Company, of West Jefferson, for $12,410. The board became interested in the possibility of developing hydro-electric power in the county and appropriated $2,000 to aid the State Department of Conservation and Development in making a survey.

Tax levies went up, the school tax reaching 54 cents on the $100; county indebtedness, 84 cents; general highway bonds, 65 cents. Special school tax districts jumped from 8 to 12. The board took a long step forward in hiring a county farm agent at $100 per month, with state and federal governments and interested farmers paying the balance. The school tax for 1926 rose to 63 cents; bonded debt, 75 cents; county roads, 10 cents.

In 1927 the board consisted of Chairman I. H. Stuart, J. C. Crawford and R. B. Brown. It voted 2 to 1 to continue the employment of a county farm agent, Chairman Stuart opposing. The board voted an appropriation of $250 to assist federal and state authorities in a campaign against tuberculosis in cattle. The tax levy went to 48 cents for schools; 75 cents for bonds; county debt, 20 cents; general county, 15 cents; sinking fund, 10 cents.

H. M. Miller was appointed tax collector.

Seeking to get a better outlet to markets, the board memorialized the Virginia State Highway Commission to construct a good road from Grassy Creek to Mouth of Wilson, Virginia.

Henry Duvall took over as manager of the county home on Beaver Creek and contracted to operate the county farm.

The 1928 board faced widespread demands for reduction of various property valuations for tax purposes.

At the January 2, 1928 session the Virginia Coal and Iron Company, owner of the large mineral rights in the northwestern part of Ashe, appealed from an assessed valuation of $35,000 on five hundred acres of land. The company, represented by attorney T. C. Bowie, was granted a reduction of valuation to $17,500 to become effective in 1929.

At its May 7, 1928 meeting, the board took action against former sheriff J. W. Hampton, whose accounts showed an apparent deficit for the years 1921 to 1926. Ira T. Johnston and William B. Austin were named as commissioners to foreclose on a deed of trust for $10,000 signed by Hampton and his wife, covering part of the alleged deficit.

In 1928 by legislative action, county commissioners were elected for staggered terms. M. E. Reeves was elected for six years; B. F. Kilby for four years and J. F. Scott for two years.

The new board undertook to induce the State to take over more road mileage in Ashe, its first effort being a petition to the State Highway Commission to take over the road from the bridge over New River by way of Ore Knob to Laurel Springs, which the county had graded at a cost of $139,744.96. It was pointed out that Ashe, with a population of 22,000, was one of the largest counties in the State, had bonded itself for road construction to the amount of $1,510,000 and yet had only 75 miles of state maintained road.

In 1929 J. F. Hartzog succeed J. F. Scott on the board. The board acted to apply all state aid for roads under the state law to the county's bonded indebtedness for roads.

The Bank of Ashe became county treasurer on June 3, 1929.

At the August term, 1929, the board levied an 80 cent tax for the county sinking fund; 40 cents for outstanding notes; county general, 15 cents; school taxes, 36 cents.

On November 7, 1929 M. E. Reeves resigned as chairman and board member and E. C. Eller was appointed to succeed him. B. F. Kilby was elected chairman.

The tax levy in 1930 went to 72 cents for schools; 70 cents for outstanding bonds; 20 cents for interest and principal of notes; 14 cents for general county.

On December 3, 1930 the claim against J. W. Hampton, ex-sheriff, for the alleged shortage in his accounts of $40,474.24, was compromised. A committee of taxpayers, headed by John A. Weaver, filed a petition in protest, and there was much controversy and considerable litigation about it.

On April 4, 1931, the board made settlement of taxes with Carl B. Graybeal, sheriff and county treasurer, and released him from all official bonds covering collections for 1929 and 1930. The First National Bank of West Jefferson was named as the county's official depository of all road maintenance and sinking funds, the bank to pay 4 per cent interest on deposits.

In 1932 the tax levy for outstanding bonds went up to $1.06, the general schools tax to 19 cents and the general county tax to 23 cents.

The board petitioned the State Highway Commission to build a hard-surfaced road from Jefferson toward Abingdon, Virginia and Bristol, Tennessee and from Jefferson to North Wilkesboro.

In an economy move, the board leased the new county home, with its 85 acres of good land, to H. H. Duvall for two years at $65 per month, the manager and his family and inmates of the home to be supported by the products of the farm.

The 1932 board, consisting of Chairman J. F. Hartzog, E. C. Eller and J. F. Scott, faced dismal prospects. Scott was to resign in June, 1933 and to be succeeded by E. B. Shepherd. The county had just begun to feel the great depression. Sheriff H. M. Miller reported frankly to the board that he had not been able to collect taxes for 1931. Under the law, taxes for the previous year not paid by May 1, 1932 subjected the taxpayer to sale of his property at the courthouse door. The sheriff laid the matter before the board, declaring that enforcement of the law would require the sale of more than half of the homes in Ashe County for taxes. After long consideration the board passed a resolution exempting Sheriff Miller from this provision of the law. Sheriff Miller, assisted by the county accountant, reported $50,271.22 cash on hand, and settlement was made on that basis.

A room in the courthouse was rented to T. C. Bowie as an office for $3 per month. The per diem of members was reduced from $4 to $3. The county accountant's salary was reduced from $100 to $90 per month. In every possible way the board cut county expenditures.

In August, 1933, the board listed uncollected taxes as follows:

For 1928, $1,479.60; 1929, $3,202.17; 1930, $6,699.13; 1931, $24,892.55; 1932, $110,962.40. Thus, unpaid taxes reached a staggering total of $147,235.85. Cutting all expenditures to the bone, the board came up with a tax rate of $1.40 for all purposes and the same levy was made in August, 1934.

On January 1, 1936, the board sold to T. M. Taylor and wife, 15½ acres of land from the county farm at $16 per acre.

Still mindful of the pressing need for economy, the board reduced the sheriff's salary to $1,500 per year, plus 5 per cent commission on the collection of taxes.

Striving to keep up with developments in the State, the board selected J. Ivan Miller as superintendent of public welfare. James Allen, county surveyor, who had been elected mayor of West Jefferson, resigned and was succeeded by Nelson Severt. E. J. Barker was appointed county accountant.

The Board did not lose its interest in roads but actually increased its efforts to interest the State Highway Commission in Ashe County roads. They asked that the road from Glendale Springs, via Obids, to Deep Gap, be made a state highway and that the road from the bridge over the North Fork of New River near Warrensville, be surfaced to a point on the state line nearest to Trade, Tennessee.

The 1936 tax levy stayed at $1.40 for all purposes and the terms of commissioners reverted to the original system. The staggered terms did not gain public approval and the board chosen was composed of Chairman J. F. Scott, R. B. Brown and Ed Davis. William B. Austin and Ira T. Johnston were elected county attorneys. There were shifts at the courthouse. It was ordered that W. E. Miller, sheriff-treasurer, have his office in the courthouse, taking the offices of H. M. Miller, tax collector, who moved into the offices vacated by out-going county attorney T. C. Bowie. Dr. B. E. Reeves became county physician and county coroner. The county accountant, resigning because of bad health, had his duties taken over by Larry P. Colvard, register of deeds. Ed Davis resigned as county commissioner and was succeeded by J. E. Oliver.

The new board coming into office in 1937 consisted of Chairman

J. F. Scott, R. B. Brown and Ed Davis. It took a forward step in the field of education by leasing the buildings and grounds of the Jefferson High School, owned by the Western North Carolina Conference of the Methodist Church and valued at $25,000, for a period of four years at $1,000 per year with interest. The title of the property was to go to the county upon payment of all principal and interest.

This deal turned out to be a fortunate one for the county, but at the time it required courage to make it because this 1937 board faced serious financial problems. For several years the county had been experiencing the effects of the old saying, "Chickens come home to roost." A bond issue in the early 1900's to build a courthouse had been easy to float and easy to pay off. During the teens of the Twentieth Century there was a natural and deep interest in securing good roads. A bond issue in the sum of $200,000 was submitted to the voters in 1919 and carried. Subsequently, because of the demand of many communities for road improvements, more bonds were issued by legislative enactment. The money was not always wisely used because of the inexperience in building roads of those in charge and because of the high prices which prevailed in the World War I era. The bonded indebtedness had grown until the principal amounted to more than a million dollars and the bonds were issued with interest rates ranging from 4¾ per cent to 6 per cent. When the depression of the early Thirties began to be felt in Ashe County, the county rapidly defaulted in the payment of interest and installments of the principal of these bonds. Suits were instituted by a number of the bond holders in the United States District Court and judgments obtained to which the cost was added. All of the judgments bore interest at the rate of 6 per cent.

When bondholders undertook to collect, Judge Johnson J. Hayes, the very able United States District Judge for the Middle District of North Carolina, was most considerate of the county and would only issue orders to pay within what he considered the ability of the county to pay in a given year. However, the unpaid balances were continually growing larger.

The Board of County Commissioners, consisting of Chairman J. F. Scott, R. B. Brown and J. E. Oliver, and their attorneys, W. B.

Austin and Ira T. Johnston, were faced with this problem and they agreed upon an effort to refinance the bonds by agreement with the bondholders. They enlisted the aid of Honorable R. A. Doughton, attorney of Sparta, former Lieutenant Governor of North Carolina. Honorable Charles M. Johnson, State Treasurer and Director of the Local Government Commission, gave valuable, continual aid in working out a settlement with the bondholders.

W. Kelvin Gray of Raleigh, who represented a majority of the bondholders, cooperated in the efforts to reach an agreement. After a number of meetings with the bondholders in Raleigh attended by the county attorneys, a refinancing plan was agreed upon and became effective on January 1, 1938. At that time the interest due on the bonds amounted to almost $275,000. As stated, the bonds bore interest ranging from 4¾ per cent to 6 per cent and all the judgments against the county bore interest at the rate of 6 per cent.

The agreement reached included a forgiveness of 50 per cent of the past due interest, a saving to the county of $137,500. The agreement also reduced the interest rate and the new bonds issued under the plan bore interest ranging from 3 per cent to 5 per cent. The bonds were spread over a period of years which would enable the county to retire them without an exorbitant tax rate. It is interesting to note that the county has not been in default in the payment of principal or interest on these bonds since the refinancing plan was put into effect. The bonds were again refunded on November 1, 1945, under a plan worked out by W. B. Austin and Ira T. Johnston, county attorneys, and the Board of County Commissioners, consisting of Chairman Wade E. Vannoy, M. G. Edwards and Edward Osborne. Under this plan the interest rates were again materially reduced, beginning at 2¼ per cent, and the bonded indebtedness was reduced to approximately $600,000.

The board concerned itself with trying to induce the State Highway Commission to take over and improve the road from West Jefferson to the top of Negro Mountain, which had been built during the depression with W.P.A. labor and funds.

The board found itself a battleground for the county's Health Department. There were many who demanded its abolition but the board continued its appropriation of $1,800 per year for the department.

The next year, 1940, found the Health Department more firmly intrenched and the board undertook to provide the county's part of the appropriation for old age assistance made available under new state welfare legislation. To take care of the budget for 1939-1940, the Board set up expenditures as follows:

Old Age Assistance	$ 6,720.00
Aid to Dependent Children	2,250.00
Cost of Administration Welfare Office	4,830.00
General County, including Health Department	29,443.00
Debt Service	42,300.00
Total	$85,542.00

It was calculated that the county would receive federal and state funds to supplement the services listed, totaling $28,067.63.

To meet these requirements the property tax assessment went to $2 on the $100, a sharp increase over preceding years. The thirteen inmates of the county home were transferred to the old age assistance roll and the county attorneys were authorized to sell the county home property and apply the proceeds on the county's bonded indebtedness.

In August, 1940 the death of W. E. Miller, sheriff and treasurer, was reported. J. E. Roland was appointed to succeed him as sheriff and Mrs. Elizabeth Miller became assistant county treasurer and tax collector.

Pending sale of the county home property, Elza Cooper was employed as keeper of the home on a temporary basis. Meanwhile, S. C. Eggers & Co., Boone realtors, were authorized to sell the county home property, not including the building itself and 13½ acres of land, for not less than $15,000.

In 1941 the county's appropriation for old age assistance and aid to dependent children, had grown to $10,650.

In 1942 the death of Walter H. Worth, former clerk of the court and for many years a leading banker, farmer and stock grower, brought about a change in the county's official family. Mr. Worth had been head of the Bank of Ashe. The directors of the bank employed Larry P. Colvard, register of deeds and county accountant, to succeed him. Charles S. Neal was elected to succeed Colvard as register of deeds.

It was in 1942 that the board donated the iron fence around the courthouse to the government drive for scrap iron for the war efforts.

In September, 1942 J. F. Scott died and W. E. Vannoy succeeded him and became chairman of the board. In December of 1942 he was elected for a full term, along with Edward Osborne and M. G. Edwards.

The sale of the county home property had not materialized and the board entered into contract with the Cumbow Land Co. to sell it.

Meanwhile tax valuations, which had been variously estimated at $4,000,000 to $5,000,000 actually went up to $4,350,000 in 1945. Even with this increase, more income was required and the tax rate rose to $2.25 per $100.

Taxable property climbed above the $5,000,000 mark in 1946, when Chairman W. E. Vannoy, M. G. Edwards and Wade H. Witherspoon constituted the board. It remained for this board to sponsor the erection of the Ashe County Memorial Hospital and Nurses' Home. The board took the first official steps toward this objective. With the main building completed it authorized William B. Austin, Jefferson attorney and Chairman of the Board of Trustees of the Ashe County Memorial Hospital, to apply to the Federal Works Agency for funds to build an adequate home for nurses at the hospital. He was successful in this effort and the result was a beautiful granite building, matching the hospital itself.

In May, 1948 the board found its tax valuation up to $5,485,500. V. C. Lillard and John Houck were members of the board, succeeding M. G. Edwards and Wade H. Witherspoon.

In May of the following year the board faced the fact that the persons over 65 then receiving old age assistance had reached 745 (average $20 per month). The county's outlay for this cause was $11,664.

In 1950 the board voted to place county employees under the State Retirement System.

In this year Ed Davis replaced V. C. Lillard as a member of the board.

The board approved its heaviest budget, up to that time, at its meeting on June 2, 1952, showing the following:

Property valuation for taxes	$8,900,000
Polls	3,465
Dogs	2,638
Tax rate, $2.10 on the $100, apportioned as follows:	
General Fund	91,410
School Tax	60,250
Social Security	305,000
Debt Service	56,409

The county's part of the old age assistance and aid to dependent children was set at $12,567.

The offer of the State to aid in the support of a county service officer to aid veterans in their claims against the Government, was accepted. The county agreed to put up $1,000 per year and the State the remainder. Leonard H. Shepherd was elected veterans' service officer.

In 1953 the county's part of the welfare fund was $14,555. The estimated number of eligibles for old age assistance and aid to dependent children was 1,260 persons from 360 families. The increase of property values for taxation had reached $9,000,000 and the board fixed the tax rate at $2.10 per $100.

At the July meeting of 1954 the board, not having been able to sell all of the county home property on Beaver Creek, turned the unsold property over to the Ashe County Board of Education, which had decided to erect in the area a building to provide an accredited high school to serve West Jefferson, Beaver Creek, Fleetwood and Elkland school districts.

The new board, meeting on December 6, 1954, was made up of Chairman Q. A. Duncan, George W. Shepherd and Ed Davis. P. T. McNeill came in as clerk of court and the board fixed his salary at $2,400 per year plus fees.

At its March meeting in 1955, the board abolished the office of county treasurer and made the Northwestern Bank of Jefferson financial agent of the county. In April the board fixed the salary of the sheriff at $5,000 per year, with $600 for expenses, plus 7 cents per mile for the use of his car.

The board took an active interest in a movement for a County Health Center, to be erected on land near the Ashe Memorial Hospital. Mrs. Jack McNeill, president of the Ashe County Womans' Club, pledged her organization to raise sufficient funds to buy the site and at a meeting on May 2, 1955 the board appropriated $5,569.45 for the building, the balance to come from state, federal and local funds.

The board elected Thomas S. Johnston and Wade E. Vannoy, Jr. county attorneys.

At the meeting of May 27, 1955 the board set up the budget for the year ending June 3, 1956. The property valuation for tax purposes had climbed to $9,500,000. The tax rate was fixed at $3 per $100. It is noticeable that for the first time, tax for health, welfare and relief caught up with tax for the county's bonded debt, both being set at 67 cents on the $100.

At its June, 1955 meeting the board asked for the resignation of Mrs. Elizabeth Miller as County Tax Collector, effective July 5, 1955. On July 6, 1955 it appointed J. T. Woodie to succeed her at a salary of $250 per month.

At the request of Miss Frances Tucker, superintendent of welfare, the board set up a special commission to examine applicants for financial assistance, composed of Dr. Roy Freeman, Dr. Ralph Tarnasky and Dr. Carson M. Keys.

At its July 6, 1955 meeting the board approved an appropriation of $8,000 for the Health Department. To deal with unfounded rumors which had been circulated when Mrs. Elizabeth V. Miller had been asked to resign as County Tax Collector the board adopted a resolution praising Mrs. Miller for her service as County Tax Collector and declaring that the board in discharging her, did not intend to reflect in any way on the honesty, integrity or ability of Mrs. Miller.

The board at its September 5, 1955 meeting, after reviewing the farming situation, directed the County Farm Agent to redouble his efforts to serve every farmer in the county in the matter of spraying for pests, dehorning cattle, soil conservation, crop rotation and diversification, and other matters vital to the agriculture program. The removal of the County Farm Agent's office to larger quarters in West Jefferson was approved.

At its regular meeting on October 3, 1955, the board took up the knotty problem of revaluation of property for taxation. It was pointed out that there had not been a revaluation since 1947. The board, after discussion, voted for the revaluation, to become effective on January 1, 1957, and Ed Osborne, prominent surveyor and real estate man, who had also served as a county commissioner, was appointed appraiser at $15 per day.

On March 5, 1956, the board was able to purchase the land needed for the Ashe County Health Center from Mrs. V. V. McConnell.

A dispute over the county line between Ashe and Alleghany, through the farm of Congressman R. L. Doughton at Laurel Springs, was referred to Ed Osborne, surveyor to represent Ashe County, and C. G. Fender, county surveyor of Alleghany. Their report was approved by the board.

On July 2, 1956 the board reduced the over-all tax rate from $3.00 on the $100 to $2.90.

John G. Gentry was appointed county accountant.

At its December 4, 1956 meeting the board, after considerable argument, approved the home demonstration work that had been started during the previous year, but was not fully convinced it was worth what it was costing. They finally decided to try it for another year. Daniels, an assistant farm agent, resigned and was replaced by Perry. Cyrus Green, assistant farm agent, resigned at the close of the year but was not replaced.

At its first meeting in 1957, held on January 7, the board became civil defense-minded and appropriated $1,500 for the cause. In February following, Sheriff Kenneth C. Miller resigned and Carl Francis was sworn in to succeed him.

At the July 1, 1957 meeting of the board there was much discussion of the tax collections of ex-Sheriff Kenneth C. Miller but there was no action. At this meeting the board took note of the fact that cattle breeders were not taking advantage of the county's expensive artificial breeding program, but it decided to continue the program for 6 months to see if the breeders wanted the service, at a cost of $1,200.

On July 1, 1957 the board announced that property valuation for taxes had gone up to $19,075,000 and the over-all tax rate was fixed at $1.45 per $100.

John G. Gentry, recently appointed county accountant, had the title Tax Supervisor conferred upon him and his salary raised to $3,600.

On September 2, 1957 the board took notice that Hanes Knitting Co., which had set up a new plant in Jefferson, had presented to the town a new fire truck. The board voted an appropriation of $200 to buy new hose for it.

The board, studying school statistics with special attention to insurance coverage, found the school properties of Ashe County to be valued at $1,862,300 as of January 1, 1958. This called for fire insurance premiums for 5-year policies amounting to $25,-633.11.

Taking note of the plague of Japanese beetles that had come upon the county, the board in 1958 appropriated $1,295 toward a spraying program. The town of West Jefferson was to put up $700 and additional funds were to come from state and federal governments. Previous boards, pleading poverty, had refused to appropriate anything for this cause, thus allowing the beetles to get a good start in Ashe.

For Ashe County's fine Central High School the board on April 7, 1958 borrowed $27,000 from the State Literary Fund for the construction of an auditorium-gymnasium addition to the school. Because of the need of fire protection for schools and other county property, the board added $400 to its original contribution of the same amount for a house for the Jefferson Fire Department. To be fair with other towns in the county the board offered to donate $200 to organized fire departments for each fire truck with standard equipment.

It is interesting to note that the county was improving financially.

The budget set for 1958-1959 was based upon a tax valuation of $20,500,000. With a tax levy of $1.55 on the $100, plus state and federal aid, the board expected total receipts to reach $894,534. Out of this they set up public assistance at $595,300; bonded indebtedness, $56,896; public schools, $87,886, leaving $154,452 for general county expense.

The new board taking over in 1959 was composed of Chairman Ed Davis, Bruce Bowlin and Bryan Kirby.

The board, having received complaints from various communities about garbage disposal, contributed $500 toward the purchase of land for a garbage disposal plant and worked out an agreement with the town authorities of Jefferson, West Jefferson and Lansing to share the expense of purchasing the site and for proper up-keep.

Thomas S. Johnston and Wade E. Vannoy, Jr. became attorneys of the board. The county accountant, E. W. Stansberry, became county purchasing agent and clerk to the Board of County Commissioners, an office that had been held from the beginning by the register of deeds.

On July 6, 1959, the county Board of Education, B. E. Sturgill, chairman and A. B. Hurt, secretary and county superintendent of schools, appeared before the Board of County Commissioners and asked for a bond issue of $400,000 to be used as follows:

A new school building at Warrensville, $330,000; for additions at Ashe County Central High school, $35,000 and for the Beaver Creek consolidated school, $35,000. The board approved the issue.

For 1960, the health budget was set at $12,000; proposed expenditures for public assistance were set at $652,080; budget for schools, $102,170.82 and for the general county fund, $146,277. The property valuation for taxes for the first time exceeded $21,000,000, and the tax rate was fixed at $1.45 on the $100.

In 1961 the Board of County Commissioners took a long step forward in voting for a county office building adequate for the housing of the county's expanding agencies. The need for such a building had been long recognized but the county's income had never permitted the accumulation of sufficient surplus funds to build it. Consequently the county's various agencies overflowed the courthouse and offices outside of the courthouse in Jefferson and in West Jefferson were rented. This situation was never to the liking of the people, who experienced difficulty in finding county officials they wanted to contact. In addition, the renting of offices was expensive.

To remedy this problem the board asked the county's representative in the General Assembly to introduce a bill to authorize the borrowing of $100,000 to erect a suitable building to meet the county's needs. The bill as passed by the General Assembly may be found in Chapter 1205, Public Laws of 1961. It authorized the Board of County Commissioners to borrow the amount needed and levy a special tax to repay the loan of 20 cents on the $100 of property valuation for 1961, 1962, 1963, 1964 and 1965.

Property was acquired adjoining the courthouse lot on the east and as this is written (1962) a beautiful two story building is nearing completion. It is contemplated that County Welfare offices, the offices of the County Farm Agent, the Highway Patrol, the Soil Conservation Service, the County Superintendent of Schools, and other agencies will be housed here. It is estimated that the new building, with the furnishings that will be required, will cost approximately $135,000.

Herewith ends the story of Ashe County's governing bodies, the "Court of Pleas and Quarter Sessions," from 1799 to 1868 and its successor, the "Board of County Commissioners," from 1868 to 1960. An earnest effort has been made to tell a connected story of the development of a great county from a handful of poverty-stricken mountaineers set down in a trackless wilderness. As the facts related here will indicate, the people of Ashe accomplished this in orderly fashion, keeping within the law and moving onward and upward, lifting themselves by their own boot straps. Not all of the names of those who should have been mentioned in this story appear here. The records are not good in many places. In fact, in many cases there are no records at all, and in many others, there were no follow-ups on important matters. A matter of vital importance would come up at a board meeting, be discussed and, lacking a decision, be continued until the next meeting. Very often, so far as the record goes, the matter never came up again.

However, sufficient information is shown above to give the reader a fairly clear idea of how Ashe grew to what it is today and a large number, but not all, of those good citizens are mentioned, who at great cost to themselves and their families furnished the leadership so vital to the county development.

III

Legislators and County Officers

While the two governing bodies mentioned in the preceding section of this chapter were first and foremost in the day-to-day life of the county, it should not be forgotten that two other groups of citizens served the county well during the same period and that without their loyal support the County Court and the County Board of Commissioners would have found the going even more difficult. These groups were Ashe County's legislators and the county officers of Ashe.

From the records in the office of the Secretary of State in Raleigh it is found that Ashe County's first senator was George Koontz, who was elected to the General Assembly of 1800. John Calloway and Nathan Horton were elected to the House of Representatives.

In 1801 George Koontz was again chosen senator and Richard Williams and Nathan Horton were elected to the House. This delegation secured the passage of an act (Chapter 85, G.A. 1801) authorizing the county to levy a special tax for destroying wolves.

In 1802 George Koontz was elected senator and Richard Williams and Jonathan Baker became represenatives.

In 1803 John Calloway replaced George Koontz as senator and Richard Williams and Jonathan Baker were reelected to the House.

In 1804 James McCaleb was elected senator and Richard Williams and Jonathan Baker again represented Ashe in the House.

In 1805 Nathan Horton was elected to the Senate, with Richard Williams and John Koons going to the House.

In 1806, Nathan Horton again became senator, with Joseph Calloway and Richard Williams in the House.

In 1807 John Calloway was elected to the Senate and Richard Williams and Thomas McGimsey to the House. This delegation secured the passage of Chapter XLV, Public Laws of 1807, limiting the number of constables in Ashe to two in each captain's company, or district; that at least seven active justices of the peace be present when constables were chosen and that each constable be required to post a $500 bond.

In 1808 the Ashe delegation, consisting of Senator John Calloway and Representatives Richard Williams and Bedent Baird, wrestled with a county line dispute with Burke. By Chapter 70, Public Laws of 1808, a survey of the line was ordered, with Bedent Baird to represent Ashe and James Murphy to represent Burke.

In 1809 John Galloway was again chosen senator and Richard Williams and Thomas McGimsey representatives.

In 1810 Richard Williams, after eight terms in the house, became senator and Martin Gambill and David Miller became representatives. A most unusual proposal was laid in the laps of this particular delegation. One Alexander Smith desired to raise $1,500 by means of a lottery, to set up a "manufactory for making steel and nails in Ashe County." The Ashe County legislators backed him in this and the General Assembly authorized the lottery in Chapter 126, Public Laws of 1810. Under the act Smith was to give bond for two thousand pounds. Named as commissioners of the lottery were John O. Johnston, Eli Cleveland, Thomas Calloway and Joshua Cox.

Richard Williams again became senator in 1811 with the same representatives in the House. This delegation undertook a movement to join with other mountain counties to secure uniform widths of roads. They aided in the passage of Chapter 47, Public Laws of 1811, aimed at bringing this about. The counties involved were Ashe, Wilkes, Buncombe, Burke and Haywood.

In 1812 George Bower, who was to serve Ashe in the Senate more terms than any other man before or since, became senator. David Edwards and Elijah Calloway were in the House.

In 1813 George Bower was senator and Elijah Calloway and David Miller were representatives.

George Bower was in the Senate and Elijah Calloway and William Horton in the House in 1814. It was reported to this session of the General Assembly that the Commissioners named to conduct a lottery for a "steel and nail manufactory" by the General Assembly of 1810, had refused to serve. By resolution the General Assembly named a new commission, composed of Montford Stokes, George Bowers and John Fulton.

In 1815 and 1816 there were no changes in Ashe's legislative delegation.

In 1817 there was no change except that Joseph Doughton took the place of William Horton.

Elijah Calloway was chosen for the Senate in 1818 and Francis Bryan and Miles Allen for the House. At this session there was much pressure for the improvement of roads across the Blue Ridge Mountains. The Ashe delegation procured the passage of Chapter 71, Public Laws of 1818 providing for a commission of eight "to lay off a public road from Jonathan Wood's blacksmith shop in Wilkes to the town of Jefferson." This commission was composed of John Finley, William Colbert, James McNeill, William Judd, of Wilkes; George Bower, Jacob Baker, Sie Poll and Absolom Bowers, of Ashe. Under the Act, the damages incurred were to be reported to the two county courts, which were authorized to levy taxes to pay any damages.

In 1819 Elijah Calloway succeeded himself as senator and Bedent Baird and Richard Gentry were elected to the House.

Elijah Calloway was again chosen for the Senate in 1820 and John Hardin and Richard Gentry for the House.

In 1821, Richard Gentry became Senator and Alexander B. McMillan and Agner Smith were elected to the House. This delegation was called on to reorganize Ashe County's militia. They secured the passage of Chapter 97, Public Laws of 1822, entitled "An Act for the better regulation and discipline of the militia of Ashe County." The Act was aimed at securing better attendance at drill and more adequate training especially for field officers, who had apparently become very negligent in their duties. The Act provided for due attention to non-coms and enlisted personnel but it went further and provided two extra drill musters every year at the courthouse for all officers.

In 1823 Elijah Calloway was again chosen senator and Alexander B. McMillan and Joshua Weaver were represenatives.

In 1824 there was no change in the delegation. The General Assembly took cognizance of the death of Nathan Horton, one of Ashe County's leading citizens and an early advocate of road improvement. He had spent a large part of his personal fortune in building the toll road from his home to the Tennesee line and the State had acquired an interest in the road. Prior to his death, Horton had offered his toll road to the State without charge. The Ashe delegation procured the passage of Chapter 37, Public Laws of 1824, which appointed John Mast to succeed Horton in the management of Horton's Turnpike. The county and superior courts of Ashe and Wilkes were given jurisdiction over the turnpike.

In 1825 Abner Smith was elected to the Senate and William Herbert and Reuben Hartley to the House. By Chapter 40, Public Laws of 1825, the General Assembly gave the county and superior courts of Ashe jurisdiction over a new road "leading from Puncheon Camp to the town of Jefferson by way of Beaver Creek."

By Chapter 27, Public Laws of 1825, the General Assembly appointed commissioners to superintend the laying off and improving that part of the "Great State Road" between the town of Jefferson and the Tennessee line. The commission was composed of George Bower, Gideon Lewis and Edward King. They were authorized to survey the road, make maps showing "the most remarkable places—and the distance from one remarkable place to another, together with the whole distance of the road." To accomplish this task the General Assembly set up an appropriation of $300.

By Chapter 72, Public Laws of 1825, the General Assembly fixed the pay of jurors in Ashe at 50 cents per day.

By Chapter 129, Public Laws of 1825, the General Assembly set up a special commission to lay off a road from John Harden's to the Ashe County Courthouse. This commission was composed of David Miller, Phillip Church, George Tatum, Thomas Brown and Richard Green.

In 1826 Alexander B. McMillan was elected to the Senate and Zachariah Baker and James Blevins to the House.

Alexander B. McMillan succeeded himself as senator in 1827 and Zachariah Baker and Anderson Mitchell were chosen as representatives.

In 1828 John Hardin was elected to the Senate and Anderson Mitchell and James Calloway to the House.

In 1829 Anderson Mitchell was chosen for the Senate and James Calloway and Zachariah Baker for the House. This delegation backed a proposal for travel regulation over the new state road from the southeast edge of Wilkes County, by way of Jefferson to the Tennessee line. They secured the enactment of Chapter 95, Local Laws of 1829, setting up a fixed scale of tolls covering all sorts of traffic, including foot-travellers. In fact, all travellers paid toll except carriers of the U. S. Mails.

In Chapter 155, Local Laws of 1829, the delegation, mindful of the battle of Ashe County farmers to get started in sheep-raising, secured the passage of an act to raise the reward for killing wolves to $2.50 for every wolf-scalp.

In 1830 John Ray was elected senator and James Horton and James Calloway were elected to the House.

John Ray was again chosen for senator in 1831. James Calloway and Taliaferro Witcher were elected representatives.

In 1832 John Ray was again elected senator and Taliaferro Witcher and Jonathan Horton were elected to the House.

In 1833 George Phillips was elected senator to succeed Ray and Witcher and Horton were reelected.

Noah Mast was elected senator in 1934 and Witcher and Horton were elected to the House again.

In 1835 John Gambill was chosen for the Senate and Witcher and Horton succeeded themselves in the House.

Effective in 1836, the General Assembly divided the state into senatorial districts. Thereafter the office of senator rotated from election to election and the senator and representatives chosen served two years instead of one. The number of representatives for Ashe was reduced from two to one.

In 1836 Ashe was in a district with Wilkes, and Edmund Jones of Wilkes was its senator. James W. Nye was elected to the House.

In 1838 there was no change in representation in either House.

In 1840 Anderson Mitchell was elected senator and Alexander B. McMillan was elected to the House. By Chapter 32, Local Laws of 1841, the General Assembly again took note of unsatisfactory conditions in the militia of Ashe and ordered the breaking up of the 46th regiment, which included all of Ashe, and the formation of three regiments, as follows: 46th regiment, including Jefferson, North Fork, Horse Creek, and Chestnut Hill; 95th regiment, Three Forks, Old Fields, Watauga, Cove Creek; 96th regiment, Cranberry, Elk Creek, Glade Creek and Gap Civil.

In 1842 Edmund Jones of Wilkes became senator again and George Bowers was elected to the House. The General Assembly, in Chapter 68, Public Laws of 1842, upon the petition of Representative George Bowers, ordered that Ashe County, having voted to adopt the State Common School System, receive its proportional share of the State Literary Fund set up by the General Assembly of 1841. This move was considered a long step forward in the field of education.

In 1844 Alexander B. McMillan was elected to the Senate and Benjamin C. Calloway to the House. They were both returned to office in 1846. Interest in roads had not declined in Ashe and representative McMillan sponsored Chapter 105, Public Laws of 1846-1847, for the incorporation of the Caldwell-Ashe Turnpike Company. The Act named Dr. Larken Jones, Robert C. Williams, George Bowers, George Hamilton, and William Dula as commissioners to sell stock.

In 1848, Colonel George Bowers was returned to the Senate and W. Reuben Mast was elected to the House. It was at this session of the General Assembly that Ashe lost the territory that is now Watauga County. The partition of the county met with the approval of Ashe County's senator, George Bowers, and of Reuben Mast, Ashe's member of the House, whose home was in the area cut off to make Watauga. Mast later was to move to Texas. The Act creating Watauga may be found in Chapters 25 and 26, Public Laws of 1848-1849.

In 1850 Colonel George Bowers was again elected to the Senate and Alexander B. McMillan was elected to the House. He was reelected in 1852, along with Representative Benjamin C. Calloway.

In 1854 Colonel Bowers was again senator and Allen Gentry was elected to the House. It was at this session that the General Assembly in Chapter 254, Public Laws of 1854-1855, passed an act to incorporate the town of Jefferson. To serve until their successors could be elected, Quincy F. Neal, James Wagg, E. C. Bartlett, Samuel C. Waugh, and James W. Gentry were appointed commissioners. The act fixed the town limits as "one-half mile each way from the courthouse."

In 1856 A. M. Bryan was elected senator and Allen Gentry was returned to the House.

In 1858 the senatorship went to Surry County and the district was represented in the Senate by Joseph H. Dobson. Ashe was represented in the House by Allen Gentry. It was at this session that the General Assembly took its next big bite out of the territory of Ashe. The act that created Alleghany by lopping off 230 square miles of Ashe's territory on the east, is found in Chapter 20, Public Laws of 1858-1859.

In 1860 Dobson of Surry again represented Ashe in the Senate and Thomas N. Crumpler was elected to the House. Despite the tensions of the time, the educational leaders of the day were active and at the legislative session that continued into 1861, secured the enactment of Chapter 55, Private Laws of 1861, being "An Act to incorporate Jefferson Academy." The following prominent citizens were appointed trustees: James M. Gentry, E. C. Bartlett, James Wagg, David Smith, James W. Hardin, N. H. Waugh and David Worth.

In 1862 Isaac Jarratt was elected senator and James M. Gentry was elected to the House.

The senate seat went to Jonathan Horton of Watauga in 1864 and F. A. McMillan was elected to the House.

In 1865 A. C. Cowles of Watauga was senator and Matthew Carson was representative.

A. C. Cowles was again senator in 1866 and Robert Gambill was elected to the House.

In 1868 Samuel P. Smith was elected Senator and Matthew Carson, representative. It was in this year that new districting, both judicial and legislative, was required under the new state constitution. Ashe County found itself in the 11th judicial district, along with Alleghany, Mitchell, Buncombe, Yancey, Watauga and Madison. Legislatively, Ashe was placed in the 34th senatorial district, composed of Ashe, Alleghany and Wilkes. This district was entitled to one senator.

In 1870 C. L. Clark of Wilkes was Ashe County's senator and J. O. Wilcox was elected to the House. In Chapter 209, Public Laws of 1870, Ashe was authorized to levy a special tax on all real and personal property, sufficient to provide a fund of $5,000 for relief of the poor.

By Chapter 66, Public Laws of 1870, Ashe and Alleghany were authorized to construct a twenty-foot highway between Jefferson and Sparta, every citizen living within five miles of said road to be liable for road duty on said road not to exceed thirty days in any one year.

In 1872 Captain Joseph W. Todd, eminent Jefferson lawyer, became senator from the 34th district and Squire Trivett was elected to the House.

In 1874 A. J. McMillan of Alleghany became senator, with Squire Trivett again in the House. At this session the thriving mining town of Ore Knob, which had reached a population in excess of 500 and was the largest town in the county, asked for a charter. It was granted under date of March 18, 1875 and may be found in the Public Laws of 1874-1875.

Henry Bingham of Watauga became senator in 1876 and Captain J. W. Todd was elected to the House.

In 1879 J. Bledsoe was elected senator and J. E. Foster was elected representative.

In 1881 Tyre York of Wilkes County became senator and L. C. Gentry was elected to the House. The Ashe delegation to the General Assembly consisting of Senator Tyre York of Wilkes, and Representative L. C. Gentry, at the request of the board, which was worried about the unpaid balance of debt carried over when the new state constitution went into effect, introduced and secured the passage of Chaper 259, Public Laws of 1881, authorizing the board to levy a property tax in Ashe sufficient to pay $2,000 per year on the accumulated debt.

For reasons not recorded the General Assembly raised the amount to $3,000 per year in 1885. In this year Captain J. W. Todd was senator and J. C. Plummer was representative in the House.

In 1883 the senatorship by rotation went to Watauga and E. F. Lovill was elected. J. O. Wilcox was elected to the House. It was in this period that interest in railroad building to connect Ashe with the outside world, reached the boiling point. Promoters had been at work through Ashe and other counties of the northwest. They sought to sell stock and bonds to build a railroad into the northwestern part of the State to connect with the Western North Carolina Railroad between Salisbury and Newton, the road to go by Wilkesboro and to cross Ashe to the Virginia or Tennessee line. Representative Wilcox secured the passage of an act (Chapter 371, Public Laws of 1883) to authorize a bond issue of $50,000 by Ashe County to aid the project, with the proviso that the proposal be submitted to a vote of the people of Ashe. The promotion collapsed and no election was held on it.

At the same session, Chapter 131, Public Laws of 1883, the county commissioners were authorized to hold an election on a bond issue to build a railroad from Taylorsville into Ashe. This venture also collapsed.

In Chapter 410, Public Laws of 1883, the General Assembly of North Carolina, for the protection of cattle-raisers in Ashe against distemper, passed a law prohibiting the driving of cattle across the Blue Ridge Mountains between May 1 and November 1 of every year.

In 1885 Captain J. W. Todd was again elected senator and J. C. Plummer was elected to the House.

Ashe's senator in 1887 was Eli M. Stephenson of Alleghany and Riley Blevins was elected to the House.

In 1891 Benjamin P. Griggsby was elected senator and H. G. Phipps was elected to the House.

In 1893 Alleghany had the senator and W. C. Fields was chosen. R. A. Hamilton was elected to the House. Ashe's legislators, representing three adjoining counties, secured legislative sanction for joint action of their counties in improving the road from North Wilkesboro to the Virginia line by way of Jefferson and from Millers Creek in Wilkes to Creston in Ashe.

In 1895 W. H. Farthing of Watauga was senator. J. B. Hopkins was elected representative. By legislative action Ashe was exempted from the provisions of the law requiring the holding of an election on a special school tax of 20 cents on the $100 and 30 cents on the poll.

In 1897 J. M. Dickson was elected to the Senate and E. Spencer Blackburn to the House. Blackburn, a Republican, was later to become congressman from the Eighth District.

In 1899 Alleghany furnished the senator, H. T. Campbell, and Ashe elected Dr. B. E. Reeves to the House.

L. H. Michael of Watauga was senator in 1901 and Hiram Weaver was elected to the House.

In 1903, H. M. Wellborn was elected to the senate and John D. Thomas to the House.

S. A. Taylor of Alleghany, was elected senator in 1905 and F. C. Young was elected to the House.

In 1907 E. F. Lovill of Watauga was again senator and G. L. Park, Jefferson attorney, was elected to the House.

In 1909 Robert L. Doughton of Alleghany was senator. Mr. Doughton was born near Laurel Springs and so close to the Ashe County line that Ashe claimed him for her own, and watched with pride as he went on from this initial venture in politics to the Congress of the United States, where he served forty-two years, the last twelve as chairman of the House Ways and Means Committee, the most powerful of all of the committees of the Congress. Ashe's choice for the House in 1909 was Thomas C. Bowie. This was his first venture in politics. Better known throughout the State as "Tam" Bowie, he too was destined to go far and become a power in state politics.

In 1911 John M. Wagoner of Alleghany became senator and Harrison C. Tucker was elected representative from Ashe. At this session a special game law was passed for Ashe, making it unlawful for a person to kill grouse or quail off of his own land for a period of five years. Also, there was special legislation concerning sheep-killing dogs and another special act was passed providing that convicted criminals sentenced to jail in the courts of Ashe, Alleghany and Watauga might be sentenced to serve on the roads of Ashe. Taking notice that interest and principal on the bonds issued to build the courthouse in 1904 had not been met, there was an act providing for a special tax of 30 cents on the $100 and 90 cents on the poll to be applied on these bonds.

In 1913 E. S. Coffey was senator and Thomas "Tam" C. Bowie was reelected to the House. Because of the continuing agitation in Ashe concerning railroads, either steam or electric, the General Assembly passed an act (Chapter 215, Private Laws of 1913) providing that the Board of Commissioners in Ashe should have authority to submit any proposals relative to railroads to a vote of the people.

In 1915 Robert L. Ballou was elected senator and Thomas C. Bowie was returned to the House. With only two terms in the House behind him (1909 and 1913) young Tam Bowie became speaker pro tem of the House in February 1915, when Speaker Emmet Wooten of Lenoir County suffered an accident that later resulted in his death. When Wooten died Bowie was elected speaker. He was sworn in on March 1, 1915. In this session the General Assembly raised the pay of county commissioners in Ashe from $3 to $4 per day; of members of the Finance Committee from $2 to $3 per day; of jurors from $1 to $2 per day, plus 5 cents mileage.

By legislative action (Chapter 176, Private Laws of 1915) the town of Jefferson was chartered again. This act reaffirmed the town boundary lines and provided for a mayor and three aldermen. Walter H. Worth was named as mayor and E. A. McNeill, Charles S. Neal and Dr. J. W. Colvard were named as aldermen, and J. E. Koontz, town constable.

West Jefferson came on to the scene by legislative action in 1915. Its charter may be found in Chapter 36 of the Private Laws of that session. It fixed the town limits in accordance with the plan of the West Jefferson Land Co., which had laid out a town east and west of the depot of the Virginia-Carolina Railway Co., one-half mile from the square where the depot is located. Donnelly Blevins was named as mayor. R. C. Barr, W. F. Hartzog, Isaac Faw and Amos Graybeal were named as aldermen, and Weaver Koontz, town constable.

In 1917 Eugene Transou of Alleghany, was senator and Ambrose Clark was elected to the House. In the Private Laws of that session, Chapter 74, the town of Jefferson was again incorporated, again without explanation. The only difference appearing was that W. T. Colvard was named as mayor, and Eugene Wagg, W. E. Gentry and W. E. McNeill as aldermen, and B. F. May, town constable.

In 1919 E. F. Lovill of Watauga was senator and Thomas A. Farmer was elected to the House. In Chapter 79, Private Laws of 1919, the General Assembly authorized the school board of Jefferson district, number 1, to enter into contract with the Board of Trustees of the Jefferson (Methodist) High School to permit the operation of public free school in the buildings of the church school.

In 1921 Dr. W. Joseph Robinson was the senator and Thomas C. Bowie was the member of the House.

In 1922 Allen Jones was elected senator and Thomas C. Bowie to the House, and with this term Ashe passed from the 34th to 29th senatorial district.

In 1924 John E. Brown of Watauga was elected senator and Thomas C. Bowie was again elected to the House of Representatives. It was at this session that the General Assembly in Chapter 427, Public Laws of 1925, directed that the Australian Ballot System be adopted in Ashe County. By Chapter 221, Public Laws of the same session, the powers and duties of the county commissioners with respect to roads, were transferred to the "Good Roads Commission of Ashe County." Good Roads Commissioners named in the act were R. L. Reeves, E. M. Osborne and Luther Miller. Under the provisions of the act it was required that all of the roads not included in the State Highway System be divided into sections, with a paid overseer, or patrolman, and at least one paid hand and team to each section. A special tax of 15 cents on the $100 was to be levied to support this program.

In 1926, Peter Thurman McNeill was elected senator and attorney William Bryant Austin was elected to the House. This term saw important action as to Ashe, particularly as to its financial situation. Chapter 372, Public Laws of 1927, set up a new schedule of fees for Ashe County officers. Chapter 624, Public Laws of 1927 undertook to fund the county's bonded debt of $220,000 for roads and bridges. It was noted that the county had $120,000 available to apply on the debt. The General Assembly authorized a bond issue of $100,000 to take care of the remainder. In Chapter 91, Public Laws of 1927, the General Assembly provided that in the future members of the Board of County Commissioners should be elected for staggered terms, one for two years, one for four and one for six, beginning with the next election. This plan, designed to keep men experienced in county government on every board, did not please and was not long continued. At this session, under date of May 16, 1928, the town of Lansing was incorporated.

In 1928, Carlisle W. Higgins of Alleghany was elected senator and Peter Thurman McNeill was elected to the House.

In 1930 W. R. Lovill of Watauga was elected senator and Ira Thomas Johnston, Jefferson attorney, was elected to the House.

Peter Thurman McNeill was again elected to the senate in 1932 and Thomas C. Bowie to the House.

In 1934 Dalton Warren of Alleghany was elected senator. Thomas C. Bowie was again elected to the House. At this session, by Chapter 165, Public Laws of 1936, the town of Todd was incorporated. At the same session, by Chapter 124, Public Laws of 1936, the town of Warrensville was incorporated.

In 1937 Roby T. Greer of Watauga was senator and J. Bruce Hash was elected to the House.

In 1938 William Bryant Austin was elected senator and Ira Thomas Johnston was elected to the House.

Eugene Transou of Alleghany was elected senator in 1940 and William Bryant Austin was elected to the House.

In 1942 H. Grady Farthing of Watauga was elected senator and Fred Blevins was elected to the House.

In 1944, Edison M. Thomas was elected senator and M. Donley Hart was elected to the House.

Wade E. Brown of Watauga was elected senator in 1946 and J. O. Blevins was elected to the House.

Dr. H. B. Perry of Watauga was elected senator in 1948 and Todd H. Gentry was elected to his first term in the House.

In 1950 William B. Reeves was elected senator and Todd Gentry was returned to the House. Mr. Reeves died before taking the oath of office. By Chapter 1184, Public Laws of 1951, the state-wide primary law was extended to Ashe County.

In 1952 Edwin Duncan of Alleghany was elected senator, and Todd Gentry was elected to the House.

Dr. H. B. Perry of Watauga was again elected senator in 1954, and Todd Gentry was reelected to the House.

In 1956 Todd Gentry was elected to the Senate and Robert Austin Jones was elected to the House of Representatives. At this session, Chapter 215, Public Laws of 1957, was enacted prohibiting the practice of phrenology, palmistry, clairvoyance and fortune-telling in Ashe. Chapter 665 of the same session prohibited the killing of deer in Ashe.

It is not to be considered that the activities listed above constitute all, or even a majority of the activities of Ashe County's representatives in the General Assembly but enough is recorded here to show that Ashe County's Court of Pleas and Quarter Sessions, and its successor, the Board of County Commissioners, found patriotic helpers in their efforts to give Ashe County the kind of government it so richly deserved.

Another group, the elective officers of Ashe County, also proved sturdy and always faithful supporters. Because they were human they occasionally made mistakes but these miscues were so few as to be almost negligible.

As near as may be determined from available records these officers were:

Clerks of Court

John McMillan, 1800-08; David Earnest, 1808-18; Thomas Calloway, 1818-32; John Ray, 1833-34; Richard Gentry, 1834-52; Robert Gambill, 1852-58; James Wagg, 1858-62; E. C. Bartlett, 1862-64; R. T. Hardin, 1864-68; J. B. Parsons, 1868-70; Robert Parsons, 1870-74; Geo. W. Ray, 1874-78; E. F. Foster, 1878, Inf. Ct.; W. H. Gentry, 1892-94; Poindexter Blevins, 1894-96; A. S. Eller, 1896-1906; W. H. Worth, 1906-12; W. E. Johnson, 1912-16; S. G. Parsons, 1916-20; J. D. Stansberry, 1920-42; C. S. Neal, 1942-54; P. T. McNeill, 1954-61, deceased; C. S. Neal, appointed 1961, resigned 1961; Don L. Francis, appointed 1961.

Registers of Deeds

Joshua Cox, 1834-35; Jonathan (J. B.) Stamper, 1835-46; Joshua Cox, 1846-56; Joseph Hudler, 1856-60; John Hardin, 1860-64; A. C. Hawthorn, 1864-68; C. Younce, 1868-70; G. W. Ray, 1870-74; Joseph Hudler, 1874-82; Naman Loggins, 1882-84; A. C. McEwen, 1884-86; Isaac (I. M.) Carter, 1886-88; M. F. Smith, 1888-96; D. A. Osborne, 1896-1902; J. D. Stansberry, 1902-04; R. K. Elliott, 1904-06; J. A. Jones, 1906-10; G. W. Sawyers, 1910-16; J. D. Stansberry, 1916-18; M. C. Roark, 1918-22; C. S. Neal, 1922-32; L. P. Colvard, 1932-40; C. S. Neal, 1940-42; J. D. Stansberry, 1942-58; John G. Gentry 1958-.

Sheriffs

John Cox, 1800-02; Joshua Cox, 1802-10; Samuel Cox, 1810-16; Shadrick Calloway, 1816-20; John Ray, 1820-28; John Gambill, 1828-34; George Phillips, 1834-44; Geo. W. Reeves, 1844; E. C. Bartlett, 1845-52; Joshua Baker, 1852-58; J. A. Reeves, 1858-60; John M. Carson, 1860-68; W. M. Latham, 1868-78; John Baker, 1878-84; T. K. Miller, 1884-90; Byron Sturgill, 1890-98; P. G. McNeill, 1898-1900; Ambrose Clerk, 1900-06; G. B. Austin, 1906-14; W. A. McMillan, 1914-16; C. R. Latham, 1916-20; J. W. Hampton, 1920-28; C. B. Graybeal, 1928-30; H. M. Miller, 1930-36; W. E. Miller, 1936-40; Everett Roland, 1940-42; John Goodman, 1942-46; W. B. Todd, 1946-50; W. R. Roten, 1950-54; Kenneth Miller, 1954-55; Carl Francis, 1955-58; W. R. Brown, 1958-1962.

There is some uncertainty about the officers who served Ashe County between 1800 and 1816. There is official record that Martin Gambill was elected sheriff and tax collector by the County Court at the May term, 1806 and as related elsewhere he gave bonds of two thousand pounds for each office, John Cox and Jesse Reeves signing the bonds. In a later entry he was reported as being re-elected and renewing his bonds. The old records show that Jonathan Baker was elected sheriff in 1808, the same year David Earnest became Clerk of Court. There is also reason to believe that Jesse Reeves served for a short period as sheriff, though the list above does not contain his name, nor is there any record that Baker served as sheriff between the terms of Joshua Cox and Samuel Cox.

This uncertainty probably came about through the confusion attendant upon all major changes in government. The new Superior Court coming into the picture, probably resulted in Superior Court judges appointing temporary officers for their courts and the old County Court carrying on, at least for a considerable period of time, in accordance with established practices.

CHAPTER SIX

ASHE COUNTY AT WAR—WAR BETWEEN THE STATES—WORLD WARS I AND II

I

Ashe County at War

Ashe County came into existence waging war. Every foot of the territory that is now Ashe had to be won and held for many years by force of arms. As related in a previous chapter, every pioneer who crossed the Blue Ridge Mountains between 1770 and 1799 took with him all that he could carry, but the bare essentials were a rifle, an axe, and a Bible. With the rifle he fought such wars as were required, killed game to feed his family, and protected his home from marauding Indians. As population increased, the first community enterprise was the organization of a militia unit. When boys reached the age of sixteen they were inducted into the military service. In various parts of Ashe you will find areas that were called "muster grounds," and here men and boys drilled assiduously at regular intervals under officers of their own choosing. To miss drill was a serious offense and brought drastic punishment. To heighten interest in drills there were annual contests for the best marksmen, the best-drilled company, and the best-drilled battalion. For the enlisted men there were contests in marksmanship, in the manual of arms, and in various other athletic activities with special attention to wrestling and foot racing.

It is true that there is no official list of Ashe County soldiers in the Revolutionary War, but it is certain that those living in the area that became Ashe in 1799 readily espoused the cause of their brethren to the east. When the British and their Indian allies sought to attack the American armies from the west they found themselves opposed by a force that they were never able to conquer. In addition to keeping the marauding British and Indians away from their homes the people of Ashe were able to lend armed forces to attack British strongholds in Virginia and, as related in Chapter Two, with only their own militia they met Ferguson at Kings Mountain and turned the tide of war. That battle was the beginning of the end for the British.

After the Revolution, Ashe County and surrounding areas remained an armed camp. Every community retained its militia unit and kept it trained for action. Their interest was increased and their ranks filled by the influx of veterans from the American army, seeking lands and new homes west of the Blue Ridge Mountains. Ashe County received many of these veterans and many of them became leading citizens of the area and rendered fine service in establishing and developing the new county. Many of them are listed in Chapter Three.

War of 1812

When the War of 1812 came on there was a call for volunteers. The federal authorities asked for two companies from Ashe. The militia of Ashe was, at the time, part of the Fifth Militia Regiment, made up of troops from Ashe, Wilkes, Burke, Rutherford, Buncombe, Haywood, Anson, Richmond, Moore, and Cabarrus counties. The provisional regiment, ordered to rendezvous at Wadesborough, found itself under the command of Lieutenant-Colonel John McGimsey of Burke; and first and second majors Jesse Allen of Wilkes and Thomas Lenoir of Haywood.

In an official publication of 1851 entitled *Muster Rolls of the Soldiers of the War of 1812* appears the list of Ashe County soldiers in the two companies. In the first company were the following:

Gideon Lewis, captain; Isaac Weaver, first lieutenant; Wm. Toliver, ensign.

Privates: Henry Graybeal, Eli Ragen, Henry Millar, James Duncan, David Graybeal, David Carpenter, Samuel Griffith, Isaac Taylor, Frederick Staley, Isaac Lewis, William Morefield, Abraham Miller, John Millar, Mark Weaver, Peter Hart, Absalom Bower, John Faw, Davis Hartzog, Aaron Owens, Peter Feese, Andrew Shearer, William Cox, Isaac Smith, Jacob Mikel, William Mink, Edward Tilley, Joshua Pennington, David Horton, Phineas Horton, Reuben Hartley, Lewis Fairchilds, Jacob Ingerham, Levi Blackburn, John Shearer, Joel Dugger, David Dugger, Thomas Swift, Henry Hately, John Vanderpool, William Brewer, Jacob Brinegar, John Hoppass, John Brower, William S. Edwards, Alex T. Conley, Enoch Passmoer, Joel Rose, Richard Perry, William Vanover, Joseph Colwell, Enoch Baldwin, John Rutherford, John Quinley, John Williams, William Taylor.

In the second company were the following:

William Horton, captain; Squire Wilcoxon, lieutenant; Phillip Baker, ensign.

Privates: William Johnston, John Kirby, William Toliver, Moses McBride, Stephen Cross, David Maxfield, James Hatt, Jacob Stamper, Alexander Cox, John Price, Elijah Smith, William Ellison, Edward Hart, Thomas Collins, Matthis Williams, Archibald Blankership, William Baker, George Crider, Samuel Wilcoxon, David Horton, Joseph Green, Lewis Trockler, James Tatum, John Bear, Henry Holsclaw, George Brown, Benjamin Chambers.

There is no record that these troops experienced any combat duty. The official call to arms set forth that they were called out "for the defence of the Southern Frontier of the Sixth Military District of the United States." As it turned out, there was never any serious British encroachment in this area, and about all they got out of it was field training.

The war was of short duration. Declared on June 12, 1812, slow getting under way and sluggish in action, it was concluded by a treaty of peace on December 14, 1814. The United States, except for a surprise raid on Washington and the burning of the new capitol, suffered few losses. The most famous engagement of the War of 1812 was the battle of New Orleans, which was fought on January 8, 1815, almost a month after the war was over. In this fight General Andrew Jackson, leading an army of sharp-shooting militia from the mountains of East Tennessee and Western North Carolina, met an invading force from the British West Indies under

General Pakenham and completely demolished it. The American loss was negligible but the British lost 2,033 in dead, wounded and captured.

How many Ashe County men served under General Jackson is not known, but it is certain that Ashe was represented in his army. For many years Ashe County troubadours, to the accompaniment of banjo and fiddle, were singing the original "Battle of New Orleans," telling of the slaughter of Pakenham's invaders by "Old Hickory" Jackson's mountain boys, shooting from behind breastworks made of cotton bales.

Mexican War 1846-1848

The Mexican War, 1846 to 1848, found patriotic fervor boiling over in North Carolina and this was particularly true of Ashe County. Two complete companies volunteered for service and a third company was ninety per cent complete within a few weeks after President Polk had called for volunteers. Getting around to apportioning quotas of soldiers to the various states, the Washington "high brass" put North Carolina down for ten infantry companies of 100 men each. There was a rush to volunteer. Many more companies qualified than were called for. Governor William A. Graham did not choose to accept the first ten companies to qualify but instructed his adjutant general, Robert W. Haywood, to hold a drawing and select by lot the companies that would make up the State's first regiment. When the drawing was held, nine of the winning counties were from the west and Ashe was one of them. Only one company was from east of Raleigh. Naturally this fact caused jealousy and friction.

As far as Ashe County was concerned, so far as may be determined from available records, the Mexican War was a dismal failure. Under the President's call the volunteers of 1846 enlisted "for the duration, or twelve months, unless sooner discharged."

There was delay after delay. Rations, uniforms, tentage, guns, ammunition, in fact everything essential to good soldiering, was in short supply. Sanitary conditions were bad. Typhoid fever, smallpox, and other deadly diseases ran through the regiment. Twelve months went by and enlistments expired. The Ashe County men, like the majority in the regiment, declined to re-enlist for the duration of the war, which was the only way Governor Graham would accept re-enlistments. Faced with what looked like a hopeless situation, Ashe County's soldiers came home, almost en masse, leaving a bare handful in the army, and these were scattered through the remnant of the regiment that was finally reorganized. This regiment was eventually designated as the "First North Carolina Foot Volunteers," under Colonel Robert Treat Payne. There is a roster of the regiment, certified as correct by Adjutant General Johnson Jones, but it contains no information as to the counties from which the men came.

The Mexican War was fought for the liberation of Texas, according to pronouncement from President Polk, but more accurately it was for the acquisition of the territory that later became the states of Texas, New Mexico, and California. This war was a study in disappointments, frustrations, and mismanagement. Before it was over the word "SNAFU," coined 100 years later by World War II soldiers would have fitted the war in every aspect: "Situation Normal—All Fouled Up."

The United States won because the Mexicans were in an even worse situation.

Probably the only gain for the United States outside of the territory acquired, was a lesson in how not to wage any sort of war. Many of the young officers participating in the Mexican War starred in the War Between the States, which was even then threatening. Among these were Captain Robert E. Lee, Lieutenant U. S. Grant, and many others.

II

The War Between the States

In recounting the deeds of Ashe County's men at war over the years, it has been difficult to single out the conflict from the Revolutionary War down to the present that had the greatest effect on the lives of the people of Ashe. There may be many who will disagree with the decision that the outstanding war was that known variously as the "War Between the States," "the Civil War," and the "War of the Rebellion," the last being the Yankee title of it.

Practically every household in Ashe County today has its cherished memories of father, grandfather, great-grandfather or other ancestor, who answered the call to arms and who fought bravely for the Confederacy. In Appendix I of this book will be found the names of the Ashe County men and boys who enlisted in the armed forces of the Confederacy.

The figures show that Ashe furnished for the War Between the States a very high percentage of its available manpower. The United States Census for 1860 showed a total population of 7,956. This figure included everybody, old and young, male and female, white and black. Of this number, 533 were listed as "non-whites." About 100 of the non-whites were free Negroes and the remainder slaves. The white male population of all ages was 3,733, and the white female of all ages was 3,681. Deducting Negroes, women and children, men too old to fight and those disabled by disease, the available manpower of Ashe when war came could not have exceeded 1,000.

The first call for volunteers was received with great enthusiasm. The ranks of five full companies were quickly filled with eager volunteers and many sought enlistment in other companies being organized in adjoining counties.

In Major John Wheeler Moore's monumental work, *Roster of North Carolina Troops in the War Between the States*, Volumes 1, 2, 3, and 4, there are lists of Ashe County soldiers in five county units which were made up almost entirely of Ashe County men. Some of the scattered sons of Ashe are listed in other companies. The all-Ashe companies were:

Company A, 9th Regiment, C.S.A.; Company A, 26th Regiment; Company A, 37th Regiment; Company L, 58th Regiment; and Company D, 58th Regiment.

The record discloses that these companies had plenty of action at Bull Run, Chancellorsville, Gaines' Mill, Cold Harbor, Brandy Station, and on many other bloody fields. No less than three Ashe county companies fought at Gettysburg. Writing of the services of North Carolina troops in this battle, a noted North Carolina historian said:

> The North Carolina troops at Gettysburg, on July 1, 2 and 3, 1863, were to reach the pinnacle of military greatness—of the 15,301 Confederates killed and wounded in this battle, 4,033 wore North Carolina uniforms.

Major Moore did not claim that his roster was complete, or entirely correct in its details. He spent many years working on it, and he did the best he could with the records available. He wrote that the roster contains the names of 104,698 men, with the records of one regiment, the 68th Infantry, missing. It was his estimate that 20,000 or more North Carolinians who served are not listed in his roster. Major Moore established the fact that North Carolina led all of the states of the Confederacy in its contribution of manpower. In addition to its fighting units, commissioned and enlisted, as shown in his roster, Major Moore sets out that the State of North Carolina furnished 32 generals and 106 executive officers.

Since it is based on Major Moore's roster, complete accuracy is not claimed for the list of Ashe County's Confederate veterans appearing in Appendix I. Careful examination of Moore's roster discloses Ashe County men, by ones, twos, and fives, scattered over a dozen regiments. Among them are the following:

In Company A, 22nd Regiment, Collet A. Green; Company H, 23rd Regiment, A. Lyal, H. Lyal, F. Maberry, W. A. Grier, and G. E. Marvel; Company C, 26th Regiment, Abram Edmonston; Company C, First Regiment, Sidney L. Witherspoon, Jonathan F. Taylor, John B. Smith; Company I, 1st Regiment, R. C. Whitfield, J. R. Whitfield, J. J. Walker; Company H, 60th Regiment, E. F. Younts; Company A, 69th Regiment, Joseph A. Brown.

Commanding Company I of the 61st Infantry was Ashe County's former Clerk of Superior Court and eminent physician, Dr. Aras B. Cox.

The Confederate States had a navy, so-called, but it is not recorded that Ashe County men wanted to do their fighting on the sea. As far as Major Moore's roster goes, only E. F. Younts of Ashe enlisted in the Navy at Wilmington. There were probably others.

It should be noted that in all of the companies listed in Appendix I there are a few soldiers not natives of Ashe, who came to the various companies to fill vacancies caused by death or disability. There seems to have been a strenuous effort to keep incoming recruits in companies from their home counties but this was not always feasible.

It should not go unmentioned that Ashe County had many citizens who were opposed to slavery and who preferred to remain loyal to the Union. The controversy between unionists and secessionists divided communities and even spread to the churches. Out of the great Baptist Church came the Union Baptists, and their churches continue to this day. The Methodists split in the same way, establishing separate conferences. The Methodists finally settled their differences and reunited, but the reconciliation came long after the war.

Eighteen citizens of Ashe openly enlisted in the Union army and very many more slipped out of the county and enlisted in a Union regiment formed in the mountains of East Tennessee. In addition to these, a great many more disappeared in the mountains and hid out for the duration of the war. It was estimated at one time that there were more than 1,500 deserters and draft-evaders in the mountains of Ashe, Alleghany, Wilkes, and Watauga. As these bushwhackers, as they were called, increased in numbers their food supply gave out and they resorted to robbery by day and night. Their strength was such that the home guard, made up of old men and boys too young for the army, could not subdue them.

It should be stated that all of the deserters and draft-evaders were not from the counties named. The mountains provided ideal hiding places and evaders came from everywhere. They made living difficult for everybody.

In spite of these burdens and annoyances, Ashe County carried on bravely. Churches and schools were not forgotten. By great good fortune, Ashe County was spared the ravages of invading troops. This enabled the county to contribute substantially to the support of the Confederacy from the products of its farms, iron mines and forges. lead mines, and other resources. Agricultural production and everything else was retarded, but did not bog down.

Old men, young boys, women, and girls took the places of the men in uniform and carried on bravely and with unexpected efficiency.

The Spanish-American War

Ashe County took part in the Spanish-American War in a small way. The United States declared war on April 25, 1898, and a peace protocol was signed on August 12, 1898. In this brief space of time Admiral Dewey destroyed one Spanish fleet at Manila, another Spanish fleet under Admiral Cervera was bottled up at Santiago, and General Shafter and Colonel Theodore Roosevelt smashed the Spanish land forces at El Caney and San Juan Hill, and the war was over. North Carolina, in that brief space of time, raised three regiments of volunteers. None participated in the fighting. So far as the records go, only one recruiting officer came to Ashe. He enlisted "for the duration" the following:

Donald B. Todd, Gilbert S. Bower, Charles P. Carson, Winfred Barr, Robert C. Barr, all of Jefferson; John B. Thomas, Sandifer; James R. Caudle, Obids; and Robert F. Cannady, Ashland.

There were probably other Ashe County men among the volunteers, but none is recorded.

III

World Wars I and II

In Appendix II of this book will be found a complete list of Ashe County citizens who were enlisted or inducted into the military forces of the United States for World War I. Appendix III has a similar list for those serving in World War II. These lists were compiled from registration cards filed in the office of the Adjutant General of North Carolina and which are presently in the vaults of the North Carolina Department of Archives and History at Raleigh.

An official list compiled in June, 1927, showing the number of veterans, based on registration cards, who were entitled to participate in the North Carolina Veterans Loan Fund, contained the following statistics about Ashe County's soldiers in World War I:

Officers, 7; enlisted and inducted, 438 white and 15 colored; killed in action, 7; died of wounds, 3; wounded, 49; died of disease overseas, 1; domestic deaths, 4; deserters, 3; dishonorably discharged, 5.

In addition there were two who served as officers in the Navy and thirty-six men who were enlisted or inducted in the Navy and five in the Marine Corps.

The complete list of those who died in World War I, in conflict or as the result of wounds or disease as shown on the Soldiers' Monument on the Courthouse Square in Jefferson, is as follows:

Charles C. Ashley, Cecil Bare, John Parker, Chester A. Brooks, Marcus W. Cockerham, Fred N. Cox, Lester Ham, Samuel C. Hardin, Brant Lewis, Luke P. Mahala, Edgar Parsons, Harrison Perry, Frank C. Porter, Enla Price, Hedrick Roark, William L. Sheets, Roscoe Thompson, Osco Tucker, William M. Wallace, John E. Yates.

On another side of the same monument is a bronze plate containing the names of the Ashe County men who died in action, or of wounds received in action, or of disease in World War II:

Marvin Arnold, Orville Baker, Clell C. Bare, Richard J. Black, Lida A. Brown, Lawrence P. Burkett, Thomas E. Burkett, Burley G. Church, Lloyd J. Church, George Todd Colvard, William A. Cornett, John Cox, Duane F. Crepps, Frances H. Crepps, Gale M. Davis, Frank M. Debord, Blan D. Dixon, Blanco Eller, Bruce Farrington, Scott J. Gambill, Herbert Gentry, Ray A. Gentry, Raymond E. Goodman, Earl W. Greer, Ford G. Greer, Ellis D. Grogan, Francis E. Grubb, Charles H. Hart, George C. Holeman, James G. Hopkins, Bowie M. Houck, Wallace G. Houck, Robert L. Howell, Vance James, Charles R. Johnson, Claude W. Johnson, Ellis H. Kemp, J. C. Krider, Albert F. Lewis, Arline Miller, Cecil M. Miller, Robert F. Miller, Roger F. Miller, Wade Miller, Alonzo L. Moretz, Ernest D. Mullis, Carl E. Oliver, Charles B. Oliver, Earl Oliver, Fred J. Osborne, Grover C. Osborne, Howard Osborne, James H. Osborne, Junior A. Osborne, Robert H. Osborne, Howard V. Parsons, Richard B. Phillips, William H. Phipps, Rexie Powers, Paul W. Rash, Cecil W. Richardson, Herman C. Roberts,

James W. Roberts, James E. Roten, James G. Russ, Claude R. Severt, Glenn D. Sexton, Verna R. Shepherd, William L. Stansbury, Shuba W. Taylor, David H. Testerman, Walter A. Trivett, Thomas E. Vought, Rex Viers, Amon D. Wagoner, Charles H. Walters, Larkin L. Witherspoon, Charles H. Wood, Lester Wyatt, Thomas N. Wyatt, James V. Yates, John H. Yearick, James R. Younce, Edwin B. Young.

There are probably other names of Ashe County men that should be added to these two lists. Also, it is highly probable that the lists of those drafted for service, and those entering the various services by enlistment, as shown in Appendices II and III, are not complete. Because of handwriting difficult to read, it is certain that there are errors in the names listed. No one will regret these omissions and errors more than the researcher, who did the best he could.

World War I

For a time, at the outset of World War I, Ashe County played in hard luck and established a reputation that it found hard to live down. It started early when draft records failed to flow in from Ashe. Governor Thomas W. Bickett, who had appointed a native of Ashe as "Federal Agent in Charge of the Draft," sent him to Jefferson to assist the local board. He found the local board eager to do the job properly but like many individuals and organizations, before and since, bewildered by government "paper work." In less than a day, the machinery was running.

This bewilderment brought no serious black mark against the county's record, but what followed a few months thereafter did. On June 24, 1918, Governor Bickett received a telegram from W. E. McNeill, Chairman of the Ashe County Draft Board, stating that there were forty deserters from the Army roaming around Ashe County and that one civilian had been killed trying to arrest a deserter. Mr. McNeill asked for troops to deal with a situation that civil authorities could not, or would not handle.

Governor Bickett called in his Adjutant General, Brigadier General Lawrence W. Young, and, after a conference, ordered him to

Ashe to make an investigation. General Young arrived and caught the prevailing hysteria before he had been in Ashe an hour. Under date of June 26, 1918, he reported:

> Situation here appears acute. I consider an outside force necessary. Reported about thirty deserters hiding out. Sheriff reported sympathetic to deserters and will not help—I am convinced that the only solution is an outside force. Please advise.

General Young got his advice quickly. The outside force was on the way and it consisted of one man, Thomas Walter Bickett, Governor of North Carolina. He directed General Young to have a car meet him at North Wilkesboro on the following Saturday to take him to Jefferson, and to get word to every nook and corner of Ashe that on Saturday afternoon at 3 o'clock he would address a mass meeting of citizens at the County Courthouse. He sent a similar telegram to Chairman McNeill, asking that he notify everybody, especially the families of the deserters.

When the Governor arrived he found one deserter waiting at the courthouse to surrender. He spoke to a crowd that packed the courthouse to the doors. Famous as an orator, Governor Bickett exceeded all expectations on this occasion. He told his hearers that the source of all of the trouble was ignorance.

"These mountain boys," said he, "are giving trouble because they have not been told the truth about this war, and they have been told a lot of lies about it. Ignorance and misinformation are at the bottom of all of this trouble and all of this shame. It is my purpose to lay before you the everlasting truth about this war—"

And this he proceeded to do.

He told of his own visits to the camps, where he ate with the men, slept on their cots and saw what was being done to protect their health and morals. He said:

"The boys in camp are better fed, better clothed, and are leading more healthful and more decent lives than the men of the same age at home."

He praised the so-called "Selective Draft Act" as the essence of the democratic process and described the old volunteer system as unjust and unwise, "placing a tax on patriotism and a premium on cowardice."

Governor Bickett made it clear in closing that the law was going to be strictly enforced and that every loafer and shirker, every evader and deserter was going to be rounded up and "given a fair chance to die for his country."

Governor Bickett's speech ended the trouble. The thirty to forty deserters hit the trail back to camp where the military authorities, for the most part, accepted Governor Bickett's explanation of Ashe County's mass desertions, and punishments were light.

The Draft Board of Ashe, thereafter, had no trouble. The desertions, the one death and the threats of the deserters and their families to kill, had attracted wide interest. The papers were full of it for many weeks but when the final records were analyzed, Ashe County showed that a total of 461 had been drafted for World War I and the county actually had sent the armed forces 536. The state average of draft evaders was found to have been 2.65 per cent, while the Ashe County percentage of draft evaders was three-fourths of one per cent. (See report of Ira T. Johnston on "Ashe County Draft Record," in North Carolina Papers, University of North Carolina.)

The local Draft Board, originally stymied by federal red tape, got down to business and no local board in the State made a better record. As noted above, W. E. McNeill of Jefferson was chairman; W. R. Bauguess, Dr. J. W. Colvard, and F. W. Testerman were the other members.

The government appeal agent was G. L. Park, Jefferson attorney. The legal advisory board for Ashe was composed of G. L. Park, T. C. Bowie, and W. R. Bauguess. On the District No. 5 medical advisory board was Dr. B. E. Reeves, representing Ashe County.

World War II

When World War II came there was no trouble in Ashe County. There was ready and complete acceptance of the provisions of the "Selective Training and Service Act." For the period of the war, covering six registrations, Ashe County's total registrations were 6,421. As of February, 1944, when they were at their peak, Ashe had 250 agricultural deferments, all white; in non-agricultural deferments (as of December, 1944, when they were at their peak) 416, six of them colored; in deferment to prevent extreme hardship in the home (as of June 1, 1944) 21; percentage rejected at the local board level and at induction stations, 1940-1945, 50 per cent. Deducting the registrations and deferments of all kinds, Ashe County men who actually were accepted for service in the armed forces through May, 1946, totaled 1,730. The rejection rate of 50 per cent looks bad and is, but the facts show that 35 counties in the state had higher rejection rates than Ashe. It is interesting to note that there were only three conscientious objectors in Ashe County, all white. (These statistics are taken from Spencer B. King's *Selective Service in North Carolina in World War II.*)

The Ashe County Local Board had functioned at Jefferson for World War I but the new board for World War II found it more convenient to set up headquarters at West Jefferson. The members of the board were: Wade E. Vannoy, John W. Luke, Robert E. Farmer, Edward Doyle Barr, Bruce Bowlin, David Harless, J. C. Goodman, Quincy Ashley, and S. W. James.

The government appeal agent was Robert L. Ballou; examining physicians, Dr. B. E. Reeves, Dr. Lester Lee Long, Dr. Deane C. Jones; re-employment committeemen, Charles H. St. Clair, J. B. Hash; chairman of registrants' advisory board, J. G. Rhodes.

This completes the story of Ashe County's participation in conflicts recognized as "wars." The United States military insisted on calling the Korean war a "police action" but those Ashe County boys participating found it close akin to war. Their names are not available now but will be later. Meanwhile, the National Selective Service System is still working and Ashe County sent its quota to Korea and other trouble spots, and today (1962) Ashe County boys are fighting so-called "cold wars" all over the world, on land, on sea, and in the air.

Indicative of the interest of Ashe County's discharged veterans of World War I in the proper care of their disabled comrades and in the general welfare of the community is the fact that they early formed a post of the American Legion. The post participated in every worthy civic enterprise for the betterment of West Jefferson and the county, and with its ranks filled anew by veterans of World War II, has continued to grow in usefulness. It is recognized as one of the county's top civic organizations today.

The officers of the post, from the beginning, have been as follows, the first named for each year being the post commander and the second the post adjutant:

In 1926, Dr. R. F. Barr, M. A. Shepherd; 1927, Charles E. Welch, B. W. Jones; 1928, Dr. R. F. Barr, J. M. Warren; 1929, Dr. R. F. Barr, J. M. Warren; 1930, Jack G. Rhodes, J. B. Hash; 1931, Jack G. Rhodes, J. B. Hash; 1933, P. G. Wright, Larry P. Colvard; 1934, P. G. Wright, Larry P. Colvard; 1935, Larry P. Colvard, E. D. Barr; 1936, Larry P. Colvard, E. D. Barr; 1937, E. D. Barr, Guy T. Badger; 1938, J. B. Hash, Charles S. McNeill; 1939, Jack G. Rhodes, Glenn Graybeal; 1940, William B. Austin, P. G. Wright; 1941, Charles H. St. Clair, Ira T. Johnston; 1942, Ira T. Johnston, P. G. Wright; 1943, A. B. Hurt, P. G. Wright; 1944, W. W. Terry, P. G. Wright; 1945, L. B. Tyson, P. G. Wright; 1946, W. Parks Colvard, P. G. Wright; 1947, Quayle Barlow, P. G. Wright; 1948, Quayle Barlow, P. G. Wright; 1949, L. H. Shepherd, P. G. Wright; 1950, James T. Capps, P. G. Wright; 1951, James T. Capps, P. G. Wright; 1952, James T. Capps, P. G. Wright; 1953, James T. Capps, P. G. Wright; 1954, U. S. Grant Bauguess, L. H. Shepherd; 1955, Henry F. Cooper, L. Albert Poe; 1956, Larry P. Colvard, William O. Ashley, Jr.; 1957 Walter R. Weaver, Harold B. Colvard; 1958, G. T. Badger, Don B. Goodman; 1959, D. B. Goodman, Larry P. Colvard; 1960, L. Albert Poe, Larry P. Colvard; 1961, Robert D. Hurley, Larry P. Colvard; 1962, John F. Hardin, Larry P. Colvard.

It is interesting to note that immediately after World War I, Upton Blevins, who lived at Crumpler and was a rugged individualist not famed for his love of officers, undertook to form a national organization of veterans composed of enlisted men only. He met with some success for a time but his organization found the American Legion and the Veterans of Foreign Wars too strong and it withered away.

It is worthy of note, also, that P. G. Wright, whose name appears 15 times in the above list of officers, died in 1956 and in his honor Ashe County Post No. 171 was renamed the "P. G. Wright Post No. 171."

CHAPTER SEVEN

RELIGION IN ASHE COUNTY
THE BAPTISTS–THE METHODISTS–PRESBYTERIANS AND OTHER DENOMINATIONS

I

Religion in Ashe County

As recorded elsewhere, historians have noted that the hardy pioneers who came to the wilderness that was to become Ashe County in 1799 were deeply religious. They brought with them as many household and agricultural necessities as could be carried on a packhorse or transported on a two-wheeled cart, but the three predominantly essential things the pioneer brought were his rifle, his axe and the Bible.

General William Lenoir, who established a home about four miles from Wilkesboro before the outbreak of the Revolutionary War, relates in his accounts of the settling of the area that when he arrived in the area there was a big church at Mulberry Fields, later to become Wilkesboro, the county seat of Wilkes, of which Ashe was a part. It was known as the Mulberry Meeting House. Built by the Baptists, it was open to the community for all kinds of meetings and all of the religious denominations and sects were free to use it.

From the records it is certain that the early settlers were deeply religious. Theodore Roosevelt, in his *Winning of the West*, took note of this fact and in his account of the Battle of Kings Mountain, which has been covered in another chapter, he tells how the little army that assembled at Sycamore Shoals to follow Colonel William Campbell, Colonel John Sevier and Colonel Ben Cleveland to meet Colonel Patrick Ferguson of the British Army, at Kings Mountain, did not move until they had held a solemn religious service and had invoked the blessings of God on their undertaking. The account reads:

On the 26th day of the month, when they were ready to march, the men assembled in a grove, and there the Rev. Samuel Doak, a Presbyterian preacher, the pioneer clergyman of the frontiers, made a few remarks befitting the occasion, closing the same with the Bible quotation: "The sword of the Lord and of Gideon," and while these stern, hardy men bowed their heads in reverence, this good man invoked on the expedition the blessings of God. He recounted the dangers that surrounded his congregation from the savages in their rear and the British in their front; and reciting the promises of mercy contained in the word of their God, he earnestly prayed for the protection of their families and success for those marching to defend their homes and liberty; and so effective were his prayers that tears stole down the cheeks of many of the rough and hardy mountaineers. After this the army mounted their horses and commenced their march for South Carolina.

From the records of the Baptist, Methodist, Presbyterian, and other churches, it is evident that the first interest of every community, as it came into existence, was the establishment of churches. The United States Census reports show that after 1850 there were enough church buildings of all denominations in Ashe to furnish a place of worship for every citizen in the county.

While the agencies for improving the educational system were slow in achieving any noticeable improvement, as the chapter relating to public schools will show, the churches continued to grow. The record will show that the churches saw the need of higher education and in addition to their purely religious activities ventured into the field of secular education and played an outstanding part in the movement for higher education in Ashe. Leader in this undertaking was, undoubtedly, the Methodist church, with the Baptist and Presbyterian churches following.

The part played by the Methodist church in Ashe was unusual. It will be dealt with in detail in the chapter on Education.

II

The Baptist Church

Reference has been made elsewhere to the fact that the Baptists of Piedmont and Eastern North Carolina moved west in steady streams in 1771 and 1772 following the disastrous Battle of Alamance. Many of them followed the comparatively easy trail, northwest through Salem and across the Blue Ridge at Fancy Gap, north of Mt. Airy. Once over the mountain they found easy going along established trails to the Watauga, Nolichucky, and Holston settlements, whence they spread back into what is now Ashe County. Others pushed up into the foothills of the Blue Ridge and eventually found or made trails over the Ridge.

The question has often been asked why so many Baptists left the lowlands and headed west. There have been many answers. Probably the best of them is that the Baptists of those days were lovers of liberty and haters of every form of tyranny. They rebelled against a tyrannical royal governor and they rebelled against the established church. The Baptist church, a pure democracy, wherein every individual church was free to join an association of churches or to join none, exactly met their needs and in the area that later became Ashe they waxed strong, and they are strong to this day.

The first Baptist Church in Wilkes County, which included Ashe, was set up at Mulberry Fields. Its membership came mainly from Baptists who were members of churches outside the county. Exactly when the church at Mulberry Fields was constituted is not known. It was there when General Lenoir moved into the community in 1770.

The next church of record that drew members from the area was Fox Creek Baptist Church in Grayson County, Virginia, which was constituted in 1782. This church was close to the North Carolina-Virginia line. The next Baptist church to be constituted in this area was Three Forks Church in the southwestern part of Ashe, now in Watauga County. The date, as set out in the church minute book which is preserved in the vaults of the Bank of Watauga at Boone, was "November the 6 Day in the year of our Lord and Saviour Jesus Christ, 1790." The following were listed as members of the new church: Richard Green, Daniel Eggers, Elender Green, William Miller, Mary Miller, Phebe Miller. Others received at the same time and added by experience and baptism were Sarah Colemon, Lois Eggers, Lidia Counsel, and Benjamin Cutbirth.

This church grew in numbers and usefulness down through the years, giving off enough members from time to time to establish other churches, eventually resulting in the formation of the Three Forks Baptist Association.

It is difficult to trace the growth of Baptist churches in the Ashe County area for the reason that many of the new churches allied themselves with the Baptists of southwest Virginia. The mighty Blue Ridge cut them off from the Baptist churches of North Carolina and they allied themselves with the Virginians and many remained so allied for a hundred years.

Semple's *History of the Baptists in Virginia* records the organization of a Baptist church, known as "North Fork of New River Church," in Grayson County in 1796. Rev. J. F. Fletcher, who wrote a history of Ashe County Baptists, made a search of the records in Virginia and North Carolina and decided that this church was doubtless within the area that became Ashe in 1799. His conclusion is supported by the fact that no part of the North Fork of New River lies in Virginia; all of it is in Ashe County. The church, according to Dr. Semple, had thirteen members.

It is highly probable that there were others, though not in the Ashe County area. In 1786 the Strawberry Association of Virginia had thirteen churches in North Carolina. These, with one church in Virginia, formed a sort of sub-association, reporting annually to the mother association in Virginia. When this set-up was effected no one knows, but it is certain that it was in effect in 1786, and it ended in 1790 when these churches petitioned the Strawberry Association to release them and permit them to form a separate association.

In the list of delegates who attended the organization meeting at Eaton's Meeting House in Rowan County on August 28, 29, and 30, 1790, were representatives from six churches in Wilkes county, of which Ashe was a part. Beaver Creek, New River, and North Fork may have been in what is now Ashe, but it is doubtful. For example, the Beaver Creek delegation was headed by the famous Colonel John Sevier, and he and his associates, John Barlow and James Franklin, were prominent in the Tennessee region. Their Beaver Creek church was probably in Tennessee.

The new association formed was the Yadkin Baptist Association and it started with fourteen churches and 340 members. It grew rapidly and in nine years was able to give off enough churches to form the Mountain Baptist Association with ten churches and eight ministers, which came into existence in 1799, the year Ashe became a county. The churches were: Rye Valley, New River, North Fork of New River, Fish River, South Fork of Roaring River, Beaver Creek, Head of Yadkin, Cedar Island, Three Forks, and St. Claire's Bottom. The first and last were in Virginia and Cedar Island later was called Fox Creek.

The Mountain Baptist Association, though divided and upset over the matter of missions, foreign and domestic, continued to grow. It gave off enough churches to start the Roaring River Baptist Association in the 1840's and also the Three Forks Baptist Association. With all this loss of churches the Mountain Association was left with twenty-four churches and 1,134 members.

The Senter Baptist Association was formed at a convention held at Senter Church, in Ashe County, named for the renowned Elder Drewry Senter and his equally famous son, Elder Nathaniel Senter. The convention met on October 21, 1853, and when it had finished its labors there was a new association, the Senter, named for the two preachers. The association was made up of four churches from Three Forks Association (Bear Creek, Beaver Creek, North Fork, and Horse Creek) and five from the Mountain Association (Big Helton, Silas Creek, South Fork, Senter, and Cranberry). To the credit of the Senter Baptist Association is the first recorded action toward bettering educational facilities in Ashe. At its session in 1857 the matter was discussed and a committee was named to "devise a plan or platform for the establishment of a school in Ashe County." At a subsequent meeting the committee reported favorably on the proposal. The committee was discharged and nothing came of the proposal immediately because the War Between the States was looming and the Baptist groups in Ashe County were busy fighting each other over issues of union and non-union, foreign and home missions, and no missions at all.

Missionary Baptists

Out of the turmoil of war came more confusion. The churches had formed hostile camps. Those favoring missions and the establishment of institutions for higher education broke away from the main body of Baptists and quickly drew others. Eventually they took the lead over those of the old order until today in Ashe, as in the rest of North Carolina, they lead in numbers. Those of the old order, generally referred to as Primitive Baptists, or Union Baptists, have not increased greatly in membership since the days when the "Missionaries" moved out, which was in 1853. Among Baptists of the area, this came to be known as the "year of the great split."

The rise of Union sentiment in Ashe, which eventually resulted in the formation of the Mountain Union Baptist Association, was for the most part an under-cover movement while the War Between the States was going on. However, when the war was over, it flamed into the open and the Union League, a secret order established by Union sympathizers, spread into Ashe County. In 1867 more than 100 Baptists, all Union sympathizers, assembled at the home of Elder R. Jones in Ashe to discuss the formation of an association favorable to their way of thinking. Out of this grew the Mountain Union Baptist Association. Many eminent Baptist leaders of the day participated in the movement, among them Elders R. Jones, John Adams, A. Powers, William Halsey, and J. A. Caudill.

The battle over missions and over church membership for those who joined the Free Masons, the Sons of Temperance, or other secret orders, disrupted many of the strongest Baptist churches in Ashe. For example, Elder Aaron Johnston of Beaver Creek Church was expelled from that body because of his membership in the Sons of Temperance, and at about the same time Elder Richard Gentry and his son, Captain W. H. Gentry, were turned out of Old Fields church for the same cause.

Naturally, these progressive leaders did not take it lying down. Elders Johnston and Gentry, with the able assistance of Elders J. J. Watts, J. H. Watts, Robert Steel, and Z. B. Adams, started the battle with the organization of the famous old Bethel Baptist church. It turned out that there were many Baptists of their way of thinking and in a very few years there was in existence a progressive association, known as the United Baptist Association, made up of three smaller associations: Lewis Fork, with eleven churches; Lower Creek, with four; and Taylorsville, with eleven.

These twenty-six churches had twenty-six ordained preachers, Richard Gentry, Aaron Johnston, J. Reed, R. L. Steel, J. G. Bryan, William Pool, J. Crouch, P. Tritt, G. Swaim, H. Holtsclaw, S. P. Smith, William Church, S. Ferguson, P. Grimes, L. Pipes, H. M. Stokes, J. H. Brown, L. Land, J. McNeill, A. W. Vannoy, J. B. Green, E. Tilley, J. H. West, D. Austin, M. Austin, and I. Oxford.

This association came out boldly for missions, Sunday schools and temperance and there was no turning back. Eventually Ashe County Baptists, with the exception of the Primitive and Union Baptists, fell in line and grew in power and influence.

Among the strong Baptist preachers of this early day were:

Richard Jacks, J. A. Davis, H. G. Brown, Stephen Ross, Elijah Tucker, Volly Bowers, N. C. Baldwin, Armstrong Blevins, Elijah Edmondson, W. C. Parks, J. Blevins, Levi Barker, T. M. Duncan, J. B. Jones, W. Franklin Barker, J. H. Brown, J. McNeill, J. H. West, Thomas Masters, J. B. Jones, J. J. L. Sherwood, B. G. Maynard, J. M. Halsey, A. S. Murray, E. Ayers, J. W. Thomas, Alex Stamey, William Fisher, W. P. Long, J. F. Maiden, L. D. Vaughn, A. S. Murray, Walter A. Hash, J. F. Fletcher, Albert G. Hash, George M. Reeves, T. F. Edmondson, Armstrong Blevins, J. A. Caudell, E. W. Reedy, C. W. Trainham, F. L. Cox, C. T. Taylor, J. H. Powers, J. R. Brown, J. L. Bishop, W. F. Brannock, N. M. Blevins, J. W. Farmer, J. M. Neaves, G. M. Pennington, M. Sturgill, A. J. Stamper, J. A. Schuyler, J. M. Walls, J. S. Murray, T. R. Warren, and many others who helped to build the Baptist church as it exists in Ashe today.

For several years, the affairs of the Baptist churches of Ashe were tied up with churches in Grayson County, Virginia in an association known as the New River Baptist Association which was organized on June 10, 1870 from churches in both states. This connection continued until 1886, when the Ashe County churches were granted letters of dismissal to join with their brethren in Alleghany to form the Ashe-Alleghany Baptist Association, which began operation with thirteen churches and with 611 members scattered over Ashe and Alleghany counties.

By 1888 the new association had grown to fourteen churches. It had started a program of progress, which had gone far by the standards of that day, though it had only seven ordained ministers, T. M. Honeycutt, T. M. Duncan, D. W. Thomason, J. F. Fletcher, Solomon Blackburn, Elihu Tucker and B. C. Swift. In the light of what will be shown in this section, it should be interesting to note that only six churches of the association paid anything for pastors' salaries and the total for the six was $178.75. As in the beginning in the Baptist church, the ministers were supposed to preach for nothing, and farm, teach school, or do common labor to support themselves and their families.

In 1898 this association had grown to a point where it was able to divide itself into two associations, the Ashe Association and the Alleghany and Grayson Association. The dividing line between the two was the county line between Ashe and Alleghany. The Ashe Missionary Baptist Association, with twenty-eight churches, held what it called its 12th annual meeting on September 27, 1898, which was, in fact, its first meeting as a separate unit, all in one county.

It should be noted here that the interest of the Baptists of Ashe in higher education, while it suffered eclipse during the war period and the first five years thereafter, did not die. As noted, the Senter Association started it but made little progress. The New River Baptist Association appointed a special committee to work on the project, consisting of William Young, Wiley G. Baldwin, William C. Parks, James Blevins, David Smith, Daniel Blevins, Andrew Dickson, Jonathan B. Young and Jesse Reeves. This committee found that while it had been lying dormant during the war years and the years immediately following, the school program had not been forgotten. It engaged their attention in 1872 and in 1873. At that time the majority of the Baptist Churches of Ashe were in the New River Association, which had churches in Ashe and Alleghany and in Grayson County, Virginia. In 1873 this association unanimously accepted a proposal from Young's Chapel Baptist Church, which was in Grayson County, Virginia, "to construct an academy at Oak Hill." The Association went into action immediately, naming a board of trustees for the school as follows:

Elder W. C. Parks, Elder J. B. Jones, W. G. Young, L. N. Perkins, William Carson, John W. Ross, James Eller, D. Blevins and W. C. Fields.

The school was established on sound principles and was fortunate in having good teachers. It was a great influence for good in Ashe and Grayson Counties. It had periods of stagnation, when students were few and qualified teachers hard to find, but the fine old school, with a very fine school plant, is still in existence today. The school has been duly incorporated into the Virginia Baptist Home Missions Board's system of mountain schools and is open to young men of Ashe and Alleghany Counties of North Carolina and of Grayson and other counties in Virginia. Because of the progress of education in both states and the establishment of public high schools everywhere, the need for church-supported high schools was lessened, but from the beginning, until well into the present century, they rendered fine service and Oak Hill Academy was, and is today, among the best in the mountains.

From its humble beginning the Ashe Missionary Baptist Association grew to its present proportions and continues to grow. It would be interesting to follow its steady climb to eminence in membership and membership activities from year to year, but space forbids. The information below will afford some idea of the growth of the Missionary branch of the Baptist Church in Ashe. It is taken from the official minutes of the Ashe Missionary Baptist Association covering the 73rd annual session of the association held August 13 and 14, 1959, at two churches in the Grassy Creek area.

The names of the churches, with their pastors, were as follows:

Apple Grove, Finley Miller; Bald Mountain, R. C. Ashley; Baptist Home, none; Beaver Creek, Joseph E. Goodman; Bethel, J. W. Eldreth; Big Flats, Garland Hutton; Big Laurel, Keen Roark; Blue Ridge, Gilbert Osborne; Bristol, Herbert McCoy; Buffalo, Frank Tucker; Chestnut Hill, Wm. Sexton; Clifton, Frank Tucker; Fairview, Douglas Parsons; Farmer Memorial, Jesse Denny; Franklin, Arthur C. Ashley; Friendly Grove, W. E. Burchette; Friendship, G. C. Burkett; Glendale, Garland Hutton; Grassy Creek, Paul Phipps; Healing Springs, Paul Phipps; Jefferson, W. T. Whittington; Landmark, A. P. Howell; Liberty Hill, Wiley Carroll; Laurel Knob, G. C. Burkett; Liberty Grove, Roe Pasley; Laurel Hill, John Davis; Little Helton, Lee Waddell; Long Branch, Earl Hartzog; Midway, M. D. Hart; Mission Home, W. E. Burchette; Mount Olive, Roe Pasley; Mountain View, none; New River, Roe Pasley;

North Beaver, John Goodman; Oak Hill, Roe Pasley; Obids, John Goodman; Old Fields, Arnold Bell; Orion, Smith Miller; Peak Valley, Frank Tucker; Phoenix, R. C. Ashley; Pilot Mountain, Roscoe Morrow; Pine Mountain, Fred Haggaman; Pine Swamp, Gilbert Osborne; Pleasant Chapel, Keen Roark; Pleasant Home, Roe Pasley; Pleasant Valley, G. L. Denny; Prosperity, none; Rock Creek, Finley Miller; Round Knob, Jewell Blevins; Sabbath Home, Roe Pasley; Smethport, Roe Pasley; Sturgill's, A. P. Howell; Three Forks, Reeves Jones; Tuckerdale, Frank Tucker; Valley Home, Noah Johnson; Wagoner, A. E. Sells; Warrensville, R. C. Ashely; Welcome Home, Frank Tucker; West Jefferson, Rexford R. Campbell.

The reader will note that only three of these fifty-nine churches reported no pastors. The combined statistical reports covering the year's activities showed 230 accessions by baptism and eighty-three by transfer. Loss by death and transfer was 172. The grand total of membership was 5,872. An interesting item is that pastors' salaries for the year totaled $48,138.50. The grand total of all expenditures including pastors' salaries was $85,253.36. Other church expenses included church staff salaries, $4,145.94; local missions, $1,323.54; and church local expenses, $28,648.57.

The Ashe association has been marked by steady progress in building new church houses and renovating and enlarging old buildings. The church plant of the West Jefferson church is valued at approximately $100,000. Next in line is probably the new Baptist church in Jefferson, valued at approximately $50,000. In passing it is well to note that the West Jefferson church, with 525 members and 385 in its Sunday school, is the largest church in the Ashe County Missionary Baptist Association.

Primitive Baptists

Reference has been made to the so-called "great split" in the Baptist church, which came about between 1853 and 1858. The issues between two schools of thought in the Baptist church were over missions, foreign and domestic, establishment of schools above the public school level for the education of young men and young women, and other matters relating to better life and living. From all accounts it appears that when the showdown came the division in Ashe County, as in the rest of the State, was about fifty-fifty. Those favoring strong missionary effort and progress in secular and religious education became known as "Missionary Baptists." The other body, made up of conservatives who thought the old ways best, came to be known as Primitive Baptists. While small in number, the Primitive Baptists have maintained an organization in Ashe for more than one hundred years. It is the "Senter District Primitive Baptist Association." The minutes of its 107th annual session, held at Horse Creek Church on August 19 to 21, 1960, shows Elder Ed Davis as moderator. In addition to Elder Davis the Association had five other elders, W. E. Hester, Blair Kilby, P. T. McNeill, G. D. Roten, and Ed Severt. There were ten churches, Bear Creek, Beaver Creek, Big Helton, Horse Creek, North Fork, Pond Mountain, River View, Roans Creek, Senter and South Fork. The total membership was 404. Total collections for the year, to cover expense of printing the minutes and expenses of visiting ministers (called Elders) amounted to $176.00. If any church paid anything to its preachers, there is no record of it.

Since 1960, Elder Ed Davis, for many years moderator of the Senter Baptist Association, has died, as has Elder P. T. McNeill. Elder G. D. Roten is presently (1962) the only active minister of the Senter Baptist Association remaining. It is interesting to note that the two elders, both of whom died suddenly, were leading political figures in Ashe, Elder Davis having been Chairman of the Board of County Commissioners and Elder McNeill having been Clerk of Superior Court.

The Union Baptists

The origin of the denomination known as the Union Baptists has been covered elsewhere and some of its activities have been recorded. Its published book of minutes for the annual meeting of the "Mountain Union Baptist Association," held at Mt. Pleasant Chapel church on September 4 and 5, 1959, states that this was the 93rd annual meeting of the Association. As related elsewhere, the differences over matters relating to and growing out of the War Between the States, became acute and seven churches broke away from the regular Baptist church, called themselves "Union Baptists," and at Silas Creek Church in August, 1867, formed the "Mountain Union Baptist Association," which has endured through the years. Apparently it took a middle course between the progressive Missionary Baptists and the conservative, stand-pat Primitive Baptists. It retained many of the old customs of Baptists, such as calling its ministers "elders," and, as far as the records go, followed the old Baptist custom of paying their preachers little, if anything at all, leaving them to preach for nothing and earn their own livings on the farm or at other labor. Evidently they spent no money for missions or other causes, as the total cash contributions from the twenty churches composing the Association, was $198.23, which went mainly to the expenses of the meeting.

The Association had the following eighteen ministers in North Carolina:

James Brown, G. W. Campbell, G. G. Carpenter, Norman Carpenter, Thomas Darrell, John Graham, Edward Hart, Howard Hicks, E. R. McClure, Harvey Price, Coy Powers, Luther Powers, D. L. Shepherd, Earl Sexton, Avery Testerman, E. E. Woods, Conley Wyatt, and Glenn Johnson.

The churches making up the Association were Baptist Chapel, Beech Creek, Baptist View, Covenant, Buffalo, Fox Creek, Little Valley, Laurel Hill, Liberty, Mt. Zion, Mt. Pleasant Chapel, New Hope, New Bethel, New Bridge, Oak Grove, Pine Grove, Rich Valley, Silas Creek, Three Top, and White Oak.

These twenty churches had 1,675 members. Ten of the churches in the Association had Sunday schools and the association went on record as advising all of its churches to become active in Sunday school work.

III

The Methodist Church

The Methodists, second in number of members and in churches to the Baptists, came into Ashe County sometime between 1815 and 1820. The famous Methodist bishop, Francis Asbury, who travelled more than 270,000 miles, mostly on horseback, preaching

16,200 sermons and ordaining more than 4,000 preachers, visited the Holston settlement more than once, but there is no record that he ever visited Ashe.

Daniel Burkett, leading citizen and devout Methodist, who was born on November 26, 1818, in the old Burkett home which stood where the town of West Jefferson now is and who lived to be 100 years, 7 months and 21 days old, said that the first Methodist "class" in the area was organized at the home of George (Paddy) Bowers near his own home in the 1820's. He was there as a small boy and remembered the details of the meeting. It was held outdoors, under an oak tree, and the officiating minister was James Hurley, great-great-grandfather of D. P. Hurley, noted Methodist minister of recent years. Daniel Burkett was destined to play a large part in the establishment of Methodism in Ashe. One of his daughters married James H. Weaver, young Methodist minister, who became one of the foremost ministers of his church in North Carolina. His son, Dr. Charles Clinton Weaver, became even more famous as a preacher than his father. He was also a successful educator.

Rev. Garland R. Stafford, who served charges in Ashe and later became superintendent of the North Wilkesboro District of the Western Conference of the Methodist Church, has written an interesting account of the growth of the Methodist Church in Ashe, under the title, *Methodism in Ashe County*. It is a scholarly treatise, exceedingly well done. Most of the information following about Methodism is taken from it.

He found that Methodism came into Ashe from the Holston conference. This area was north and west of Ashe County and as early as 1783 one Jeremiah Lambert had "appointments on the headwaters of New River, in Grayson County, Virginia, or in Ashe County, North Carolina." (Price, R. N., *Holston Methodism*). Lambert was followed by Henry Willis in 1784, Richard Swift and Michael Gilbert in 1785, Monk Whittaker and Mark Moore in 1786, and Jeremiah Martin and Nathaniel Moore in 1787. In 1785 Rev. Henry Willis became presiding elder of a district embracing the Yadkin and Holston Circuits and although Ashe County lay almost in the center between them, there was little activity in Ashe. The first official notice of the presence of Methodists in Ashe appears in the book, *Holston Methodism,* previously referred to, where it is recorded that there were 100 Methodists scattered over Ashe. Steps were taken to organize them into a circuit in 1817. Rev. Jesse Green was assigned to the task. It should be remembered that these pioneers of Methodism started with nothing in the way of financial means. There were no church houses. Meetings were held in homes, barns, under the shade of trees—anywhere groups of people could be assembled.

Ashe County has been part of several Methodist conferences. The year 1796 witnessed the establishment of the "Western Conference," which was the beginning of annual conferences with fixed boundaries. (See I. P. Martin's *History of Methodism in the Holston Conference.*) In 1812 the Western Conference was divided into the Ohio and Tennessee Conferences, Ashe being included in the latter, and twelve years later in 1824, the Holston Conference was formed out of the Tennessee.

In the Methodist church, as in the Baptist church, as above related, the issue of slavery brought dissension and as early as 1844 the Methodist Episcopal Church became two churches—the Methodist Episcopal Church and the Methodist Episcopal Church South. The Holston Conference, of which Ashe was a part, was not divided. It elected to be part of the Methodist Episcopal Church South and it so remained throughout the War Between the States. After the war, as had been the case with the Baptists, union sentiment resulted in disruption. The Holston Conference was divided into two churches—one Methodist Episcopal and the other Methodist Episcopal South. Most of the Methodist churches in Ashe County adhered to "South," but several were established by people with Union sympathy. The two factions got together, settled their differences, and found themselves in agreement in the Western Conference formed in 1890. Agreement on a national scale was reached in 1939 when the two churches reunited to form the Methodist Church, and Ashe County Methodism is, therefore, in the western North Carolina Conference of this united church.

The arrangement of the churches into circuits for pastoral oversight and service has changed many times. All the churches of the Methodist Episcopal Church South in Ashe, with the exception of

Sutherland, Grassy Creek and possibly one or two others, were on the Jefferson Circuit until 1886. That year Creston Circuit was formed, and others have followed as membership grew and the work load increased. As of 1960 Rev. Garland R. Stafford, District Superintendent, lists the arrangement of the churches in circuits, with the pastors assigned, as follows:

Creston-Green Valley Circuit: R. Clifton Summey, pastor; P. E. Bingham, associate. Churches: Big Laurel, Creston, Green Valley, Little Laurel, Martin's Chapel, Mountain View, Peak Grove, Pleasant Hill, Riverview, Roaring Fork, Rock Creek, Roundabout, Sutherland.

Helton Circuit: W. Ralph Surratt, pastor. Churches: Ashley's Chapel, Grassy Creek, Greenwood, Helton, Lansing, Trinity.

Jefferson Circuit: Ray C. Stephens, pastor. Churches: Bethany, Jefferson, Orion, Zion.

Nathan's Creek Circuit: S. E. White, pastor. Churches: Chestnut Hill, Nathan's Creek, Transou.

Todd Circuit: J. O. Pritchard, pastor. Churches: Blackburn's, Calvary, Cranberry, Stephen's Memorial.

Warrensville Circuit: Keith Tutterow, pastor. Churches: Clifton, Fairview, Mill Creek, Rich Hill, Smethport, Warrensville.

West Jefferson (station): Charles A. Rhinehart, pastor.

These thirty-seven Methodist churches in Ashe County reported a total membership for 1960 of 2,561. Total contributions for all causes for the year were $66,598.00, a little more than $26 per member. Mr. Stafford notes that based upon census figures for 1960, this membership was almost thirteen per cent of the total population and the ratio of giving was well above the comparable ratio among Methodists of the State.

From all accounts the Methodists were among the first to promote camp meetings, where people came together annually, or oftener, for religious services. The meetings lasted usually a week, but often longer. The worshipers lived in covered wagons, or under improvised shelters, and services were held under an arbor or a shed roof. There was preaching all day long, every day.

Dr. Elisha Mitchell, head of the chemistry department of the University of North Carolina, left an account in his diary covering two official visits to Ashe in 1827 and 1828, in which he wrote of traveling many miles to attend a Methodist camp meeting near the home of Timothy Perkins, on Big Helton Creek. He admired the worshipers' earnestness and religious fervor but, being a reserved, strait-laced Presbyterian and a lay preacher in that church, he was shocked by the shouting of the women and the excitement around the "mourner's bench."

He found, as he admitted, that end results were good and generally beneficial.

Mr. Stafford could not find evidence of a campground near the Timothy Perkins home but he did find evidence of such a place in the Helton community. Later there was a campground near Warrensville on the North Fork of New River, nearly opposite the place where the Sprague Electric Company now stands. This campground, according to Mr. E. C. Eller who lives at Bina, was supported mainly by David Worth and Wiley P. Thomas, well-to-do Methodist laymen, who erected there a building, forty feet by sixty feet in size. Both of these men erected comfortable buildings there for their own use. There was a campground at Sutherland, forerunner of the Methodist church there, and another at Riverside near Fig, and still another at Little Laurel. A quarterly conference of the Ashe and Watauga Circuits was held at Little Laurel on September 9, 1877. From there and other outdoor meeting places came many of the early churches of the Methodist and Baptist denominations.

In his *Methodism in Ashe County*, which has been referred to, Rev. G. R. Stafford undertakes to give sketches of all of the Methodist churches in Ashe. It is to be regretted that there is not space here for all of them.

He has arranged them in alphabetical order, beginning with Ashley's Chapel, one mile west from Bina. There is no information except that it has thirty-six members and contributed $1,379 to all causes in 1960.

The second church, Bethany, located at Baldwin, has a remarkable record. It was organized in 1849 under the name of Lebanon and for three years met in the homes of its members. It erected a log building in 1852, which served the church until 1870. Then it was abandoned, and the church moved into a vacant store building back of which the church of today stands. Mrs. Elizabeth Edwards and her children donated land for a new church building, which was dedicated in 1875 by the presiding elder, Rev. I. S. Ross, who renamed the church Bethany. The church grew and in 1915 a third building was erected. This served the church for thirty-seven years. The present church building was undertaken in 1952, under the leadership of Rev. W. Grady Burgin. The moving spirits behind the movement for a new church were G. W. Edwards, M. G. Edwards, Raner Edwards and Frank Edwards, all grandsons of Mrs. Elizabeth Edwards. The chairman of the building committee was M. G. Edwards. The other members were Ward Ray and Roger Holman. The finance committee was composed of Mrs. G. W. Edwards, Mrs. Roger Holman, Mrs. Raner Edwards, Mrs. Worth Gentry, Mrs. Bruce Houck, Mrs. M. G. Edwards, Robert Colvard, Rayburn Houck, Ross Houck, and Homer Gentry. The architect for the new church building was H. N. Haines of Durham. The building was constructed of the famous Crab Orchard stone and it is one of the most beautiful rural churches in America. A story about it with pictures, has appeared in the *Saturday Evening Post* and in other papers and magazines of national circulation. The cost of the building was in excess of $70,000. With the exception of West Jefferson Methodist Church, Bethany's church building is the most expensive church building of the Methodists of Ashe. It was dedicated on September 4, 1960, by Bishop Nolan B. Harmon.

Big Laurel Church, built of logs on land donated by Eli Graybeal in 1855, erected the present frame building in 1885. An unusual feature of the building was that the builder, Rev. George Dillen of the Creston Community, was a skilled carpenter and also a Baptist preacher.

Blackburn's Chapel at Todd was organized in 1860. It was named for Levi Blackburn, one of the founders. Originally it occupied a small log house at Elk Cross Roads. In 1900 land for a new church was given by Rev. Hamilton Blackburn. After the coming of the railroad, the name was changed from Elk Cross Roads to Todd and in 1948 a brick veneer church building was erected. A brick veneer parsonage was added in 1953.

Calvary Church, located at Fleetwood, was organized by Rev. E. P. Stabler in 1914.

Chestnut Hill, Crumpler, Clifton, and Cranberry, all active churches, had no records of their early days and activities.

Creston Church, located at Creston, was organized before the War Between the States. The land for it was donated by David Worth. It was originally known as Worth's Chapel. Its present building was built about 1902 and a new parsonage, on land donated by Mr. and Mrs. Todd Price, was built in 1960.

Fairview, located in the northwest corner of the county, is an active church but has no records of its beginnings.

Grassy Creek Church, located at Grassy Creek, was organized sometime prior to 1900. It is located close to the North Carolina-Virginia line and at one time its meeting place was in Virginia. In 1904 a new building was erected in the North Carolina side of the line, but the church remained attached to the Virginia Methodists until 1925, when it was transferred to the Western North Carolina Conference and became part of the Helton Circuit. This church produced many progressive Methodist leaders, among them S. L. Duvall, W. J. Pugh, Dr. A. W. Wagg, W. C. Greer, Scott Jones, J. A. Dickson, Mrs. Irene Dickson Cox, E. A. Ashley, and Paul Graybeal.

Greenwood Church, organized in 1884, drew most of its members from Old Helton. Leader in organizing the church and securing a proper building was William P. Young. Three of its young men became preachers, Cecil and Wiley Akers and Aaron Phipps. All of them became Baptist ministers.

Greer's Chapel on Little Horse Creek ceased to be a Methodist church and became a Primitive Baptist Church.

No information was available concerning Green Valley, except that it had eighty-seven members in 1960 and contributed $907 to all church causes.

Old Helton Church, situated about halfway between Greenwood and Helton Churches and the mother of both, was the first Methodist church in the Helton area, and served the needs of its community well through a trying period. When it was formed is not known, but it was an active church long before the War Between the States. Its building was used as a school beginning in

1863, when Rev. John Wesley Bowman came into the county. He undertook the work of the church and also established the school, which he carried on for three years. He farmed for a living in the summer and taught school in the winter, while looking after his pastoral duties as well.

The church grew and prospered and in 1885 was able to give off enough members to start two churches, Helton and Greenwood. On November 19, 1885, a committee, consisting of Calvin Young and Dr. Stephen Pennington, was named to divide the membership between the two churches.

The new Helton, which was set up about a mile below Sturgill's, was assigned these members from the old congregation: Elizabeth Blevins, David Dixon, Pheba Dixon, America Hurley, James E. Neece, Sarah Neece, Rosa V. Neece, Catherine Perkins, Lucy Perkins, Belle Perkins, Dr. Stephen Pennington, Johanna Pennington, Orlean Pennington, Clayburn Pennington, Charity Pennington, Davie Pennington, Martha Sturgill, Eli Weaver, Polly Weaver, and Amanda Weaver.

The church building was erected about 1856 and remodeled in 1939.

The Helton Circuit came into existence in 1902 and by great good fortune there was assigned to the circuit Rev. Samuel Weldon Brown, an M.A. graduate of Trinity College (now Duke University) and a dedicated educator. He moved to Sparta in 1881 and remained there thirty-four years. He was the first college graduate in Alleghany County and, by choice, a lay preacher. He was brought into full conference connection when assigned to the Helton Circuit and he served effectively, while keeping his school connections. Through his efforts the Helton High School, one of Ashe County's first high schools, came into existence and served many hundreds of Ashe County boys and girls.

Notable among the leaders who made the school and church outstanding were Eli Weaver, W. W. Osborne, J. N. Baldwin, E. F. Perkins, Herbert Littlewood, Wade Eller, E. C. Francis, W. T. Pennington, Dr. Pardue Bunch, and others. Out of the Helton church, and Old Helton, came the following preachers: Ambrose Weaver, Tivis E. Weaver, and Oscar Eller. Green Weaver, Enoch Osborne, and Granville Weaver became useful lay teachers.

The Jefferson Church came into existence some time before 1827. In that year the Ashe Circuit had its name changed to the Jefferson Circuit, indicating, as Rev. G. R. Stafford says in his treatise, that Jefferson had become the base of Methodist operations in the county. Where the church worshiped for the first twenty years or more is not known. The first deed to land for a Methodist church was executed by William P. Waugh, dated November 27, 1847. George Bowers, N. H. Waugh, Eli Graybeal, and George Hawk were named as trustees. The land was west of Jefferson, "adjoining the lands of James Vannoy." A second deed, believed to cover the site of the present church, was executed February 23, 1860, by James P. Waugh to Rev. Abram Weaver, David Worth, and Johnson Perkins, trustees for the Jefferson Methodist Church. It is a family tradition that the church erected on this site was built by Colonel George Bowers with slave labor and that the bricks were made at a kiln that stood near where the residence of William B. Austin now stands.

In 1895 Mrs. Etta Hall, aunt of two famous educators born in Ashe, the late B. B. and D. D. Daugherty, executed a will bequeathing $1,500 toward the erection of a new Methodist church in Jefferson under the supervision of Captain J. W. Todd, Major J. E. Foster, Captain John Dent, John Neal, and the preacher in charge. With this as a starter the church raised additional funds and the building was completed in 1904. Other building activities consisted of additions to the church buildings for growing Sunday school needs and providing adequate parsonage and other facilities. In 1960 the church had 178 members and raised $10,036 for all purposes.

The Lansing Church was organized by Calvin Graybeal in 1876. From this church three young men entered the ministry. They were Adolphus Graybeal, W. A. Patton, and Cicero Graybeal. Others to be licensed to preach at this church were David W. Haga and Kelly L. Haga. The famous hunter, Wilburn Waters, was a member of this church. In 1934 the congregation started a campaign to build a new church. The foundation for it was laid on July 31, 1938, and the building was completed in 1944. Membership in 1960 was sixty-six and contributions to all causes amounted to $1,020.

Little Laurel is located on Little Laurel Creek and is worshiping in the third church to be built on the same site. The first was built in 1868 and it was preceded by a camp meeting ground. The second building was erected in 1887 and the third in 1945.

Little or no data was available about Martin's Chapel, Mill Creek, Mountain View, Nathan's Creek, Pleasant Hill, Peakview, Rich Hill, Roaring Fork, Rock Creek, Roundabout, Transou, Trinity, Snider's Chapel, Stephen's Memorial, and Warrensville.

Orion Church made its start under the ministry of Rev. J. T. Stover on February 10, 1886. The following constituted the membership: George W. Perkins, Dobson Bare, Katie Ann Wyatt, Alice Coldiron, Captain John Dent, Christian Burkett, Catherine Burkett, Sallie Colvard, Rose Colvard, Laticia Perkins, Nancy Witherspoon, Martha Jane Witherspoon, Alice Speaks, and Ella S. Dent. W. T. Colvard and wife conveyed to the church the present site by deed dated October 20, 1900. In 1960 the church had ninety-three members and had contributed $1,016 to all causes.

Smethport is a church which grew out of a Sunday school organized in 1910 in the old log schoolhouse, Bee Branch, on Buffalo Creek. Ransom Johnson, Sam Lemly, Mitchell Faircloth, and John W. Weaver were leaders. In 1923 a small group of Methodists living in the community organized the Smethport Methodist Church. The Bee Branch schoolhouse was used as a meeting house, as later was a store building, until the church acquired a lot and built a church building. Trustees under the deed for the property were Gwyn L. Park, Jefferson attorney; Daniel Weaver; J. I. Weaver; G. W. Shatley; and A. G. Caudill. A building program in 1958 resulted in brick veneering for the building and the addition of rooms for an educational department. The church reported seventy-eight members in 1960 and total contributions of $9,002.

Sutherland is another Methodist congregation that grew out of a camp meeting. It was immediately after one of these religious gatherings, during which there had been many conversions, that Rev. Mr. Cooper, the Methodist minister in charge, started the movement for a church. Alfred Sutherland and Aras Cox took the lead. The church was organized following the meeting referred to, which was in 1851 or 1852. The church building was completed between 1854 and 1856. This building served the church until 1885 when a new site was chosen and a new building erected. Leaders in this movement were James Hardin, William Phillips, Thomas Sutherland, Andy Lewis, John Wilson, and Alex Boyer.

This church has been a force for righteousness in its area and has produced many leaders of the Methodist church. Probably the most famous was Rev. W. A. Wilson, who preached his first sermon at Sutherland, later was pastor of the church, and still later a missionary to Japan, where he served for forty-two years. Other preachers to come out of this church were Joshua Cole, Alex Sutherland, Lorenzo Cole, George W. Osborne, and William Rominger.

West Jefferson Methodist, the largest Methodist Church in Ashe, came into existence in 1921. West Jefferson, a new town built around the station of the new railroad, had many Methodists but they were served by the Jefferson Methodist church some two miles away. They decided that a Methodist church was needed in their new town and met with Rev. T. E. Wagg, pastor of the Jefferson charge, at the home of Mr. and Mrs. James Allen for discussion of the matter. A decision was made to proceed with organization and the following became charter members of the new church:

Mr. and Mrs. R. E. Faw, Mrs. A. E. Graybeal, Miss Jennie Graybeal, Mrs. Edgar D. Jones, Miss Nona Kirby, T. E. Parker, J. A. Roland, Mr. and Mrs. J. L. Segraves, and Mr. and Mrs. James Allen. J. E. Shumate offered his theater as a meeting house and West Jefferson became a point on the Jefferson Circuit. The theater, owing to lack of light and room, was used only two months and the church moved to the schoolhouse. The congregation was growing and took steps to acquire a suitable lot for a church building. Rev. J. L. Reynolds came to the church in 1922. During his pastorate the membership passed the one-hundred mark and the present church building was begun. The building was free of debt by 1934 and in that year it was formally dedicated by Bishop Kern.

The Western North Carolina Conference in 1936 separated the church from the Jefferson Circuit and it became a "station" charge. Because of continued growth of the church it was decided to buy adjoining property and in 1957 the present educational building, which cost $52,000, was put into use. Including the church edifice, the additional property purchased and the parsonage, the church plant is conservatively valued at $150,000. It was dedicated on May 25, 1958, by the district superintendent, Rev. Garland R. Stafford.

The church had 245 members in 1960 and its contributions to all causes amounted to $16,580.

Zion church, located near Todd, in the Mill Creek community, was organized in 1896 and held its services first in a log schoolhouse, later in a new frame schoolhouse, and then in its own building which was dedicated by Presiding Elder Rev. M. H. Vestal in 1913. Out of this church came three ministers, Rev. W. L. Scott, Rev. T. Hobson Houck, and Rev. W. K. Greer. In 1960 the church had 216 members and raised $2,503 for all causes.

In *Methodism in Ashe County*, referred to above, Rev. Garland R. Stafford lists twenty men who entered the ministry of the Methodist church. "The strength of a church is measured," says he, "by the number of those who enter its ministry. By this measure, Ashe County Methodism is well above the average."

Mr. Stafford proceeds to line them up alphabetically and to give a brief sketch of their lives, where information was available. It is to be regretted that space will permit little more here than a list of their names. The list follows:

H. A. Blankenship, local preacher at Pond Mountain, 1911-1916.

Oscar Lester Brown, Sutherland; famous as a pastor; a church administrator; and a builder of churches.

Martin P. Carico, Edmonds; a preacher of unusual ability who served several of the biggest churches; presiding elder for twelve years.

Jack Leon Caudill, Bina; licensed in 1959; died in 1960.

J. W. Caudill, father of Jack Leon and Russel H. Caudill; builder by trade but a devoted local preacher.

Thomas E. Goodman, transferred to the Holston Conference; died in 1934.

Adolphus Graybeal, Lansing; filled many important assignments in North Carolina and Kansas; died in 1917.

David M. Graybeal, Lansing; preacher and educator; died in 1924.

Winifred Alexander Graybeal, Lansing; served in North Carolina and in the Holston Conference.

Thomas R. Handy, Grassy Creek; served mostly in Tennessee,

where he was a presiding elder for twelve years; member of the Holston Conference for seventy-one years.

George Fielder Houck, Baldwin; active and successful pastor and good church administrator.

Thomas Hobson Houck, Todd; served churches at Sparta, Roaring River, Warrensville, Danbury, and Flat Rock; withdrew in 1941.

Thomas Jackson Houck, Baldwin; active in the ministry for twenty-nine years; retired in 1905, he continued to serve in many capacities for twenty-three years more.

David P. Hurley, Helton; noted as a teacher; became a minister in 1889.

Roy Presley Jones, Rich Hill; licensed to preach in 1916; retired after nine years as a pastor.

John Nicholas, of Ashe.

Robert Edward Lee Plummer, Helton; local preacher; served one year as pastor at Warrensville. His first interest was teaching and he had a notable career in this field. He led the fight for the establishment of an effective public health service in Ashe and was prominent in the movement that brought about the establishment of the Ashe County Memorial Hospital. He made Healing Springs High School, of which he was principal for many years, one of the finest high schools in the State.

William Lee Scott of Todd became a preacher in 1911 and served eight or more charges, but his greatest interest was in Christian education. A more complete account of his work in this field appears in the chapter on education.

James Wagg, Jefferson; a local preacher and a physician.

John D. Wagg, Jefferson; son of Dr. Wagg; entered the ministry in 1858; served large churches in Bristol, Tennessee, and Asheville.

Herman E. Haire, born in Virginia and reared at West Jefferson; licensed to preach in 1951; presently serving as pastor of the Valdese Methodist Church.

Thomas Eugene Wagg, Jefferson; son of Dr. James Wagg; served many churches in the Western North Carolina Conference.

Abram Weaver, Jefferson; pastor at Jefferson in 1863.

Ambrose Weaver, Jefferson.

James Harvey Weaver, Helton; son of Hiram Weaver, a local

preacher. He was mainly self-educated and entered the teaching profession. While teaching at Jefferson Academy he entered the ministry. He served the church at Jefferson for four years and later held pastorates in several districts. In 1893 he was made presiding elder of the Greensboro District. The following year he was appointed pastor of West Market Street Church and completed its building. Many important assignments followed, including the First Methodist in Salisbury, Central Church in Asheville, Central in Monroe, presiding elder in the Shelby, Statesville, Hickory, and Greensboro Districts. Seven times he was named delegate of the Western Conference to the General Conference.

Dr. Charles Clinton Weaver, son of Rev. James H. and Jennie Burkett Weaver, was born on Little Helton Creek. Mr. Stafford, in his *Methodism in Ashe*, expresses the opinion that he was "one of the most eminent sons of Ashe and certainly the most eminent Methodist minister born here."

There are those who remember him and his father and who might argue the point. Dr. Weaver was graduated from Trinity College, where he was Phi Beta Kappa, and from Johns Hopkins University with a Ph.D. degree. He entered immediately the field of education and served three years as president of Rutherford College, followed by the presidency of Davenport College for seven years and of Emory and Henry College, Emory, Virginia for ten years. He left the educational field for the ministry and served pastorates at Central Methodist in Monroe, Central in Asheville, First Methodist in Charlotte, and Centenary in Winston-Salem. In the last named church he served nine years and brought together two large downtown Methodist churches and led in building the cathedral Centenary Church on West Fifth Street in Winston-Salem. After this he served as presiding elder in the Greensboro District for one year and for four years in the Winston-Salem District. He was long a member of the General Board of Missions of the Methodist Church, a trustee of the annual conference, member of the North Carolina Council of Churches, and member of the Board of Managers of the Pastor's School. He was an influential member of several General Conferences and of the Uniting Conference. He was a trustee of the Hugh Chatham Memorial Hospital at Elkin and when he retired from the ministry he accepted employment as superintendent of this hospital. He died there on February 19, 1946.

Other Weavers to serve as Methodist preachers were Granville Weaver of Helton church, Hiram Weaver of Bina, J. S. Weaver of Jefferson, R. Green Weaver of Helton, and Tevis E. Weaver of Helton.

William Albert Wilson, mentioned as a preacher coming out of Sutherland Church, entered the ministry in 1886 and joined the Holston Conference. He offered himself as a missionary to Japan and was accepted in 1890. The Southern Methodist Mission to Japan had been organized only three years before his arrival. He was literally "in on the ground floor" and had much to do with the growth of the mission. He became presiding elder in Kyushu, Kobe, and Hiroshima and for a time was in charge of the missionary work among the Japanese in Korea. He was retired in 1932.

Mr. Stafford lists the following local preachers about whom he could gain little information:

Cicero Graybeal, Joshua Cole, Alex Sutherland, Lorenzy Cole, George W. Osborne, William Rominger, W. Kelly Greer, Enoch Osborne, of Helton; Billy Osborne, Big Laurel; Hilton Lewis, Ashland; L. D. Osborne, Trade, Tennessee; T. W. Arnold and D. F. Cole, Ashland; J. D. Campbell, Thomas A. Farmer, and Samuel Gambill, Lansing; Rufus Graybeal, Mountain City, Tennessee.

This completes the story of Methodist activities in Ashe except its part in the educational awakening that came to the country about the turn of the century. That story will be told in the following chapter on education.

IV

Presbyterians and Other Denominations

Historians are generally agreed that the first settlers, who came to Ashe before the Revolutionary War, were primarily Irish Presbyterians with occasional Episcopalians. They came south, down the Blue Ridge from Virginia. The Baptists and Methodists poured in between 1771 and 1775 from eastern and piedmont North Carolina and completely overwhelmed the Presbyterians.

According to Presbyterian records, a start at organizing a Presbyterian church was made at Grassy Creek. In 1773 Rev. John Black, noted pioneer minister located at Abingdon, Virginia, preached what was probably the first sermon ever preached in the Ashe County area. He preached in an oak grove. He continued to visit the area and laid plans for a church building. Logs had been cut for the erection of such a building but the Revolutionary War came and the project was abandoned. The end of the war left the area and the entire State of North Carolina in a serious situation economically and otherwise, and the temptation to follow Daniel Boone and other pathfinders into the wilds of Kentucky was too strong for the Scotch-Irish settlers, ever a pioneer people. The movement started by John Black to establish a Presbyterian church among them failed.

Dr. Elisha Mitchell, in his diary covering a trip through Ashe County in 1828, wrote that he spent the night of July 6 in the home of Colonel and Mrs. John Finley near Jefferson. Colonel Finley informed Dr. Mitchell that he and his wife were the only Presbyterians in Ashe County.

From 1857 through 1871, there were sporadic efforts, with little success, on the part of several Presbyterian evangelists to gain a foothold in Ashe. Between 1857 and 1863, Rev. Jesse Septimus Rankin, evangelist for the Concord Presbytery, spent much time preaching in Ashe and he actually organized a Presbyterian church at Jefferson on August 29, 1863. Ministerial leadership was not available and the church was soon discontinued. The records show that Benjamin H. Neal was an elder in this church. Other circuit-riding Presbyterian preachers between 1857 and 1871 were Rev. William McEwan, 1862-63; Rev. Mr. Wilson, 1867-68; Rev. B. L. Beall, 1867-71. Rev. Mr. Beall served as a chaplain in Lee's army in 1864-65, and after the war he returned to his work of the ministry, where he continued for four or five years.

There is no record of Presbyterian church activities in Ashe, after Rev. B. L. Beall left the ministry for other work in 1869, until 1896. Mrs. Elizabeth Neal Foster of Jefferson is credited with reviving Presbyterianism in Ashe by bringing into the county Rev. C. W. Robinson, a young Presbyterian minister who was serving charges at North Wilkesboro and Elkin. He was able to create much local interest and he aroused Orange Presbytery to the importance of missionary effort in the mountains. In 1897 Rev. E. E. Gillespie was assigned as home missionary in Ashe. Aided by another young minister, John H. Grey, he established Ebenezer Presbyterian Church near Wagoner. Organized on January 1, 1899, it is known as the "Mother Presbyterian Church of Ashe County."

When Mr. Gillespie was transferred to South Carolina, he was succeeded as permanent pastor by Rev. Allen Jones, who had an active part in establishing the next Presbyterian church, Jefferson, which started off with twenty-two members on July 15, 1900. Obids Presbyterian Church, the third permanent Presbyterian church in the county, was organized by Allen Jones.

To this young minister, Rev. Allen Jones, Jr., should go credit for establishing the famous Presbyterian Mission School at Glade Valley. He had a burning zeal for education and he was able to sell the idea to Orange Presbytery. It was thought at first the school would be established in Ashe but it finally went to Alleghany. The school has done wonderful work and is still going strong.

Mr. Jones was succeeded by Rev. S. Calvin Smith, serving Ebenezer, Jefferson, and Obids churches.

Following Mr. Smith's retirement because of bad health in 1902, there was another lack of ministerial leadership and the work lagged until Rev. R. K. Moseley took charge. When he left in 1908 there was another period of inactivity, for the same reason, lasting until 1914, when Rev. J. C. Brown came to the field to begin a successful pastorate of two years. He was succeeded by Rev. E. Wayne Thompson, who, working out of Glade Valley, took over the work in Ashe. He organized Peak Creek Presbyterian Church on October 3, 1921, with the aid of S. M. Rankin and C. W. Irwin and Elders E. B. Eldredge, D. C. Bare, and George W. Bowlin.

In 1922 Mr. Thompson was succeeded by Rev. R. H. Stone. During his period of service Mr. Stone began the publication of the *Ashe Presbyterian*, which has meant much to the Presbyterian churches of the county. He fostered and promoted the "Christian Chatauqua" program, which covered the county. From these meetings came several new Presbyterian churches, among them West Jefferson in 1925, Lansing in 1926, Foster Memorial in 1931, Gillespie in 1932, Stone's Chapel, and Big Ridge. Mr. Stone left the field in 1941 to join Mecklenburg Presbytery.

His leaving coincided with the coming of Rev. John W. Luke, fresh from college and Union Theological Seminary, who has been in the county since. He has been instrumental in building the following Presbyterian churches:

Low Gap in 1929, Laurel Fork in 1932, Glendale Springs in 1936, Bethel and Millers Creek (both in Wilkes County). He brought about the rebuilding of the mother church, Ebenezer, and served for four years as supply pastor for West Jefferson. The J. W. Luke, Jr., Memorial Building, a community building and gymnasium, has been erected at Glendale Springs as a memorial to Dr. Luke's son, who died suddenly at age sixteen.

The Presbyterians made fine headway in Jefferson, West Jefferson and Lansing. Among the ministers who furnished the inspiration and leadership and who did the hardest work were these:

Rev. D. F. Helm in 1932; Rev. R. H. Stone in 1935; Rev. J. W. Luke in 1942; Rev. W. P. Boyle in 1945; Rev. C. M. Voyles in 1950; Rev. Russell Burns in 1954; Rev. T. S. Smith in 1958; Rev. W. P. Boyle in 1946; Rev. Cecil Callis in 1949; Rev. R. F. Brown, Rev. J. R. Jackson in 1954; Rev. H. H. Culler in 1956. The last-named left the field for a charge in the Concord Presbytery in 1960. This left the Jefferson field without a minister but West Jefferson, which had been made a separate field in 1945, was served by Rev. T. S. Smith.

Between 1940 and 1960 there had been fine growth in the Lansing field. Lansing had been cut off from the Jefferson field. The first pastor was Rev. Carl H. Stark, who took over in 1941. He served until he entered the Army as chaplain in 1944. Those who followed him were Rev. J. S. Johnson, in 1944; Rev. Kenneth Foreman, Jr.; Rev. G. W. Hollenhead in 1948; and Rev. John B. Stanley in 1959.

While the story of Presbyterianism in Ashe, up to the present, may appear to be confined to ministers, a study of the record discloses fine work by ministers' wives and by trained and dedicated women who assisted these ministers. Mention should be made of the late Miss Myrtle Williamson, assistant to Rev. R. H. Stone; Miss Betsy Tinley, who took over in the Lansing charge when they had no minister, and Miss Kathryn Hunt, who performed a similar service when Rev. G. W. Hollenhead left the same field. Also active in the field have been Miss Katherine O'Neal, Miss Lois Calhoun, Miss Evelyn Acheson, Miss Maxie Weaver, Miss Annabel Corry, Miss Delphine Brown, Miss Ruth Bowlin, Miss Kate DuBose, Miss Annie Walker, Miss Virginia Smith, Miss Laura F. Steel, Miss Helen Stacy, Miss Agnes Peacock, Miss Alice Neal Wilson, Miss Eurice Thompson, Miss Lucille Moore, Miss Julia Finley, Miss Ruby Hudler, Miss Irene Baldwin, Miss Shirley Caudill, Miss Martha Rose Miller, Miss Cleo Osborne, Miss Ruby Wyatt, Miss Mary E. Shaw, Mrs. R. H. Stone, Mrs. Mary F. Luke, Mrs. Evelyn Brown, Miss Lucille Moore, Miss Peggy Joe Miller, and many others.

Men workers, all worthy of mention, include James Sydnor, Bob White, Charles Moore, De Armord Moore, A. N. Moffett, J. B. Spillman, Ross Faw, C. W. Williams, and many others, representing all of the Presbyterian churches in Ashe.

Out of the churches of Ashe have come the following ministers: Rev. W. Carty, Rev. Denver Blevins, Rev. Dawes Graybeal, all of the Lansing charge; Rev. John Bare from Big Ridge Church, near Glendale Springs.

The Presbyterian churches in Ashe County, in order of organization, present membership, and those leading in the work of organization, are listed below. It is not intended as a complete list of those who aided in establishing the churches, but painstaking research, covering the records of every church, revealed the information here set down which is believed to contain the names of the Presbyterians, lay and ministerial, who laid much of the groundwork for the Presbyterian church of today in Ashe County.

Ebenezer, organized January 1, 1899, by Rev. E. E. Gillespie, Rev. John H. Grey, Rev. C. E. Hodgin. Elders: Franklin Atwood, John Burgess, Calvin Severt, N. L. Brooks, George Farrington; deacon: Cornelius Bare; present pastor, Rev. Allan Jones, Jr.; present membership, twenty-four.

Jefferson, July 15, 1900. Dr. Robert E. Caldwell, organizer; elders: John T. Bledsoe, E. A. McNeill, Anson R. Vail; deacons:

Richard T. Gentry, James R. McEwen, William H. McNeill.

Obids, December 3, 1904. Rev. M. C. Arrowood, organizer; elders: Jesse Baker, James M. Calloway; deacon: Robert McNeill.

Peak Creek, October 3, 1921. Rev. E. Wayne Thompson, organizer; elder: George W. Bowlin; deacon: Green Wingler; twenty members.

West Jefferson, July 12, 1925. Rev. R. H. Stone, Rev. C. W. Robinson and Rev. J. H. Carter, organizers; elder: O. L. Naas. The original members of this church were Mesdames W. J. Price, T. C. Bowie, and T. P. Tudor, and Miss Elizabeth Bowie. Very recently, this church has been consolidated with the Jefferson and Obids churches under the name of the Mount Jefferson Presbyterian Church. It has a total membership of 155 and Rev. T. I. Smith is pastor.

Lansing, September 26, 1926. Rev. R. H. Stone, Dr. D. Clay Lilly and Rev. J. H. Carter, organizers; elders: Daniel T. Jones, J. Ross Weaver, James Campbell; deacons: Elbert McCarter and Ernest Carty; membership, sixty-four; present pastor, Rev. John Stanley.

Low Gap, Jefferson, Route 2, June 22, 1929. Organized by Rev. John W. Luke, Rev. C. W. Robinson and Rev. R. H. Stone; elders: F. M. Allen, Will Bare; deacon: Isaac Bare; membership, twenty.

Foster Memorial, Husk, November 29, 1931. Organizers: Rev. R. H. Stone, Rev. J. W. Luke, Rev. E. W. Thompson; elders: L. B. Ham, N. W. Graham; deacons: Felix Ham, A. L. Carter; present membership, seventeen; present pastor, Rev. John Stanley.

Laurel Fork, September 25, 1932. Organized by Rev. John W. Luke, Rev. C. W. Robinson, Rev. J. W. McFall, Rev. DeWitt Helm; elder: Hiram Woody; deacon: Ola Long; membership, twenty.

Gillespie, at Apple Grove, November 27, 1932. Organized by Rev. R. H. Stone, Rev. C. W. Robinson, Rev. DeWitt Helm, Dr. E. E. Gillespie; elder: Conley Thompson; deacons; Vance Miller, Walter Calhoun; present pastor, Rev. John Stanly; membership, thirteen.

Big Ridge, September 29, 1934. Organized by Rev. R. H. Stone, Rev. John W. Luke, Rev. De Witt Helm; elder: J. W. Farrington; deacon: A. E. Bare; inactive.

Glendale Springs, August 12, 1939. Organizers: Rev. John W. Luke, Rev. T. F. Haney, Rev. R. H. Stone, Dr. E. E. Gillespie; elder: Delmer Rose; deacons: Otto Wilcox, J. E. Whitely; membership, seventy-two; present pastor, Rev. John W. Luke.

Because John W. Luke is not only a prominent minister of his church, but also because he is an unusual citizen in many respects, Dr. R. H. Stone, Executive Secretary and Stated Clerk of the Orange Presbytery, when asked to comment on his services, submitted a statement from which the following is taken:

> "There was a man sent from God, whose name was John." Many people in Ashe and Wilkes Counties would like to take that verse, modernize it, and say, "There was a man sent from God, whose name was John Luke." In 1927, just out of Union Theological Seminary of Virginia, Rev. John Luke came to make his home in Ashe County. He had accepted the calls of Obids, Ebenezer and Peak Creek Presbyterian Churches. Then he began to organize other churches—Low Gap and Glendale Springs in Ashe, Millers Creek and Bethel in Wilkes, and Laurel Fork on the Alleghany line, all with substantial church buildings. He was an indefatigable worker and his life was identified with the people whom he served . . . . During World War II Dr. Luke (given the honorary degree of Doctor of Divinity by his Alma Mater, Hampden-Sydney College) was a member of the Draft Board in Ashe County for the entire length of the war. For a part of the time he was chairman of the board. It was for him a civic and patriotic duty to which he brought the concern of religion. Every man sent to service was a matter of prayer. No winter morning could be too dark or too cold to prevent his coming to Jefferson to see the outgoing group, have a prayer with them and place a Testament in their hands. He has been and is God's good man, rendering through the years a sacrificial and unselfish service.

Other Denominations

The Episcopal Church

The Episcopal church came to the mountains at an early unrecorded date. Back in the days when Watauga was part of Ashe the Episcopal church undertook to establish a training school for young priests and others at Valle Crucis. This work was discontinued in 1851, and thereafter for several years during and following the War Between the States, there was little ministerial activity in Ashe. Rev. Milnor Jones, Episcopal minister, took over the work at Valle Crucis in 1894. He was active as a missionary and by 1897 had organized a school and leased a large school building at Beaver Creek. He started the first Episcopal church in Ashe, naming it the Church of St. Simon the Zealot. It was later named St. Mary's. It had nineteen candidates for admission. A building was erected on land donated by the Hamilton family and occupied on December 23, 1905.

It is interesting to note that the Episcopal church did not receive a warm welcome in Ashe. At its organization on June 21, 1896, with Bishop Joseph Blount Cheshire of Raleigh present to conduct services, they were denied the privilege of holding services in the school building, which they had under lease. These are the Bishop's own words about the occurrence:

> It was on Sunday, the 21st day of June last, at Beaver Creek, that I was assaulted and forcibly prevented from entering this building by a mob of between fifty and one hundred men which had been gotten together for the express purpose of preventing our service that day. And the reason they gave for this action was that they "did not like Mr. Jones' doctrine" and they understood that I taught the same doctrine taught by Mr. Jones. These facts require no comment.

The service that had been planned was held in the yard of the nearby home of Mr. W. H. Hamilton, and despite the opposition the church was duly set up and has been functioning ever since. Bishop Cheshire, a man of great courage and a church leader of great ability, found the going in Ashe a bit hard at first, but the new church grew and made a place for itself in the religious life of Ashe. This end was not attained easily, for as Bishop Cheshire wrote in the record book of St. Mary's, he "met with the most violent opposition, accompanied with bitter abuse from Methodists and Baptists, especially the latter." In 1901 the Church of the Holy Trinity at Venus, later called Glendale Springs, came into existence. A church building was erected and a residence built for the minister. This church is presently a mission point, served out of North Wilkesboro. Later a church was established at the village of Elk Cross Roads, which became known as Todd with the coming of the railroad in 1914.

Smaller Denominations

The Church of the Brethren, though small in numbers in Ashe County, has been long established. A traveling preacher of the Moravian Church, originally known as the Unitas Fratrum, or Unity of the Brethren, records a visit to Ashe in 1804, where he was hospitably received in the home of John Bauer, an adherent of the Church of the Brethren, who had come from Rowan County to the area that became Ashe. Bauer was counted in the United States Census of 1790. His brother Adam Bauer, or "Bower" as it was anglicised, was the man from whom the land for the location of Jefferson was bought in 1800. Wade Eller, local historian and genealogist of established reputation, traces the origin of the Bower family to this Bauer, who was a member of the Church of the Brethren. Elder Clayton B. Miller, present pastor of Flat Rock Church of the Brethren, states that his research discloses that the church was formed under the guidance of Jonathan Miller, who came into the county from Salem in 1802. Peak Creek Church of the Brethren, with 102 members, is located five miles southwest of Laurel Springs. The pastor is Elder Rex Sheets. The church was organized by Adam Sheets and Martin Owen. Pleasant Valley Church of the Brethren, with Elder David Cleary as pastor, has thirty-four members and is located one and one-half miles from Cranberry Creek Road. There were churches at Mt. Carmel and Ben Bowlin Creek, in the Three Top area, but these became disorganized and ceased activities.

One of the newest of all the denominations operating in Ashe County is the Mennonite, a denomination not well known in North Carolina but very strong in parts of Pennsylvania. Its first Ashe County unit, known as the Big Laurel Mennonite Church, stands by Big Laurel Road near Fig. It was the denomination's first church in North Carolina and Rev. Aquilla Stoltzfus was the pastor. They erected their first church building there in 1951. Their second, known as Meadowview, was built in 1955 on Little Horse Creek near Lansing and has Paul Mast as pastor. These two churches, and the surrounding country, have been declared a "needy area" by the mother church in Pennsylvania, and two Pennsylvania Mennonite churches, the Maple Grove and Conestoga congregations of Chester and Banks Counties, Pennsylvania, are supporting their missionary effort in Ashe.

At Todd there exists what has come to be known as a "Holiness" church. It is, by name, the Blackburn Memorial Church. It was established more than fifty years ago as a Methodist Church by Rev. and Mrs. Alexander Blackburn, who might properly be identified as fundamentalists, since they proclaimed the doctrines preached by John Wesley. The church has existed through the years and now owns a tabernacle on a hillside at Todd big enough to seat 400 people. About twenty years ago, Rev. Edd Blackburn (son of Alexander) and his wife decided to open up the place for an annual camp meeting. A kitchen and dining room were built, and as the fame of the place spread, a dormitory with toilets and bathrooms, and cottages were added to accommodate campers. These buildings are filled to capacity every summer. The church and its camp are not connected with any organization but are wholly supported by freewill offerings.

There are several Holiness, Pentecostal Holiness, and Nazarene congregations in the county and there are several "Christian Unity" Baptist churches not affiliated with the Missionary, Primitive, or Union Baptists.

So far as can be learned there is one Catholic church at Jefferson and one Christian church. The Christian church has a beautiful new church building on the old highway to Boone, about six miles from West Jefferson. It was organized in 1908 in the Three Top section and later moved to its present location. It has 108 members.

CHAPTER EIGHT

EDUCATION IN ASHE 1784-1868
DEVELOPMENT OF PUBLIC EDUCATION 1868-1962
CHURCH SCHOOLS ESTABLISHED

I

Education in Ashe 1784-1868

As related in Chapter 1, Thomas McGimsey, a recognized leader in the years between 1800 and 1820, who served once as clerk of court and twice (1807 and 1809) as representative from Ashe in the House of Commons, wrote a letter to Thomas Henderson, editor of the Raleigh *Star*, dated May 3, 1811, in which he bemoaned the illiteracy of Ashe County. He found the people generally to be devout Christians. He approved this fact but he lamented that they "improved more in religion than in the arts and sciences." However, he expressed the fervent hope that "more pains will soon be taken to improve youth in one as well as in the other." (Thomas Henderson's Letter Book, 1810-1811.)

Little is known about the beginning of schools in Ashe County. There were no public schools in the year preceding the establishment of Ashe, or for many years thereafter, but there was an effort toward providing schools. The *Northwestern Herald*, published at Jefferson in the 1920's, had as its editor Walter C. Johnston, who was also a leading teacher of the county. He was interested in education in the early days and produced some interesting articles. Most of his information he got from the diary of one David Woods, who was himself a schoolmaster and "kept school," as he called it. Woods wrote in the period between 1784 and 1796. There is no record of schools prior to that time but it is highly probable that there was teaching among families and joint efforts in conducting local schools when teachers were available.

In 1784, according to Woods' diary, four schools were "kept" in Ashe County, one on Grassy Creek, one on Helton, one on North Fork of New River near Creston, and a fourth on Beaver Creek. Evidently, progress was being made in the field of education for he noted that in 1789 schools were maintained at the following places:

Grassy Creek, Helton, two up North Fork, one on Naked Creek, one on Beaver Creek, and two others, location unknown to Mr. Woods.

Schools were kept open only in summer. The buildings in which they were held were of crude construction and not suited for winter use. Generally they were bark-covered and open at the sides and ends. Logs served as seats for the pupils.

The salaries of the teachers had to be paid by the patrons of the schools. As an indication of the remuneration of teachers in that day, the following account is taken from the diary of David Woods, listing his pay for six months of teaching at Nathan's Creek in 1789:

> 37 shillings in Virginia money (about $4.75); 5 deer hams; two bear-skins; 4½ yards of woolen cloth and one cooking pot. (*Northwestern Herald*, March 27, 1924.)

It is not recorded that material progress was made in schools, teachers or teaching methods for many years after Ashe became a separate county in 1799. As late as 1823 Ashe had no resident attorney-at-law, no physician, no notary public, no academy, and no newspaper. (*N. C. Register*, 1823.) There is no record that there was even a movement to establish academies in Ashe, such as those being established in other counties of the state. The United States Census report for 1840 indicates very little progress. There were two primary common schools in Ashe with an enrollment of forty-eight. The Census of 1850 showed 1,476 attending school but fails to give the number of schools. There must have been several private schools in operation but the census report makes no mention of them. There had been state legislation in support of public schools, notably the Public School Law of 1839 (Public

Laws of 1839), but there is no record that Ashe qualified prior to 1858 for state assistance under the Literary Fund set up to aid counties. Under the law setting up the Literary Fund, as amended in 1839, it was provided that the fund should be divided equitably among the counties and each county was to receive its share, whether or not it levied the tax provided by the law. There is record that Ashe was paid $1,505.70 from the Literary Fund in 1843-1844 and varying amounts thereafter, but the county made no report of expenditures and there is no record of how it was spent.

The General Assembly of 1857, tiring of such slack methods of doing business, passed an act amending the Literary Fund Law by inserting the following section:

> The Court of Pleas and Quarter Sessions of every county, a majority of the justices being present, shall levy a tax in the same manner as other county taxes are now levied, which shall not be less than one-half of the estimated amount to be received by said county for that year from the Literary Fund.

Ashe County fell into line when this amendment carried and its governing body in 1858 levied its first county-wide tax for public schools. There was no public enthusiasm for it and Ashe's representatives in the General Assembly were found opposing the election of a State Superintendent of Public Instruction and the appropriation of funds to provide for the education of teachers. In this attitude they were representing an electorate bitterly opposed to anything that called for increased taxation.

In spite of the opposition of Ashe and other backward counties, the General Assembly created the office of State Superintendent of Public Instruction in 1852 and Calvin H. Wiley was appointed to the office.

Edward W. Knight, in his book, *Public Education in North Carolina* (p. 160) has the following to say of education in the period between 1852 and 1861:

> Conditions were so improved that at the outbreak of the war in 1861, the state laid just claim to educational leadership in the entire Southern States. This was accomplished largely through the resourcefulness, versatility and indefatigable toil of the superintendent.

In Wiley's report for 1853 Ashe County reported thirty-six districts, with school being taught in every district. The total number of children being taught was 2,078, with an average attendance of 1,055. The average length of the school term was 2.94 months and the salaries of teachers ranged from $9 to $15 per month. (Annual Report, State Superintendent of Schools, 1854.)

The annual report for 1857 shows that the number of districts in Ashe had increased to eighty-seven and schools were taught in fifty-six districts. The number of children in school increased to 4,226, with an average attendance of 2,480. Fifty-six teachers were licensed for the year, two being females. The average length of school term was 2.6 months.

A year later the report showed that the number of districts in Ashe had increased to ninety-three, and that schools had been taught in fifty-eight districts. The number of children increased to 4,371 with average attendance of 2,223. The average salary of teachers was $17.

In 1860 the average number of children in school was 2,388. The number of districts had decreased to seventy-one, but the number in which schools had been taught was increased to sixty-one. The average school term was three months.

The ninth report of State Superintendent Wiley, for the year 1861-62, shows that the county started the year with more funds than ever before, but there is no record of how they were spent. If the county made any progress in the field of public education, there is no record of it. Dr. Wiley's annual report for 1863 presents a stark and rather hopeless situation, which was true of the State in general and particularly applicable to Ashe. Dr. Wiley said:

> The present generation does not need to be told that it was hard to keep up a general education system during 1863; the character of the times and the nature of the obstacles interposed to moral progress of every kind, are well understood. Considering the trials through which the country is passing, we are prepared to hear without surprise of the temporary suspension of enterprises with which our best hopes are bound up.

Dr. Wiley issued another annual statement after the War Between the States which contained little but his recommendations for improving the State's educational system. There is nothing in it of direct interest to Ashe County. With the collapse of the Confederacy many things "went down the drain" and among them was the State Literary Fund. It had been inactive during the war and had built up to goodly proportions in Confederate money. Because that money was worthless, the educational forces had to start at the bottom and begin building up again.

The North Carolina General Assembly of 1866-67 enacted laws to authorize towns and cities to establish public school systems "to be supported by taxes collected for cooperation purposes," and required every county to appoint a qualified superintendent of schools. A four-month school term was required. A school tax was to be levied, a prescribed course of study set up, and every county was to have a competent examiner of teachers.

Under the circumstances, the new system did not find the going easy at first. Mrs. Mary Sutherland of Sutherland is authority for the statement that in 1866 she taught the first school at Sutherland after the war. She got no part of her salary from public funds. It was all paid by the parents of her pupils.

The first official report on Ashe County's school system after the war, issued in 1868, showed that the county had fifty schoolhouses, all in bad condition. The county's apportionment of public school funds amounted to $1,915.50. However, the report of Captain J. W. Todd, Jefferson lawyer, who had been appointed county examiner of teachers, indicated that no part of the fund had been used in 1868-69. There were no public schools in operation. His report for 1870 shows four public schools had been opened for white children after October 1, 1869, with 150 children attending. The pay of the teachers was set at $20 per month for first grade and $17 for second. For 1870 the teachers were Alex McEwen at North Fork, William Brooks and Edward Barker at Piney Creek, and H. Squire at Staggs Creek. Their salaries for the school terms totaled $132. The report of the State Superintendent of Public Instruction for 1870, from which these figures are taken, goes on to show a high rate of illiteracy in Ashe. Out of a population of 9,575 ten years old and older, there were 3,386 who could not read or write.

The official report for 1877 shows little or no gain. During that year only six schools were in operation. The so-called "Reconstruction Period" which followed the war was considered to have closed in 1876, but improvement in schools was slow in coming to Ashe. However, in spite of difficulties and lack of interest on the part of school patrons, the annual report of the Superintendent of Public Instruction for 1879 showed that there were 106 school districts in Ashe for white children and six for Negroes. There were thirty-one publicly owned schoolhouses, all for white students. As there were eighty-three schools taught during the year it appears that many schools were taught in private homes, vacant store buildings, or other places. The school census for the year showed 5,153 white and 232 colored pupils. The average attendance for white was 1,610 and for Negroes, 110. All public school property was valued at $1,707 and the average monthly salary for teachers was $15.40.

Complete and authentic school records for this period are hard to find, but the office of the County Superintendent of Schools contains an interesting record of the school taught at Jefferson by John B. Hands in 1879-80. The school committee consisted of Major Qunicy F. Neal, Nathan H. Waugh, and George W. Reeves. The following subjects were taught:

Webster's Speller, McGuffey's Readers, Davies' Mathematics (including algebra), Mitchell's Geography, Smith and Bullion's Grammar, Holmes' History, and the New Testament.

II

Development of Public Education 1868-1962

The item in the preceding section relative to the Jefferson public school in 1879-80, is indicative of an arousing consciousness of needs that a public school system should provide. A. B. Hurt, late superintendent of schools, quotes William Perkins of Warrensville as saying that eagerness for learning beyond the public school level resulted in the establishment of a school at Jefferson by Prof. J. P. Marlin, assisted by a Professor Lawrence, where French, Latin (through Virgil), Greek, and algebra were taught.

The General Assembly touched off a quick forward advance in education by an act abolishing the office of county examiner and requiring the election in every county of a superintendent of schools. (Acts of the General Assembly, 1881, Chapter 200.) Major Quincy F. Neal, leading attorney, appears to have served as superintendent *pro tem*, on a part-time basis, until duly elected superintendent in 1885.

Interest in education picked up all over the county. In District No. 3, Peak Creek Township, J. F. Greer and nine other white citizens petitioned the county commissioners to order an election in their township on the matter of levying a special tax in aid of local schools. The election was held but there is no record of the result.

The movement for private schools gained momentum and the State Superintendent of Schools in his Annual Report for 1890 was able to report the following well-established private schools in Ashe:

Jefferson Academy, E. F. Winfield, principal; enrollment sixty.

Beaver Creek Academy, J. C. McEwen, principal; enrollment seventy.

Creston Academy, B. P. Grigsby, principal, enrollment fifty.

Sutherland Seminary, W. A. Wilson, principal; enrollment sixty.

Graybeal Chapel, Cicero Graybeal, principal; enrollment fifty-five.

Helton Academy, D. P. Hurley, principal; enrollment fifty.

Sutherland Seminary was probably the most popular of these schools. It was fortunate in having a noted teacher, J. C. McEwen of Nashville, Tennessee, whose teaching ability and qualities of leadership drew students from a wide area. Among its graduates were Congressman Spencer Blackburn, noted attorney W. R. Lovill of Boone, and William A. Wilson, Methodist missionary in Japan. McEwen departed and the school languished until 1896, when W. H. Jones became principal. He restored the school's prestige and drew students from afar. Enrollment reached 175, of which forty or more were admitted without examination to Trinity College, Emory and Henry College, and the University of North

Carolina, a distinction no other Ashe County School could claim at that time.

As an earlier chapter relates, the regular meetings of the Board of County Commissioners recorded continued interest in special school taxes. Many elections were petitioned. Some elections were defeated, but the number that met with the approval of the voters continued to grow.

In compliance with the legislative action requiring the naming of a county superintendent, Major Quincy F. Neal, a leading attorney, was elected. Entries in the book of minutes of the County Board of Education record that he was paid the sum of $6 for two days of service in the months of February and March, 1882. He was relieved of the responsibility of visiting every school and the board reduced his salary to $2 per day, for time actually spent in meetings and other official duties.

Major Neal served as superintendent from 1882 to 1887. He was succeeded by another prominent lawyer, George W. Bower, who held the office from 1887 to 1892. From the beginning of the new system in Ashe the office of superintendent of schools became increasingly important and the two eminent lawyers who devoted time and talent to the poorly paid and exceedingly difficult job, set high standards for their successors to follow. Their successors were:

M. M. Blevins, 1892 to 1897; J. W. Jones, 1897 to 1901; J. O. Goodman, 1901 to 1905; W. H. Jones, 1905 to 1911; C. M. Dickson, 1911 to 1923; J. O. Goodman, 1923 to 1929; R. E. L. Plummer, 1929 to 1931; J. B. Hash, 1931 to 1935; J. Ivan Miller, 1935 to 1937; J. B. Hash, 1937 to 1943; A. B. Hurt, 1943 to 1945; B. H. Duncan, 1945 to 1947; A. B. Hurt, 1947 to 1962; Frank James, 1962 to present.

For the most part these men set themselves to learn school administration as well as school teaching, and they kept in close touch with the State Superintendent of Public Instruction at Raleigh and his experts in all fields of education. The position of county superintendent of schools quickly graduated out of the part-time class and became a job requiring full time and all of the ability the superintendent possessed. The development of these dedicated public servants brought about a new era in Ashe County's school system.

Governor Zebulon B. Vance saw in the reorganization of the schools the State's best hope for progress. He undertook the task of reorganizing the system and the idea of a school system headed by a state superintendent, with a county superintendent on a full-time basis in every county, may have been his. Certain it is that he put schools first in his program of recovery from the War Between the States. He demanded schools for the training of teachers and strict examination and inquiry into the fitness of those who applied for license to teach. He saw no hope for the future except through the improvement of teachers.

The county superintendents, as they came into office, began to follow the precepts of Calvin Wiley and Governor Vance, and there followed marked improvement in teaching personnel and interest in the proposal to consolidate the small one- and two-teacher schools. Those superintendents, teachers, and other progressive persons who favored consolidation of the schools did not find life a bed of roses. The populace, brought up to consider the one-room school adequate, generally saw no reason to change. It was a project that would close many community schools and call for burdensome taxes to construct the larger schoolhouses that would be required.

The first breakthrough in the campaign for the consolidation of small schools came in 1929 when R. E. L. Plummer was superintendent of schools. He had preached the gospel of consolidation far and wide. To get the project under way at Healing Springs (Crumpler post office) he donated a large tract of valuable land for the school which was to be the first consolidated school in Ashe. The following small schools were brought together: Oakdale, Oak Hill, Fairview, Laurel View, and Old Fields. The people in this area, under the leadership of Superintendent Plummer, constructed a modern school building and Mr. Plummer was prevailed upon to retire from the office of county superintendent to become principal of this school. It was known in the beginning as the Healing Springs High School and it is still rated as one of the best elementary schools in the Ashe County system.

The successful launching of this project aroused interest in nearby Nathan's Creek community. In 1930, in the depths of the depression and with no money, the people of this area set their hearts on building a consolidated school at Nathan's Creek. Most of the land for the school was donated by S. H. Absher. The labor on the building and the lumber to build it were largely donated by the families that would be served by the school. The small schools consolidated in what came to be known as Nathan's Creek High School were Nathan's Creek, Dog Creek, Huckleberry Ridge, Chestnut Hill and Rocky Flat. The new consolidated school began its work with A. B. Hurt as principal.

The following table, compiled from the records in the office of the County Superintendent of School, gives the number of schools, white and colored, at intervals from 1933 to 1961, indicating the trend away from one-teacher schools:

1933		1936		1940	
Total white	73	Total White	65	Total White	59
One-Teacher	40	One-Teacher	36	One-Teacher	31
Two-Teacher	19	Two-Teacher	14	Two-Teacher	16
Others	14	Others	15	Others	12
Colored		*Colored*		*Colored*	
One-Teacher	7	One-Teacher	7	One-Teacher	4

1945		1950		1960	
Total White	56	Total White	33	Total White	14
One-Teacher	29	One-Teacher	12	One-Teacher	0
Two-Teacher	16	Two-Teacher	9	Two-Teacher	0
Others	11	Others	12	Three-Teacher	2
Colored		*Colored*		Four-Teacher	1
One-Teacher	4	Three-Teacher	1	Others	11
				Colored	
				Three-Teacher	1

The above tables give an interesting picture of school consolidation in Ashe County. As may be observed, there was a total of seventy-three schools for whites in 1933 as compared with a total of fourteen in 1960. In 1933 there were forty one-teacher schools and nineteen two-teacher schools as compared with none of either in 1960. As late as 1936 there were seven one-teacher colored schools as compared with one three-teacher school in 1950. The schools indicated in the tables as "others" represent the larger elementary and high schools, to which reference will be made later.

Beginning about 1933, through Works Progress Administration assistance, several school buildings were constructed. The central buildings at Jefferson, West Jefferson, Riverview, Lansing, and Virginia-Carolina were constructed or remodeled. Additions to the buildings at Healing Springs and Nathan's Creek were made under this program. Also, gymnasiums were built or remodeled at Riverview, Jefferson, Lansing, Elkland, Fleetwood, Virginia-Carolina, Nathan's Creek, Healing Springs, and West Jefferson.

During this period of construction very little in the way of public funds was available for school buildings. The property valuation was very low and little or no levy was made for schools.

In 1951 a four-teacher school was established at White Oak through the consolidation of several small schools in that section. The students from Little Helton and Chapel were transferred to Helton and a new three-room building constructed. A four-room elementary building was erected at Elkland. This building was a joint project with Watauga County. New lunchrooms were built at Riverview, West Jefferson, and Fleetwood. All schools in the county now operate lunchrooms.

In 1949 a School Plant Improvement and Construction Fund was made available to the State through a state-wide bond election. Ashe County's share in this fund was $408,000. All projects had to be approved by the State in order to share in this fund.

In order that Ashe County could have a building program that would best serve its needs, a survey committee headed by Dr. W. H. Plemmons was invited to study and make recommendations for such a plan. On the basis of the recommendation of this committee a new consolidated high school was built at Beaver Creek. The high school departments of West Jefferson, Fleetwood, and Elkland were brought into this new school which opened in the fall of 1954 under the principalship of Paul Bingham. A gymnasium-auditorium was built the following year. A music building was built later as a local project.

During this same period the following buildings were constructed:

An eight-room elementary building at Riverview, an eight-room high school building at Lansing, a six-room elementary building at Jefferson, and an auditorium and lunchroom at the Virginia-Carolina School in cooperation with Grayson County, Virginia. This school is maintained and operated jointly by Ashe and Grayson counties.

In 1954 about $185,000 was allotted to Ashe County from the proceeds made available to the state through a second bond election. With the aid of this fund the following improvements were made:

A four-room addition at the Riverview School, a seven-room elementary building at Fleetwood, and a four-room elementary building at West Jefferson.

The high school departments of Jefferson, Nathan's Creek, and Healing Springs were brought together by the establishment of the Ashe Central High School located near Jefferson. This school opened in 1957 under the principalship of Orville Jackson. An auditorium-gymnasium was later built at this school. In 1959 a new auditorium-gymnasium was built at Lansing to replace one destroyed by fire the previous year.

Ashe County has never provided funds for school facilities through issuing bonds, and there have been periods when no levy was made for school purposes. In recent years the county commissioners have made a substantial levy and borrowed money from the State Literary Fund to aid in the school building program. However, with the limited public funds Ashe County could not have gone forward educationally as it has without the financial assistance it has received individually from its citizens. Reference has been made to how the people cooperated financially in the first two major consolidations. That same spirit of cooperation has existed throughout the entire school building program in Ashe County. In some of the major school projects thousands of dollars have been donated by the people, not only for construction of buildings but also for otherwise maintaining and improving facilities.

A. B. Hurt, who was in the middle of his ninth two-year term (a longer period of service than any other superintendent) as county superintendent of schools when death claimed him, had much to do with this great record. Ever humble, he was prone to give credit to others for achievements that would not have been possible without his wise guidance and his unfailing faith and courage. He sought no personal credit, but was content to remain in the background. He was proud of the success of the long battle for consolidated schools and of the new buildings, but in a letter written the day before he died, he said:

> After all it is not the physical facilities of schools that count as much as the type of boys and girls who go out from these schools and the training they have received. The students of the Ashe County Schools make records wherever they go. Many receive various scholarships and other awards and rank at the top in college.

Tribute should be paid here to the many dedicated and devoted teachers who gave freely of their time and talent to the building of the public schools, but space limitations permit little more than the mention of their names. Mention has been made of Robert E. Lee Plummer, A. B. Hurt, James O. Goodman, J. B. Hash, Gwyn B. Price, Charles M. Dickson, and others. A most unusual school man, who had much to do with improving educational facilities for Negroes, was Oddie Cox of Nathan's Creek, a Negro teacher who led the fight to reduce the number of one-teacher schools for Negroes from seven in 1933 to none in 1950. Cooperating with the county superintendent, he brought about the consolidation of all of the Negro schools in the county into one three-teacher school at Bristol, which he headed very efficiently. He was the subject of a fine story in *Readers' Digest.*

III

Church Schools Established

As related in another chapter, the churches of Ashe became interested in higher education and, despairing of any progress in establishing public schools above the elementary school level, undertook to establish private schools for higher education. The Baptists of the old Senter Baptist Association started the movement prior to the War Between the States. It died when the war came on and was not revived thereafter.

The Baptists of the New River Baptist Association, with churches in Ashe and Alleghany Counties in North Carolina and in Grayson County, Virginia, established Oak Hill Academy near Mouth-of-Wilson, Virginia, in 1873. One of the first principals of the school was J. F. Spainhour of Morganton, later to be a member of the North Carolina State Senate. Hon. W. C. Fields of Sparta headed the board of trustees. James Eller of Ashe was for many years a trustee.

Like all private and church-owned high schools, Oak Hill suffered ups and downs through the years but it still exists on the original site, which has been expanded to 250 acres of land, with buildings that would do credit to a junior college.

The Presbyterians made a try at locating a high school in Ashe but the school was finally located at Glade Valley in Alleghany. It is a successful school to this day.

The Episcopalians undertook to establish a school at Beaver Creek, using a school building which had been built by a private school group, but it went out of business.

In 1910, the Methodists moved to fill a long felt need for high school education. A group proposed to the Western North Carolina Conference of the Methodist Church the establishment of a "collegiate institute" at Jefferson. The Conference was interested but appropriated only $500 for the undertaking with the provision that the Conference Board of Missions appropriate a like amount and "that the promoters of this enterprise shall raise not less than $10,000." At the 1911 conference, Dr. James H. Weaver, a son of Ashe, reported that $4,825.50 had been raised by popular subscription and that Mrs. Eula J. Neal of Jefferson had deeded to the Methodist church six acres of very valuable land in the outskirts of Jefferson as a site for the school. The land was valued at $1,200.

The Conference proceeded to get things under way and in December, 1911, Dr. J. H. Weaver of Monroe, Dr. H. K. Boyer of Statesville, and Rev. E. L. Baine of Winston-Salem were named trustees for the Conference. Trustees representing the Methodists of Ashe were Dr. J. W. Colvard, Frank H. Neal, R. L. Ballou, Presiding Elder M. H. Vestal, and J. M. Edwards. This board employed architect W. L. White of Hickory to draw plans for a building with seven classrooms and furnace heat. The board named a Building Committee composed of Dr. J. W. Colvard, J. N. Baldwin, R. L. Ballou, F. H. Neal, and W. E. Johnson.

Rev. W. L. Scott, noted educator, native of the Todd area and a graduate of Appalachian State Teachers College and Trinity College, was the first principal of the school. For the first year of its operation, 1913-1914, Wade E. Eller shared administrative and instructional duties with Mr. Scott but did not return for the 1914-1915 session. Ira T. Johnston became co-principal beginning in 1915 and continuing until 1918 when he resigned to enter the United States Army. J. B. Colvard, postmaster at Jefferson, taught classes in mathematics in 1917-1918. Following Rev. W. L. Scott, Rev. E. M. Jones became principal in 1922 and served two years. He was succeeded in 1924 by another son of Ashe, Gwyn B. Price, graduate of Emory and Henry College, now chairman of the Rural Electrification Authority in Raleigh. He held the position of principal until 1941.

It is generally agreed that the school reached its zenith under Rev. W. L. Scott. Enrollment at the school reached nearly 200 before World War I but dropped to 120 during the war. After the war enrollment picked up for a time, the all-time high being 262 in 1920, at which time the school had a faculty of seven.

The increase in the number and quality of state-supported high schools in the 1920's brought about the decision to discontinue the school as a Methodist church institution. In 1926 the Conference appointed a committee, composed of Walter H. Worth, G. L. Park, and Rev. John F. Kirk, with authority to sell the school property, at that time valued at $33,000. This committee, not finding a buyer, turned the property over to the Ashe County Board of Education to be operated as a public high school. Eventually the property was deeded to the Jefferson Methodist Church and by the church to the Ashe County Board of Education.

At the time of this school's beginning in 1913, Ashe County had no accredited high school and there was no reason to believe that there would be one available soon. Rev. Garland R. Stafford, in his story of "Methodism in Ashe" says that while the school lasted only about ten years as a church institution, it was distinctly worthwhile and furnished education to hundreds of Ashe County boys and girls who would otherwise have faced life with little education. In this venture, Mr. Stafford says:

"The church, through this school, fostered the elements of an advancing culture."

Today, Ashe County has five duly accredited high schools. These schools, with the dates of their accreditation, are the following:

Virginia-Carolina High School, Grassy Creek, 1922; Lansing High School, Lansing, 1927; Riverview High School, Fig, 1935; Beaver Creek High School, West Jefferson, 1954; and Ashe Central High School, Jefferson, 1958.

CHAPTER NINE

AGRICULTURE IN ASHE–PIONEER LIVESTOCK, DAIRYING, AND CHEESE-MAKING– LONG PERIOD OF SMALL PROGRESS– MODERN AGRICULTURE COMES TO ASHE– FUTURE OF AGRICULTURE IN ASHE

I

Pioneer Livestock

Those who came first to the wilderness that in 1799 became Ashe County were interested primarily in land suitable for farming. In the beginning they did not go into agriculture extensively, clearing just enough land around their cabins to produce the corn, beans, potatoes, and other vegetables necessary to feed their own families and the livestock which every thrifty pioneer managed to acquire. Nearby forests furnished ideal grazing for cattle and abundant nuts, roots, and grazing for hogs. To supplement the meats that required effort to grow, the pioneers had the game of the forests and abundant fish in the streams.

That the pioneer took advantage of what nature offered is indicated in the writings of Dr. Elisha Mitchell, who in 1828 wrote that he found the farmers of Ashe "lazy, content to subsist on small patches of land around their cabins and on hunting, after the game was practically all gone."

That the game should be considered as "all gone" only twenty-nine years after the County of Ashe was established indicates that hunting must have been the favorite occupation of the male pioneers of the era and that game conservation was the least of their worries.

Dr. Mitchell, who had come to North Carolina from Connecticut, had an appreciation of good soil and was quick to note and set down in his diary that Ashe County had boundless opportunity to go forward in the production of clover and other grasses and that the black, rich soil along its creeks and rivers would produce an abundance of food for man and feed for hogs, cattle, and sheep.

As has been noted, the first man to lead an exploring party into the Ashe County area, back in 1752, was equally impressed by the possibilities. This was Bishop Spangenberg, whose diary is in the Archives of the Moravian Church at Winston-Salem. In his party he had a wheelwright to assess possibilities of the use of water power, and other skilled persons, including a farmer, to evaluate farm land. The wheelwright found abundant favorable sites for the utilization of water power and the farmer found the soil admirably suited to the growing of corn, wheat, oats, flax, barley, rye, buckwheat, hay, and other crops. They surveyed land in the Ashe area and were greatly pleased with it, but they were seeking a big tract of 100,000 acres or more, and this they could not find in Ashe.

Another writer of the era, who antedated Dr. Mitchell, was Thomas McGimsey, representative of Ashe in the House of Commons in 1807 and 1809. He wrote to Thomas Henderson in 1810 that the people of Ashe marketed cattle, sheep, butter, cheese, lard, beeswax, venison, honey, deerskins, and ginseng to the "amount of upwards of thirty thousand dollars yearly."

The United States Census reports record progress in farming and other occupations. There is not space for full accounts, from census to census, but the Census of 1840 is typical. That Census reports produce as follows:

Wheat, 10,836 bushels; corn, 150,279 bushels; buckwheat, 10,970 bushels; rye, 17,805 bushels; oats, 108,805 bushels; potatoes, 57,982 bushels.

There were ninety-seven distilleries, producing 25,573 gallons of whiskey. The production of maple sugar was 16,193 pounds and the value of the ginseng sold was $735.

Ginseng, commonly known as "sang," was one among many medicinal roots and herbs found in Ashe which became articles of commerce and gave employment to many people. For thirty years or more, ginseng was a top product and sold for prices as high as $7 per pound. As far as modern research has been able to determine, the plant had no medicinal value whatsoever, but it was highly esteemed by the Chinese and eventually the mountain area was stripped of ginseng. Scores of other plants of established medical value were gathered in season, air-cured or cured in the sun, and sold to local merchants who found ready market for them in establishments making medicines. The medicinal root and herb business is still a flourishing business in Ashe. Many rural mercantile establishments still have root and herb warehouses in connection with their stores.

Tanbark, widely used for tanning leather, was for many years a leading crop from the forests of Ashe. It was nearly used up by 1912, the date of the Hardison-Perkins *Soil Survey of Ashe* later referred to, and with it went millions of feet of prime oak and chestnut oak lumber for which there was no profitable market. Small tannic acid plants in the county started the slaughter of the oaks, but the tanbark business zoomed to monumental proportions after the Southern Railroad came to North Wilkesboro in 1890. Soon thereafter, C. C. Smoot & Sons set up their big tannery at North Wilkesboro and the small plants went out of business.

The first comers to Ashe were land seekers. Their first concern was to acquire land suitable for farming. As intimated elsewhere they were not eager to toil in the sun, with fishing and hunting so attractive and so available, but they wanted the land also. There was keen competition for balds on the mountains where grass and clover grew and for the level lands along the streams of the county.

In the diary of Dr. Elisha Mitchell for August 1828 there appears his evaluation of Ashe as an area for producing cattle, sheep, and hogs. He predicted that the time would soon come when the great forests of oak, pine, poplar, walnut, hickory, and maple would be stripped from the valleys and the mountains and great herds of cattle and sheep would be produced.

Elsewhere in a chapter relating to the geography of Ashe, there is an analysis of the county's soils, setting out the acreage of each variety and the particular crop, or crops, that do best on the various types of soils. It is not recorded that the pioneer settlers paid any great amount of attention to this. Probably they went ahead with settling and developing the land, learning the hard way how to get the best out of the lands they were blessed with.

The herds of cattle came quickly. By the time of the Census of 1810, butter was an article of commerce. How many cows there were in Ashe is not known, but butter was being shipped out.

It is worthy of note that the pioneers who came from the North and those who came from Piedmont North Carolina after the Battle of Alamance (1771) brought with them a breed of cattle named Devon, developed in Devonshire, England, and called the "Ruby Reds." In 1623 the good ship "Charity" put ashore the first shipload of the breed in America, consigned to Edward Winslow, one of the Pilgrim fathers and agent for the Plymouth Colony. From that shipload of Devons came what is known in America as the "Shorthorn" line. The first registered bull of the line was bought by R. Hargrave, of Lexington, North Carolina, in 1841.

The Devon, or Shorthorn, breed was ideally suited for the pioneer settlers, for it was a great producer of milk and meat. Work oxen of the breed were best for farm work, because of their superior activity and intelligence. Breeders of pure-bred Shorthorns in Ashe included the Greers at Grassy Creek, the Hamiltons at Beaver Creek and the Duvall and Perkins families on Helton Creek. The Shorthorn was the ideal pioneer cow and gave fine service to the hardy pioneers who found them exactly what they needed for the production of meat, milk and fine oxen to till the virgin soil.

Herefords were introduced about 1900, and for a time there was mixture of the two breeds, resulting in the "white faces" now seen everywhere in Ashe.

II

Dairying and Cheese-making

The Shorthorn was a great producer of milk and butter in summertime, but not so good in winter. The cross-bred Shorthorn-Hereford had the meat-producing qualities but was not satisfactory for milk the year round. Gradually the farmers of Ashe realized that there were Jerseys, Guernseys, Ayrshires, and Holsteins, all great milk producers, and soon there were herds of these fine cattle. Interest in dairying and cheese-making spread through the county as the milking herds increased. (See *History of Livestock in North Carolina*, by Dr. R. S. Curtis.)

The Dairy Extension Service of the North Carolina Department of Agriculture had been conducting a study of conditions in Ashe with a view to increasing milk production. With the increase of milk-producing cows in the area and the interest that had been aroused by the study, the department decided to promote the establishment of cheese factories in Ashe and adjoining counties. The department set up a working team consisting of its best men in this field, headed by John A. Arey. They secured an expert cheese manufacturer from the Middle West named F. R. Farnham. He made a careful study of the situation and came to the conclusion that Mr. Arey and his committee were on the right road and so reported to the North Carolina Extension Service.

Cheese-making demonstrations were conducted first at Grassy Creek and following soon after at A. R. Vail's farm at Crumpler. The demonstrations created more interest and enthusiasm and Farnham was designated to direct the work of setting up local cheese factories in Ashe. The first in Ashe was the factory at Grassy Creek in 1915. This factory turned out $1,500 worth of cheese during its first year. Another factory at Beaver Creek was established in 1915. The Helton Cooperative Cheese Factory at Sturgills, the New River Cooperative Cheese Factory at Crumpler, and the Sutherland Cooperative Cheese Factory at Ashland were all completed and put in operation in 1917. It is recorded that Grassy Creek produced between $14,000 and $15,000 worth of cheese in 1917.

For a time all went well. Dr. Curtis' *History of Livestock in North Carolina* records that the first carload of cheese from a Southern state was shipped from West Jefferson in 1919. Naturally, Mr. Arey and his associates were pleased with the results. Gradually, however, the hard facts were driven home to the expert dairy and cheese men of the North Carolina Department of Agriculture and their fine group of dairy farmers in Ashe that their venture, which had started off so well, could not succeed with small widely scattered factories, and roads that were difficult at all times and absolutely impassable a great deal of the time. In addition, economic conditions were greatly disturbed by World War I. In the end the little factories closed, one by one. No amount of hard work could produce a profit from their operation.

But the movement did not die. The end results were far-reaching and lasting. Building on the foundations laid by John A. Arey, A. C. Kimrey, F. R. Farnham, R. H. Ruffner, W. L. Clevenger, and Dr. C. D. Grinnells, of the North Carolina State Extension Service, who had spent much time in Ashe County promoting pasture improvement, the Kraft-Phoenix Creamery established a big, modern plant in West Jefferson. It is presently operated by the Kraft Food Company, a division of National Dairies, with H. G. Vanderford as manager. The plant today maintains milk routes covering the county and has fifty employees. It buys from Ashe County dairy farmers more than 1,500,000 pounds of milk per month in spring, summer and fall months and approximately 750,000 pounds per month in winter. Their purchases do not constitute the full milk production of Ashe County farms, as Coble Dairies, Carnation, and Pet Brand creameries also operate routes in the county from points outside.

There was not complete agreement of cattlemen on the matter of dairying. The beef cattlemen on and off the Board of County Commissioners were not in favor of dairy cattle and cheese-making. They opposed the introduction of dairy cattle and for a long time the board could not be interested in shifting from beef cattle to dairy herds.

A strong supporter of beef cattle was W. M. Bledsoe of Nathans Creek, who was a member of the State Board of Agriculture during the administration of Governor W. W. Kitchen. Through his efforts the State purchased several very fine pure-bred bulls, which were leased to responsible Ashe County breeders of beef cattle, thus laying the foundation for today's beef cattle industry in Ashe. This undoubtedly resulted in enabling the beef producers of Ashe to keep step with the increasing dairy herds and to firmly establish Ashe County as the largest producer of beef in North Carolina.

The controversy may be credited with beginning farm demonstration work in Ashe. The Board of County Commissioners had been hostile to the idea of employing a county farm agent but the beef cattle-dairy cattle disagreement served to indicate the need of skilled men to help with all farm problems and to keep all interests working together. A small group, mostly dairy farmers, led by W. Lynch Dent and R. W. Hardin, started a movement to hire a county farm agent. The State Extension Service agreed to provide a competent person if the county would pay his salary. The board would not make the appropriation but Messers Dent and Hardin would not take no for an answer. They prepared petitions asking for the appointment of a farm agent and pledging funds to pay his salary for a year.

With the money available, the board proceeded to employ E. C. Turner of Alamance County as its first county farm agent.

While they eventually brought about many lasting benefits, the end of the dairying program and the wreck of the cheese-making plans of Mr. Farnham and of his associates in the North Carolina Extension Service, resulted in the loss of a large number of good citizens, which the county feels to this day. Not willing to abandon their plans for dairying and cheese-making, a large group of Ashe County's best citizens disposed of their farms and moved to Bel Air, Maryland. Among these were W. C. Greer, Ed Greer, Cleve Greer, John Greer, John Jones, Wilburn Thompson, Charley Jones, Robert Livesay, and Columbus Young, all of the Grassy Creek section. They were joined later by good farmers from Helton, Crumpler, and other communities. In fact, there were so many of them that the area around Bel Air became known as an Ashe County community and was so considered for several years. Many Ashe County boys, finishing high school, went to Bel Air for experience in dairying and general farming before going on to college. A noted example of this group was Dr. Dean W. Colvard, who finished high school at Grassy Creek and found a job with friends at Bel Air. He went on to graduate at Berea College in Kentucky and later won degrees at Missouri University and at Purdue University. He came back to North Carolina to work with the State-Federal Extension Service in Western North Carolina. Working with W. B. Austin, a member of the State Board of Agriculture during the administration of Governor R. Gregg Cherry, and other leaders of the area, he aided in establishing the "Upper Mountain State Farm Experiment Station" at Transou in the eastern edge of Ashe. He became the first superintendent of this farm. From this position he went to North Carolina State College as dean of the School of Agriculture, and from State College he was called to the presidency of Mississippi State University, one of the South's greatest educational institutions.

In passing it should be noted that Ashe County has lost many of its talented sons and daughters to other counties and other states. Among these was Dr. John E. Foster of Jefferson, who taught Animal Husbandry at State College and became Director of the Beef Cattle Division. The University of Maryland picked him to head its Department of Animal Husbandry, where he has been highly successful and has won wide fame.

Another Ashe County man who graduated at State College, with B.S. and M.S. degrees in Animal Husbandry, and followed graduation with highly satisfactory service in State-Federal Extension Service, was John C. Pierce of the Grassy Creek community. He was picked for an important post in the United States Department of Agriculture, where he has been highly successful. At last accounts he was serving as Deputy Director of the Livestock Division, Agricultural Markets Service, Washington, D. C.

Worthy of preservation here are the names of the men who gave their time and energy to qualifying as cheese-makers and managers of the little cheese factories. They took their training under Mr. Farnham. His list of his helpers in the records of the Extension Service is as follows:

Grassy Creek, Clayborne Baker; Beaver Creek, George Hamilton; Chestnut Hill, Cleve Pierce; Creston, Sheriff C. R. Latham; Sturgills, Tom Pennington; and Sutherland, W. M. Sutherland.

When their small factories collapsed because of conditions beyond their control these men and the farmers they served were, for a time, discouraged, but events proved that their labors had not been in vain. The milk and cheese business of the county today was made possible by their efforts.

Incidentally, the Grassy Creek High School mentioned above is noted for many things. It is situated exactly on the line between North Carolina and Virginia, half of it in Ashe County and half in Grayson County, Virginia. The two counties support it. The school has done outstanding work in many fields, particularly in agriculture. It led in the community's general awakening about road improvement, joined in the promotion of cheese manufacturing, backed rural telephones and rural electrification, and led the county in soil conservation. It was the first school in Ashe and Grayson to establish a vocational agricultural department with a full-time teacher, a graduate of an agricultural college. They were fortunate in having William C. LaRue to fill the post. He did a fine job and has continued his interest in agriculture through the years. He is presently associate editor of *The Progressive Farmer*, Raleigh, N. C. His record discloses that he has done fine work in the field of agricultural education in the classroom and on the editorial staff of a great paper, but it is doubtful if he has done better work anywhere than he did on the job at Grassy Creek. The results of his service are visible in the Grassy Creek community to this day.

III

Long Period of Small Progress

Under a cooperative agreement with Hon. D. F. Houston, Secretary of Agriculture, and Hon. William A. Graham, North Carolina Commissioner of Agriculture, a soil survey of Ashe County was conducted during the season of 1912. In charge were R. B. Hardison, representing the federal government, and S. O. Perkins, representing North Carolina.

According to their report, the chief agricultural pursuits of the people of Ashe had been stock raising and the growing of hay and grain crops. The earliest settlers cleared small patches of upland soil and cultivated it by scratching the surface with crude homemade implements. When the cleared patches decreased in productiveness they were said to be "worn out" and new land was cleared and brought under cultivation. Within one or two seasons the abandoned land became covered with grass, mainly clover and blue grass. This development tended to increase stock raising but, as a matter of fact, there was no great demand for livestock for many years. Apparently each settler was interested in just enough work stock for his individual use, and cattle, sheep, and hogs were raised to supply the home demand for beef, milk, butter, mutton, and bacon.

Hides were tanned for making shoes, and wool was produced, spun, and woven at home. Flax was grown for home use. Because at that time the seasons were considered too short and cool for corn and the soil not well adapted to wheat, the settlers grew only small amounts of these crops—just enough to meet their individual needs.

While there was a slow gain over the years, it is not recorded that Ashe made any considerable progress along agricultural lines before 1880. The experts found that a few good plows had been brought to Ashe as early as 1872. These were the exceptions. Prior to this time all plows, hoes, shovels, and other implements used in Ashe were homemade from iron ore taken from the mines of Ashe and forged in Ashe County forges.

The cutting and shocking of corn was first practiced in 1882, and corn and wheat growing took on new life. Improvement in yields of both corn and wheat was brought about by the introduction of better seed and the adoption of improved methods of cultivation. The first grain drills came into Ashe in 1884. Commercial fertilizer was not used prior to 1891. While the use of commercial fertilizer increased from year to year thereafter, the use of it was more or less haphazard. It took the grain, corn, and grass growers many years to learn that different types of soils and crops require different kinds of fertilizers. There were no facilities for soil testing in those days and Ashe County farmers saw no need for it. To them commercial fertilizer on any crop on any patch of ground should be equally effective on any other crop on any other patch of ground and they acted accordingly, often with discouraging results.

About this time the production of corn increased. In 1880 it became Ashe County's chief crop, with a production of 277,027 bushels from 15,616 acres. In 1900 the acreage was 20,907 and the production 381,510 bushels.

This placed corn production well out in front among agricultural products of Ashe. The crop of second importance was hay, which the Census of 1880 placed at 7,349 tons of hay from 9,439 acres. In 1910 there was a yield of 14,590 tons from 17,994 acres.

Wheat also felt the upsurge of this era, as did rye, oats, barley, and buckwheat. By 1910, wheat was the crop of third importance.

The farmers of Ashe found themselves blessed with a climate favorable to the raising of livestock, and with soil admirably suited for pastures and for the production of corn, oats, and hay for feeding them. Quite naturally they expected livestock and stock raising to become the most important agricultural industry in Ashe. While the major part of the industry was in cattle and sheep, there was also activity in breeding horses and mules. Altogether, the domestic animals in Ashe reached a value of $1,043,338 in 1910. An encouraging tendency of the time was toward pure-bred breeding stock in cattle, horses, hogs, and sheep.

The government experts found that Ashe soils were admirably adapted to apples. Every farm had its orchard. The most popular summer varieties were Red June, Summer Rambo, Early Harvest, and Yellow Transparent. The favorite winter apples were Stayman Winesap, Red Limber Twig, Smoke House, Virginia Beauty, Rome Beauty, York Imperial, Ben Davis, and Winesap. The latter varieties were best for shipping. According to the Census of 1910 the total fruit yield of the county was 142,528 bushels, of which 133,065 bushels were apples.

In their report to the United States and North Carolina Departments of Agriculture, the government experts neglected to mention cherries. Ashe had been famous for cherries for many years before this survey was made. No homestead was complete without its cherry orchard. There are those who will remember Main Street in Jefferson, 100 feet wide, with a row of cherry trees down the center of the street and two more rows down the sides of the street. These trees added immeasurably to the beauty of the little town. With the coming of good roads most of the trees came down in the name of "progress" and if anything of beauty has taken their place, it is not discernible to the naked eye.

The report of Hardison-Perkins, on page 10, records the beginning of a new era in the marketing of agricultural products. Here it is recorded that "beans for market are produced to some extent in the county." In fact, bean production had reached such proportions that the United States Census for 1910 reports a total of 622 acres of beans and a production of 2,120 bushels for market.

IV

Modern Agriculture Comes to Ashe

The bean business grew and prospered. With the improvement of roads and the coming of the Norfolk and Western Railroad, markets for beans, potatoes, cabbage, tomatoes, and other vegetables opened up. Very soon corn, which had been the leading agricultural crop in Ashe for many years, had to give way to beans. Both had to give way later to a newcomer on the agricultural front which made its appearance about 1925, burley tobacco. Ashe County farmers had produced tobacco for home consumption but it had never occured to them that they could produce it commercially. There was a period between 1925 and 1930 when the production of burley tobacco was tried in Ashe. The tobacco, sun and air cured, was marketed outside the county. Finally it was decided to erect a tobacco warehouse and sell at auction in West Jefferson. Establishing the auction was not easy. The influence of Robert L. Doughton of Alleghany County, at that time representative in Congress from the Ninth District, was finally effective and the auction was set up.

The beginning was modest. The report of the Department of Agriculture for 1930 shows seventy acres harvested, yielding 1,093 pounds per acre, and selling for 15.6 cents per pound, for a total of $11,950. From that the tobacco business grew. A second warehouse was erected. The latest figures, for the year 1958, show 1,065 acres harvested, yielding 2,083 pounds per acre, producing 2,218,000 pounds of tobacco, which sold at an average of 64.3 cents per pound, for a total of $1,426,000.

Somewhere along the line, between 1945 and 1950, "King Corn" was dethroned. The record of the corn growers was not to be laughed at, however, for it showed intelligent effort and real progress. In 1939, for example, Ashe growers planted 15,280 acres and harvested 357,650 bushels, producing twenty-four bushels per acre, which was valued at $305,000. The figures for 1958 show only 4,350 acres harvested, producing 261,000 bushels, valued at $405,000. The average yield was sixty bushels per acre.

The production and marketing of beans, referred to above as the first breakthrough toward modern farming, continued to grow. Eventually the output of beans on Ashe County farms reached a point where open markets were required. Among the pioneers in encouraging bean growing and marketing were Wick Vannoy, Everett Roland, and Burl Vannoy, who are credited with the establishment of the first bean market in 1942. That year they sold the output of 800 to 900 acres, a total of about 100,000 bushels. Today bean markets are operated in West Jefferson by Charles Pritchard in his tobacco warehouse and by Kermit and Wayne Jones operating the Appalachian Growers, Inc. The bean crop fluctuated from year to year and in the late 1940's and early 1950's the average acreage was about 3,000, yielding 150 bushels per acre. In 1961 the acreage was 1,000 and for 1962 it has been estimated at 1,500.

That bean production is playing no small part in the agricultural picture is shown by the fact that in 1961 Pritchard's "Farmers Warehouse" sold 200,000 bushels which grossed around $400,000. No report is available to show what the other warehouse did in 1961. Mountain City, Tennessee, has a bean market and much of the bean crop of Ashe goes there.

Wheat, which, after a slow start, came to be grown on every farm and which for many years was rated as the third crop in value, went steadily down. Once there were prosperous roller mills at Jefferson, Beaver Creek, Helton, and other places, but the production of wheat continued to go down and the mills closed. By 1925 the acreage of wheat in Ashe had been reduced to 1,650, producing 19,600 bushels valued at $32,040. By 1958 the acreage had been reduced to twenty, producing $910 worth of wheat.

Oats dropped from 398 acres in 1926, producing 65,940 bushels, to 140 acres producing thirty bushels per acre in 1958.

It is recorded that farmers of Ashe tried many adventures in crop diversification between 1925 and 1958, among these being the production of soy beans, peanuts, lespedeza for seed, Irish potatoes, tomatoes, cabbage, lima beans, and sweet potatoes.

In Irish potatoes there was marked progress. The famous "Sequoia" potato, developed on the farm of Fred N. Colvard, won national fame. The North Carolina Department of Agriculture in a statement showing the producion of Irish potatoes from 1949 to 1958, notes that 700 acres harvested in 1949 produced 53,700 hundredweight of potatoes and that 550 acres produced 59,000 hundredweight in 1958. In 1955 there was an attempt at growing sweet potatoes when eighty acres were harvested, producing 500 hundredweight per harvested acre. Only forty acres were harvested in 1958. The yield per harvested acre was sixty-two hundredweight in 1955 and fifty-nine hundredweight in 1958.

A new crop, coming on fast and promising to be a money-maker, is strawberries. The county farm agent's office started it with a small plot planted by Don Sturgill, a 4-H Club boy in Helton. It was successful and from this small beginning in 1952 the acreage has grown to twenty-five to forty acres. Fred N. Colvard alone had fifteen acres in 1962 and the county income from strawberries for 1962 will exceed $50,000.

Hay, once rated as Ashe County's number two crop, continued important because of the increase of livestock. It is noted that beginning with 1950 Ashe had 20,600 acres in hay crops and harvested 25,900 tons of hay valued at $756,420. These figures had increased to 23,250 acres harvested in 1958, producing 32,550 tons of hay valued at $911,000.

In livestock, according to data reported for taxation to the North Carolina Revenue Department, there has been a steady downward trend since 1925 in horses, mules, and sheep. There were 3,700 horses in 1925 and 1,583 in 1958, 600 mules in 1925 and ninety-two in 1958, 14,325 sheep in 1925 and 3,182 in 1958.

In cattle there is a different story. Cattle kept for milk production totaled 8,100 in 1925 and 11,800 in 1958. Cattle kept for beef or other purposes, were 12,000 in 1925 and 11,700 in 1958.

All hogs on the farms totaled 5,300 in 1925 and 5,425 in 1958.

Hens and pullets of laying age totaled 62,010 in 1925 and 44,278 in 1958. By estimates, commercial broilers were placed at 196,900 in 1958.

It is well to note right here that after a prolonged sleep and satisfaction with old ways, Ashe County began to wake up. There had been influences at work to have Ashe join the progressive counties of the State in the State-Federal Extension Service but it was not until June 1, 1925, that the Board of County Commissioners agreed to employ a county agent. The fact, astutely presented, that for a sum not much in excess of $100 per month, which would be paid by local subscriptions for the first year, the county would receive more than twice that amount, tipped the scales in favor of progress and a county farm agent was engaged. The vote for him was not unanimous in the board and official support of the new agency was far from enthusiastic.

The first county agent was E. C. Turner, who went into office on June 1, 1925. He found that much of the farm acreage was devoted to the production of small grains, mainly wheat, oats, and barley. Much of the land used to produce it was too steep and its cultivation resulted in soil erosion. Part of this problem has been solved, but there are still many areas of Ashe that bear scars. This erosion polluted the streams with silt and lowered the water holding capacity of the soils. A lot of acreage was used to raise corn to feed horses, mules, and cattle. When the county agent and his associate, the federal soil conservation agent, started working in Ashe, it took ten to fifteen acres of corn to feed a team of horses. By working together over the years new methods of production have been introduced by the extension agent and the county farm agent and today less than one acre of corn will feed a team of horses for a year.

Working together to inject new methods of crop production, to avoid hillside plowing by strip cropping, and to get more steep land in grass, the state extension agents and the United States soil conservation men greatly increased the production of grass, so that the average acreage of blue grass and white clover required per cow per year is now one and one-half to two acres, as against five acres at the beginning of the 1920's. Government aid, in the form of Tennessee Valley Authority phosphate and lime, which Ashe

County sorely needed and which came through the Soil Conservation Service, helped immeasureably in bringing about these improved conditions.

The first cattle market, established at West Jefferson and presently managed by Basset Young, had fine success and is still doing business. A second was required and in 1955 a cooperative livestock market was established on the new North Carolina Highway No. 16 east of Jefferson, at a point where it is easily available to the stock raisers of Ashe and Alleghany Counties. The stock of the corporation formed to provide stockbarns and other facilities, the Farmers Cooperative Livestock Market, Inc., was sold to farmers of the two counties. The proceeds of the stock sale were used to purchase and landscape the site for the sales barn, which cost $17,900. Since it was built in 1955 approximately $2,500 has been spent on improvements. The preferred stock sold at $10 per share and it is encouraging to note that over a period of six years, including the first year of operation, the stock had paid five per cent dividends.

The market started out in 1956 by selling 592 head of yearling steers, 504 steer calves, 407 heifer calves, a total of 1,503 head, for $149,829.11. In 1957 the total was 1,182 head for $135,388.01; in 1958, 1,636 head for $243,653.06; in 1959, 1,963 head for $278,575.73; in 1960, 2,722 head for $334,869.81; and in 1961, 2,099 head for $286,501.61. The grand total of sales for six years has been 11,105 head for $1,425,757.35.

Through the influence of the county agent's office, an Agricultural Workers Council was set up in the early 1950's. It meets monthly and is made up of extension workers, agriculture teachers, home economics teachers, FHA representatives, and Kraft field men. This body, led by the county agent, conceived the idea of organizing communities for promoting better farming and better living. Beginning with one or two in the early 1950's, the number had increased to twenty in 1960. Thirteen of these were judged in the finals of that year's competition in community development. No county in the State equaled that record.

Competing against the whole State of North Carolina, Ashe County won the $1,000 prize offered by *The Progressive Farmer*,

Raleigh, for the most outstanding achievement in community development in 1955. Entering a second contest fostered by *The Progressive Farmer* in 1958, Ashe County again won first prize, $500. This was awarded on the basis of increased farm income, home improvement, youth program, and over-all community development.

A spokesman of the county farm agent's office, who came to Ashe in 1948, points to the following achievements notable from his point of view that have come to Ashe since that time:

First, alfalfa acreage has increased from nothing, or nearly so, to 3,000 acres. Added to the increase of corn ensilage, which has been climbing year by year, he says that this should increase Ashe County's income from livestock by more than $1,000,000 per year.

Second, after an uphill struggle, artificial breeding of both dairy and beef cattle has finally taken firm hold. Ashe is presently breeding 1,000 cows per year. The county agent believes that the number will increase and he pronounces the artificial breeding program as "the best friend a dairyman ever had."

The county farm agents who spearheaded the fight for farm improvement were:

E. C. Turner, who served from June 1, 1925, to July 15, 1930; C. J. Rich, June 22, 1936, to February 4, 1942; H. D. Quessenberry, April 16, 1946, to September 30, 1949; Dana F. Tugman, January 16, 1950, to June 30, 1952; A. B. Addington, September 1, 1952, to the present.

V

The Future of Ashe Agriculture

As pointed out elsewhere, the Census for 1960 reported a decrease in the population of Ashe over the preceding ten years, of 9.6 per cent. The census reports all farm dwellers and residents of towns of less than 1,000 as rural. There was no appreciable gain in the one town, West Jefferson, which held its own at about 1,000. Therefore, the Census statisticians rated the county's decline in population, from 21,878 in 1950 to 19,678 in 1960, as wholly rural.

Part of this came about through the mechanization of farms. During this ten-year period mechanization constantly increased. The latest figures available, for 1958, show 1,234 motor trucks on Ashe County farms and 452 tractors. In one year, 1957 to 1958, the number of automobiles on the farm increased from 1,099 to 1,547.

This meant, of course, that the horse and mule were on their way out and that one man, plus the proper machines, could do the work formerly done by ten men or more. There was no farm work waiting for the boys finishing high school, and older farm workers were being crowded off the farms and forced to seek employment of any kind anywhere it could be found.

In Ashe, as will be shown in another chapter, industrialization has started, but more than ninety per cent of the jobs created have been for women and girls. There is nothing to indicate that any upward swing in employment for males is in prospect.

Dr. Dean W. Colvard, because he knows more about agriculture in Ashe and in the State than any other man in the field, was asked to comment on the agricultural picture as he sees it and to predict what may lie in the future for his beloved county. He wrote:

"Unfortunately, it was not possible for me to make a trip to Ashe County this summer. I am not surprised that the Census figures show some loss of population for the county in the past decade. While I had hoped that the industrial employment might prevent out-migration of the magnitude indicated, it has been clear for some time that the young people are leaving the farms. For example, in my home community a very large percentage of the people remaining are the old folks.

"Unfortunately again, I can find no basis for predicting that this trend will change until the total population is greatly reduced. The developments of technology in agriculture have been such that the greater rewards seem to accrue to those who operate on a sizable scale and who use a considerable investment in machinery and capital. Unless drastic changes take place in the general economy, it would seem that the subsistence type of farming is likely to continue to decline.

"There was a time when the mountain pastures provided the basis for more livestock than were found in any other county in the state. Here again we have come into an era when it is necessary to plant and fertilize pastures, and I am afraid that some of the areas that were once considered fine grazing areas but which were quite inaccessible for the application of cultural practices have been allowed to grow up in briers and bushes. Since World War II the explosion in agricultural technology has been such as to make it unnecessary to make large investments in human drudgery and labor in order to obtain food from the land.

"To illustrate that Ashe County is not in a unique position, let me point out just a few figures which tell quite a dramatic story in Mississippi. In the twenty-year period from 1940 to 1960 Mississippi lost 107,000 farms, over two million acres of harvested cropland, 600,000 farm people, a large percentage of its tenants and sharecroppers, and 191,000—or more than half—of its mules. This loss of 600,000 farm people becomes more striking when it is realized that the total population of the state both at the beginning and at the end of the period was approximately two million. While these adjustments were taking place, total farm income increased from less than two hundred million dollars in 1940 to almost seven hundred million in 1960.

"It seems to me that Ashe County is almost certain to continue to decline in population unless its industrial employment increases sufficiently to keep its people employed at home or even to attract people from outside the county. There is one other hopeful factor. In my opinion, the time will come when a much larger proportion of the resources of the county will be used for tourists and recreational purposes. As a matter of fact, I would like to see some planning which would capitalize on the precious but scarce climatic resources of the county. There are few places in the United States which can provide a more beautiful and pleasant environment during the summer months. People are spending money for summer homes, for fishing, golfing, and other recreational activities. I would like to see a dam or dams constructed on New River for the primary purpose of developing water sports and improving the scenery. There are ideal locations for such structures. This would encourage people who have moved away from the county to come back and purchase property and to develop it.

"I have been quite frank in my expressions. Some of the opinions may not be correct. I believe the county will continue to produce vegetables and perhaps an intensive search should be made for crops which are suited to the county and which could be produced on a scale comparable to Fred Colvard's cabbage and potato operations. This is one of the best areas of the country for white pines. If much of the land which is now idle or in scrub timber could be set in white pines, it would increase the wealth of the county but would not discourage the out-migration of the people. It will require some means of really putting technology and capital to work in conjunction with the resources if intensive operations are to be successful."

Dr. Colvard does not paint an alluring picture for farming in Ashe, but it should not be overlooked that the present farm leaders of Ashe are awake to the best practices and they are doing something in the way of making the most out of the situation they face. For example, the exhausted grass lands that Dr. Colvard referred to are being reseeded and fertilized by airplane in many sections. In others, old fields withdrawn from cultivation have been cleared of briers and underbrush, and set in white pines and poplars. The present programs, if carried out, will plant millions of seedlings in Ashe.

The figures he gives about his new state, Mississippi, are about the same as for North Carolina, where there has been a steady decline in population, particularly in the rural areas, but no decrease in the value of agricultural products produced. Figures of 1960 Census for the counties have not been published but it is not expected that even with a 2,300 decline in rural population between 1950 and 1960, Ashe will show any marked reduction in farm income.

All of which indicates a resiliency and resourcefulness that has characterized the people of Ashe from the beginning and no one should be downhearted about prospects for the future. It is well, however, to face the facts and ask the question, "Where do we go from here?"

In 1950 there were 260,608 acres of farmland in Ashe, of which

35,632 acres were harvested (excluding pasture land). For the year 3,886 farms reported 44,494 acres of improved pasture and 84,591 acres unimproved. Comparing these figures with those for 1958, from the records of the North Carolina Department of Agriculture, there were 255,585 acres listed as farmland, of which 31,538 acres were harvested. The number of farms had decreased to 3,754 in 1955. In 1958 improved pasture land had dropped to 25,434 acres and unimproved open pasture was estimated at 92,900 acres. The number of farm operators classified as full owners was 3,190, part owners, 357, and non-white owners 48 in 1950. In 1955, the latest figures available, the full owners were down to 2,198, part owners increased to 600, and non-white dropped to 28.

That the people of Ashe are moving forward and doing things is indicated by the general improvement of rural homes evident along every highway in the county. Television and radio antennas are everywhere visible and automobiles and trucks are fast taking over the county's transportation needs. When asked for the latest figures on rural telephones, the North Carolina Department of Agriculture reported their latest compilation, made in 1955. It showed 171 telephones on the farms. They also reported a total of 3,317 farms with electricity. The data for 1960, which will appear elsewhere, shows increases of these figures.

Dr. Colvard might find comfort as to Ashe County's future if he could review the activities of the county's high schools. Here the boys and girls, farm-born and farm-reared, are studying farming as it affects their daily living and their future.

As an example, he might take the Beaver Creek High School, some two or three miles from West Jefferson. This school's chapter of the Future Farmers of America, fostering cooperative activities, won the $500 cash award offered by the Farmers Cooperative Council of North Carolina for 1961. The contest, aimed at stimulating study of farmer cooperatives and developing more effective working relationships between vocational agriculture and cooperatives, covered the entire State.

Among other things, the chapter was able to show that in the school year of 1960-61 every class at Beaver Creek High had devoted twenty-two hours to the study of cooperatives; that chapter representatives had visited local cooperatives and talked with management and personnel and observed them in action; that members had studied the functions and operations of the FCX, the Blue Ridge Electric Membership, the Skyline Membership Association (telephone), the Ashe County Farmers Livestock Market, and other cooperatives. Members even journeyed to Salisbury to inspect the FCX fertilizer plant and to Statesville to see the FCX feed mill. Completely sold on the cooperative operation, they collected their own products at a central point and sold them cooperatively.

In doing this they learned another valuable lesson—that cooperation is not a one-way street. If they wanted the best results for the school and for the community, they should buy their seed, fertilizer, tools and other supplies from dealers in their own community, most of whom had wholeheartedly supported their efforts toward cooperation.

In this one school, as in others in the county, the program for cooperation in the community spilled over and spread from school projects to community business, and the chapter took over the work of improving school grounds and providing equipment the school and community needed but for which there were no public funds available.

It is encouraging to note here that this chapter of the FFA won high place in the wool and lamb contest and took first place in North Carolina in the corn contest, with a yield of 133.6 bushels per acre. This record was good enough to stand thirteenth in the nation in the FFA contests.

While perfection has not been reached, there is reason to believe that the future of agriculture in Ashe County may be safely entrusted to the boys and girls that Ashe County's high schools are graduating in ever-increasing numbers from year to year. As they mature they will adjust to changing conditions and all will be well.

CHAPTER TEN

IRON ORE DISCOVERED–MANUFACTURE OF IRON–COPPER MINING–FUTURE OF MINING IN ASHE

I

Iron Ore Discovered

The mining history of Ashe County begins with iron and ends with copper. Bulletin No. 32, of the North Carolina Geological and Economic Survey, authenticated by Dr. Joseph Hyde Pratt, Director, and written by Dr. W. S. Bayley of the University of Illinois, states that as early as 1802 iron was being produced and forged in Ashe from siliceous magnetites and shipped as far as Charleston, South Carolina, "where is enjoyed an enviable reputation." How the very heavy Catalan forges required in this process got across the Blue Ridge in those days neither history nor tradition explains, but the fact remains that Catalan forges were brought in and installed some time prior to 1800. Ores from Ashe County mines continued to be used locally until about 1887 when cheaper transportation allowed cheaper iron to enter the county and the local product, much better but also much more expensive, was driven out. During the War Between the States, tons of Ashe County iron were used to manufacture gun barrels.

Because nearly all of the agricultural instruments required by Ashe County farmers called for iron in their manufacture, iron mining and forging was an important industry in Ashe until around 1887. Mining practically ceased in 1887 or 1888, mainly because of transportation costs. The opening of the Virginia-Carolina Railroad in 1914 caused a flurry of mining interest and some ore was shipped from mines near Lansing. By 1922, however, this activity had ceased and no mines were operating.

II

Manufacture of Iron

It would be interesting to know who discovered that there was iron in the mountains of Ashe and who set about mining the ore and buying the forges necessary for the production of iron, but there is no record. Probably the most interesting character among the settlers of Ashe who may be classified as "pioneer iron men" was Meredith Ballou, who was born in Amherst County, Virginia, and who came to Ashe in 1800. His father was French and a mining engineer by profession and when Meredith Ballou came to Ashe it was in search of iron. In the area along the North Fork of New River and in the Helton area he found what he wanted and set about acquiring land where there were outcroppings that promised iron. Eventually he acquired much property and at his death in 1847 he owned hundreds of acres of land and mineral rights on many more acres.

He was a most unusual person. In addition to leading in the mining of iron ore and the operation of forges, he served various terms as county surveyor and many times as a member of the County Court of Pleas and Quarter Sessions.

He built a commodious home on the North Fork of New River and eventually filled it with children. There were thirteen children in his home, the oldest and the youngest being girls, with thirty years between their ages.

Much of the information about the early forges came from him, through Dr. Elisha Mitchell, leading geologist in the State at the time, who spent much time with Meredith Ballou in 1827 and 1828, and who admired him immensely.

Dr. Mitchell wrote of the Harbard Bloomery Forge, built at the mouth of Helton Creek in 1807 and washed away in a flood ten years later; another forge built in 1802; the Helton Forge, which was under construction and would be operating in 1829; and Meredith Ballou's own forge on New River, built in 1817. Ballou's forge was washed out in 1832.

From other sources it is learned that the Helton Forge above referred to was washed away in 1858, that John Ballou built the Paisley forge on Helton in 1848 and that it was rebuilt in 1871, that Laurel Bloomery (one mile west of Jefferson) was built in 1847 and abandoned in 1853, and that New River Forge on South Fork of New River was built in 1871 and washed out in 1878.

In the light of things that came to pass over the years it is worth recording here that among the tracts of land acquired by Meredith Ballou was one of about 300 acres that came later to be known as Ore Knob. He thought he had found promise of iron there but abandoned it after he had determined that whatever iron was there "was so badly adulterated with copper that it was useless."

Mr. Ballou himself and his sons thought the tract worthless and neglected to pay the taxes. These piled up and eventually the county sheriff sold the tract for taxes. It brought enough to pay the taxes and cost of sale, leaving a balance of $11. This amount was divided equally among the eleven surviving children of Meredith Ballou, who received $1 each.

Later Ore Knob came into the possession of Jesse Reeves, who sold it to the Buckhannon Company of Virginia four years before the outbreak of the War Between the States. This company operated it as a copper mine until after the war began, hauling the ore in ox-drawn wagons to Wytheville, Virginia.

III

Copper Mining

Copper mining in Ashe had its ups and downs but in very recent years has emerged as the leading mining industry of the county. What happened to the Buckhannon Company is not known. It probably collapsed with the economy of the times when the war ended with the complete destruction of the business and industry of the South.

There was a period after the war when no one moved, not even by ox-cart. Mining for copper, along with all other ventures for profit, ceased, and the people of Ashe found it hard to eke out a bare existence.

It was about 1870 that two capitalists from Baltimore, Maryland, S. S. and J. E. Clayton, heard of the Ore Knob Copper Mine and launched an investigation. There was, at the time, a growing need for copper and the metal was bringing a high price. The findings of their engineers were exciting and they moved to acquire the mine and some 500 acres of land around it.

Soon after operations started they were fortunate to secure the services of a talented English mining engineer, Captain John Dent, who took over as superintendent. Very soon the mine was a going concern and the operation was firmly established. Naturally it drew workers, and some time before 1875 the population of the village surrounding the mine exceeded 600. It had become the county's biggest town and it was thought wise to have the town incorporated and establish a town government. The North Carolina General Assembly, by special act ratified March 18, 1875, incorporated Ore Knob as a town, with its limits extending one-half mile from the company store in every direction. The following were named as town officials:

John Dent, Mayor; David Murray, James Williams, H. E. Alcott, and James E. Clayton, commissioners.

For ten years or more the mining operation was successful and grew in importance. For most of this time Ore Knob mine was the leading copper producer of the United States.

That the owners of the mine had visions of growth and great expansion in their activities is indicated by their decision to incorporate the operation and authorize a capitalization of $1,500,000. By Act of the General Assembly of 1881 (Private Laws, Chapter 29, page 636) the Ore Knob Copper Company of Ashe County was created. Its incorporators were John S. Williams, Washington Booth, James E. Tyson, George Small, S. S. Clayton, Herman Williams, and James E. Boyce, all of Baltimore, Maryland, and James E. Clayton of Ashe County, North Carolina.

That the incorporators were thinking big and planning big is indicated by another certificate of incorporation which appears in Chapter 121, Public Laws of 1881. This act created the Ore Knob Mineral Railway Company, with an authorized capital stock of $500,000. The incorporators were the same as those for the mining company, with the addition of Albert Fairfax and L. C. Gentry. The corporation was authorized to "construct a railroad of two or more tracks, beginning at a point in the Virginia state line somewhere in the counties of Surry, Alleghany or Ashe, and then in the general direction to or near Asheville, and then to the Georgia or Tennessee state line."

For ten years or more the mine prospered. The company provided its personnel with the best equipment available and their product was the best in the market and brought the highest prices. The mine was always hard to operate and as time went on copper-bearing ore became more difficult to mine and process. Then in about 1882 or 1883 the great copper deposits in Michigan, Idaho, and Montana were discovered, and copper went down in price to six cents per pound, a price decline of fifty per cent. With high labor costs and transportation costs going higher all the time, the Ashe County mine was finally closed, to the great distress of the town of Ore Knob and the workers living near the mine. The mine had produced for its owners more than $2,000,000 worth of copper and had furnished employment for many hundreds of Ashe County men.

In the years that followed, there were sporadic efforts by various owners at operating the mine. The Garretson Furnace Company, manufacturer of mining equipment, claimed to have new, patented equipment and new and improved processes for mining copper and undertook to de-water the old mine workings and resume operations in 1900. The effort failed. Later, the Garretson Company tried again with no success.

There was an effort to resume mining in 1917, which did not succeed, and another failure in 1927. During World War II there was a flurry of interest when engineers of the United States Bureau of Mines descended upon the mine and the surrounding area to make borings and try to locate the veins of paying ore which had been "lost" to previous operators. Nothing came of it at the time, but their reports, filed in Washington, D. C., furnished the basis for more recent developments.

The Ore Knob property finally came into the possession of a local group, composed of the heirs of G. C. Green, Thomas C. (Tam) Bowie, W. S. Morrison, R. C. Barr, and W. B. Austin. They, in turn, sold it to R. G. Lassiter, of Oxford, North Carolina and Miami, Florida, for $36,000.

Mr. Lassiter, an astute businessman and a careful investor, had made his fortune in the sand and gravel business, furnishing these commodities to contractors building state highways and bridges and other structures, public and private. He became interested in Ore Knob and that interest was intensified by what he learned from the files of the Bureau of Mines. With their findings to back him he was able to interest the Nipissing Mines, Ltd., of Toronto, Canada. This great mining company, devoted primarily to silver mining, had been forced out of that field when the price of silver dropped in 1931 almost as drastically as copper had dropped in 1883 and 1884. They were looking for new ventures and on the findings of their experts they formed a $3,500,000 corporation to take over the reopening of Ore Knob. The corporation was named the Appalachian Sulfides Co., Inc. Mr. Lassiter's interest was purchased for $150,000 and mineral rights were purchased on 1,475 acres of land adjacent to the mine tract of 500 acres.

The new owners picked Phillip Eckman of Winnipeg, Canada, as mine superintendent. Mr. Eckman brought with him a skeleton crew of experts and a few trained foremen but depended upon the local supply for most of his labor to operate the mine. After cleaning away debris and reopening mine shafts that had long been obstructed, the company got under way, on a twenty-four hour basis, operating three eight-hour shifts. With a labor force of 225 men, plus new and improved mining machinery and new methods, they were soon able to produce thirty-five loads of copper ore concentrate per month, the equivalent of one million pounds of copper per month.

In contrast with the operation of the 1870's by the Claytons, the new owners made no move to establish a town at the mine, preferring that their workers continue to live at their homes and walk or drive to the mine.

In recent months the Nipissing Mines, Ltd., sold the Appalachian Sulfides Co., Inc. to the Copper Range Co., Inc. of New York. There was no change in management at the local level and it was hoped that the operation would continue as before the sale. However, it developed that the new company found, after a few months, that the copper ore reached by the present shafts was being exhausted and that what remained was becoming extremely hard to mine and, therefore, more expensive. The mine was adjudged to be no longer a profitable operation and the announcement came about December 1, 1962, that the mine would close by the end of the month.

IV

Future of Mining in Ashe

It is not easy to determine, or even to forecast with any degree of certainty, what lies ahead for mining in Ashe County. As related above, mining for copper was abandoned for fifty years or more, in the face of expensive operation, reduced prices for copper, and costly transporation. The Ore Knob copper mine, which closed in December, 1962, has survived several earlier closings. Competent mining engineers do not agree that there is no more copper at Ore Knob and it would not be surprising to see copper back in the picture some day and going strong. Mining for iron ore suffered an even more complete eclipse than copper-mining. Great deposits of iron ore were discovered in Pennsylvania, Michigan, and other states, close to cheap water transportation and also close to the coal fields, making smelting and other manufacturing processes cheaper. This resulted in producing iron for agricultural implements and for other uses at a price that made it no longer profitable to operate the local mines and forges.

That the iron ore is in Ashe in quantities so great that few dare to estimate it, is certain. The Virginia Iron, Coal and Coke Co. invested heavily in Ashe County lands and mineral rights and the reports of its mining engineers caused the company to hold on to its Ashe County properties. They are planning for the future, believing that the day will come when the iron fields now being worked, will be exhausted. It is their firm belief that when that day comes, Ashe County will be able to furnish iron for a large part of the nation's requirements. Consequently, the company hangs on to its acreage and its mineral rights, paying taxes from year to year. An indication that this company's faith may be well founded is found in the 1958 *Minerals Year Book* of the U. S. Bureau of Mines, which reports that the old Cranberry Magnetite Iron Mine may be opened soon. This mine is in nearby Avery County and it ceased operation at about the same time as the Ashe County iron mines and for the same reasons.

In order of their value, the *Year Book* reports the minerals produced in 1957 and 1958 in Ashe as copper, mica, gold, silver, sand, and gravel. Ashe County ranked fifth in the State in value of mineral production. The copper, gold, and silver came from the operations of Appalachian Sulfides, Inc., at their Ore Knob mine. Eight sheet mica mines were operated, the leading producers being the Duncan Mining Co. (Duncan Mine) and Lewie Aldridge (Tucker, Littleton and Jackson Mines). The North Carolina State Highway Commission mined 60,800 short tons of paving sand and gravel in 1957 and 9,500 short tons in 1958.

It does not yet appear that there may come a resurgence of copper as the county's most important mineral product. It is certain, however, that only iron can challenge copper, and the day for challenge seems fairly remote. There is at least one son of Ashe who has never lost faith in iron and it is interesting to note that he bears the name of Ballou and is a direct descendant of Meredith Ballou. He is Dr. James L. Ballou, retired lieutenant commander in the United States Navy, World War II, and also retired medical officer on the staff of the United States Veterans Administration. He and his wife came back to the old Ballou home on the banks of the North Fork of New River. He acquired the interests of various relatives in the family property, which included the home place and some 320 acres surrounding it. Running through the place is one of the richest veins of iron in Ashe. In addition he acquired mineral rights in various properties in the area covered by the map printed in the picture section and furnished by courtesy of the North Carolina Geological Survey.

Dr. Ballou and his wife, who have no children, conceived the idea of leaving their interest in land and mineral rights in trust for the education of boys and girls in Ashe. Through the trust department of the University of North Carolina they set up a trust fund, starting it off with a gift from their savings, to receive the income from the property for the education of qualified boys or girls, beginning with members of the Ballou family and followed by high school graduates from Ashe and other counties of North Carolina. The winners of annual awards are to be determined under scholarship regulations of the University of North Carolina.

In addition, Dr. Ballou is withdrawing from cultivation as much acreage of the home place annually as can be handled with available help and planting it in seedling white pines and poplars. Many thousands of these plants have been set out and many more will follow, if his plans are carried out. These seedlings will eventually produce an income from lumber that will greatly increase the scholarship fund and make it a very valuable county asset, even if mining for iron ore is never resumed in the area.

However, Dr. Ballou has iron in his blood. His father, Uriah Ballou, was an iron man. Uriah's father, Napoleon Ballou, a son of the original Ballou who came to Ashe in 1800, was also an iron man. There is a family tradition that Napoleon was offered $50,000 for his mineral rights, which was "big money" in his day, but he refused it. The family's life had been wrapped up in iron and their fortunes were based on it. Consequently, Dr. Ballou felt that it was entirely fitting that what was left of the family fortune be dedicated to the education of the sons and daughters of Ashe. Believing as he does that iron will come back and that his foundation will subsist on it and continue to grow through the years, he finds pleasure and satisfaction in the prospect.

CHAPTER ELEVEN

PIONEER INDUSTRY—ELECTRIFICATION FOR INDUSTRY—POWER AND LIGHT AND TELEPHONE FOR EVERYBODY

I

Pioneer Industry

To establish a town, county, or state there must be industry and it must follow close on the heels of the first settlers. Today, conditions are such that industry often comes ready-made. It was not so in 1799 when Ashe became a county. Ashe County citizens learned early that progress is the sum of small victories won by individuals and that if they waited for big enterprises to come from outside, Ashe would continue to be a wilderness. They expected no help from an impoverished state, or from an equally distressed federal government. Their progress toward security and comfortable living would depend upon themselves. If they conquered the wilderness and established a unit of government fit to live under, they would have to do so by their own efforts. It was up to each individual citizen to make himself and his family self-supporting and in all ways self-sufficient.

Probably the greatest need of the newcomers in Ashe was farming implements. With no roads behind them or before them, and no transportation except by two-wheel carts and pack animals, the problem of getting iron farming implements across the Blue Ridge looked insoluble, but somehow they solved it.

Undoubtedly the settlers' first need was iron, and iron working was the county's first industry. The pioneers set about prospecting for iron and they found it in abundance. As related in the chapter on mines and mining, adventurous miners from Virginia, Pennsylvania, and other eastern states began prospecting in Ashe. The North Carolina General Assembly aided in exploiting the mining of iron ore and the setting up of forges to manufacture iron, by passing a law providing for a state grant of 3,000 acres of land to any person who would produce 5,000 pounds of iron in a year.

This brought much activity in mining and in setting up forges to extract the iron, and as early as 1808 there were six or seven forges in operation in Ashe. The forges turned out sufficient iron for local needs and provided a surplus to ship out by cart or wagon.

With iron of high quality available, men who had developed skill in working it set up shops at their homes, or at crossroads, or wherever people were accustomed to assemble. These establishments quickly developed into service stations of their day, where mule or horse could be shod, and broken hoes, plowshares, and wagons could be repaired.

With increase of skill many of the blacksmiths branched out into the manufacture of plows, hoes, wagon wheels and tires, adzes, axes, mattocks, scythe-blades, shovels, and other tools and equipment. In a short while the little factories were all over the county, in reach of every farmer, and they were to continue to serve the farmers' needs for nearly a century.

Another early industry was the manufacture of cloth. There was the beginning of textile industries in the New England states in 1799, but they were far away and their product was out of a poor man's reach. Consequently, the farmer undertook to grow his own wool. His wife and daughters carded it, spun it on homemade spinning wheels, and wove the thread into cloth in their own loom house. Almost every home in the early days had its own little cloth factory.

As time went on some genius invented a carding machine to be operated by water power, and carding machines were set up at Creston, Warrensville, on Dog Creek, near the South Fork of New River, at Sutherland, Helton, and other places. This took much of the hard work out of cloth making.

Shoemaking and shoe repair was an immediate necessity. Every head of family had to learn how to repair shoes. For years there also were itinerant shoemakers who went from house to house with their equipment in packs on their backs. Eventually the industry as localized in shops that fairly well covered the county.

Likewise, in the early days there were tailors who went from house to house with the tools of their trade to fashion into clothes the cloth woven on the homemade looms.

A son of Ashe, who died in 1946 at the age of eighty-eight, said that he remembered when there was a hat factory in Ashe. It was located on the Beaver Creek road at about where the road to Obids branches off. It had only one hatmaker, who made wool hats for men.

The Moravian explorers who came with Bishop Spangenberg in 1752 were loud in their praises of Ashe County's water-power possibilities. The new settlers in Ashe were quick to appreciate them, and water-driven grist mills went up all over the county. Elsewhere there is a picture of a typical grist mill of the period, which was built in 1825 by Absolom Bowers. This was not the first mill in Ashe, but it is the earliest that is still in service. It no longer grinds corn to make meal for human consumption but it is available to grind corn to make feed for cattle, sheep, and hogs on the big Colvard Farm, which is located a few miles east of Jefferson. The man in the picture, which appears in this section, is Fred N. Colvard, owner, and the old mill is located near his home on North Carolina Highway No. 16.

Mr. Colvard states that farther down the same stream that furnished water power for his old mill, was another structure which housed carding machinery. This set-up antedated his grist mill. Some of the original timbers that went into the building are still visible in the stream.

Merchandising kept pace with the spread of population, and local stores sprang up. Very early the firm of Finley, Waugh, and Murchison, which had caught the chain store idea and had set up stores at Wilkesboro, Lenoir, and other points, came into county and established a branch at Jefferson. David Worth, employee of a drug firm in Greensboro, came to Ashe to buy ginseng and other medicinal herbs and liked the area so well that he spent the rest of his life there. He married a daughter of Stephen Thomas at Creston and soon set up a general store. Later, in partnership with a Mr. Eller, he operated several stores under the firm name of Worth and Eller.

Probably the most famous store of the early days was the big general store operated at Gap Creek by the Cowles family. It was the biggest store in the county, was housed in the largest building in the county and carried the largest stock of goods. It furnished the leading market for medicinal roots and herbs in Ashe and surrounding counties. It continued to lead in this field until well up in the 1890's, but was closed when Arthur Cowles died.

Worth Knox, great-grandson of David Worth, who operates the Knox Knitting Company at Creston, told a research man engaged in digging up information about the early days, that "Creston has been an industrial center for a long time."

The remark was intended to be facetious but facts confirm it.

The first industry at Creston was set up by Elizabeth Thomas Worth, daughter of Stephen Thomas and wife of David Worth. She set up a cloth-making business, trained slaves and others to fashion the cloth into clothing for men and boys, and sold the clothes in her husband's store.

Hand carding was a laborious but necessary process in the preparation of wool for spinning until Mrs. Worth was able to procure a machine to do this work. Designed to operate by water power, the machine was installed on Three Top Creek, where it operated successfully for many years. The 1940 flood washed away the last traces of the dam that impounded the water used to operate it.

Another industrial venture at Creston was a carriage and furniture factory housed in a large frame building on the banks of Three Top opposite the present site of the Knox Knitting Company. It was operated by Worth and Lillard, with T. J. Lillard as manager.

Coming along later, to further support Creston's claim to having been an industrial center, was a roller mill, also built on Three Top Creek and driven by two turbine wheels. It was built by J. D.

Thomas and Felix Barr. Mr. Barr was manager and operator. This venture went the way of the other roller mills of the county when wheat production dropped off and there was no grain to grind.

These things support the statement, made in jest, that Creston was an industrial center early in its history. It is interesting to note that in the years that followed similar activity was to take place all over Ashe. Outstanding among these communities was Helton, where John R. Littlewood, an Englishman skilled in textiles, induced Will and Win Perkins to establish a small woolen mill on Helton Creek. They were joined later by Herbert Littlewood, who had operated the woolen mill, at that time owned by Frank McMillan, at Mouth of Wilson, Virginia. The Helton mill made woolen blankets and turned out vast quantities of wool thread which thrifty housewives knitted into socks or wove into cloth on their own looms. The mill is still standing with most of its machinery in place, but it has not been operated regularly for several years. It belongs to the Littlewood and Francis families.

The Perkins brothers, Will and Win, after disposing of their woolen mill interests, built and operated successfully a big roller mill. The mill is still standing but has not operated for several years.

For many years, beginning as far back as 1800, Helton was the iron-making center of the county, turning out sufficient iron to satisfy local demands and shipping a surplus by wagon to Fayetteville and other points in eastern North Carolina, and to Charleston, South Carolina.

And so the county grew. Its citizenship from the very beginning realized that if they wanted the comforts and conveniences of civilization they would have to work for them. They could not look to government—local, state, or federal — for help, no matter how great their need. From home industry to community industry they have moved by slow steps. Content with their independent way of life, they were slow to give up their little home shops and factories and they were slow to switch from home gardens and farms to grocery stores for food and to general stores for raiment and household and farm necessities. Consequently, industrialization on a large scale was slow in coming to Ashe.

II

Electrification for Industry

The industry of Ashe today would not be possible without electricity, but it did not wait for electricity. Water power was put to work whenever possible and when steam engines were invented they were laboriously hauled into Ashe to operate its grist and flour mills, its carding machines, sawmills, wood-working plants, and various other enterprises.

Ashe County's largest homemade and home-grown industry, the Phoenix Chair Manufacturing Company, began with water power. Its founder and president, Robert C. Barr, became interested in the wood-working business early. His first venture was a mill to manufacture locust pins for supporting telephone and light wires. He built a mill on Phoenix Creek, about two and one-half miles north of Jefferson and operated it with power from swift-running Phoenix Creek. He also had at this site a well-equipped mill for grinding grain. He gradually expanded his operations, and in 1935 opened the Phoenix Chair Manufacturing Company in a small one-room house on North Carolina Highway No. 16, opposite the mill. He started with three employees, who turned out 100 chairs per month. Today the plant employs 280 persons, mostly men. They work on two shifts of eight hours, five days per week, and produce 700 chairs per hour. From the humble beginning to its present status, with a nationwide market and an authorized capital of $400,000, this has been an all-Barr operation. Robert C. Barr has been president from the beginning and his sons, one by one, have joined him in the business. Frank Barr and Robert G. Barr are vice-presidents of the corporation and R. W. Barr is secretary and treasurer. The present plant is in the town of West Jefferson and is pictured elsewhere in this section.

A smaller enterprise in the manufacturing field, previously mentioned, is the Knox Knitting Company of Creston. It was organized at Conover, North Carolina, in 1937, by Worth Knox and other members of the Knox family. Descendants of David Worth, they had deep roots in the Creston area and they were probably haunted by the thought of the water power going to waste in Three

Top Creek. They wanted to build a dam there and set up a hydro-electric plant. Finally they packed up their machinery and moved to Creston.

They set up their first plant in August, 1940, and began operations. The machinery was driven by a six-horsepower steam engine, coupled to a twenty-five horsepower boiler, fueled by slabs purchased from various saw mills operating on Three Top Mountain. Three Top Creek, along with all of the water courses in Ashe, went on a rampage a few days after they started. When the flood subsided, the Knox Knitting Company's little mill was down the creek, lodged in a group of trees. The machinery was covered with mud and the whole situation looked hopeless. But the Ashe County spirit was there and the Knoxes set to work to dig out of the mud. Instead of tearing down the building, they put new stone pillars under it, leveled up the floors and set to work again at the new location. For power, they later abandoned the steam engine and acquired the engine of a Model T Ford, which already had served long and honorably on the trails that Ashe called roads in those days. This old motor served until a broken crankshaft ended its usefulness and it was succeeded by an ancient Chevrolet motor. The Chevrolet carried the factory until electricity came. The idea of harnessing Three Top Creek was abandoned.

The iron manufacturing industry is another example of the never-say-die spirit of Ashe County's citizens. It was essential that the forges in use in the beginning and on up to the time when iron ore mining and the manufacture of iron were abandoned be built where water was available. The history of the forges shows that the majority of them were washed away many times by flash floods, for which Ashe County's swift rivers and creeks are still famous, and as many times rebuilt. It never occurred to the citizens to quit.

When the Norfolk & Western Railroad came to Ashe in 1914, it was aimed for a point in the edge of Watauga County. Elk Cross Roads was the spot chosen for the end of the line and the name of the place was changed to Todd, honoring Captain J. W. Todd, eminent lawyer and a leading citizen of Ashe. The location of the line in the vicinity of Jefferson brought on a spirited contest. The

Norfolk & Western, interested only in freights and aiming at getting as close to abundant timber resources as possible and with the least possible outlay of capital, had brought its line in from Abingdon, Virginia, along devious and crooked streams. After the first few seasons and after disastrous experience with flash floods, most of its bridges along these streams were anchored to granite boulders to keep them in place.

It was taken for granted, at first, that the line would be run by Jefferson and there was spirited competition among Jefferson property owners for the location of the depot. The railroad's engineers favored the location of the depot at its present site, the center of the town of West Jefferson. The compelling reason for this decision, from the railroad's standpoint, was that a change in the line to touch Jefferson would cost an additional $50,000.

While the contest was being waged at Jefferson about the location of the line and the facilities the railroad needed, a corporation had been formed to promote the establishment of a new town, southwest of Jefferson and some two miles away. It was known as the West Jefferson Land Company and it had acquired title or options to the land where West Jefferson now stands. This company was composed of H. C. Tucker, Thomas C. (Tam) Bowie, Mr. and Mrs. W. E. Menges, and E. A. McNeill. The coming of the railroad brought a string of new towns – Smethport, Warrensville, Lansing, Sturgills, and others, and all of them began to think of electricity. West Jefferson led off, when H. C. Tucker acquired a generator, connected it to a steam engine, and started to put up power lines and supply electric current to the rapidly growing town. Down Buffalo Creek at Warrensville, Charles Hamby installed a small hydro-electric plant and extended his lines to several homes and places of business in Warrensville. The Northwest Carolina Utilities Corporation came into the picture in 1927. It established a plant at West Jefferson in 1927, powered by two diesel engines with a capacity of 240 horsepower, producing 150 kilowatts. It acquired H. C. Tucker's lines and equipment, which consisted of a small generator powered by a steam boiler and serving approximately fifty customers, started building lines in 1927, and were ready for business in 1928. When the corporation got under way it had between fifty and sixty miles of line and 150 customers.

The company acquired a site on the North Fork of New River for a hydro-electric plant at Sharpe Falls and let the contract for the plant to Colonel Basil Barr, of West Jefferson, in 1931. The plant was completed in 1931 and by early 1932 it was in successful operation, greatly increasing the company's capacity.

The next ten years saw steady growth in West Jefferson. As has been related, the Phoenix Chair Manufacturing Company, first in its field, moved to West Jefferson and continued to grow.

Mack Edwards and G. W. Edwards, brothers from the Baldwin community, established the Appalachian Flooring Company, Inc., later selling to Worth Gentry and associates, who still operate it.

W. E. Vannoy and associates established the flooring business now known as the Oak Flooring Company, with a plant in the edge of West Jefferson near the John Parker home, in 1935. They sold in July, 1945, to the present owners, who took over with Mack Edwards as president, G. W. Edwards as vice-president, and Todd Gentry as secretary and treasurer. W. J. Rader was plant superintendent. The corporation had a capital stock of $150,000. It employed fifty people and was selling $500,000 worth of oak flooring per year until March 9, 1956, when the plant was completely destroyed by fire. The loss was in excess of $200,000, with insurance of $75,000. The company was back in business in October of 1956, with a new plant capable of handling and processing six million feet of lumber annually, which is purchased from farmers living within seventy-five miles of the plant. The plant is presently owned and operated by the Edwards brothers, Todd Gentry having sold his interest to them.

Another thriving industry, whose growth and success was made possible by the increase of electric current, was the Peerless Hosiery Company, first known as the Skyline Hosiery Company, which came to West Jefferson in March, 1953. With adequate power, the operation was immediately successful. The plant became a subsidiary of United Hosiery Mills Corporation of Chattanooga,

Tennessee. Robert Meador of Hickory is division manager and the plant employs 160 people, sixteen of whom are men.

The Phoenix Chair Manufacturing Company, the Kraft-Phoenix Cheese Manufacturing Company, the Parker Tie Company, the Ashe County FCX, Blevins & Powers Feed Mill, Midway Lumber Company, Colonel Basil Barr's furniture manufacturing establishment, which has won wide fame, and many other establishments benefited by the increase of electric power. Establishments outside of West Jefferson, located at Jefferson, Lansing, Warrensville, Smethport, Beaver Creek, and other points felt the effects of it as well.

Big Industrial Plants

The first big industrial plant to be established in the county outside of West Jefferson's town limits, was the Sprague Electric Company's factory on the banks of the North Fork of New River between Warrensville and Bina. It is located on a thirty-acre tract and adjoins the right-of-way of the Norfolk & Western Railroad. The original building had 50,000 square feet of floor space when built in 1953, but the operation has been so successful that three additions have been made to it, bringing the square footage total to 82,651. An additional building known as the Etch house, added 1,500 more square feet in 1960.

William B. Austin, Jefferson attorney, serving on the North Carolina Board of Conservation and Development, was helpful in bringing the Sprague Electric Company to Ashe. The company's chief products, dry electronic capacitors (or condensers), are devices used for storing electric energy and releasing it when required. They are used by manufacturers of television sets and many other kinds of electrical equipment. In their manufacture an immense quantity of clean water is required, and when Mr. Austin showed the company representative the prospective site, New River was on its best behavior and showed crystal clear.

The investigator found an abundance of labor eager to learn the new business and quick to acquire the necessary skills. An official of the company wrote this about the Ashe County labor they encountered:

"It was the availability of solid, energetic mountain people that was an important point in Sprague Electric Company's decision to establish a plant in Ashe County."

Another compelling factor was that there was immediately available an abundant supply of electric power. Without this there would have been no Sprague Electric plant in Ashe.

The company brought to the new operation a bare minimum of outside specialists. The first manager, Robert Lee Parrish, was raised and educated in Asheville and the second and present manager, Urcle M. Sheets, is a native son of Ashe, an honor graduate of Jefferson High School with a B.S. degree from Fairmont College, West Virginia. The plant employs around 825 men and women, and the annual payroll is in excess of $2,000,000. Practically all the workers are from Ashe and live within twenty-five miles of the plant. Five or six live in Grayson County, Virginia.

Sprague Electric Company has its home office at North Adams, Massachusetts, where it has four plants. In addition there are plants at Concord and Nashua, New Hampshire; Bennington and Barre, Vermont; Los Angeles and Visalia, California; Grafton, Wisconsin; Rockville, Maryland; Ponce, Puerto Rico; Milan, Italy; and Mexico City, Mexico. At last account the company had more than 8,500 persons on its payroll and was producing capacitors that sold for $77,650,000 per year. Sprague Electric Company is a stable enterprise and the county is justly proud of it.

Another industrial activity that came to the county in 1956 was the P. H. Hanes Knitting Company of Winston-Salem. This company, of national reputation, in 1953 had established a plant in Sparta, Alleghany County, which had been remarkably successful, so much so that the company was considering establishing another plant in the northwestern part of North Carolina. It was learned that Hillsville and Wytheville, Virginia, were being considered, as well as Burnsville and other towns in North Carolina.

As good fortune would have it, P. Huber Hanes, Jr., president of the P. H. Hanes Knitting Company, had long been an admirer of Ashe and had purchased land near Glendale Springs. He was quick to advise the citizens who approached him that his company would consider Ashe County provided the community would erect a building according to plans and specifications to be furnished by the company and lease said building to the company.

When Mr. Hanes said that the local community would have to raise a minimum of $250,000 for the project, gloom descended upon the promoters. It was not believed that so much money could be raised locally. However, there were some who refused to give up. They went to Edwin Duncan of Sparta, president of the Northwestern Bank, which has two branches in Ashe and serves the entire county. They laid the proposition before him and he advised them to proceed with the venture, raising as much money as possible for the purchase of land and the building of a plant, and to come back when they had done that. He promised that his bank would help in every possible way.

Thus encouraged, the community woke up. A committee—composed of Edwin Duncan, president of the Northwestern Bank; Larry P. Colvard, its cashier; W. E. Vannoy, Sr., chairman of the Board of County Commissioners; R. Austin Jones, member of the North Carolina House of Representatives; and William B. Austin—arranged a meeting at Winston-Salem with Mr. Hanes, which was successful. They returned home and went to work.

They secured options on many sites for the mill, including one in West Jefferson, one in Jefferson, and two or more in Bristol. The mill officials came and inspected the sites and chose the one in Jefferson. The promoters then proceeded to fall back on the old Ashe County way of doing business, lifting themselves by their own boot-straps. They set up the Ashe County Development Corporation, a non-profit organization, with four incorporators. These were W. E. Vannoy, Sr., R. A. Jones, Larry P. Colvard, and W. B. Austin. The charter of the corporation provided that

> ...the general welfare of society and not individual profit being the object for which this corporation is created, the corporation shall have no capital stock, shall pay no dividends or salaries to its incorporators, or board of directors, and the said incorporators, or its board of directors, shall not share in any of the profits of the corporation in any way. All income or profits of the corporation over and above those necessary to pay debts and interest of the corporation, or to carry on the conduct of its business, shall go either to hospital, recreational or

other charitable purposes, as may be determined by its board of directors.

The campaign for the sale of the corporation's four per cent notes resulted in $150,000 being taken locally. The balance was subscribed by the P. H. Hanes Knitting Company. The notes sold to the company are subordinate to the notes issued to individuals. The total cost of site and plant was $254,262.93. The plant, complete and modern in every detail, was in operation early in the spring of 1957.

The operation was so successful that the P. H. Hanes Knitting Company, in the fall of 1958, asked for an increase of capacity. An addition was built, doubling the plant's capacity at a cost of $166,832.87. Of this amount $101,832.87 was raised locally, with P. H. Hanes Knitting Company subscribing the balance.

In 1959 the P. H. Hanes Knitting Company again asked for additional space to expand its operations in Ashe and the corporation agreed to double the capacity of the plant. This was done at a cost of $286,367.00, of which $150,000 was raised locally, with the company subscribing for the remainder needed.

The total raised locally for this one industrial plant exceeded $400,000. It now has 93,000 square feet of floor space and the land and building represent an investment of $650,000. There are 525 full-time employees and the total annual payroll is in excess of $1,000,000.

The president of the company recently made this statement about the personnel:

"The company is most pleased with the fine spirit and interest of the citizens of Ashe County and our employees have been found to be most intelligent, cooperative and eager to learn whatever jobs were assigned."

III

Power and Light and Telephone for Everybody

As the towns grew and increased the use of electricity for power and lights, people living outside the limits of the various towns became interested in electric light and power. Very slowly, as lines were extended, farmers within reach of distribution lines began to seek connection, and rural electrification was on its way.

It was not easy. As noted elsewhere, Ashe County citizens suffer long, endure patiently, and move slowly. Once convinced and committed to a project or program, they go places and do things. From 1914 to 1935 there had been movements backed by R. E. L. Plummer, Thomas C. (Tam) Bowie, A. B. Hurt, and others, to build hydro-electric plants to provide the additional power needed for the towns and for rural areas also. These met with determined resistance from the Northwest Carolina Utilities Company, Inc., whose district manager, George Robbins, proposed that the conflicting forces get together and help in the development of existing services. Little came of this except talk, but there was plenty of that.

It was in 1935 that the tables turned and the General Assembly of North Carolina, in Chapter 288, Public Laws of 1935, took cognizance of the need for electric light and power in rural areas and established the North Carolina Rural Electrification Authority, with the stated purpose of securing "electrical service for the rural districts of the State where service is not now being rendered." The Rural Electrification Administration was established by Executive Order No. 7037, signed by President Franklin D. Roosevelt on May 11, 1935. That Act had made $100 million available to the President for rural electrification activities. This gave encouragement to the group that had been fighting for rural electrification but there remained more than two years before real progress was made.

Because the Caldwell Mutual Rural Electric Association had access to adequate power and was willing to have Ashe share in it, the Ashe County leaders decided to try to effect a union with Caldwell. This began in 1936 and it was two years later, in 1938, that the union was brought about. The Caldwell Mutual extended its field to include Ashe, Alleghany and Watauga. Established in 1940, the name of the new corporation was the Blue Ridge Electric Membership Corporation.

When the merger was made, three Ashe County men were appointed to the board of directors, these being Gwyn B. Price,

R. E. L. Plummer, and A. B. Hurt. Joseph Charles Goodman later succeeded Mr. Plummer on the board. It is significant that all three were outstanding school men. Price was later (July 1, 1941) to be appointed chairman of the North Carolina Rural Electrification Authority, a position which he now holds. Goodman and Hurt were to serve long terms as presidents of the cooperative. Goodman became president in 1945 and served until 1952. He was succeeded by A. B. Hurt in 1952, who served until his death in 1961. The present president, incidentally, who succeeded the late A. B. Hurt, is an Ashe County man, William B. Austin, long-time director of the corporation and vice-president from 1958 to 1961.

The battle, however, was not won in 1936. To complete the merger, which had been approved by the leadership, Ashe County was required to have 1,000 members on at least 164 miles of line. R. E. L. Plummer and the directors above named put on a strenuous campaign to obtain the required number of subscribers and topped it off with a mass meeting in the Ashe County courthouse the first week in September, 1936. Congressman Robert L. Doughton came down from Washington to make the principal speech. At the conclusion of his address, committees were named from every township in the county to put the drive over. These committees were:

Jefferson township: Fred Little, A. G. Witherspoon, Fred Colvard, Ambrose Bare, George Bower.

West Jefferson: C. Walter Phillips, W. G. Vannoy, Emmet Stanley, Walter Ray, Harry Koontz.

Pond Mountain: Will Elliott, B. F. Kilby, Walter Joines, Charlie Eldreth, S. R. Greer.

Old Fields: A. J. Houck, R. W. Hardin, Rev. T. J. Houck, J. W. Duncan, E. A. Ray.

Elk: W. G. Cook, R. T. White, R. B. Brown.

Laurel: W. A. Graybeal, T. J. Graybeal, Fred C. Graybeal, J. E. Oliver, T. W. Pennington.

Clifton: Austin Jones, G. B. Price, Ed Osborne, Wade Eller, J. C. Little.

Helton: E. C. Francis, W. W. Dickson, Q. R. Young, L. E. Emerson, Bryan Pennington.

Grassy Creek: John A. Dickson, J. W. Halsey, C. F. Spencer, A. F. Paisley, Charles St. Clair.

Chestnut Hill: J. B. Pierce, E. V. Pierce, Arch McMillan, Bob Caldwell, Dane Gambell, Al Perkins.

Walnut Hill: T. W. Blevins, S. V. Alexander, F. N. Ballou, J. R. Phipps, J. E. Fender.

Peak Creek: R. L. Austin, W. B. Scarborough, W. M. Transou, D. C. Bare, Tom Cox.

Creston: Rev. A. G. Lackey, Todd Price, V. C. Lillard, Robert Baker, Dr. Robinson.

Horse Creek: Thomas I. Goss, Earl Ball, Everett Stansberry, Howard Stansberry, J. L. Gilley.

North Fork: Max Barlow, R. P. Lewis, Witt Wilson, Earl Martin, S. S. Graybeal, Joe Stansberry.

Pine Swamp: H. H. Lemly, C. M. Yates, D. A. Faw, Bob Watson, C. B. R. Hartsog.

Hurricane: A. A. Perry, W. M. Little, Ed Davis.

Obids: Luther Woodie, J. H. Colvard, Wiley Burgess.

Piney Creek: B. W. Jones, G. M. Baldwin, Ed Eller, J. E. Tucker.

This effort afforded a fine example of democracy in action, as it put the issue squarely up to the citizens of every township.

Every civic group in the county joined heartily in the drive. Ashe County's excellent newspaper, the *Skyland Post*, gave the project wide publicity in its news columns and able and effective support on its editorial page. With all this, the campaign was no whirlwind success. It went slowly and it was not until October 1, 1938, that Ashe County's goal was reached. On that date the number of subscribing members reached 1,000 and they were living along 164 miles of road.

A Rural Electrification Authority office was set up at Jefferson January 1, 1939, with Gwyn B. Price in charge. There were many details to be attended to involving federal funds for construction work, meeting state and federal membership requirements, and other things, and it was not until March 15, 1939, that the first pole in the line that had been surveyed from Todd to Sparta was set at Todd. The line was reported completed on October 1,

1939. The total mileage of electric power lines in the two counties on that date was 393, there were 1,500 members and the corporation had qualified for a federal loan of $310,000 for the project.

By September 1940, eighty additional miles of lines had been added in Ashe and there was widespread demand for more. In October 1941, Ashe had reached 331 miles of power line, with a total of 1,441 members, making Ashe the thirty-eighth county in the State in rural electrification. Other counties in the Blue Ridge Electric Membership Corporation had done as well as Ashe, and the corporation attained the distinction of being the largest rural electric membership corporation in North Carolina.

Slow to start any new program or project, as heretofore stated, Ashe County proved to be hard to stop once the merits of the venture were demonstrated.

On October 30, 1941, the long drawn out negotiations between the Blue Ridge Electric Membership Corporation and the Northwest North Carolina Utilities Company, Inc., came to an end with the purchase by the Blue Ridge Electric Membership Corporation of the power lines and hydro-electric plant at Sharpe Falls, near Warrensville, and all other facilities of the Northwest North Carolina Utilities Company in Ashe, Alleghany, Watauga, and Caldwell Counties. The total purchase price was $170,000.

On July 1, 1948, the Blue Ridge Electric Membership Corporation announced that increasing needs for electric power for enterprises large and small and for power and lighting for homes made it necessary that a new 44,000 volt transmission line be run from Boone to a new sub-station to be built at Beaver Creek. This would enable the corporation to extend service to 1,082 new members on 218 additional miles of power line.

As of July 1, 1962, the Ashe County unit of the Blue Ridge Electric Membership Corporation, under the management of Hugh A. Crigler, was able to report 6,619 meters in Ashe County, 5,212 of them in the homes of rural members, 571 in town homes, 103 classed as seasonal, 432 (all county) small commercial, schools 10 and churches 184. The Ashe unit now operates 1,084 miles of power lines.

Mr. Crigler was enthusiastic about prospects for the future. The use of electric appliances in homes, on farms, and in small shops was increasing. In the previous year electric ranges bought through the membership reached fifty-one and additional major household appliances totaled 251. Ninety-eight homes had installed electric heating.

With the present installations Mr. Crigler's unit of the membership uses 10,000 kilowatts of power and has a total capacity of 30,000 kilowatts, providing a bountiful supply of power for future development.

All of this has cost a great deal of money, but no part of it created bonded indebtedness. The membership borrowed the money, obligated themselves to pay two percent interest to the federal government and to repay the loan from the earnings of the membership corporation.

Another venture coming along with the power and light development and financed in the same way, was the Skyline Telephone Membership Corporation, authorized by Congress by amendment of the Act that made possible the Electric Membership Corporation. This Act was passed in October, 1949, and a telephone system, built along the same lines as the electric power and light system, came into existence very soon thereafter to serve Ashe, Alleghany, Watauga, and Avery counties, and Johnson County, Tennessee.

This corporation started business in June, 1957, with 400 members. It had, at last account, 1,300 members in Ashe, served by central exchanges at Lansing, Nathan's Creek, Baldwin, and Creston. Connection with outside lines is through the Central Telephone Company. The corporation provides direct distance dialing for members in Ashe and Alleghany through Central at Elkin, North Carolina.

G. W. Edwards is the president of the Skyline Telephone Membership Corporation. John H. McGuire is general manager. They have twenty-one employees operating their facilities in Ashe and expected to add 200 members to their Ashe County system in 1962.

As may be seen from the above, the stage is set for the development so ardently advocated by Dr. Dean W. Colvard and other agricultural experts. After years of study and experience they would have the young men and women of the future hold on to the old home place, cultivating as much of the land as possible while depending for their support upon paying jobs in industry. The employees at Hanes, Sprague Electric, Peerless Hosiery, Phoenix Chair Company, and other industrial plants are leading the way. Good roads and the automobile are making it possible for the worker to live twenty-five miles or more from his job, work at it eight hours a day for five days a week, and still keep the home farm going. There is no need to move to town, or to the plant site, in these days.

Most of the county's industrial workers, however, still are women and girls. The pressing need today is for industries that will employ men and boys. There should be many concerns that would be attracted to Ashe if they knew about its climate, its good roads, its abundance of capable labor, and the unlimited electric power available.

CHAPTER TWELVE

WEST JEFFERSON, ITS ORIGIN AND GROWTH – SURVEY OF AVAILABLE LABOR AND EMPLOYMENT – BANKS AND BANKING

I

West Jefferson, Its Origin and Growth

The previous chapter, concerned mainly with the larger industrial establishments and with rural electrification and rural telephones, lacked a great deal of telling the whole story of how Ashe County grew in and around the town of West Jefferson. As already related, the Norfolk and Western Railway Company, with the Virginia-Carolina railroad, at long last provided an outlet for Ashe County products of farm, mine and forest. The railroad placed its depot some two miles from Jefferson, the county seat, where the county's stores, banks and other businesses were located. At the headwaters of Little Buffalo Creek they found a beautiful little valley, off the main highway from Jefferson to Beaver Creek. bounded on the east by Negro Mountain (Mt. Jefferson) and on the west by Paddy Mountain. At the turn of the century this valley had the following five families in it:

John Parker and family, whose home still stands across the road from the Oak Flooring Company; Amos E. Graybeal and wife, Daisy Burkett Graybeal, whose house still stands and is occupied by their son, Bernard B. Graybeal; Rev. James Floyd Fletcher, who lived in a double log house located where the residence of Mr. and Mrs. Jesse A. Reeves now stands; Daniel Hartzog, whose home was closer to Paddy Mountain; and Calvin Graybeal, whose house was located near the present site of the Appalachian Flooring Company. Characteristic of the county, every one of these homes had its orchard, in which cherry trees predominated.

Few people know that Colonel Ben Cleveland, hero of the Battle of King's Mountain, at one time owned the entire valley where West Jefferson now stands. He received it by State Grant No. 27, dated March 3, 1779, and signed by Richard Caswell, Governor of North Carolina. It was signed at Kingston (Kinston), at that time the capital of North Carolina, and, as what is now Ashe was then a part of Wilkes, the grant is registered in the office of the Register of Deeds of Wilkes County. It called for 320 acres, more or less, bounded on the south by a line running along the crest of the ridge dividing the waters of Beaver Creek and Buffalo Creek. The west line was along the base of "Paddy's Nobb." The boundary markers, or monuments, are lost and cannot be located today. Mr. Bernard B. Graybeal has in his possession ancient deeds to the lands of his grandfather, Calvin Graybeal, which contain a sketch of the area granted to Colonel Cleveland and which refer back to this grant as a basis of title to the Graybeal holdings.

Incidentally, it may be noted that the controversy over where Paddy Mountain got its name is not settled by these ancient documents, but at least they make it certain that it was not named for George (Paddy) Bowers, who lived close to the base of the mountain and was called "Paddy" to distinguish him from George Bowers of Jefferson. From Paddy's Nobb the name changed to Paddy Mountain. Seen from the east or the west, it is a mountain of surpassing beauty. Any one who has seen it from its south end can understand why it was called a Nobb. Who Paddy was and what he was doing in Ashe prior to 1779, nobody knows.

With the coming of the Norfolk and Western in 1914 the hoped-for millennium did not come. It was still 202 miles to the state capital and the railroad was not interested in passenger traffic, which is true of it to this day. By a roundabout way, one could reach Raleigh in approximately two days and nights by rail.

The new community that began to grow around the depot accepted the plans of the West Jefferson Land Company and began to build. They called on the North Carolina General Assembly for a charter and it was granted in Chapter 36, Private Laws of 1915.

By this Act the plan of the West Jefferson Land Company was made official and town limits were fixed at "one-half mile north, south, east and west of the Virginia-Carolina depot, which shall constitute a square."

The Act provided for a governing body consisting of Donnelly Blevins, Mayor, and R. C. Barr, W. F. Hartzog, Isaac Faw, and Amos E. Graybeal, aldermen.

The Act was duly ratified on February 9, 1915.

The new town, which was destined to drain away from Jefferson practically all of its business activity, leaving it only the county government, did not get going without dissension, jealousy, and harsh words. But with the passing of the years better feeling has developed between the two towns. West Jefferson has experienced no great increase in population for the past ten years or more, but its increase in buisness establishments of importance and standing has been more than anybody expected. Its tobacco, livestock, and bean markets are fast becoming famous. It has an adequate elementary school plant, with the new Beaver Creek Consolidated High School nearby. Three handsome churches, the Baptist, Methodist, and Presbyterian, would do credit to any town in the State. The town has a satisfactory water and sewer service. Its streets are well-lighted and well-kept. Its stores, shops, and industries are geared to the needs of West Jefferson and the county surrounding it.

Originally said to be two miles apart, West Jefferson and Jefferson have practically grown together. Main Street, West Jefferson, may be regarded as an extension of Main Street, Jefferson, and it is inevitable that eventually the two will grow together and become one.

A son or daughter of Ashe, returning after long absence, will note that the consolidation today (1962) is well on the way. A supermarket is under construction between the two towns, with restaurants, mercantile establishments, lumber plants, and other places of business. Handsome new brick homes are fast filling up every vacant lot between the towns and spreading out along the road that leads up to the State Park at the top of Mount Jefferson, and along the highway toward Beaver Creek.

On the beautiful fields around Jefferson there are scores of new homes, and the growth has extended eastward until now there is an East Jefferson.

A uniting influence is the beautiful granite Ashe Memorial Hospital which serves both towns and the entire county. It stands between the two towns and is one of the best small hospitals in North Carolina.

Other towns began to grow along the railroad. Lansing was chartered May 16, 1928. Todd was incorporated in Chapter 165, Private Laws of 1936. Warrensville was chartered by Chapter 124, Private Laws of 1936. Smethport, which is just north of West Jefferson, came along about the same time. Tuckerdale, Sturgills, and other stations began to grow into villages with stores and other facilities.

II

Available Labor and Employment

Mention has been made that the new town of West Jefferson drew to itself most of the business that had kept Jefferson going. With the coming of the Hanes Knitting Company the so-called "Old Town" appears to be waking up, but West Jefferson, at this writing (1962) is still miles ahead.

The Bureau of Research and Statistics (Hugh M. Raper, director), North Carolina Employment Security Commission, gives some interesting facts and figures about Ashe County's insured establishments. The following are all of the establishments in Ashe at the end of the first quarter of 1962 listed as insured establishments (employing four or more persons):

West Jefferson Livestock Company, Appalachian Sulfides, Inc., M. D. Mullis, Lewis and Lewis, Luke Blevins, James R. Vannoy, Blevins Building Construction Company, Lyall's Stone and Grading, Victor Gass, Inc., Modern Heating and Sheet Metal Company, R. Taylor Well Drilling Company, Bare Company, Inc., National Dairy Products Corporation, Dr. Pepper Bottling Company, Liggett & Myers Tobacco Company, Peerless Hosiery Company, Knox Knitting Company, P. H. Hanes Knitting Company, W. W. Lumber Company, Howard E. Jones, Grant Jones, Charles

C. Edwards, Rayner L. Scott, William Jordan, G. Pell Bower, Cecil W. Yates, Oak Flooring Company, Inc., Appalachian Flooring Company, Inc., Phoenix Chair Company, Inc., Weaver Manufacturing Company, *The Skyland Post,* Gentry Brothers, Sprague Electric Company, Miller Produce Company, Central Telephone Company, Skyline Telephone Membership Association, Radio Station WKSK, Blue Ridge Electric Membership Corporation, Segraves Motor Company, Bare Little Company, Colvard Oil Company, Inc., Midway Lumber and Supply Company, Parker Tie Company, W. P. and R. C. Shoaf, Bower and Hurley Trading Company, Ashe Hardware Company, Inc., Rose's 5, 10 & 25 cent Store, Thompson's, Belk's Department Store, N. B. Smithey Stores, Bare's Department Store, Ben Franklin Store, Davidson's Central Food Market, G. F. P. Chevrolet Company, Inc., Payne Truck and Tractor Company, Jackson Truck and Rambler Company, Duncan Motors, Inc., Colvard's Truck Stop, West Jefferson Esso Station, Frazier's Stores, Blackburn Department Store, McNeill's, Burgess Furniture Store, Gray Brothers Furniture Company, W. J. Electric Company, Bo Jo Drive-In, Sprague Electric Cafeteria, Coffee Cup Grill, Roberts Drug Store, People's Rexall Store, Farmers Cooperative Exchange, Northwestern Bank, First National Bank, Ashe Savings and Loan Association, Barr Insurance Agency, Colvard Hotel, Hodges Ideal Laundry, City Barber Shop, Reins-Sturdivant Funeral Home, Hodges Body Shop, Elam S. Kurtz, Grandview Rest Home.

From the same source comes the information on page 254 about insured employment and wage payment data for Ashe County from 1937 through 1961.

These figures are interesting. It will be noted that the trend in covered employment and wages, from the beginning in 1937 up to and including 1961, has been upward, with only a few brief periods of decline. Starting with a monthly average covered employment of 257 and total wages of $134,536 in 1937, the monthly average employment in Ashe reached 586 in 1953, with total wages of $1,108,111 for that year. It should be remembered that during these years and for two years more the law only required reports from employers of eight or more persons. In 1956 the law was amended

Year	*Monthly Average Employment*	*Total Wages*
1937	257	$ 134,536
1938	173	79,181
1939	286	99,064
1940	226	131,101
1941	247	148,417
1942	275	172,705
1943	271	212,241
1944	300	260,456
1945	297	315,379
1946	389	479,851
1947	403	544,440
1948	439	618,454
1949	428	611,044
1950	467	714,908
1951	470	783,781
1952	508	911,746
1953	586	1,108,111
1954	701	1,335,262
1955	831	1,699,994
*1956	1,172	2,572,263
1957	1,385	3,514,747
1958	1,578	4,084,703
1959	2,056	5,553,740
1960	2,230	6,096,589
1961	2,395	6,905,470

*Coverage extended to include employers of four or more workers instead of eight or more.

to cover employers of four or more persons. This boosted the average monthly employment figure to 1,172 for 1956, and total wages for the year to $2,572,263. As the table shows, progress since 1956 has been nothing short of sensational. The total monthly average employment at the end of 1961 was 2,395 and the total of wages paid to Ashe County workers was $6,905,470.

This wage total lacks a great deal of covering all wages paid to Ashe County workers gainfully employed, as there are many places in the professions and in business and trade that employ fewer than four. Such employers include offices of lawyers and doctors, automobile service stations, insurance agencies, farms, country stores, motels, and many other establishments. The total employed in such establishments would add probably a thousand or more persons gainfully employed in Ashe to the 2,395 listed for 1961 in reporting establishments.

The North Carolina Employment Security Commission undertook in 1960 to make a survey of the labor supply available in Ashe for new industries seeking production-type employees for manufacturing plants. In this survey the state agency had the support of *The Skyland Post* of West Jefferson, the county schools, the Rotary and Lions Clubs of West Jefferson, Radio Station WKSK of West Jefferson, West Jefferson Merchants Association, and other groups.

The Employment Security Commission prepared a questionnaire and gave it wide distribution. There were 1,307 individuals who sent in completed questionnaires, about equally divided between males and females. A study of the completed questionnaires discloses these facts:

Approximately seventy-five per cent of those who responded (973) live within fifteen miles of West Jefferson; over sixty per cent of the respondents were seventeen to twenty-four years of age and about eighty-five per cent were under forty-five years of age; nearly 950 respondents reported that they were not currently employed (of these, 495 had previous work experience); about seventy-four per cent (962) of all respondents have had at least some high school education, slightly more than forty-nine per cent (474) being high school graduates and thirty-five per cent college graduates; approximately twenty-eight per cent of the respondents (362) are experienced in various specific manufacturing occupations; experienced respondents, both currently and formerly employed in non-manufacturing industries, totaled 521, or about forty per cent; of the 353 respondents who reported that they had never worked, seventy-five per cent were women, primarily housewives.

As of January 1, 1961, the total labor force as revealed in the survey, consisted of 644 males, of whom 271 were not at the time working and eighty-eight who had never worked, and 651 females, 279 not working and 263 who had never worked.

In its survey the Employment Security Commission could not concern itself with investigating the skills of every worker who signed and returned the questionnaire, but there is reason to believe that employers would find those filing the forms to be interested in new employment promising a future, and that they would qualify quickly for most of the places in industry that they would be asked to fill. As has been noted elsewhere, Ashe County's two biggest and newest industrial plants, Sprague Electric Company and P. H. Hanes Knitting Company, experienced no difficulty in getting their establishments into full and satisfactory operation, using nearly all local labor. They found the workers applying for jobs eager to work and teachable beyond all expectations.

The Employment Security Commission's report made no mention of the friendly attitude of Ashe County workers toward their employers, which may be best illustrated by an account of what happened when the Weaver Manufacturing Company at Smethport burned to the ground. The company was not financially strong at the time and its employees knew it. They volunteered to devote full time, without pay, to rebuilding the plant. In record time the Weaver Manufacturing Company was back in business and going strong, as it is today (1962), with forty-five full-time employees.

The commission's "Labor Force Summary," under the heading of West Jefferson, which included all of Ashe, is worth noting here. It showed the following:

Total labor force as of March, 1960, 7,225; March, 1961, 6,795.

Unemployment 1,475 in March, 1960, and 1,175 in March, 1961.

Employment total for March, 1960, 5,750; for March, 1961, 5,800.

Non-agricultural, wage and salaried workers (excluding domestics), 3,060 for March, 1960; 3,110 for March, 1961.

Total for manufacturing for March, 1960, 1,550; for March, 1961, 1,560 (including workers in food processing, textiles, apparel, furniture and lumber, printing, machinists, and all other manufacturing).

Total for non-manufacturing for March, 1960, 1,510; for March, 1961, 1,550. (This classification covered workers in construction, transportation, communications, service, and government. The total for agriculture for both March, 1960, and March, 1961, was 1,940.)

The employers of four or more in other employment covered by law had 2,170 employees in March, 1960, and 2,220 in March, 1961.

A significant entry appears at the bottom of the commission's wage summary:

"Persons involved in labor-management disputes 1960, 1961, none."

The facts set forth above make it clear that there is available manpower in the county to staff and operate many manufacturing enterprises. Furthermore, these records support the local claim that Ashe County labor is friendly to industry, new and old, and eager for work.

III

Banks and Banking

The need for banking facilities in Ashe brought out again the Ashe County do-it-yourself spirit. A group of forty or fifty persons met in Jefferson on June 16, 1903, to discuss the problem. Three interested persons in the group were not from Ashe—Hon. Robert L. Doughton of Laurel Springs, W. C. Fields of Sparta, and J. E. Finley, an experienced banker of high standing from North Wilkesboro.

After discussion it was decided to apply for a charter for a corporation to be known as the Bank of Ashe. Stock was to be sold in the amount of $20,000, made up of 200 shares of the par value of $100. Subscriptions were called for and those present subscribed the full amount. The subscribers were the following:

J. E. Finley of North Wilkesboro; R. L. Doughton of Laurel Springs; W. C. Fields, Sparta; George P. Pell, Jefferson; J. D. Thomas, Jefferson; Thomas K. Miller, Ore Knob; J. E. Foster, Jefferson; W. M. Transou, Jefferson; John Dent, Jefferson; J. B. Councill, Jefferson; J. W. Colvard, Jefferson; F. H. Neal, Jefferson; J. J. Thomas, Vernon; Elisha Graybeal, Graybeal; E. A. McNeill, Jefferson; J. C. Testerman, Jefferson; T. M. Calhoun, Roten; Ambrose Weaver, Sturgill's; T. C. Bowie, Jefferson; W. H. Hamilton, Beaver Creek; and W. J. Perkins, Helton.

The charter was duly granted and at a subsequent meeting, held July 28, 1903, J. E. Finley was elected president; Thomas K. Miller, vice-president; and Walter H. Worth, cashier. The stock subscribed had been paid in and, except for proper quarters, the bank was ready for business. This obstacle was overcome and the Bank of Ashe opened for business on October 17, 1903.

The Bank of Ashe prospered and found it advisable to increase its capital stock to $25,000 in July, 1919. Walter H. Worth continued as cashier of the bank until 1920, when he became president. Thomas K. Miller remained as vice-president and W. E. Johnson was elected cashier. Joe Worth became assistant cashier.

The Bank of Ashe continued in active and useful operation until June 25, 1938, when it was merged with the Northwestern Bank of North Wilkesboro.

Thus ended thirty-five years of service to Ashe County through a period of depression such as the world has not seen, before or since. The only official statement of the Bank of Ashe available for this period is the statement dated December 31, 1937. It showed that the Bank of Ashe, immediately prior to its merger with the Northwestern, had preferred capital stock amounting to $30,000; common stock, $25,000; undivided profits, $5,135.71; reserves $2,500. Its total resources were listed $437,789.41, some of doubtful value. About the only tangible asset of value the Bank of Ashe had to turn over to its successor was its banking house in Jefferson. The Bank of Ashe, which had served as liquidating agency for three state banks, later referred to, found its financial structure weakened by the three liquidations but had assumed the burden, at the urging of the North Carolina Banking Commission, and did the best it could to remedy a distressing situation not of its making.

Faith in the management of the Bank of Ashe was shown by the action of the board of board of directors of the big Northwestern Bank in naming Walter H. Worth as cashier of its Jefferson branch. The Northwestern, a very strong and ably managed bank, has two branch banks in Ashe today, one in the old banking house of the Bank of Ashe in Jefferson and the other in West Jefferson.

Walter H. Worth, cashier of the Jefferson branch of the Northwestern, died December 16, 1941. He was succeeded in January, 1942, by Larry P. Colvard, for many years Register of Deeds for Ashe County, who held the position for eighteen years. Mr. Colvard was elected assistant to the vice-president of the Northwestern in 1959 and later was named vice-president in charge of Ashe County operations. He held this position until January, 1961, when he retired, having served the bank for a period of twenty years. His son, H. B. Colvard, was elected cashier of the Jefferson branch of the Northwestern and is still so employed.

The coming of the Northwestern proved to be a blessing to the county. It kept its local affiliations and thereby kept the confidence of the people of Ashe. Its local board in Jefferson is composed of William B. Austin, W. G. Vannoy, and J. D. Stansberry. In West Jefferson, where Gwyn Bowers is manager, it has a local board composed of Carl F. Colvard, Sr., Dwight I. McGrady, and W. G. Vannoy. These men have the great satisfaction of knowing that they are backed by one of North Carolina's strongest banking chains with about forty offices in thirty-six towns and cities. As of June 30, 1963, the Northwestern Bank had paid-in capital stock of $2,269,750, a surplus of $7,730,250, and undivided profits of $2,759,764.58. Reserve for possible loan losses was $3,701,397.97 The Northwestern's deposits as of June 30, 1963 totaled $142,218,-821.99 and total resources were $162,852,160.68.

The Northwestern had its beginnings at Sparta. Many men of note and of sterling character have been connected with it, including the late Lieutenant Governor R. A. Doughton, who was president until his death August 4, 1945; his brother, nationally famous Congressman Robert L. Doughton, who served as chairman of the board of directors; Dr. B. B. Daugherty, president of Appalachian State Teachers College, who succeeded R. A. Doughton as president, serving until his death on May 27, 1957; E. C. Duncan, executive vice-president, who succeeded Dr. Daugherty and as of December 31, 1961, was still holding the office.

The second banking institution to come upon the scene in Ashe was the First National Bank of Jefferson, which was chartered December 1, 1906. Its capital stock was fixed at $25,000 and the following were listed as stockholders:

S. G. Parsons, B. O. Edwards, Ambrose Clark, T. H. Sutherland, F. H. Neal, W. S. Edwards, J. J. Thomas, E. A. McNeill, T. C. Bowie, W. C. Greer, T. K. Miller, J. B. Councill, Julia L. Smith, Mollie Edwards, J. W. Calloway, G. W. Brown, H. M. Brown, John Dent, John F. Jones, F. C. Young, F. M. Young, Isham Thompson, W. W. Greer, C. F. Segraves, J. W. Jones, T. G. Bauguess, Thomas J. Jones, David Graybeal, W. W. Turner, W. H. Perkins, J. A. Graybeal, J. M. Graybeal, Lee Eller, C. A. Jones, and Oscar Lewis.

At the first stockholders' meeting following the granting of the charter for the new bank, the following officers were elected:

T. H. Sutherland, president; W. C. Greer, vice-president; S. Greer Parsons, cashier; B. O. Edwards, E. A. McNeill, J. B. Councill, F. H. Neal, J. J. Thomas, John Dent, J. W. Calloway, W. H. Perkins, W. M. Brown, F. M. Young, T. K. Miller, Ambrose Clark, T. H. Sutherland, W. C. Greer, S. Greer Parsons, T. C. Bowie, and J. M. Graybeal, directors. All of the stockholders and directors were Ashe County citizens except F. M. Young, who was from Grayson County, Virginia.

The problem of finding suitable quarters for the new bank was solved when the Ashe County Board of Commissioners voted to rent it office space, on a temporary basis, in the new county courthouse. The board of directors were instructed to have the new bank open for business on March 1, 1907.

At the second stockholders' meeting, held June 10, 1907, the appointment of Harry Procter as assistant cashier was announced and he was placed under a bond of $15,000. A bond of the same amount was required for the cashier.

The minute books of the bank show that the following served as cashiers of the bank in the order named:

S. Greer Parsons, H. C. Tucker, B. C. Segraves, G. P. Cox, J. A. Roland, J. Lester Segraves, and Herbert Francis.

The bank has had as presidents T. H. Sutherland, J. J. Thomas, and Edison Thomas.

J. Lester Segraves joined the bank's official family as assistant cashier on April 1, 1920, became cashier in 1924, and executive vice-president in 1957, a position he still holds.

On August 9, 1915, the bank moved to West Jefferson and changed its name to First National Bank of West Jefferson. It has been a prime factor in making West Jefferson what it is today. Always conservative and averse to get-rich-quick promotions, the bank has stayed close to the business life of the county, advising and cautioning when needed and helping where help was required. As of a recent report to the federal banking authorities, the bank had a capital stock of $50,000, a surplus of $350,000 and undivided profits of $40,000. Its total resources are $4,191,897.14.

In the interest of economy the bank has occupied cramped quarters from the beginning, the West Jefferson quarters being no great improvement over the rooms in the courthouse at Jefferson. The bank has recently acquired real estate in the heart of the town and is building an adequate banking house.

There were other banking ventures in Ashe that met hard times in the years around the era of the great depression and failed to stand up under the pressure.

The Bank of Lansing was the first of these, being incorporated in March, 1916. It had authorized capital stock of $25,000 but was authorized to begin business when $5,000 had been paid in. The stockholders were J. W. Graybeal, J. F. Miller, S. A. Hartsoe, T. A. Farmer, Thomas J. Jones, E. L. Childers, J. D. Childers, J. H. Gentry, Monroe Welch, and E. H. Higginbottom. The first president was Daniel Joines and E. H. Higginbottom was the first cashier. The bank was finally liquidated by the Bank of Ashe. Banner Segraves was cashier at the time of liquidation.

The new town at the end of the Virginia-Carolina Railroad, named Todd, felt the need of banking facilities and interested citizens filed an application for a charter for the Bank of Todd on November 16, 1918. The bank was to have an authorized capital of $25,000 but could begin business when $5,000 had been paid in. The incorporators, holding fifty shares paid in, were H. J. Toliver, Robert B. Jackson, Samuel C. Miller, B. K. Barrs, Willet S. Miller, and H. G. Miller.

Todd, however, was not destined to grow. Very quickly lumbering operations stripped the area of its merchantable timber and the railroad ripped up its tracks to West Jefferson. The bank operated for only a short time before it, too, was liquidated by the Bank of Ashe.

The Peoples Bank and Trust Company of West Jefferson was organized in January, 1924. It had an authorized capital stock of $50,000, but was authorized to begin business when $20,000 of stock had been subscribed and paid in. The incorporators were H. C. Tucker, G. M. Donnelly, George A. Hopkins, Dr. J. C. Gambill, W. R. Bauguess, J. B. Councill, C. M. Dickson, W. W. Dickson, Dr. M. Blevins, A. F. Rose, W. F. Tucker, Dr. E. D. Jones, G. B. Doggett, J. E. Shumate, W. M. Caudill, J. A. Roland, E. F. Sheets, W. M. Wyrick, W. M. Peel, Ira W. Francis, E. M. Jenkins, D. P. Jones, Ed Mullis, and J. C. Jones.

The bank organized for business in February, 1924, with the following officers: President, H. C. Tucker; vice-president, C. M. Dickson; and cashier, J. A. Roland.

This bank operated for several years but ran into difficulties in the 1929-1933 depression and closed its doors. It was liquidated by the Bank of Ashe.

The above, as nearly as can be determined from available records, is the story of banking in Ashe County. The banking casualties were due in the main to economic difficulties of the period, though some of the trouble was due to local disagreements and jealousies that are sure to develop in every growing community. The net result, however, may be set down as a definite gain and a long step forward in the field of finance. The conflicts resulted in the strengthening of the county's only national bank and the firm establishment in Ashe of two branch banks of the Northwestern Bank.

Conservatively managed and alive to the needs of Ashe County, these banks offer every facility that interested industrialists could ask for.

CHAPTER THIRTEEN

TOLL ROADS AND RAILROADS–LOST PROVINCES RECOVERED BY HIGHWAYS–GROWTH OF POSTAL SERVICE

I

Toll Roads and Railroads

In the chapter relating to the activities of the County Court of Pleas and Quarter Sessions and of its successor, the County Board of Commissioners, there are scores of entries indicating the interest of a growing population in building new roads and improving old ones. Progressive citizens favored the construction of toll roads by private subscriptions and formed corporations to build the roads. It is not recorded anywhere that the stock issued for these enterprises ever paid dividends, or that any toll road long existed. Eventually the roads so contructed were absorbed by the public roads system and Ashe County sank deeper into the mud.

Ashe, Watauga, and Alleghany counties, shut off from the rest of the State by the Blue Ridge Mountains, and with roads that were red trails over almost impassable grades, became known as the "Lost Provinces." Their trade and business relations were with Virginia and Tennessee, which were easier of access. As has been recorded, frequent efforts were made to issue bonds for the construction of a railroad into Ashe, usually from Tennessee or Virginia, but at least once for an intrastate line to run from the Southern Railway's line at Morganton, or near by. Bond issues were duly submitted to the people at various times and every time defeated, not because the voters were opposed to railroads but because they lacked faith in the promoters and, in addition, they saw that they might become more than ever citizens of a lost province with the building of a railroad to the north or west. The projected railroads offered no promise of closer connection with other parts of North Carolina.

As a matter of fact, time has proved the voters right. The Norfolk and Western pushed its Virginia-Carolina line from Abingdon, Virginia, through Ashe to Todd, on the line between Ashe and Watauga. Literally hundreds of sawmills soon were established in Ashe and the railroad profited by hauling millions of tons of freight headed north and northeast, no part of it for North Carolina. When the timber supply was exhausted in the western part of Ashe, the railroad track from West Jefferson to Todd was ripped up. Only recently the Norfolk and Western has sought permission of the Virginia and North Carolina Utilities Commissions to discontinue passenger service between West Jefferson and Abingdon. The permission was granted in Virginia but denied in North Carolina, and today a traveler may ride by rail from West Jefferson to the Virginia-North Carolina line, but no farther. From there on to the Norfolk and Western's main line the traveler must hire a taxi or take a bus.

A further indication of the present attitude of the Norfolk and Western, now that the timber is gone, was found when Ashe was trying desperately to secure the location of the Sprague Electric Company's plant on property adjoining the railroad's right-of-way near Warrensville. Norfolk and Western representatives, at a conference held on the site of the big plant, expressed complete indifference and declared that they were not interested in promoting industry in Ashe County. They said their company planned to abandon the line. The first step toward this end has already been taken in the discontinuance of passenger service in Virginia.

The coming of the railroad and the sawmills that accompanied it served as a temporary stimulus for a sluggish economy. The wholesale cutting of Ashe County's oaks, maples, walnuts, chestnuts, poplars, and other trees admittedly brought money into the county but it left the area bereft of much of its beauty and also much of its wealth. Timber tracts that would bring thousands of dollars today were sold for a fraction of their present value. Incidentally, many of the denuded areas are being reforested and eventually Ashe County's beauty and much of its dissipated wealth will be regained, but with no thanks to the railroad that helped to despoil it.

There is nothing of record to indicate that the depots established along the line of the railroad in 1914 benefited in the long run, with the exception of West Jefferson and, perhaps, Smethport and Lansing. The others were designed to serve as loading points for outgoing lumber and were located where they would best serve the sawmill men.

II

Lost Provinces Recovered by Highways

Hon. Thomas C. (Tam) Bowie, for many years Ashe County's dynamic, hard fighting representative in the General Assembly, did not let a session of that body go by, when he was a member, without introducing legislation providing for railroads in Ashe County. For years he was obsessed with the idea that Ashe could be brought back into the sisterhood of counties only through the building of railroads. It was his firm belief that until they were built Ashe would remain a lost province.

The reunion of the "Lost Provinces" with North Carolina, a thing Mr. Bowie and his followers so ardently favored, came about eventually not because of the coming of the lone railroad from Virginia, but because of a system of good roads such as the county has today.

In 1900 Hon. Charles Brantley Aycock, candidate for Governor, crossed the Blue Ridge in a horse-drawn vehicle and came to Jefferson seeking votes. He was the first gubernatorial candidate to visit Ashe since 1876, when Zebulon Vance and Thomas Settle staged a debate on the square in front of the courthouse. Aycock had never been in Ashe before that time and he was struck by the fine herds of cattle, the beauty of the fields, mountains, and streams, and by the fine quality of Ashe's citizenship. He was quoted at Jefferson, and at many other places later, as saying that Ashe County was "the best county in the State." Before leaving Jefferson he pledged that if he was elected "Ashe County should have a road letting it out at its front door." (See North Carolina Papers, University of North Carolina, Ira T. Johnston.)

Governor Aycock did not forget his pledge. In the early part of his administration he backed a proposal to incorporate the North Wilkesboro-Jefferson Turnpike Company, which provided for the sale of stock to citizens on both sides of the Blue Ridge. He brought the State into the undertaking by providing that convicts would be assigned to build the road. The two counties involved, Ashe and Wilkes, were to furnish guards and food and shelter. The resulting road, built with pick and shovel and wheelbarrow, was a vast improvement over any roads previously built in the area but it was not an all-weather road. Over the first five or six years of its life there were wet spells, flash floods and the like that made the new turnpike almost as bad as the old trail, except that its grades were easier. The flood of 1916 completed the turnpike's destruction.

But the seed had been planted. In spite of setbacks, Ashe County citizens refused to quit. When the battle for the governship came in 1920, with Cameron Morrison, O. Max Gardner, and R. N. Page vying for the Democratic nomination, none of the candidates came to Ashe. However, Cameron Morrison visited North Wilkesboro. A large group of Ashe County citizens went over the ridge to hear him and present the cause of good roads. He was more than friendly to their pleas. He declared that he favored an all-weather road from North Wilkesboro to Jefferson and on to Grassy Creek at the Virginia line. The news spread in Ashe and it was the majority of eighty-eight votes that Ashe gave him that put Morrison in the lead in the first primary and led eventually to the Governor's chair. Cameron Morrison became North Carolina's first "good roads Governor" and he did not forget the promise he had made. Highway No. 16 gradually crept up the Blue Ridge, over its crest at the "Jumping Off Place," down in to the beautiful valley of the South Fork of New River and on to Jefferson and West Jefferson. Ashe County was no longer a lost province.

The good roads contagion seized Ashe. It ventured into the bond business and before the enthusiasm had cooled the county had done what it had previously been loath to do. It had issued road bonds for $1,500,000 or more, and with its own Ashe County Good Roads Commission had set out to build roads. Not all of the proceeds of the bonds were wisely spent and, as was inevitable, trouble followed.

In spite of difficulties the road building went on. As of January 1, 1962, Ashe County had 108.9 miles of paved rural primary road, and 7.6 miles of paved municipal road, a total of 116.5 miles of paved primary roads. Of secondary rural roads, Ashe County had 90.1 miles of paved road and 579.9 miles of unpaved. Of municipal roads of the secondary system, 3.9 miles were paved and 1.5 miles unpaved. The total mileage of state secondary roads in Ashe, paved and unpaved, was 675.4 miles.

Since all of these roads of the primary and secondary systems are maintained by the State, it follows that Ashe is well out of the mud. Even the secondary unpaved roads are well kept and may be considered as all-weather roads. They are a little muddy in long wet spells but always passable and always quickly repaired.

Because the network of good roads now in Ashe has been growing and is expected to continue to grow, there has been a decided increase in the number of cars and trucks. There has been no compilation of the number of licensed vehicles for Ashe County for 1962, but as of December 31, 1961, Miss Fay Ingram, head of the North Carolina Automobile License Bureau, reported that there were 4,631 licensed automobiles and 2,034 licensed trucks. With a total population of 19,768, as shown by the 1960 census, that means that there were enough automobiles in Ashe on January 1, 1962, to transport every man, woman and child, allowing an average of slightly over four to the car.

The more than 2,000 licensed trucks indicate the further replacement of manpower and mule and horsepower by mechanized muscles on the farms of Ashe County. Wagons and other horse-drawn equipment are fast disappearing and trucks and tractors are taking their places.

III

Growth of Postal Service

The preceding sections have been devoted to the coming of the first railroad and its effect on the county's economy and the county's road system, and its effect on the way of living in Ashe.

An influence taken for granted in these days is the postal system. In tracing the county's development from raw frontier to its present status, the part its postal service played should be considered along with the coming of railroads and the sale of the county's most valuable assets, its timber, and the building of roads to serve the public needs.

The first available annual report of the United States Postmaster General was contained in a manual dated April 1, 1831, a copy of which is on file in the North Carolina Department of Archives and History. In that year Ashe County had six post offices, as follows:

Bower's Store, Wyatt McBride, Postmaster; Councill's Store (now Boone), Jordon Councill, Jr., Postmaster; Cove Creek, John Mast, Postmaster; Jeffersonton, Winston Somers, Postmaster; North Fork (now Creston) Stephen Thomas, Postmaster; and Old Field, Robert Hamilton, Postmaster.

It should be remembered that at that time Watauga and Alleghany were parts of Ashe and these six widely scattered offices had to serve the entire area. The federal governmnt designated the county seat of Ashe "Jefferson," instead of Jeffersonton or Jeffersontown, sometime after 1831. The next available official report, dated 1849, called it Jefferson.

According to the 1849 report the number of post offices had not increased but there were changes, as follows:

Gap Civil, Allen Gentry, Postmaster; Jefferson, Roderick Murchison, Postmaster; Laurel Springs, John Reeves, Postmaster; Moretz Mill, John Moretz, Postmaster; North Fork, David Worth, Jr., Postmaster; and Valle Crucis, W. W. Skiles, Postmaster.

The number of post offices in the county climbed to twenty in 1859. It dropped to eleven in 1869 and to eight in 1879. The number increased to twenty in 1889 and reached a peak of sixty-eight in 1899. Thereafter, the number decreased from year to year as rural free delivery spread over the nation and finally reached Ashe County. Every part of the county wanted free mail delivery and scores of Ashe County young men sought jobs as rural mail carriers.

Those who are prone to complain about present day postal rates and services should take a look at postal costs and practices as set out in the manual above referred to. There were only six post offices in a county that spread over 977 square miles of mountains. Note these rates:

Single letter, composed of one piece of paper, for any distance up to thirty miles, six cents; about thirty miles and up to 400 the rate increased gradually to twenty-five cents. Two pieces of paper, double rate; three pieces, triple rate; four pieces, quadruple rate. To mail a one-piece letter from Jefferson to Raleigh cost 18¾ cents.

The abandonment of old post offices brought about a change in rural life in Ashe. The local post office had become a part of community life. Usually it was set up in a country store, or shop, or in the postmaster's own home, and citizens found it a convenient place to linger, talk politics or religion, gossip a bit, pass the time of day, and discuss crops and the weather. The post office gave name and recognized boundaries to communities. Some of the names still linger. Perhaps the list that follows, covering the post offices in 1899, may serve to bring back to mind many of these communities that have been forgotten. The post offices listed by the United States Post Office Department, with their postmasters in 1899, were:

Algiers, W. B. Carson; Apple Grove, John N. Barr; Ashley, Christian Powers; Baldwin, James M. Edwards; Blevins, M. M. Blevins; Beaver Creek, William H. Hamilton; Berlin, James Eller; Blys, J. S. Miller; Brandon, W. S. Graybeal; Burnthill, Fannie A. Shepherd; Bud, Charles M. Mikel; Clifton, Jesse G. Miller; Comet, R. K. James; Concert, Millier Hinson; Creston, Ruth C. Worth; Crow, Armstrong Clark; Crumpler, Maude C. Lambert; Dresden, W. H. Wilcox; Dyson, Emma Brown; Eugene, J. U. Ballou; Eye, W. M. Miller; Fig, A. M. Maxwell; Fleetwood, John L. Bowen; Furches, Emma V. Richardson; Gale, Jennie C. Bledsoe; Gap Creek, W. A. Tomlinson; Grassy Creek, S. Greer Parsons; Graybeal, James M. Graybeal; Grayson, J. W. McGrayson; Grigsby, R. P. Grigsby; Grimsley, Alfred Barker; Helton, Jacob Eller;

Husk, Amos Sullivan; Hermitage, Lydia Dolinger; Idlewild, John S. Yates; Idol, Barnet V. Idol; Jefferson, Julia L. Smith; Jones, Riley A. Jones; Lamar, A. M. Reeves; Lansing, W. H. Perkins; Linney, William Porter; Nathan's Creek, Hugh Tillery; Nettle Knob, J. J. Goodman; Obids, Joseph W. Calloway; Orion, William H. Graybeal; Oval, Lowry A. Vannoy; Parker, John F. Parker; Pinckton, Drury Elliott; Roark, Ivey L. Roark; Roberts, William J. Roberts; Riverside, G. H. Tatum; Roten, Thomas M. Calhoun; Scottville, John C. Woodie; Silas Creek, W. S. Jones; Solitude, Louis J. Maxwell; Sturgills, Byron Sturgill; Sussex, Wilson Hudler; Sutherlands, Guss M. Donnelly; Thaxton, James A. Martin; Todd, Ishmael Graham; Trausou, Sinie A. Trausou; Treetop, William F. Perkins; Trout, Joseph Powell; Vernon, Elizabeth C. Young; Wagoner, John H. Wagoner; Weasel, Marion Miller; Weaversford, James O. Parsons; and Wheeler, Moses D. Caudill.

Today Ashe County's postal service leaves little to be desired. Until recently, the Abingdon-West Jefferson Railway Post Office brought in a large part of Ashe County's mail but on February 5, 1949, the Post Office Department established highway post office service between Greensboro and Boone, running through Jefferson and West Jefferson. A bus, equipped for postal service, leaves Greensboro every day except Sunday at 2:15 A.M. It arrives at West Jefferson at 7:45 A.M., bearing the morning papers and other mail from Raleigh, Greensboro, Winston-Salem and Charlotte. It goes to Boone and, returning, leaves West Jefferson at 3:50 P.M., arriving in Greensboro at 9:10 P.M.

This makes for fast mail service, as the mail gets to Jefferson and West Jefferson in time to catch the eastbound highway post office, in the same day.

It is worth noting that Ashe now has only sixteen post offices. These, with their postmasters, are the following:

Creston, Mary Baker; Fleetwood, Lillie A. Howell; Glendale Springs, Carl F. Miller; Husk, Ruth Vannoy; Jefferson, Irene Morphew; Lansing, Ed Eller; Scottville, Carrie D. Maines; Todd, Eleanor M. Moretz; Apple Grove, Vance Miller; Crumpler, Frank McMillan; Fig, Ocie Sutherland; Tuckerdale, J. E. Tucker; Warrensville, John Eastridge, acting postmaster; and West Jefferson, Sam Davis.

Two of Ashe County's post offices, Jefferson and West Jefferson, are rated as second-class post offices; six are third-class – Grassy Creek, Crumpler, Warrensville, Todd, Lansing, and Creston; eight are fourth-class – Fleetwood, Glendale Springs, Husk, Scottville, Apple Grove, Fig, Grayson, and Tuckerdale.

This postal system has brought all parts of the county closer together, and, along with good roads and telephones, has resulted in the creation of a citizenship free from disputes and differences that often produce bitter hatreds and prejudices. Moreover, there is no such thing in Ashe County as racial trouble, and there never has been. By the United States Census of 1860, there were 391 Negro slaves in Ashe and 142 free Negroes. If there are violations of law in Ashe, few of the defendants are Negroes, and it has always been so.

True, the last public hanging in Ashe was the hanging of Will Banks, a Negro, for the killing of a relative, one Frank McMillan who, from all accounts, richly deserved killing.

The story, though slightly irrelevant, is interesting and may as well be told here. Will Banks, who was rated as a good citizen, claimed self-defense, but he was convicted after a hard-fought trial in which Thomas C. (Tam) Bowie aided the solicitor in the prosecution. He was sentenced to be hanged and the biggest crowd ever to assemble in Ashe County gathered behind the county jail to witness the show.

George B. Austin, who was sheriff from 1906 to 1914, and who had just assumed office, had what he called the toughest experience of his official career in hanging Will Banks. He found no one in his office, or in the county, who knew how to tie a hangman's knot and had to send to Johnson City, Tennessee, for an "expert."

Because of his feeling in the matter he offered Banks unlimited time to address the crowd. Banks spoke eloquently for forty-five minutes, during which he bitterly attacked Mr. Bowie and other lawyers and was highly critical of Sheriff Austin. He stoutly contended to the end that the killing was in self-defense and maintained complete control of himself. His last words, spoken cooly and calmly, were:

"Mr. Austin, I am ready to hang."

In Ashe County today there is no prejudice against the Negro. Whites and non-whites work side by side on farms, in wood-working plants, automobile service stations, machine shops, and other undertakings, including schools.

Mention has been made of Oddie Cox, highly respected colored schoolteacher, who perished in the fire that destroyed his little home at Nathan's Creek. He had worked unceasingly, and with success, to do away with one-room schoolhouses for the Negro boys and girls scattered over Ashe County and had finally secured a commodious central school building big enough to take care of all of the Negro pupils in Ashe, served by buses and staffed by good teachers, as were schools for white children. When he died, many hundreds of people attended his funeral. His pallbearers were three young white men and three Negroes.

Many will remember Dewey Poe, the friendly colored merchant who operated a store on old Highway 16 just over the ridge north of Jefferson. In addition to selling foodstuffs, he prowled the highways of Pennsylvania, New York, and Maryland, bringing back truck load after truck load of furniture and household goods, some of it antique but most of it just old and decrepit. He never misrepresented his goods, but conducted a business that won and held the respect of his white neighbors and his influence kept a community, slightly given to violence, in good order.

There are many others of his kind in the county and all of them have the friendship and support of their white neighbors. Their numbers have decreased from year to year, declining from an all-time high, according to the Census of 1880, of 963 to its present 191, according to the Census of 1960. The decline in colored population can not be attributed to social causes. It has been due to economic pressures and nothing else. The Ashe County colored youth, like the young whites, left Ashe because there were few job opportunities for them and in many cases the departing young folks drew the old folks after them.

CHAPTER FOURTEEN

ASHE COUNTY DEPARTMENT OF PUBLIC WELFARE — ASHE COUNTY DEPARTMENT OF HEALTH — THE ASHE MEMORIAL HOSPITAL AND ASHE'S PHYSICIANS

I

The Ashe County Department of Public Welfare

There are those who speak disapprovingly of the "welfare state" and condemn it as a dangerous socialistic concept, bordering on communism. They quite overlook the fact that the constitution of the State of North Carolina says that "beneficent provisions for the poor, the unfortunate and the orphan (is) one of the first duties of a civilized and Christian state." From the beginning, or at least from the adoption of the present State Constitution in 1868, it may be assumed, it was not vastly different, if the practices followed in Ashe County were general.

Ashe County, newest and poorest of the State's counties, was "welfare minded" from the beginning, as it is today. Minutes of the sessions of the Ashe County Court of Pleas and Quarter Sessions in 1806 provided for a "poor tax." Minutes of most of the sessions of the court prior to 1806 are not available, but it is likely that the first and subsequent tax levies contained levies for the poor. It is certain that they did after 1806.

Through periods of dire poverty, war, and economic and political upsets, Ashe County remained welfare-minded. In 1870, the new Board of County Commissioners, which succeeded the Court of Pleas and Quarter Sessions, asked for legislative sanction to levy a special tax on all real and personal property sufficient to raise $5,000 for the poor. Authority was granted in Chapter 209, Public Laws of 1870.

A reading of the accounts of the activities of the Board of County Commissioners will disclose that the board busied itself with the affairs of the County Home and with the welfare of indigent widows and orphans.

Those who keep up with the doings of the County Board of Welfare these days find frequent cases of dependent children being placed in foster homes. This may be rated as a fine activity but it is by no means new. More than 150 years ago, the County Court was performing similar service in Ashe County. Orphan children in need were "bound out" to citizens of high standing who were required to furnish bond guaranteeing to the unfortunates humane treatment, adequate support, proper clothing, and schooling up to the standards of the day. For the girls, there was the pledge of household equipment and clothing on marriage. For the boys, at twenty-one, to quote the usual stipulation in the bond, "a horse, saddle and bridle, valued at $50, and a freedom suit when free."

Upon the execution of the bond, the youngster became a member of the bondsman's family, the only difference being that the bondsman had to report regularly to the court as to how the provisions of the bond were being carried out in case of the orphan. No reports were required about his own children. There were few abuses of the system and, in the main, it worked well.

It was in the 1890's that North Carolina began to show concern for the welfare situation. Ashe County had been drifting along, taking reasonably good care of its unfortunates, but in the larger, more thickly populated counties there were problems that loomed large and resulted in new state laws on the subject. To assist in solving these problems new statutes required, among other things, the appointment of county welfare committees. The first of these committees in Ashe was composed of T. W. Perkins and B. P. Grigsby, who served from 1891 to 1896, when Mrs. L. C. Gentry and Mrs. J. W. Wayman were added. Attorney George P. Pell of Jefferson became attorney for the committee in 1900. In 1904, B. P. Grigsby went off the committee and was succeeded by R. L.

Shoaf. T. W. Perkins and R. L. Shoaf appear to have been the active members of the committee from 1904 to 1907.

It was about this time that the committee came to be known as the County Board of Welfare. Walter H. Worth of Jefferson appears to have been the first chairman. He held this position until 1916. Up to this time all board members had served as volunteers. The ever-increasing load of duties caused the General Assembly of 1917 to set out in detail the responsibilities and duties of the superintendent of welfare and the members of the board. The record is not complete as to activities between 1917 and 1920 but it is recorded that W. R. Bauguess became chairman of the board in 1920.

In 1924, by operation of law, the county superintendent of schools became ex-officio superintendent of welfare in those counties not having a full time superintendent of welfare. J. O. Goodman, county superintendent of schools, took over as acting superintendent of welfare. Attorney Ira T. Johnston was chairman of the board and E. L. Tucker, assistant superintendent.

The County Board of Commissioners in the administration of Superintendent J. O. Goodman, 1926 to 1928, made the first grant of record for mothers' aid, amounting to $217. In 1928-29, when Robert E. Lee Plummer was superintendent, the board set up $299 for mothers' aid.

In 1931, with Robert E. Lee Plummer as superintendent, Miss Ruth Reeves, daughter of Dr. and Mrs. B. E. Reeves, came into the welfare picture as assistant to Superintendent Plummer on a part time basis. The county superintendent of schools remained ex-officio the superintendent of welfare, but Miss Reeves was designated as federal relief agent and was charged with the responsibility of receiving, storing and distributing to the needy, under the Federal Civil Works Administration, such articles of food, clothing, and other things as the agencies allocated to Ashe County. In her work she had the assistance of Rev. R. H. Stone as a volunteer worker.

Miss Reeves resigned her position on November 6, 1933, when J. B. Hash was superintendent of schools. Presumably these welfare duties again became one of the major concerns of the county superintendent of schools, as they had been before. If any one was named to the post in the remainder of Mr. Hash's term of office, or during the term of office (1935-1937) of his successor, J. Ivan Miller, there is no record of it.

Mr. Hash began a new term of office as county superintendent of schools on July 1, 1937 and with his term new statutes relating to public welfare became effective in Ashe. The new laws required the appointment of a county director of welfare and of a County Welfare Board.

The county commissioners appointed J. B. Hash, W. B. Oliver, and H. H. Burgess to the County Welfare Board. Miss Ruth Tugman became the first director of the County Welfare Department as it exists under the present administrative setup. Her appointment became effective on July 1, 1937, and she served until June 30, 1948, when she was succeeded by the present director, Miss Frances Tucker. The present County Welfare Board is composed of Chairman George W. Shephard of Laurel Springs (appointed by the Board of County Commissioners), J. Tatum Brown of Todd (appointed by the State Board of Public Welfare), and John W. Knox of Creston (appointed by the other two).

The County Welfare Department continued to grow and became more and more useful as the years went by. Aided by state and federal welfare funds, it began to take off of the heavily burdened shoulders of the county commissioners much of their load. Eventually the County Home was closed, as elsewhere noted, and the home and its fine farm were put up for sale. The support of the inmates was taken over by the state-federal-county aid program. The site of the County Home is presently occupied by the Beaver Creek Consolidated High School, one of the finest high schools in North Carolina.

As he considers the statistics set out below, the reader will be astonished at what has happened to the welfare program, if he will keep in mind the early years heretofore mentioned. From statewide experience, new laws brought about changes that promise well for the future. Wisely, the lawmakers built the Welfare Department into a locally administered, state supervised agency of government.

It is good to be able to report that insofar as Ashe County is concerned, the welfare agency is working well. It has grown from the meager beginnings herein recorded to an agency expending in the year ending June 30, 1960, a total of $569,290.37 on a total of 953 welfare cases. Of these there were 445 cases of old age assistance receiving $217,499; 781 dependent children in 276 families, $248,393; 203 totally and permanently disabled, $97,984; general assistance, two for $342.03; medical care and hospitalization, $3,244.05 for twenty-three cases; boarding care for children, four for $1,768.29; all other listed at $60. In addition, as an indication of the agency's other activities, the report lists seventy-nine cases not involving finances but requiring service only.

These figures are from the biennial report of the North Carolina State Board of Public Welfare for the period July 1, 1958, to June 30, 1960.

These large amounts of money do not come from Ashe County alone. They are provided by the State of North Carolina, the federal government and the county of Ashe.

II

Ashe County Department of Health

It is entirely possible for a County Welfare Department to carry on, after a fashion, without a County Department of Health but it is hard in these days to even imagine such a condition. The two go together and supplement each other in many ways.

By being vigilant, an active Department of Health reduces the welfare load for the medically indigent; reduces the need for welfare services in dealing with maternal and child welfare; and reduces expenditures for crippled children; checks and controls the ravages of diabetes, tuberculosis, cancer, heart and cardiovascular ailments; all of which, along with many other activities, tend to reduce the case load of the County Welfare Department.

The records shown elsewhere disclose that Ashe County was not only welfare minded at an early date but was public health minded, too. The limited funds available prevented continuous employment of a county health officer but from time to time it is noted that various physicians were designated as county health officers.

According to the thirty-eighth Biennial Report of the North Carolina Board of Health, covering the years 1958 to 1960, Ashe County is listed as having completed its organization within the framework of the North Carolina health laws enacted in 1938. It is presently in a district of three counties, the other two being Alleghany and Watauga. The present superintendent is Dr. Mary Michal and the district office is at Boone. Dr. Michal visits the three counties on regular schedule and in Jefferson has an adequate, well equipped county health office. This new building was erected near the Ashe Memorial Hospital. It is built of granite, like the hospital, and with the same style of architecture. It was formally dedicated on December 10, 1957. State and federal funds paid for part of the building and the remainder was raised by private subscription. The total cost was $33,000.

For the fiscal year ending June 30, 1960, according to the Biennial Report above referred to, the total health budget for Ashe County was $19,961. Of this amount $12,068 was the county appropriation; $6,869 was the state allotment to the county, which included allotment for mental health; $1,024 in federal funds for mental health and other services. Using the latest United States Census figures available at the time (1950) this budget called for an expenditure for health purposes of a little more than 91 cents per capita.

Considering what the county gets for this amount, few citizens will complain and the majority will readily fall in line to support the addition of personnel in the county's Health Department. The Biennial Report showed Ashe sharing the services of a director with Watauga and Alleghany. In addition there was a sanitary officer and two clerks in the Ashe County office. These have done good work, but there is pressing need for additional help in the fields of maternal and child welfare, in aid to crippled children, in preschool examination, in oral hygiene for school children and treatment for defective hearing and sight, in detection and control of communicable diseases, and in many other fields where trained health workers, always available and ready to serve, could alleviate suffering and save lives. The filling of this need is already on the way and should not be long in coming.

Asked for data on births and deaths in Ashe for a period as far back as reliable figures are available, the North Carolina State Board of Health responded with a copy of the Annual Report of Public Health Statistics Section, showing live births and deaths from 1920 to 1958 inclusive. The information is given year by year, but for sake of brevity is broken down in ten year periods, as follows:

1920-1929, live births, 6,272; deaths, 1,664. Difference, 4,608.
1930-1939, live births, 5,404; deaths, 1,696. Difference, 3,708.
1940-1949, live births, 5,343; deaths, 1,545. Difference, 3,798.
1950-1958, live births, 4,286; deaths, 1,504. Difference, 2,782.

For this period of thirty-nine years, Ashe County's birth rate continued high, the death rate low. The total differences showed that there were 15,596 more live births in Ashe than there were deaths between 1920 and 1958, and yet the population decreased from census to census.

It cannot be maintained that the ravages of disease carried away the indicated surplus population, as that is not true. Many living today can remember when typhoid fever, scarlet fever, tuberculosis, smallpox, and other contagious diseases wiped out families and decimated communities, but that does not happen in Ashe any more.

The statistical report above referred to noted 160 white deaths in 1958 and two non-white. Only two of the deaths were from tuberculosis and none at all from those dreaded diseases, typhoid fever, scarlet fever, diphtheria, smallpox, meningitis, and other ailments that were formerly accepted stoically as a pattern of life. It is interesting to note that the diseases claiming the lives of twenty or more Ashe County citizens in 1958 were:

Malignant neoplasms, twenty-three; vascular lesions, affecting central nervous system, twenty-three; arteriosclerotic heart disease, including coronary disease, twenty-eight.

The remainder of the 160 come from pneumonia, seven; endocarditis, eight; hypertension with heart disease, eight; accidents, six; suicide, eight; homicide, two; and others, totaling forty-seven, which are spread over a variety of diseases accounting for one to four deaths each.

Ashe County's Health Department deserves a fuller account of its activities than has been given above and the official records in the office of Dr. Mary Michal, present district health director, bear this out.

The Ashe-Alleghany-Watauga District Health Department was first organized in 1938, and Dr. Robert R. King, Sr., was the first district health officer. He resigned in 1944 to return to his work as a missionary of the Presbyterian church in Africa. The position was vacant until Dr. Robert R. King, Jr., accepted it in 1946. He resigned after two years to resume special studies in Public Health Administration. The position remained vacant until Dr. Mary Michal accepted it in February 1950. She had served in similar positions in seven western North Carolina counties. In 1951-52, she served as director and took advanced courses in Public Health Administration at the University of North Carolina, receiving the degree of Master of Health from the university's School of Public Health. She became ill in 1959 and had to resign. Dr. James T. Googe succeeded her and served for two years, resigning to accept another position. The office was unfilled for the following year and Dr. Mary Michal, her health restored, again accepted the office and since July 1, 1962, has been in charge.

Dr. Michal is immensely proud of the handsome Health Building, built on a lot adjacent to the Ashe Memorial Hospital. The records in her office show the money for putting up the new building came from the following sources:

Medical Care Commission, with Hill-Burton and state funds, $25,500; Ashe County funds, $5,500; land for the building, $2,000. In addition, the West Jefferson Woman's Club contributed $465.

The county assumed responsibility for water and sewage disposal. The County Board of Commissioners at the time were Chairman Quincy A. Duncan, George Shepherd, and Edd Davis. The two first named happened at the time to be members of the District Board of Health, along with Thomas F. Cockerham.

Dr. Michal is pleased with the Ashe County office and with the progress made in recent years. She has two competent public health nurses now, Mrs. Carrie T. McNeill and Mrs. Virginia Adderton, and an additional public health nurse for work in the schools, Mrs. Margaret Bower. She has one sanitarian in Ashe, Bower E. Campbell, and the part time service of Jack Cobb, district supervising sanitarian. Her secretary-clerk, who runs the district office at Boone, completes her staff. She is asking for two more public health nurses and other trained personnel.

III

Ashe County Memorial Hospital and Ashe County's Physicians

It seems fitting that along with the sections devoted to Public Welfare and Public Health should be told the story of the Ashe County Memorial Hospital, housed in a beautiful stone building on a beautiful hilltop at the edge of Jefferson and close to the town limits of West Jefferson. From its front door is visible the town of Jefferson, with magnificent Mount Jefferson looming over it and to the north and northeast, Big Phoenix and Little Phoenix mountains.

The county's need for such an institution had been long known and felt and talked about, but action was lacking. Many people helped to build sentiment for a hospital in Ashe County. Among the very first and probably the most eloquent and persuasive of these advocates was Robert E. Lee Plummer, great teacher, great school builder and administrator, a dynamic leader in all movements for the betterment of Ashe County. Another to render fine and unselfish service was Wade E. Eller, presently disabled and in a United States Veterans Hospital at Johnson City, Tennessee.

Dr. Dean C. Jones, native of Ashe, who has been connected with the hospital since it started, combining the duties of chief surgeon, head physician, and superintendent, was asked to write a brief account of the establishment of the hospital and its operations. The account he gave was interesting, but his innate modesty made it impossible for him to tell the whole story. The fact remains, however, that from the beginning up to now (1962) Dr. Dean C.

Jones has been the motivating force behind the project and without his help there would have been no hospital in Ashe County today. Dr. Jones would be the last to agree to such a statement, but it is absolutely true.

In his brief account Dr. Jones stated that he could not list and give credit to all who had a part in the program, because, to use his words, "it was truly a community project and had the cooperation of a great portion of our people."

He pays tribute to Robert E. Lee Plummer and Wade E. Eller; William B. Austin, who served as president of the association set up to build the hospital and later as chairman of the board of directors; R. R. Badger, treasurer of the building committee; and L. L. Scott, business manager, who gave nearly all of his time to his hospital duties for several years for little or no salary. Dr. Jones emphasizes that there were many more.

Dr. Jones credits a Presbyterian minister, Rev. R. H. Stone, with arousing his own interest in the hospital. He came to Dr. Jones and inquired if he would run a hospital if the minister got one built and furnished. These are Dr. Jones' own words:

"As this was the thing I desired most for the county, I readily agreed."

With this assurance, Rev. R. H. Stone, with characteristic energy, got busy. Within a few weeks he laid before Dr. Jones a list of pledges for the construction of a hospital. It appeared entirely feasible to go ahead with plans for the building.

At this juncture, Mr. Stone was approached by the Ashe County Rotary Club, which had been considering plans for getting a hospital started. They suggested a merger, and a pooling of efforts and resources. After conferences and careful study, Dr. Jones and Mr. Stone and their supporters agreed to join forces with the Rotary Club and the project was on its way.

Dr. Jones does not hesitate to praise Mr. Stone for his part in getting the project started. While others had tentative plans and good intentions, they did not move. There had to be a "prime mover" and in Dr. Jones' opinion, Mr. Stone was such person. Because his church assigned him to work outside of the county he was not so active in the later program. But Dr. Jones said, "it took his enthusiasm and aggressive approach to get it started."

The original building was constructed with Works Progress Administration labor and a great deal of the material needed in construction was donated by citizens of the county. When the building was opened for patients in 1941, an appeal to the public went out and community vied with community in collecting canned goods and other food supplies for the early months of operation.

The task of operating a hospital, after it is built and furnished, is not easy. About his own experience along this line Dr. Jones says:

"When the problem of operating our hospital was considered, it was realized that there was no one here with experience in this line and also no visible means of financial support for the operation. Being determined that our county should have a hospital, if within my power, I offered to take the responsibility of running the hospital, both medically and financially and receive my income from the income left over. This offer was accepted by the Board and the hospital was run on that basis for several years. It was done, of course, by my subsidizing the hospital with a great proportion of my professional fees, but it was done willingly and I have no regrets for it.

"After a few years, when financial developments made it feasible, I was given a regular salary, which was yet much less than the income from my fees, but this was also due to my willingness and desire to have it this way until the hospital was well enough established on its own. I am happy to say it has so proven its ability in the past two years."

Dr. Jones, a well-established physician, did not find it easy to give up a growing private practice for the meager returns the hospital program offered and the pinch must have been felt by his wife, who joined him wholeheartedly in his undertaking. Unofficially, she became good-will officer for the hospital, taking upon herself the task of selling the hospital's services to the general public and producing in the hospital a homelike atmosphere. Most of this was done without pay. In recent years she has received a small salary.

Dr. Jones has praise for Mrs. Theresa Badger, who has been cook from the beginning; for Mrs. Kate Duncan, who has been with the hospital almost from its opening and who, with totally unskilled aides, managed nursing duties almost alone for a large part of World War II; for Miss Virginia Ashley, a trained nurse, who donated her services for several months at the beginning; and for many others.

The hospital has shown satisfactory growth in plant, equipment, clientele and personnel. Its most recent financial statement for the year ended September 30, 1962, laid before the stockholders by the administrator, Thomas F. Cockerham, shows total receipts of $265,949.82 for the year, as against $237,282.92 for 1961. Total disbursements for the year reached $264,399.05 as against $234,-162.86 for the previous year. The hospital closed the year with $6,493.86 in savings account, as compared with $5,000 the previous year and a general operating fund balance for the year of $8,732.85, as against $7,182.07 for 1961. During the year, new equipment to the amount of $10,850.06 was bought and paid for. The hospital had rendered during the year 2,155 certified charity days of care and had recovered from all sources for charity patients the sum of $36,564.18. Its loss from charity patients was $4,307.89.

The administrator's report pointed out that "organizations in the county, along with the Ashe County Memorial Hospital Auxiliary, had refurnished and redecorated all of the rooms in the hospital, fixed up the doctors' lounge, helped control visiting hours and had performed many other worthwhile services."

Dr. Jones and his staff are understandably proud of this record. His hospital is one of the few in the country to operate "in the black." Most of the smaller hospitals operate at a loss from year to year, and expect nothing else. Probably an explanation of Ashe County Memorial's success may be found in the Ashe County do-it-yourself spirit, as exemplified in the founding of the hospital and in the services of the Association and the members of the Ashe County Woman's Club and of the West Jefferson Woman's Club.

Typical, also, of the spirit that has made Ashe County great, are the citizens chosen recently by the stockholders for 1963:

Trustees for three-year terms – Mrs. Norman Duvall, West Jefferson; A. A. Perry, Lansing; E. O. Woodie, West Jefferson; V. C. Lillard, Jefferson; Miss Frances Tucker, Jefferson; Frank James, Jefferson.

Officers for one-year terms: J. Gwyn Gambill, North Wilkesboro, president; Edison M. Thomas, Grassy Creek, first vice-president; Mrs. Ed M. Anderson, West Jefferson, second vice-president; Frank James, Jefferson, third vice-president; G. W. Edwards, West Jefferson, secretary; Thomas F. Cockerham, Jefferson, treasurer.

Executive Committee, for one-year terms: Ira T. Johnston, Jefferson; W. B. Oliver, Jefferson; W. B. Austin, Jefferson. Finance Committee, for one-year terms: Mrs. Ed M. Anderson, West Jefferson; L. P. Colvard, Jefferson; Frank James, Jefferson.

There is an interesting item about Ashe County in Table 3 of the Annual Report of the Public Health Statistics, State Board of Health for 1958. This tables shows live births for the preceding year of 382 children in Ashe, 361 white and four non-white, all of whom were delivered in the Ashe County Memorial Hospital. The other seventeen white were attended by a physician but not in the hospital. Midwives are credited with five white deliveries. This makes for better maternal and child care and marks the passing of the midwife, once such a vital factor in rural life.

Dr. Jones would be the last person on earth to claim credit for the remarkable success of Ashe Memorial Hospital. He attributes it to the united effort of the community and the dedicated service of his staff and the fine cooperation of Ashe County's practicing physicians. These are: Doctors C. E. Miller, Ritz C. Ray, Sr., Roy O. Freeman, D. C. Jones, Jr., Ritz C. Ray, Jr., Carson M. Keys, and E. S. Kurtz. Other physicians listed as semi-retired but available for consultation are Doctors James L. Ballou, Robert L. Dickson, and C. R. Eller.

It may be true that the beautiful and efficient hospital, now recognized as successful beyond all expectations, should be set down as a community achievement, but the fact remains that the driving force behind the movement to establish it, get it going and keep it going was Dr. Dean C. Jones.

The medical profession did not find it easy to carry on in the old days. Dr. James L. Ballou, who came back from medical school to practice in the area around Crumpler, found it necessary to keep five horses to carry on his practice in an area where there were no roads.

Most of the young men aspiring to be physicians in those days arranged to "read medicine" in the office of some established physician. Only a few of them were able to go to a medical college. There are those still living who remember the home medical schools of that day. One of these was at the home of Dr. J. O. Wilcox, who lived on the North Fork of New River, near Creston.

Dr. Wilcox was an able physician and he had a big practice. Many classes of young doctors graduated from his school and became successful practitioners.

It is related of him that he had regular lecture dates and prior to his lectures he would make a round of visits to selected patients, making note of what he found and the treatment recommended. Following the lecture he would assign pupils to visit these patients, diagnose their ailments, prescribe for them and bring the report of their findings to him. With the cooperation of his patients he was able to give the young man in his "school" at least some of the experience that the young intern gets in a modern hospital today.

This, at best, was sketchy schooling and training and did not meet the standards later set up by law for the up-grading of physicians. Many of the most successful practitioners found it difficult to qualify for the practice of medicine under the new laws. There was a grand hullabaloo about it, including bills in the General Assembly and bitter fighting. Some of the "home-made" doctors came out of the melee with no licenses at all and others emerged with so-called "limited licenses."

The disturbance turned out to be a "tempest in a teapot." The old and established physicians kept their practices and the "limited license" designation did them little damage.

It is impossible to give a complete list of the physicians who have served in Ashe. A diligent effort has been made to name as many as possible and in the list that follows appear the names presently available. No effort has been made to separate the old and the new, the living and the dead. All that is claimed for this list is that it contains the names of some of the doctors who at some time lived and served in Ashe:

Doctors S. E. Pennington, Arthur L. Jones, B. C. Waddell, Fieldon L. Osborne, B. E. Reeves, B. W. Tugman, W. J. Robinson, Manly M. Blevins, Clyde Jones, Douglas Powers, Joseph Cutri, Breece Pennington, Ralph Tarnasky, A. J. Kennel, R. R. Rosen, C. Pardue Bunch, Aras B. Cox, James Butler, Rufus Jones, L. L. Long, Joe Tucker, J. Reeves Gambill, Jr., Quincy Tucker, Dr. Barton, L. C. Gentry, Dr. Houston, Robert Baker, C. R. Eller, James M. Nye, E. G. Jones, Dr. Bahnson, Everett Martin, J. L. Ballou, R. L. Dickson, George Todd Colvard, Alfred Wagg, J. O. Wilcox, Floyd Long, Thomas J. Jones, Lester L. Jones, Arthur L. Jones, U. S. G. Jones, Robert L. Waddell, I. T. Lemly, William Lawrence, Joseph Lawrence, J. B. Hagaman, J. W. Colvard, Joseph Tucker, E. F. Foster, Dr. Stauffer, Simp Osborne, Mack Anders, Oscar Black, James B. Roberts, Walter Graybeal, Billy Reece Graham, Elmer Jones, James Wagg, S. A. Perkins, Millard Graybeal, W. A. Tucker, Glenn L. Dickson, J. C. Testerman, B. O. Edwards, J. R. Gambill, James F. Gambill, A. B. Graybeal, Robert R. Garvey, Roby Blackburn, and Larkin Jones, and J. C. Gambill, dentist.

Add to this list the name of Dr. Dean C. Jones and the names of the physicians active in the practice today, as they appear above, and you have all of the names of Ashe County's physicians, living and dead, of which there is record or remembrance. It is admitted that the list above is by no means complete. The writer is grateful to Dr. Dean C. Jones, Mrs. B. W. Tugman, and others for aid in compiling it.

CHAPTER FIFTEEN

HOMEMADE REMEDIES – INHERITED SKILLS – ANCIENT SUPERSTITIONS, BELIEFS, AND CUSTOMS

I

Homemade Remedies

Those who have read Chapter 14 have doubtless wondered how Ashe County "got along" over a period stretching from 1799 to 1962 with not more than seventy-five physicians practicing their profession in Ashe in all that time. It is highly probable that there were others whose names have been lost in the mists of time, but diligent research has not revealed them.

That the work-toughened settlers of the early days were largely immune to many of the ailments that afflict their offspring of this day and time is certain, but there was doubtless need of medication for many diseases and many injuries, while others were given scant attention. For example, the common cold was generally ignored. Physicians of today admit generally that there is no cure for it, a fact that the pioneers knew more than a hundred years ago. You just keep quiet and wait it out.

The settlers brought with them, or acquired very early, a knowledge of home remedies. These were made in the pioneer kitchen, or in the back yard if the odors were too objectionable for inside the house, using the so-called medicinal roots, barks, leaves, and herbs that grew wild in the woods.

Mention has been made elsewhere of the growth of the medicinal root and herb business which brought considerable money to Ashe and surrounding counties. Manufacturers in the North and East found the chemicals they needed in the plants and there was a ready market for them, which continues to this day.

Gradually local "doctors," male and female, worked out prescriptions for various ailments. They had the courage to tackle the most formidable diseases. The following taken from the diary of a leading citizen, dated February 4, 1883, is an example:

> To cure consumption: Take a handful of heart leaves and a handful of ground ivy and a handful of wild cherry (the young growth). Put in two gallons of water, boil down to three quarts; then strain and add one-half pint of honey and boil down to one-half a quart; then take about one teaspoonful three times a day.

In the same diary is a "Cure for Diphtheria" (labeled as 'a certain cure'), which required:

> . . . crain's bill, or wild alum, chestnut oak bark, red dogwood bark, and beechwood bark — five parts of chestnut oak bark to one of dogwood, with as much beechwood as dogwood, in eight or ten gallons of water. Boil down to one gallon. Add enough wild alum to make very strong. Boil out the strength and strain. One pint will commonly cure the hardest case.

The diary gives also what is labeled as a "sure cure for cansors" [*sic*] which was as follows:

> Take one ounce of quicksilver, two ounces of aquafortis. Mix in a glass tumbler and let it stand until the quicksilver is killed. Then add one pound of lard. Stir until it becomes a salve. Then wash cansor in casteel soap and take a linen cloth and spread salve and apply once a day. It will not fail.

Still another, which was described as a prescription "that would take the soreness out" and effect what the writer called a "present cure of rheumatism," was as follows:

> Take two pounds of tobacco, six Indian turnips, twelve pods of red pepper. Put in a quart of water and boil down to one pint. Then strain it well. Then take one gill of beef-foot oil and one of spirits of turpentine, and shake every time you use it, which is three times a day. Rub well above the pane [*sic*].

Aside from these major afflictions there were set out in this diary remedies for various ailments of domestic animals. One particularly puzzling one was labeled "To cure murin (an animal disease). Three spoonfuls of buckhorn, three of pepper, three of sut, three of hen dung, three of tobacco, three eggs and a beef gall."

What disease this was and how the remedy was to be administered, the prescription does not say. Veterinarians of today do not know of any such animal disease.

There are those still living in Ashe who will remember that terrifying remedy for colds, coughs and fevers, "boneset tea." Nothing tasted worse, or was harder to take, but the concoction literally sweated your ailment out of you. That is, if you could get it down!

There were less objectionable medicines made from bloodroot, Balm of Gilead buds, blisters on balsam trees, yellow and white sarsparilla, liverwort, spearmint, pleurisy weed, poke weed, Queen Anne's lace, elder blossoms, "Pennyrile" (penny royal), "sassefact" (sassafras) root, dogwood roots and barks of various kinds. From these came various medicines and teas. Some of these were teas made from sassafras root and spice wood, which were a "must" for every family in the springtime, as they were said to "thin and purify the blood." Sulphur and molasses was a sovereign remedy for many ills, and a required medication for everybody in the spring. A particularly trying experience was the wearing of a little bag of asafoetida suspended from the neck of the victim by a string. Its odor, variously described by Webster as fetid, stinking, like garlic, etc., was supposed to ward off diseases of the respiratory organs.

Sulphur and lard, mixed in a salve, was sure cure for itch and other skin eruptions.

These were supplemented by homemade medicines, including among other remedies red worm oil, mutton tallow, onion poultice, lye poultice, burdock tea, catnip tea, fodder tea, lady slipper tea, and mullein, the last being good for man or beast.

Physicians of today and the chemists upon whom they rely for the medicines which they prescribe, will not admit that the local prescriptions above set out for those great killers, consumption (tuberculosis), diptheria, cancer, and rheumatism, would be effective today, but for a host of minor ailments they will admit that the plants listed above and others produce many of the medicines that are used today for "the ills that flesh is heir to."

It is nowhere related how the pioneers learned the virtues of these leaves, barks, roots, and herbs, but they learned and lived. J. P. Arthur, in his *History of Western North Carolina* (p. 257) says that "medicine was at a crude stage, many of the so-called cures being as old as Egypt, while others were borrowed from the Indians." Perhaps he is right, but it is easier to believe that, coming from rural areas rather than cities, the early settlers brought with them knowledge acquired by their ancestors as to the medicinal values of various roots, herbs, barks, animal fats, and the like and how they could be made into effective medications.

II

Inherited Skills

There are those who marvel at the dexterity and versatility of the young women who came from all parts of Ashe County to operate the machinery that knits hosiery, underwear, and other textile products in the plants springing up in Ashe. Many who have come into the county for the setting up of these new plants and training available workers, are astonished at their speed in acquiring necessary skills. They overlook the fact that weaving, knitting, and sewing are in their blood. It comes naturally to Ashe County young women to learn how to operate modern machines, which, while more speedy and more efficient than those ancient spinning wheels and looms operated by their grandmothers and great-grandmothers, operate on the same principles as the machines of a hundred years or more ago.

In the old days there was no exception to the rule. Every girl, as soon as she became four or five years old, began to learn how to operate the little home factory that was part of every home, no matter how humble and no matter how crude the homemade machinery she had to work with. By the time she reached marriageable age, she was adept in this phase of homemaking.

Mr. Arthur pays tribute to the men of the early days who were necessarily "handy" at every trade known at that time and needed in the area that is Ashe.

> They made shoes, bullets and powder [p. 255], built houses, constructed tables, chairs, cupboards, harness, saddles, bridles, buckets, barrels and plow stocks. They made their own axe and hoe handles, made nails on the anvil, burnt wood charcoal, made wagon tires, bolts, nuts and everything needed about the farm.

But Mr. Arthur found, after research and study, that the women of this mountain section were the true heroines and that they did most of the back-breaking labor around their cabins. Their husbands concerned themselves not at all with house work but in their spare time, if they had any, hunted or fished, or loafed around the country store or blacksmith shop. In the work classed as "women's work" were such things as feeding and clothing the children; carding wool and spinning thread for the weaving of cloth on the crude looms of the day; the making of soap from lye leached out of wood ashes and blended with animal fats; planting and tending the family garden; keeping a watchful eye on the chickens and pigs, to see that hawks and other "varmints" did not feast on them; gathering medicinal roots and herbs and curing them for market; drying vegetables and fruits from garden and orchard for winter use, and scores of other chores, not to mention that when the husband got behind with his work in the fields the wife was expected to lend a hand there also. She was handy with a hoe in the garden, which was her exclusive domain, but she was expected to be equally handy in the corn field.

Withal, the women of that era did not forget beauty and evidence of that quality was found in their improvement of skill and art in their weaving, their making of quilts, making clothing, doing needlework, and homemaking in general. Every cabin, no matter how remote, had its vegetable garden producing an abundance of food in season and providing a surplus to dry and store for the winter. Food came first but there was always room for morning glory vines, cockscomb, sweet William, pansies, zinnias, marigolds, princess feather, sunflowers, verbenas, larkspur, hollyhocks, and other hardy flowers around their homes.

Tiring of sameness in the colors available for making dresses for the females of the household, they experimented in making dyes and there was always a "dye pot" sitting on the kitchen hearth. They found that madder dyed red and burnt copperas dyed nearly red. "Walnut bark and walnut roots," says Mr. Arthur, "dyed brown, beechwood bark dyed purple, dye flowers and snuff weed dyed yellow."

Thus they brought a touch of color into their lives in the midst of hardship and adversity and the women of Ashe have kept it up to this day. They still go in for bright colors in the flower garden.

It may as well be mentioned here that the vegetation of Ashe County, including wild flowers and ferns and trees and shrubs, early attracted botanists of America and Europe. One John Frazier, a Scotchman, came into the area that became Ashe and discovered the Carolina rhododendron in 1787. One William Bertram, of Philadelphia, traversed the county in 1776. It appears that either he or John Frazier was responsible for naming the purple rhododendron "Catawbiensis." Andrew Michaux, representing the French government, came to the area in 1794 and is credited with taking back to France with him more than 2,500 specimens of trees, shrubs, and plants. Andrew's son, F. A. Michaux, followed in his father's footsteps. He came in 1802 to the mountain area including Ashe and what is now Alleghany and Watauga, and spent several years in botanical research and study. The results were included in his book, *Forest Trees of America,* which was published in 1857.

The scientific world of that day was, in fact, greatly excited over what these explorers found in the mountains of Ashe and her sister counties. There is a historical memorial in the eastern edge of Jefferson, honoring Dr. Asa Gray, noted botanist of Harvard University, who was associated with the explorers named, and who came to Ashe in 1840 and 1841.

To add to their scanty stock of domesticated flowers – scanty because seeds were hard to come by – the women did not neglect the beauties of nature that flourished in the woods and fields about them. There were the evergreens, rhododendrons, kalmia (mountain laurel), sweet bells, arrowood; the deciduous shrubs, flame azalea, elderberry, gooseberry, huckleberry, sassafras, witch hazel, sweet shrub, yellow root, hawthorn; evergreen vines, including trailing arbutus, partridge berry, galax; and the wealth of perennials, among them golden rod, wild asters, iron weed, many varieties of ferns, queen of the meadow, butterfly weed, bleeding hearts, daisies, lady slipper, may apple, anemones, Queen Anne's lace, and many others. Many of these found their way into yards and gardens of the pioneers.

II

Ancient Superstitions, Beliefs, and Customs

Various persons writing about the people of the mountains have described those living in secluded areas, such as Ashe was for the first hundred years or more of its existence, as backward and superstitious, believing in the existence of witches. It is claimed that they believed disaster was sure to follow bad dreams, eclipses of the sun, falling stars, the croaking of ravens, and the howling of dogs.

It has been said that ancient beliefs and superstitions die hard and it is true that some of them linger to this day. These are some of them concerning that universal topic, the weather: "Fire treading snow," a sound made by a wood fire and resembling the sound made by shoes in hard, dry snow. This meant snow within twenty-four hours.

The number of fogs in August determines the number of heavy snows in the following winter.

The first killing frost will come twenty-one days after the first cricket chirps on the hearth.

It will snow if the turkeys sit in the trees and will not come down, or if black clouds gather in the north in winter.

It will snow or rain if cats wash their faces.

It will be a hard winter if the leaves hang on, or if squirrels grow unusually bushy tails.

A quick cold snap is on the way if hogs pick up straw, leaves and sticks and carry them to their beds and huddle together there.

A storm is coming if rabbits take to the woods and birds get quiet.

It will rain if cats cry a lot, or if smoke hugs the ground.

It will "fair off" if spiders spin new webs and ants make new hills, or if there are red clouds at sunset.

It is probably true that the early settler brought with him, stored in his mind, many beliefs as to growing crops of various kinds. These beliefs were passed from one settler to another and gradually there grew up a system of planting and growing foodstuffs which was rigidly followed. The sun and the moon, with its phases, governed all plantings. For example, it was established that root crops must be planted on the dark of the moon and other seeds on the light of the moon and that tan bark could only be taken on the new moon in June.

Very early these beliefs about planting, harvesting, and storing crops, all governed by the sun, or the moon, or by some particular planet, were gathered by some wise person and published in a booklet named *Blum's Almanac,* printed first in Old Salem, North Carolina, 135 years ago, and still going strong. Old timers will remember that *Blum's Almanac* held an honored place in every home and the wise and prudent householder always made sure that the "sign was right" for every venture in field or garden. Any deviation from this rule, they believed, was sure to cause failure.

A feature of the early editions of the Almanac, as it is today, was bold predictions, a year in advance, as to the weather from day to day, which, upon examination, will be found to measure up in accuracy to the weather forecasts of United States Weather Bureau of today. Another carefully worked out feature is the monthly schedule of plantings and other operations in field and garden, which the North Carolina State Department of Agriculture would not change materially today.

In truth, learned men of today are finding sound, scientific basis for many of the so-called superstitions of the early days, just as modern physicians are finding merit in the remedies used to combat diseases in the days when qualified physicians were few and far between and hospitals and drugstores did not exist at all.

Customs and usages change with the passing years and in the health field it does not yet appear that human beings are much better off with drugstores on every corner filled with nostrums guaranteed to cure, than they were in the old days when all the medication you got was concocted in the kitchen or came out of the rural doctor's saddle pockets.

It should not be overlooked that springs producing mineral waters came into the picture. The most famous of these springs was

Healing Springs, originally called "Thompson's Springs" after one Captain Thompson, of Saltville, Virginia, who purchased the springs and twenty-eight acres of land around them in 1887.

The original spring was discovered one hot summer day in 1883 when Willie Barker, son of Mr. and Mrs. Eli Barker, was helping his father in the corn field nearby. His father directed him to find a spring along the branch and bring him some water. The following is little Willie's story as related by Ed M. Anderson (North Carolina Papers, University of North Carolina, in the *Charlotte Observer* of July 23, 1939):

> I went across the road and got in the branch and walked down it, stooping along under the bushes and grape vines until I felt cold water under my feet. I then commenced looking for and soon found the cold water running down the rock. I scratched around until I found a place large enough to get a cup of water for my father. He sent me back for more and said it was the best he had ever drunk.
>
> My hand and arm were very badly sore. The next morning they were almost well. We went back the next day and father worked in the spring with his hands which had sores on them. The following day they were almost well ... Then everybody got to using the water and it has cured a power of folks. ... Sometimes 300 came here in one day.

Little Willie's story was verified by his father and the fame of the water spread.

Accounts of it reached Captain Thompson, who, after investigation, purchased the springs and twenty-eight acres around them for $5,000. He saw possibilities of profit and moved to establish a summer resort. He started an advertising campaign that quickly became almost nation-wide. He described the water as "a medicinal beverage performing miraculous cures—nature's remedy for the alleviation and cure of many of the ills to which the human family is subject. Through its action in purifying the blood, it imparts health to the skin and gives clearness to the complexion—all stomach and bowel diseases yield at once to this delicious spring water—the most remarkable discovery of the 19th century."

It is related that many medical journals and newspapers all over the country treated it as a sensational discovery. Hundreds of physicians approved it and prescribed the use of the water for their patients. It became profitable commercially and at one time Mr. Anderson said that "an average of fifty wagons per day were engaged in hauling the water, put up in cases containing six half-gallon bottles of water, costing $6 per case, from the spring to Marion, Virginia, the nearest railroad station, some thirty-five miles away."

This activity continued from 1888 until 1898. The nearby Plummer Springs, developed by R. E. L. Plummer, noted educator, claimed to have the same properties as the original springs and their water was bottled and sold over a wide area.

Shatley Springs, three or four miles from Healing Springs, was discovered by Martin Shatley on land which he owned. Afflicted by a skin ailment which physicians had pronounced incurable, he happened to wash his face and hands in water from a bold spring. Within a short time he noticed marked improvement and continued bathing in the water resulted in complete cure.

As in the case of Willie Barker's discovery, news of it spread abroad and backed by the famous Thomas Dixon, of Shelby, a movement was started for a resort to be established at the site. The water is not shipped out from the spring but thousands of gallons are carried away every year by people who believe in its curative powers.

There are at least two other so-called "mineral springs" in the same area, these being the Foster Springs and Eureka Springs, both famous locally for the fine qualities of their waters.

In fairness to those who praised the waters of Ashe and professed to find healing in them, be it said that they submitted their claims to government chemists and invited them to examine the bottled waters and to come to Ashe and analyze the water as it came from the earth. In case of the Healing Springs water, Henry Froehling, analytical chemist, showed the chief property of the water to be bromine and arsenic. He found that the water contained sodium, calcium, lithium, copper and zinc carbonate, sodium and potassium chloride, sodium fluoride, iodide and forate, ferrous sulphate, and silica.

The promoters of Shatley Springs also brought government

chemists into the picture who found in Shatley Springs water most of the chemicals they found at Healing Springs, plus ammonium and radium.

The owners of Healing Springs, in a twenty-four page booklet, called their water "the most remarkable discovery of the 19th century; truly the Eighth Wonder of the World." On the back cover of their booklet, which would be called a "brochure" today, they named thirty-two diseases and boldly challenged the medical profession "to report any of these diseases they fail to cure with this wonderful water." It is not recorded that Shatley Springs owners have claimed as much.

Another change that has come over life in the mountains of Ashe and adjoining counties is the change in speech. Only a few years ago, writers from the North and East professed to find in the area a group of people talking in the language of Chaucer and Shakespeare and in the border English and Scotch dialects of Queen Elizabeth's day. Prior to 1900 there was some basis for their claims, because Ashe was really isolated, shut off from the world. Fifty miles were a "far piece" and few traveled that distance. Fewer ventured as far as a hundred miles.

But not today. Radio and television have wrought a change. By their magic, Nikita Khrushchev, Harold Macmillan, General De Gaulle, John F. Kennedy, and a host of others come right into the mountain homes. Listening to outsiders, local and national, the people are losing the so-called "mountain brogue" and it will soon be heard no more. The Ashe County mountaineer is not ignorant about world happenings; he knows about state, national and international events as they occur. Much of this passing show he sees and all of it he hears, leaving to local newspapers and the telephones that now go everywhere in Ashe, the spreading of purely local news and gossip.

Old-time dances, frolics, and hoedowns that drew all of the people, young and old, are known no more. To the music of phonograph records or radio the boys and girls dance the twist and other modern dances, while the old-time dances, with banjo and fiddle music, are things of the past.

CHAPTER SIXTEEN

SECRET ORDERS IN ASHE—JEFFERSON LODGE A. F. AND A. M.—JEFFERSON LODGE NO. 38 I.O.O.F.—ROTARY, LIONS, AND WOMAN'S CLUBS

I

Secret Orders in Ashe

The citizens of Ashe, from the beginning, were moderately temperate people, in so far as the use of alcoholic liquors was concerned, but there was constant demand for corn whiskey. Scores of thrifty citizens set up stills and made their own, generally with a surplus left over to sell to their thirsty neighbors. There was no stigma attached to the man who made whiskey and sold it. In those days there was no law against making or selling alcoholic liquors. In the chapter relating to the county government there is frequent reference to the granting of licenses to sell liquor in Jefferson, and the licensees were the county's leading citizens, among them such men as Colonel George Bowers, long-time senator from Ashe and for forty years or more probably Ashe's leading citizen.

Consequently, the making and selling of whiskey was entirely respectable and those who opposed it were regarded as public enemies. Ashe County was a free-drinking county and wanted so to remain.

There is evidence of record that the authorities sought to reduce drunkenness and rioting around places of worship and that the churches themselves, particularly the Baptists and Methodists, asked for the incorporation of various church sites, limiting drinking within one-half or one mile of the church. In addition the churches passed rules requiring their members to "maintain order at their still houses," under pain of expulsion. The movement in the churches to get at the root of the trouble by declaring it sinful for a member to drink alcoholic beverages and grounds for expulsion from the church, was slow to prevail. Many devout Baptists and Methodists, despairing of ever getting action from their churches, joined in a secret society known as the Sons of Temperance. This caused quite an uproar. For example, at the 1851 meeting of the Mountain Baptist Association, the assembled delegates voted to recommend to the churches that they "exclude from their membership any member, or members, who join any Division or Order of the Sons of Temperance."

It is worth noting here that the Baptists took the recommendation seriously, as indicated by their quick expulsion from the church of the two leading ministers of the Association, Rev. Aaron Johnston and Rev. Richard Gentry. The latter's son, Captain W. H. Gentry, leading Baptist layman and Clerk of Superior Court of Ashe, met a like fate. Incidentally, these good men found their way back into the Baptist denomination by organizing the famous Old Bethel Baptist Church whose members held similar views on the liquor issue.

The Baptists were to be disrupted again when a secret society known as the Union League began operating in the county during the closing years and immediately after the War Between the States. The decree of the Mountain Baptist Association was invoked and there was bitter fighting in the local churches. In the end there was a clear-cut division and a new association to be known as the Mountain Union Baptist Association came into existence. From it came the Union Baptist denomination of today.

As early as 1848 there had been determined opposition to the Masonic Order. The Baptists finally came around to accepting the Masonic Order, the Knights Templar, the Sons of Temperance, and similar orders at what it termed a "general convention" in September, 1867. On that occasion they passed this resolution:

"That the benevolent institutions of the day should not be any bar or test of fellowship but all should be free to sustain or not to sustain, as they may choose."

A Baptist historian, who spent many years studying the records of this era, came to the conclusion that church opposition to the Sons of Temperance and other "secret orders of the day," was due in the main to their conviction that the orders named, particularly the Sons of Temperance and the Masons, were taking over the duties of the churches and lessening their influence on the lives of men. They were opposed to excessive drinking and carousing and disorder at the still houses of their members and eventually decreed expulsion from church for second offenses. They came to look upon these orders as allies.

This did not, of course, affect the relation of the churches to the other secret order named above, the Union League, which was purely political. The Baptists and Methodists of that day did not consider the League a "benevolent institution."

II

Jefferson Lodge, A. F. and A. M.

It was inevitable, of course, that the Masonic Order, everywhere strong in North Carolina, should come to Ashe County. It came in a period of storm and stress and when the county was at its lowest point. The War Between the States was dragging its weary way to a finish that everybody knew would be disastrous to the South. With religious organizations divided to the point where brother fought brother and with a population split asunder by political differences, there were those who thought that a great organization such as the Masons might serve as a bridge between warring factions and that unity might again be achieved.

So far as the record shows, there was no Masonic Lodge in Ashe prior to the War Between the States. There were, however, many Masons in the county. Who thought up the idea of establishing a Masonic Lodge is not known, but this group of Masons signed a petition to the Grand Lodge of North Carolina for a dispensation for a lodge to be known as the "Jefferson Lodge." The dispensation was duly granted by the Grand Master of North Carolina Masons and the first meeting of record was held on December 8, 1863. The original minutes book for the new lodge was found in the library of Major U. S. G. Bauguess and, by gift of his widow, Ruby Pennington Bauguess, is now among the archives of the Grand Lodge of Masons at Raleigh. The first page is devoted to the first meeting and lists officers pro tem as follows:

Abram Weaver, worshipful master; J. D. Wilson (Liberty Lodge No. 45) senior warden; J. P. Waugh, junior warden; James Wagg, secretary; J. S. Forrester (Liberty Lodge), junior deacon; Blake Ballew, senior deacon; B. G. Willis (Friendship Lodge No. 9, Charleston), tyler.

It is recorded that Rev. Abram Weaver, Rev. John Prather, and James P. Waugh signed as members of the lodge. As to the others who had signed the petition for the dispensation, there is an entry that "the way was not open for the other brethren to connect themselves with this Lodge at this time."

Presumably they signed subsequently but there is no mention of it. The first entry on page two tells of petitions for the degrees of Masonry from Major Quincy F. Neal, Dr. E. F. Foster, Rev. Squire Trivette, and J. N. Ballew. At this meeting the by-laws of Perseverance Lodge, No. 59, Plymouth, N. C., were adopted for the lodge "until different provisions are made."

The new lodge moved fast. For example, Major Quincy F. Neal was an entered apprentice on December 8, 1863. On December 9, he and Dr. E. F. Foster became master masons. On December 10, Major Neal was serving as junior deacon and Dr. Foster was tyler of the lodge. Before the month was out Major Neal had become secretary of the lodge and soon was to be master.

The lodge also speeded up the conferring of degrees to qualified citizens home from the war on furlough and it was not at all uncommon to find it recorded that all three degrees were conferred upon an applicant in one day. Among these were Colonel George W. Ray, Captain William H. Gentry, Colonel James M. Gentry, John S. Lapp, Johnson Perkins, Captain A. B. Duvall, James M. Duvall, Colonel George W. Reeves, David Hines, Lieutenant Poindexter Blevins, H. H. Ray, James N. Duff, Melvin Campbell, J. B. H. Ray, F. Hardin, Captain S. L. Blevins, N. G. Turner, Hiram Baker, B. P. Snitzer, and John W. Wayman.

Ministers found the lodge and the teachings of Masonry to their liking and many joined. In every case their membership fees, which totaled $20, were refunded. Among the early ministers becoming members were Abram Weaver, Squire Trivett, James E. Neese, Thomas Duncan, William H. Weaver, David Smith, H. P. Waugh, T. F. Smith, and John Prather.

The last recorded meeting in this original book of the minutes of the Jefferson Lodge was dated August 12, 1864. Dr. E. F. Foster was recorded as the master of the lodge; S. Trivett, senior warden; J. P. Waugh, junior warden; J. E. Foster, junior warden; R. T. Hardin, senior deacon; N. H. Waugh, junior deacon; N. H. Weaver, tyler; and William Weaver, secretary.

Just what happened to the lodge is a matter of conjecture. The little group had undoubtedly found the going difficult. Major Quincy F. Neal, who had been most active in the lodge from the beginning, found it necessary to resign his post as secretary on March 24, 1864. The situation, statewide and locally, worsened from day to day and by August 12, 1864, the date of the last recorded meeting, the people generally must have reached bottom, and it is not strange that the lodge ceased operations. That there were members of the lodge who wanted to carry on, in spite of all the difficulties, is indicated in this valedictory, inscribed with pencil inside of the back cover of the minute book:

"And finely [*sic*] this lodge went to nothing from the cause of soriness [*sic*] in its membership."

This notation was signed by B. H. Neal, elder brother of Major Quincy F. Neal. He was later to become active in the rejuvenated lodge, which was built on the ruins of the old, but at the time he was disgusted with what was happening and expressed that disgust forthrightly.

With the end of the war the men who had set up the lodge and had accepted its teachings could think of no finer influence for the wartorn county than their old lodge. They set about re-establishing the lodge on a stronger basis. Exactly when the lodge was again set up is not known but early in 1866 they were fully organized, and had been duly christened as Jefferson Lodge No. 219. Their first return to the Grand Lodge of North Carolina was dated December 3, 1866.

Because out of this membership list came many of Ashe County's leaders for most of the century that has followed, their names should be recorded here. It will be noted that many of those who were members of the original group were listed on the return for December 3, 1866. The list follows:

Officers: Q. F. Neal, worshipful master; W. V. Armfield, senior warden; James P. Waugh, junior warden; D. S. Windle, senior deacon; L. C. Gentry, junior deacon; D. B. Murchison, secretary; S. C. Waugh, treasurer; J. E. Foster, tyler.

Members: Dr. E. F. Foster (past master), S. Trivett, William Weaver, James Wagg, James Gentry, J. M. Carson, Alex McEwin, Alex Dickson, G. W. Reeves, David Worth, N. H. Waugh, William Gentry, G. H. Hamilton, Hiram Baker, John Baker, James M. Duvall, A. M. Duvall, Thomas Duncan, E. McCarroll, Johnson Perkins, David Smith, Jackson Blevins, Joshua Smith, W. H. Campbell, H. C. Ray, Melvin Campbell, John Whittman, G. W. Ray, Carlton Blevins, J. W. Boman, J. M. Duff, W. S. Watson, R. T. Hardin, Calvin Brinegar, David Dickson, Frank Harden, Martin Hardin, John Hardin, James Blevins, James Liggins, A. Wyatt, H. W. Hardin, J. W. Shepperd, C. W. Osborne, S. Pennington, Asa Weaver, A. C. Southerland, David Black, A. B. Cox, J. F. Greer, J. B. Parsons, James Oliver, Jacob Graybeal, James Wilson, R. R. Pierce, J. H. Park, L. C. Stump, B. H. Neal, William Baker, Samuel Jones, A. P. Wilson, W. L. Bryan, C. A. Greer, J. W. Todd, W. H. Wilcoxen, A. M. McEwin, Horton Dougton, G. W. Houck, W. Thompson, W. P. Thomas, James Garvey, Rev. Aaron Johnston, James Eller, G. W. Burkitt, Gid Weaver, B. F. Baker, Simeon Graybeal, Poindexter Blevins, George W. Price, James Smith, Jr.

The report showed that the lodge had experienced a busy year, with eight initiated, thirteen passed, eleven raised, four rejected, one expelled and seven withdrawn by demit. Three entered apprentices awaited the conferring of other degrees, these being C. K. Miller, John McEwin, and James W. D. Weaver.

Space forbids the listing of the good men who found opportunity for service in Lodge No. 219 and its successors. There were periods when interest waned and the lodge dragged along. On March 26, 1933, its charter was "arrested" by the Grand Lodge. Helton Lodge

No. 594, at Sturgill's post office, was chartered January 1, 1911, and for a time Jefferson Masons served in this lodge. They later were chartered as Ashe County Lodge No. 671, dated April 18, 1934. On June 13, 1944, Ashe County Lodge No. 671 was consolidated with Helton Lodge No. 594, which was given the title of Ashe County Lodge No. 594. The lodge had its hall at Jefferson until it was moved to West Jefferson. Below will be found a list of the men who have served Lodges 219, 671, and 594 as masters and as secretaries. The first named for each year is master of the lodge and the second is the secretary. Owing to confusion during periods of inactivity and other periods when the process of consolidation was under way, there may be errors in exact dates of service. It is believed, however, that the list is approximately correct.

Some of the officers are mentioned in the old original minute book of Lodge No. 219 but the list which follows is based upon official returns to the Grand Lodge of North Carolina which are on file in the record room of the State Masonic Headquarters in Raleigh, and they begin with the year 1866. The list follows:

1866: Quincy F. Neal, worshipful master, D. N. Murchison, secretary; 1867: same officials; 1868: J. W. Todd, J. E. Foster; 1869: same officials; 1870: J. W. Todd, Q. F. Neal; 1871: J. W. Todd, J. P. Waugh; 1872: J. W. Todd, L. C. Gentry; 1873 to 1889, inclusive: no record; 1890: Joseph W. Todd, H. A. Currin; 1891: Joseph W. Todd, C. E. Graybeal; 1892-1893: no record; 1894: Walter Williamson, A. C. McEwin; 1895-1896: same officials; 1907: J. W. Todd, W. H. Gentry; 1908: John P. Shepherd, Quincy F. Neal; 1909: E. J. Johnson, W. S. Carner; 1910: J. D. Baker, J. E. Walters; 1911: J. D. Baker, Charles S. Neal; 1912-1913: same officials; 1914: W. E. McNeill, W. R. Bauguess; 1915, W. A. Williams, R. F. Gentry; 1916: W. E. McNeill, Charles S. Neal; 1917: W. E. McNeill, W. R. Bauguess; 1918: same officials; 1919: W. A. Williams, R. L. Ballou; 1920: Charles S. Neal, R. L. Ballou; 1921 to 1923; Charles S. Neal, T. K. Luther; 1924: W. R. Bauguess, T. K. Luther; 1925: William B. Austin, Joe Worth; 1926: T. B. Grayson, S. C. Blackburn; 1927: E. A. Ray, S. C. Blackburn; 1928-1929: W. L. Hughes, S. C. Blackburn; 1930: W. J. Bare, S. C. Blackburn; 1931-1932: W. J. Bare, E. D. Barr.

There is a notation in the records that the charter of Lodge No. 219 was arrested on March 26, 1933. It is evident that efforts were made after that date to keep the Lodge alive. There are records on file of reports made after that date, as follows:

1934: W. A. Campbell, worshipful master, and Gwyn B. Gambill, secretary; 1935: Ira T. Johnston, C. S. McNeill; 1936: no change of officers; 1937: T. B. Grayson, Troy I. Jones; 1938: no change; 1939: William B. Austin, W. D. McMillan; 1940: T. B. Grayson, William B. Austin; 1941: W. D. McMillan, Ira T. Johnston; 1942: Ira T. Johnston, W. B. Austin; 1943-1944: R. H. Holt, W. B. Austin.

Helton Lodge No. 594, Sturgill's post office, was chartered January 1, 1911. Eventually it was to retain its number and take into membership the Masons of the two other lodges. Its officers were:

1911: W. M. Stuart, worshipful master, M. F. Kerby, secretary; 1912: W. M. Stuart, A. H. Perkins; 1914: no change in officials; 1915: J. M. Ballou, M. F. Kirby; 1916: no change; 1917: L. M. Sturgill, M. F. Kirby; 1918: F. M. Goss, M. F. Kirby; 1919: R. G. Weaver, M. F. Kirby; 1920: J. M. Sturgill, M. F. Kirby; 1921: Baxter Blevins, M. F. Kirby; 1922: C. M. Dickson, M. F. Kirby; 1923: R. V. Pennington, Bryan Pennington; 1924: R. E. Farmer, R. V. Pennington; 1925: Bryan Kirby, R. V. Pennington; 1926: R. E. Farmer, A. D. Testerman; 1927: John Ballou, A. D. Testerman; 1928: J. M. Ballou, A. D. Testerman; 1929: Bryan Kirby, R. E. Farmer; 1930: Lester M. Sturgill, R. E. Farmer; 1931 to 1933, inclusive: J. C. Blevins, R. E. Farmer; 1934-1935: W. R. Francis, R. E. Farmer; 1936: J. O. Blevins, R. E. Farmer; 1937: R. G. Weaver, R. E. Farmer; 1938-1941: Bryan Kirby, J. O. Blevins; 1942-1943: L. M. Sturgill, J. O. Blevins.

The consolidation above referred to came into full force and effect in 1944, when the lodge became Ashe County Lodge No. 594. J. K. Hunter became master of the lodge and Ira T. Johnston, secretary. Since that time, officers have been:

1945: Gwyn P. Little, worshipful master; Ira T. Johnston, secretary; 1946-1948: Forest L. McMillan, James H. Payne; 1949: Sharpe S. Shoemaker, James H. Payne; 1950: Wiley Dean McMillan, James H. Payne; 1951: Gwyn P. Little, James H. Payne;

1952: Raymond G. Childers, James H. Payne; 1953: Forrest L. McMillan, Hamilton Gentry; 1954: Joseph M. Graybeal, J. Harvey Payne; 1955: William Grady Burgin, Wiley D. McMillan; 1956: Forrest McMillan, Willard F. Bumgarner, Jr.; 1957: J. K. Hunter, James H. Payne; 1958: Wiley D. McMillan, James H. Payne; 1959: James M. Graybeal, James H. Payne; 1960: Spencer Lee Bryan, James H. Payne; 1961: Sharpe S. Shoemaker, James H. Payne.

III

Jefferson Lodge No. 38, I.O.O.F.

Another secret organization to invade Ashe was the Independent Order of Odd Fellows. This grand old order had its beginning in England in the eighteenth century. It came to America in 1819 and found a fine field for its activities. It now has grand lodges in every state in the union and a membership in the neighborhood of five million in 20,000 lodges.

According to Larry P. Colvard, secretary of Jefferson Lodge No. 38, who has been an active member of the Lodge for thirty-eight years, there were several lodges of Odd Fellows in Ashe in the early days but all have disappeared except the Jefferson Lodge. Jefferson Lodge was organized by E. Leff Wagoner of Alleghany County, a great teacher and leader of men, and was chartered on August 21, 1908.

The charter members were: Dr. B. O. Edwards, Dr. J. C. Testerman, Harry Proctor, E. L. Tucker, J. L. Thompson, Edwin J. Johnson, W. L. Luther, W. E. Gentry, Felix Barr, Quincy F. Neal, E. A. McNeill, David Burkett, and Jacob Burkett.

During its more than fifty-four years of service Lodge No. 38 has had more than 500 members. Secretary Colvard is unable to find complete records of membership or of officials from year to year but he has vivid recollections of these outstanding citizens who have been members of Lodge No. 38:

Thomas C. Bowie, Robert C. Barr, T. E. Parker, M. M. Blevins, C. S. Neal, D. B. Todd, Phillip L. Shore, Wade E. Eller, J. D.

Stansberry, David Weaver, U. S. Grant Bauguess, W. H. Jones, R. Austin Jones, Roy R. Badger, Paul Jones, Bernard B. Graybeal, and Zeb V. Weaver.

Jefferson Lodge at the present has seventy-five members. They are active in civic affairs but their particular interest is in the welfare of children of deceased Odd Fellows. They support a Children's Home at Goldsboro, rated as one of the top institutions of its kind in the State. Here the children are not only fed and clothed but have the advantages of a good graded school and an excellent high school. Following graduation from high school, children are free to leave. If they want college and can qualify for entrance, the order will find a way for them to go.

IV

Rotary, Lions, and Other Clubs

One of the finest developments in the last fifty years has been the growth of the so-called civic clubs. They were designed to further the development of sense of brotherhood, as in the fraternal orders, but they went further by building organizations that represented every profession and every type of mercantile and industrial activity. Most of these clubs limited membership to one representative for each profession or business, in the beginning, but by splitting up occupations into divisions calling for specialists, it became the custom to accept more than one from a classification.

The first of these clubs to come to Ashe was the Rotary Club of the Jeffersons, which was organized on April 4, 1938, and became Club No. 4686 of the 188th district of Rotary International. The charter night program was held on May 26, 1938 at the old Healing Springs Hotel, recently (1962) destroyed by fire.

The first officers were: president, Lavern Johnson; vice-president, Ed Barr; secretary, Dean McMillan; and treasurer, Ed M. Anderson. The charter members were the following:

Ed M. Anderson, William B. Austin, Ed Barr, Russel W. Barr, Rufus W. Colvard, Roy R. Badger, T. G. Duncan, Wade E. Eller, Gwyn Gambill, Glenn E. Graybeal, Dr. J. K. Hunter, J. B. Hash,

A. B. Hurt, Dr. E. D. Jones, Lavern Johnson, Ira T. Johnston, Clint Jarvis, Mont E. Little, W. Dean McMillan, Joe F. Neal, Gwyn B. Price, C. J. Rich, John Reeves, Sharpe Shoemaker, Eugene F. Scott, Langdon L. Scott, Guy Snow, J. Lester Segraves, and Wick G. Vannoy.

The new club wasted no time in getting under way. It instituted a program of good works that has continued to grow throughout the years. Elsewhere is recorded the fact that the first organized group in Ashe to plan for an Ashe County hospital was the Jeffersons Rotary Club. It also assumed responsibility for supporting and treating crippled children. The club later broadened its service to poor and needy children in Ashe by aiding in their education. Every year for many years the club has had two worthy students at Appalachian State Teachers College at Boone, not on a student loan basis, but with all of their expenses at college paid by the club.

The club can point with pride to its work in helping to establish the county's fine tobacco, vegetable, and livestock markets and to its unselfish service in many other community undertakings, regardless of what individual or organization started them.

The club's present officials, serving for 1962-1963, are president, Frank James; first vice-president, Eugene Sloop; second vice-president, Dana Tugman; secretary-treasurer, A. B. Addington; and sergeant-at-arms, Dewey Davidson. Directors for the year are Larry P. Colvard, Don Francis, Frank James, Tom Roberts, Ardell Sink, Eugene Sloop, and Dana Tugman.

As everybody knows, and particularly those who have served as president of a civic club, the load that a club president carries from his induction into office until the last fall of his gavel is trying in the extreme. Much depends upon the president and for that reason the names of the past presidents of the Jefferson Rotary Club are here recorded:

Laverne Johnson, 1939; Ed M. Anderson, 1940; Langdon Scott, 1941; Dr. J. K. Hunter, 1942; John Reeves, 1943; Ira T. Johnston, 1944; Gale McMillan, 1945; Sharpe Shoemaker, 1946; W. B. Austin, 1947; Hoyt Wood, 1948; Dean McMillan, 1949; Jake Caudill, 1950; Tom Duncan, 1951; Jim Graham, 1952; Jim Owens, 1953; Thomas Johnston, 1954; Austin Jones, 1955; Gilbert Ward,

1956; Coleman Payne, 1957; Wick Vannoy, 1958; Orville Jackson, 1959; Phil Eckman, 1960; Ed Barr, 1961; and Larry P. Colvard, 1962. It is interesting to note that of the twenty-four past presidents here listed all are living except Ed M. Anderson, editor and owner at the time of the *Skyland Post* and other newspapers.

Noting that the club's membership has rarely exceeded thirty during its twenty-five years of service, one wonders how the club could have achieved so much in such a short time. The answer may probably be found in the kind of men that make up the club's present membership, which is as follows:

A. B. Addington, Bill Ashley, F. L. Barker, Jr., Ed Barr, J. D. Boone, James Church, Hal Colvard, L. P. Colvard, Dewey Davidson, Phil Eckman, Don L. Francis, Glenn Graybeal, Glenn Hentschel, Earl Hightower, Dr. J. K. Hunter, Dean Hurley, Gale Hurley, Orville Jackson, Frank James, Ira T. Johnston, Thomas Johnston, Dr. D. C. Jones, R. A. Jones, Dean McMillan, Gale McMillan, C. M. Payne, J. Harvey Payne, John Reeves, Tom Roberts, Dale Shepherd, Sharpe Shoemaker, Eugene Sloop, Ardell Sink, Dana F. Tugman, Lawrence Tyson, Herman Vanderford, and Wick Vannoy.

Another civic club to come to the county is the West Jefferson Lions Club, organized on the same plan as Rotary and appealing particularly to younger business and professional men. This club was chartered in 1949 with twenty-three members. It grew rapidly and at last accounts had a membership of fifty-four. For the past ten years its average membership held at forty to forty-five.

Lions International concerns itself with sight conservation and problems of the blind. The West Jefferson Lions Club has not neglected this international objective but has contributed heavily to the local needs of the blind and those threatened with blindness. The club's contribution to this cause exceeds $2,887. Through its "white cane project" the club raised $2,428 for the State Association for the Blind. In addition, for this period the club has raised $532 to be distributed to the blind of Ashe along with Christmas packages, $192 for the State Eye Bank, $200 for the Lions Boys' Home, $1,025 for the general Community Development program, and $514.36 for needed equipment at Ashe Memorial Hospital.

The West Jefferson Lions Club as presently constituted, is headed by Charles E. (Chuck) Gardner and the secretary is A. D. Goodman. A list of the members follows:

Lee Absher, Dale Baldwin, James Baldwin, Talmage Baker, Don Blackburn, Gwyn Bowers, George Burgess, Rexford Campbell, Tom Cockerham, John D. Cook, Hugh Crigler, Carl Crouse, Bob Davis, Kyle Dickson, James Gambill, C. E. Gardner, Jack Garner, John Gentry, Don Goodman, A. D. Goodman, Eugene Gray, G. C. Greene, Edwin Houck, Gene Hunsucker, Tommy Johnson, Wayne Johnson, Worth Knox, Larry Linker, Henry Lum, Vernon McCarthy, John McIntyre, Bill McNeill, R. C. Miller, Rex Morton, Lester Overbaugh, Woodrow Rogers, E. V. Searcy, Bill Shatley, James Paul Sheets, Urcle Sheets, Douglas Shelton, Bill Spencer, Darwin Walker, A. B. Weaver, C. E. Welsh, W. C. Wells, Don Wiles, Robert Woodie, and Gwyn Yates. Honorary member, Colonel Arthur L. Fletcher; members-at-large, John Christy, Bill Francis, Roy Freeman, John McGuire, Charles Rhinehart, and Edwin Roland.

No story of civic service in Ashe County would be complete without some account of the activities of Ashe County women. From records available it has not been easy to tell the story.

Ashe County is blessed with two active woman's clubs, the Ashe County Woman's Club which came into existence in 1929 and made its first report to the North Carolina Federation of Woman's Clubs in 1931, and the West Jefferson Woman's Club, which filed its first annual report to the State Federation in 1943.

The first president of the Ashe County Woman's Club was Mrs. James Allen of West Jefferson, who held office until 1933. She laid a solid foundation for the new club, reaching out beyond the town limits of West Jefferson to bring into the club's membership progressive women from all parts of Ashe County. In this she had the backing of Miss Ruth Reeves and a pioneer group that established early in the game the fact that the woman's club was not a social organization but a working outfit, ready to serve town and county in every undertaking for the public good.

One of the club's outstanding achievements was the establishment in 1932 of the Ashe County Public Library. Leading in this project were Mrs. Chessie Neal and Miss Ruth Reeves. Mrs. Neal became the librarian and held that position until 1962, when she resigned. The Ashe County Woman's Club continued its sponsorship of the library, paying rent on the quarters it occupied, until the project was taken over by the county and the State.

Among the other projects the club sponsored were the annual sale of T. B. seals for many years; assistance in sponsoring the Ashe County Fair; conducting a health program for schools, including medals for athletic achievements; placing scales in all of the schools to keep check on weights of the children; providing scales and other equipment for the Ashe Memorial Hospital; participating actively in the Rotary Club's work for crippled children; providing Christmas gifts for crippled children and for patients at the State T. B. Hospital at Black Mountain; beautification of homes in town and county; establishing a little park with seats and tables for the use of shoppers in West Jefferson; and furnishing a room in the Community House.

For these and other activities too numerous to mention the Ashe County Woman's Club won state and national federation citations.

Early in the 1940's the club was abandoned, or practically so, and no report was made to state headquarters. The club was reorganized in 1943.

So far as available records go the Ashe County Woman's Club has been headed by the following women:

Mrs. James Allen, 1929-33; Mrs. R. H. Stone, 1933-35; Mrs. Clifford Ray, 1935-36; Miss Nancy Ruth Reeves, 1936-38; Mrs. L. G. Johnson, 1938-39; Mrs. A. B. Hurt, 1939-40; Mrs. Ed M. Anderson, 1940-41; Mrs. B. L. Hafer, 1943-44; Mrs. A. B. Hurt, 1944-45; Mrs. John Wilkins, 1945-46; Mrs. W. D. McMillan, 1946-47; Mrs. Sam Diggs, 1947-49; Mrs. Claude Auman, 1949-50; Mrs. E. R. Sturdivant, 1950-52; Mrs. W. D. McMillan, 1952-53; Mrs. John Hardin, 1953-54; Mrs. John Rhodes, 1954-56; Mrs. W. D. McMillan, 1956-57; Mrs. Leonard Shepherd, 1959-60; Mrs. Robert Pugh, 1960-61; Mrs. E. R. Sturdivant, 1961-63; and Mrs. Nell Bare, 1963.

In 1943 the West Jefferson Woman's Club came on the scene.

It was organized under the direction and leadership of Mrs. Ed M. Anderson, who was its first president. The club has experienced steady growth through the years and has gained steadily in power and influence. Its presidents from 1943 to the present have been as follows:

Mrs. Ed M. Anderson, 1943-45; Mrs. Jennings Rader, 1945-47; Mrs. J. A. Reeves, 1947-48; Mrs. Gale McMillan, 1948-51; Mrs. Clyde Jones, 1951-53; Mrs. W. E. McNeill, 1953-56; Mrs. Robert Draughan, 1956-58; Mrs. Elizabeth Barlow, 1958-62; and Miss Blanche Pugh, 1962-63.

This club has to its credit many fine achievements, including an area award winning community clean-up program; the beautification of grounds and interior of the Community Building and the beautification of roadsides; the furnishing of a room at Ashe Memorial Hospital; the backing with cash donations and much hard work of the building of the County Health Center; the sponsorship of Brownie Scout troops; the support of annual chest X-rays and cancer tests; the promotion of public safety programs; the support of the Ashe County Trading Post project; the active support of the County Welfare Department, and service in every area where help was needed.

Probably the most spectacular of its many projects has been the annual "Autumn Leaf Excursion," a trip by rail from West Jefferson to Abingdon, Virginia, over the Virginia-Carolina Railroad, which is staged in October, when the leaves are at their peak in coloring. Every year hundreds of people come to Ashe to make this exciting journey. It has brought to the club treasury many hundreds of dollars, all of which has gone into the club's treasury for public service. Credit for this project goes mainly to Mrs. Ed M. Anderson, who has been in charge of it from the beginning.

It should be mentioned here that Mrs. Anderson has had notable success in woman's club work. Her activity in Ashe has not waned, and her fame has spread beyond the bounds of Ashe County. She was chosen District Vice-President of the North Carolina State Federation in 1943. This achievement was followed by her election to the presidency of the North Carolina Federation of Woman's

Clubs. She was later elected treasurer of the General Federation of Woman's Clubs and chairman of the budget committee of the General Federation of Woman's Clubs, which positions she still holds (1963).

Looking to the future, the Jefferson Woman's Club is undertaking, as its newest project, the organization of a Junior Woman's Club.

CHAPTER SEVENTEEN

LAWYERS AND LEADERSHIP – ASHE COUNTY NEWSPAPERS

I

Lawyers and Leadership

It is axiomatic in North Carolina that no county makes appreciable gains in its economy without an enlightened and dedicated bar to furnish wise leadership and sound advice. The lawyer is depended upon not only to represent citizens charged in criminal courts but to help with legal entanglements in civil courts and out. Generally the practicing lawyer acquires a grasp of his county's needs and what is best for its citizens, and without regard to fee or other remuneration, he becomes sponsor and spokesman for needed reforms and improvements. In North Carolina, long before there was ever a chamber of commerce, a civic club, or a merchants association, the lawyer was looked to for leadership in every movement for community uplift and betterment.

For many years Ashe County, because of its isolation, suffered from lack of lawyers. From the records available it does not appear that Ashe had even one resident practicing lawyer as late as 1843. There were plenty of lawyers from Salisbury, Statesville, Lexington, and other towns who rode the circuit with the presiding judge and were available for trial of civil and criminal cases, but they were not citizens of Ashe and, therefore, not greatly concerned about county progress and development. The United States Census of 1840 reports no lawyer resident in the county.

The Ashe County Bar was asked to make a study of records at the county courthouse and elsewhere, and compile a list of the lawyers who had been born in Ashe, who had come to Ashe after being licensed, or who had practiced their profession in Ashe from offices in adjacent counties. The compilation, which appears below, required the examination of North Carolina Supreme Court Reports up to 1962. The list has been studied by every member of the Ashe County Bar and has their unanimous approval. It is given without change.

II

Ashe Bar List

"For a number of years after the establishment of Ashe County in 1799, attorneys were licensed by the County Court of Pleas and Quarter Sessions upon presentation of a certificate of qualification signed by two judges of Superior Court. The applicant for license 'read law' in the office of a licensed attorney and was examined by two judges. There were no law schools.

"There is record in the minutes of the Court of Pleas and Quarter Sessions that Robert H. Burton was licensed by the Court to practice in Ashe in 1806 and Burton McQueen in 1807. The minutes state that Thomas McGimsey 'resigned as attorney' in 1807 and was 'succeeded by James Maxwell as prosecuting attorney.' Sanders Donaha was licensed in 1807 and elected county attorney. Henry Young Webbs was admitted to the Ashe County bar in 1809. Adolphus L. Eulin was admitted to the bar in 1812 and became solicitor of the Court. W. W. Alexander, licensed in 1828, became solicitor of the Court the same year. Anderson Mitchell, later to become a Supreme Court judge, was practicing in Ashe in 1828.

"That practice in the courts and the need of legal services must have continued unabated through the years that followed is certain, but our researchers found a gap, so far as the records are concerned, in the licensing of attorneys until 1866 when this function was taken over by the Supreme Court of North Carolina.

"Two attorneys who were licensed prior to 1866 and who became leaders at the Ashe County Bar immediately following the War Between the States were Captain Joseph W. Todd and Major

Quincy F. Neal. Both had outstanding war records and both were destined to see distinguished service as citizens and as lawyers for many years.

"The following is a list of the attorneys who were practicing in the courts of the county, had offices in the county, or were natives of the county when they obtained license to practice law, together, where available, with the year they were licensed:

"W. Horton Bower, Caldwell, 1870; W. C. Fields, Alleghany, 1873 (served in the North Carolina State Senate); George W. Bower, 1873; W. W. Barker, Wilkes, 1879; John T. Morphew, 1880; Rufus A. Doughton, 1880 (served for many years in North Carolina General Assembly, Speaker of the House and Lieutenant Governor); W. C. Newland, 1881 (served in General Assembly and as Lieutenant Governor); H. M. Wellborn, 1881; W. B. Councill, 1881 (Superior Court judge); S. E. Morphew, 1883; T. J. Hackler, 1884.

"E. F. Lovill, 1885 (served several terms in State Senate); T. B. Finley, 1885 (for many years a Superior Court judge); S. Porter Graves, 1887 (for many years solicitor); J. F. Spainhour, 1887 (served as solicitor); H. L. Greene, 1887; M. L. Mott, 1888 (served as solicitor); W. R. Lovill, 1888 (served in State Senate); R. N. Hackett, 1888 (member of Congress); James J. Perkins, 1888; E. Spencer Blackburn, 1889 (member of Congress).

"J. Hayden Burke, 1892; Moses N. Harshaw, 1895 (served as solicitor); James W. McNeill, 1895; J. B. Councill, 1896; T. H. Jones, 1897; G. L. Park, 1897 (served in General Assembly); George P. Pell, 1897 (served as Superior Court judge and member of the North Carolina Corporation Commission); Floyd C. Cox, 1898; Robert H. McNeill, 1898 (Republican candidate for Governor and for Supreme Court justice); T. C. Bowie, 1901 (served many terms as member of North Carolina House of Representatives, as Speaker of the House and as Superior Court judge); R. L. Ballou, 1903 (served as member of State Senate).

"A. E. Tilley, 1904; John C. Bower, 1905 (served many years as solicitor of his district); Arthur L. Fletcher, 1907; Donald B. Todd, 1910; Charles B. Spicer, 1910; Alfred J. (Fred) Fletcher, 1910; Walter R. Bauguess, 1912; Albert T. Bare, 1913; Carlisle W.

Higgins, 1914 (served as member of State Senate, as solicitor, as U. S. District Attorney and now [1962] Justice of the Supreme Court of North Carolina); Cyrus H. Smithdeal, 1914; Ira T. Johnston, 1917 (two terms in General Assembly, where he was chairman of the House Committee on Education; presently [1962] senator-elect for his district).

"William B. Austin, 1919 (served in both houses of North Carolina General Assembly, member of State Board of Agriculture and State Board of Conservation and Development); William Thomas Graybeal, 1923; Paul G. Parsons, 1923; R. Floyd Crouse, 1923; Paul Swanson, 1931; Major U. S. Grant Bauguess, 1931; Zeb V. Gambill, 1932; Athel P. Phillips, 1932; T. C. Bowie, Jr., 1933; Sidney B. Gambill, 1932; Robert H. Gambill, 1936 (now [1962] serving as Superior Court judge); Carmon J. Stuart, 1938; Thomas S. Johnston, 1949; Wade E. Vannoy, Jr., 1950; Brice B. Gambill, 1951; Allen Worth, 1952; Robert Phillip Haire, 1961.

"Other attorneys who practiced in the county and were known to everybody, were Romulus Z. Linney, noted Republican leader and member of Congress; Worth Folger, who had an office in the county at one time; J. Earl McMichael, solicitor; Harvey A. Lupton, present (1962) solicitor; Allen H. Gwyn and Walter Johnson, who served many years as solicitors of the district and are now (1962) Superior Court judges; Joseph M. Prevette, who had an office in Jefferson for some time during the 30's.

"Two natives of the county who have had distinguished careers at the bar and otherwise are Colonel Arthur L. Fletcher, for many years Commissioner of Labor of North Carolina and a veteran of both World Wars, and his brother, Alfred J. (Fred) Fletcher, a prominent attorney in the city of Raleigh. Colonel Fletcher had an office in Jefferson at one time.

"Noted lawyers, who have appeared in cases in Ashe and are remembered with pleasure by the older members of the Ashe County Bar, are Cyrus B. Watson, of Winston-Salem; Charles B. Aycock, of Goldsboro, Governor from 1901 to 1905; O. Max Gardner, who was Governor from 1929 to 1933 and who was appointed, just prior to his death, as ambassador from the United States to the Court of St. James, Great Britain."

This completes the contribution of the Ashe County Bar to the Ashe County history and one is constrained to marvel at their modesty. Major John H. Wheeler, of Lincoln County, who was State Treasurer from 1843 to 1845, wrote a fine *History of North Carolina,* which was published in 1850. He lamented the fact that he did not have space to give credit to the members of the legal profession for their contributions to the welfare of community, state and nation, but he expressed the hope that "a history of the bench and bar of North Carolina, will at some period, be published. Its members have been, at all periods, the firm friends of popular rights, and ready defenders of the privileges of the many against the encroachments of the few. They, as a body, are remarkable for their assiduity, fidelity and *poverty*."

Major Wheeler, in the section dealing with lawyers and judges, told an amusing little story, which had an Ashe County connection, though he does not say so. He credits the story as taken from the *Greensboro Patriot* "of many years since" and says that it took place in a western county.

He said that James R. Dodge of Lexington, Clerk of the North Carolina Supreme Court at the date of the history's publication, but who at the time of the incident, was prosecuting attorney in his district, which included Ashe, was making a speech. Three idle lawyers, named Hillman, Swain, and Dews, got their heads together and composed this "Epitaph on James R. Dodge, Esq., Attorney at Law":

Here lies a Dodge, who dodged all good,
And dodged a deal of evil,
Who after dodging all he could,
He could not dodge the Devil.

When Solicitor Dodge had finished his speech and resumed his seat, he found the epitaph in front of him. He read it hurriedly, turned the sheet over and wrote "Another Epitaph on Three Attorneys":

Here lie a Hillman and a Swain,
Their lots let no man choose;
They lived in sin, and died in pain,
And the Devil got his Dews.

Some of the older inhabitants may remember Peter J. Earnest of the Helton Community, who lived to be eighty or more, and was the son, or grandson, of David Earnest, who was Clerk of Court from 1808 to 1818. He claimed to have been in the courtroom at Jefferson when this incident occurred.

II

Newspapers in Ashe

Another uplifting influence that was slow in gaining fast hold in Ashe was the press. For many years legal notices that had to be published in newspapers of local circulation were printed in newspapers of Salisbury and other towns. In comparatively recent years, the only paper of wide circulation in Ashe was the *Alleghany Star*, published at Sparta. For many years, and until he followed Hon. R. A. Doughton to Raleigh to serve as his assistant in the North Carolina Department of Revenue, the *Star* was edited by A. S. Carson.

There were many attempts to establish newspapers in Ashe and many failures. Probably the paper to last the longest, excepting the present county newspaper, *The Skyland Post*, was the *Jefferson Recorder*, owned and edited by T. W. Adams. It flourished in the late 1890's and the early 1900's. Following the death of Mr. Adams the *Recorder* was taken over by Walter C. Johnston and Melvin Campbell, who had started a newspaper at West Jefferson known as the *Northwestern Herald*. Johnston, a well-known teacher, became editor and Campbell was publisher. In 1922 D. Clinton Nance came into the picture and acquired title to both papers. He sold them to Ruth Reeves, able daughter of Dr. and Mrs. B. E. Reeves of West Jefferson, who set up the county's present excellent newspaper, *The Skyland Post*. She ran it successfully until other interests made it difficult for her to carry on and she sold it to Mr. and Mrs. Ed M. Anderson.

The Andersons, young and energetic, and fresh from the School of Journalism at the University of North Carolina, built a sizeable newspaper and radio station empire in western North Carolina, with *The Skyland Post* as its basis. Most regrettably, Ed M. Anderson died at the peak of his powers, but *The Skyland Post* continues to grow, with his widow, Stella W. Anderson, as editor and owner.

Typical of the newspapers that came and went, leaving a bare trace of their existence, was the *Republican Patriot* which existed for a few months in 1900 and 1901. It was set up by Robert H. McNeill, young Republican lawyer from Wilkes County who was later to acquire statewide and national importance in his party. It is famous because one of its first editors was James Larkin Pearson, of Moravian Falls, widely acclaimed as the poet laureate of North Carolina.

Mr. Pearson now lives at North Wilkesboro. He is eighty-three years old, but he has vivid recollections of his first venture into the newspaper business, which began at the end of his thirty-five mile walk across the Blue Ridge, carrying a cardboard suitcase and ended the same way six or eight months later, with his trudging the same weary thirty-five miles back to Moravian Falls.

Pearson's account of the equipment the impecunious young McNeill (who, by the way was his cousin) had gotten together for publishing a newspaper, was illuminating. It had about half enough body type, old and worn, and almost no display type. Its press was an ancient Washington hand press, a fugitive from some junk heap, which broke down every other week. Pearson says they missed about as many issues as they printed. However, he credits this ill-starred venture with getting "printer's ink on his fingers." Here he learned to set type and eventually he achieved marked success as a newspaper man and national recognition as a poet, with many books of poetry to his credit. He still sets type, and prints and binds his own books in his own shop.

CHAPTER EIGHTEEN

ASHE COUNTY AND THE W.P.A. – PUBLIC HEALTH AND W.P.A. – COUNTY SCHOOLS AND W.P.A. – ASHE COUNTY WOMEN AND W.P.A.

I

Ashe County and the W.P.A.

Ashe County, famed for its capacity for taking punishment and standing up under it, found the so-called "great depression" of the 1930's hard to endure. In previous brushes with hard times, the people had been able to tighten their belts and carry on, but in this one they found that the resources that they had been able to draw on in the past were gone. For example:

As everybody knows, Ashe County with close to 4,500 farms, has never been a farming county. In 1930 more than eight per cent of the so-called farms had ten acres of land or less, and 14.6 per cent of the farms had less than twenty acres. Over forty per cent had twenty to fifty acres. Frugal and thrifty Ashe County farmers supplemented the income from their few acres by raising cattle on that part of their land which grew grass in abundance but was unfit for cultivation. The depression killed the cattle market, as well as the hog, sheep and poultry markets.

It had been established custom for many Ashe farmers to go to the coal mines of Virginia, West Virginia and Kentucky, after their crops were "laid by" in the summer, returning home for spring planting. The bottom dropped out of the coal market, and mining almost completely stopped. Thus a second source of income disappeared.

As has been stated elsewhere, hordes of timber buyers had swarmed into Ashe on the heels of the Virginia-Carolina Railroad, which came in 1914. Their assault on the vast timber resources of Ashe had been ruthless and devastating. Ashe County farmers themselves had aided in destroying the county's forest resources. The price they got for their timber was a pittance but the sawmills that came with the timber men furnished employment for hundreds.

By 1930 the damage had been done. The landscape was dotted with abandoned, decaying sawmills. As far as Ashe was concerned, the devastation of her forests had been completed in approximately sixteen years, and such remnants as remained were not marketable. So, another source of income was closed.

Very quickly unemployment became a problem in Ashe. County leaders, both men and women, became interested in the federal government's assault on unemployment, and formulated plans for worthwhile public improvements that could be done under the Works Progress Administration. These were approved and without undue delay, W.P.A. was operating in Ashe. As has been related elsewhere, Ashe County citizens have never believed in accepting charity from any source but in accepting pay from W.P.A. for work for the common good, they found no charity, and were not ashamed. They went to work gladly.

The men and women who directed the program in Ashe were wise in choosing projects that could serve the public interest best and win acceptance and approval from the general public. They were wise, too, in making generous use of state agencies in their projects.

For instance, Ashe County's long felt need of all-weather roads came in for immediate attention. The W.P.A. officials did not work alone. They invited the State Highway and Public Works Commission to lead the way and the end result was 416 miles of improved road in Ashe. Very little of the money allocated to highway work was wasted because it was spent under the watchful eyes of competent state highway officials, who made every dollar count.

Major attention was given to farm-to-market roads, but main arteries of travel were not forgotten. Included in this class were

U. S. 221 and North Carolina Highway 16. The effect of these improvements in lifting the county out of the mud, in making roads passable for school buses and for transportation of all kinds, served to give impetus to the good roads program which did not die when W.P.A. funds were no longer available.

A monument to the W.P.A. workers, who labored to build it with pick, shovel, wheelbarrow and dynamite, is the road to the top of Mt. Jefferson. The State is presently finishing their work with modern road building machinery, widening the road which the W.P.A. built and hard surfacing the road to the park area at the summit. The State is completing this job, and when the road is finished and hard-surfaced, any type of car will find the trip to the top of Mt. Jefferson, with all of its rugged beauty and 5,000 feet of elevation, a very easy undertaking.

The W.P.A. did not confine its interest to rural areas. It undertook to provide the town of Jefferson with sidewalks and in West Jefferson it helped with the construction of water mains and sewage treatment plants. When the project was completed West Jefferson had four and three-fourths miles of sanitary sewers with 489 service connections and seventy-two manholes. (Report of *The Charlotte Observer*, May 25, 1941, North Carolina Collection, University of North Carolina Library.)

The W.P.A. did not confine itself to roads, streets, and sanitary facilities but went further in the effort to improve transportation by building nine bridges over rivers and creeks and 306 culverts. A mile of road drainage pipe was laid.

II

Public Health and W.P.A.

In the field of public health and welfare the Works Progress Administration did probably its finest service in Ashe. The present health and welfare setups, which have been mentioned elsewhere and are well-nigh perfect for a rural county, might have come to Ashe County eventually, but without the impetus given by the W.P.A. they might not have come for many years.

For example, the present very efficient, very beautiful, and very useful Ashe Memorial Hospital owes its beginning to the W.P.A. The hospital and its other buildings built since W.P.A. days, required the finishing touches put on them by private contributions, public funds, and grants from various agencies, but the W.P.A. started actual construction, and it was done without the charge so frequently leveled against this great federal agency that precious federal funds were being wasted. The derisive term, "boondoggling," invented by would-be comics to heap derision on the heads of W.P.A. workers, who were alleged to be lazy and to spend most of their time leaning on their shovel handles, never at any time applied to Ashe County W.P.A. workers. Almost invariably they gave a day's work for a day's pay, and the result was real achievement.

The W.P.A. forces, advised and directed by state highway personnel, constructed a hard surface highway to connect the hospital with two of the county's main highways.

Another W.P.A. activity, which was widely criticized and much laughed at, was the project aimed at abolishing the outdoor open privy, or "back-house," admittedly a source of danger to health. The W.P.A. reported to *The Charlotte Observer* that the campaign up to June 1, 1941, had resulted in the construction of 246 sanitary privies in Ashe. These, serving as models, have served to greatly reduce the number of dangerous, old-fashioned privies. Hundreds of new homes had water piped in, and plumbing and septic tanks installed. These, added to the sanitary privies built by W.P.A. and the many others built after the W.P.A. pattern, make rural life reasonably safe from ailments caused by faulty sanitation.

Ashe County Schools and W.P.A.

The road improvement helped to bring about a notable acceleration in the consolidation of schools. With the main highways made into all-weather roads and many secondary roads greatly improved, it was possible to operate more school buses and opposition to consolidation mentioned elsewhere disappeared. W.P.A. workers built or improved schools at Crumpler, Lansing, Grassy Creek, and

Riverview. All of these schools were purely rural. None of them had running water and sewage facilities. W.P.A. workers provided them.

West Jefferson was provided with a large addition to its school plant, not to mention the handsome community building which the W.P.A. helped to build. Playgrounds were provided at many schools and two gymnasiums were built. The W.P.A. may properly be credited with the movement, which has spread over the entire county, to improve school grounds by planting shrubbery, and by grading and building stone retaining walls.

Adding the figures for improvements provided under W.P.A. to June 1, 1941, the total reached was $1,655,564. The major part of this went into the pockets of the W.P.A. workers and right out again for food, clothing, medicines and medical attention, and other necessities of life. This cycle meant, of course, a shot in the arm for the local economy, and merchants, landlords, farmers, and many others who were supplying human needs were benefited, too.

Ashe County Women and W.P.A.

The W.P.A. did not confine itself to providing work on worthwhile projects for men. It sought to enlist the help of Ashe County women. There was pressing need for clothing in Ashe and elsewhere, and the W.P.A. found eager response when it proposed to set up sewing rooms in Ashe and there manufacture clothing for the needy. Many of those who reported for this service already knew how to turn out acceptable work, but there were a great many who did not know and needed to be taught. They were found to be apt and quick to acquire the necessary skills, which were to serve them well in the established sewing rooms and to make them more efficient housewives after the project closed.

According to the W.P.A. statistician, the women of Ashe as of June 1, 1941, had produced 71,630 garments, all made to specification. These clothes were turned over to the County Superintendent of Public Welfare and from there they went to other needy adults, school children, and babies in homes where there was no money to purchase such apparel.

The women did more than sew and learn to sew. They found a genuine need of good books in school libraries, and nobody to assist boys and girls in the use of such books as were available. They sought to remedy this in as many schools as they could find qualified personnel to do the work and were able to report that they had furnished library workers for Fleetwood High School, Healing Springs High, Riverview High, Riverview Elementary, Virginia-Carolina High, and West Jefferson High.

Finding that many children came to school hungry and brought no lunches with them, the women moved to establish lunchrooms in seventeen schools. They proved immediately successful and they were soon serving an average of 27,136 lunches per month. For those who could not pay, the W.P.A. "picked up the tab" to the total of 12,208 lunches. Others, totaling 7,144 lunches, were paid for by produce from the farm. The remainder were paid for in cash. The serving of lunches at schools was something new at the time. Today every school in the county has its lunchroom.

The operations of W.P.A. in Ashe did not cease on the dates above referred to but continued for a considerable period. The facts set out above are considered sufficient to give the reader some idea what W.P.A. meant to Ashe County at a critical time in its history.

CHAPTER NINETEEN

A NEW CASH CROP–MOUNT JEFFERSON STATE PARK – CONFERENCE AND RECREATIONAL CAMPS

I

A New Cash Crop

Those who have read the preceding chapters of this brief history of Ashe County have been made aware of the county's greatest problem. In agriculture, industry, mining, and other pursuits, Ashe has little or nothing to offer its young men and young women who graduate from high school or college. For the young women, new industries have offered work opportunities for some, but job openings for men, young and old, are practically nonexistent. Naturally the young men seek work opportunities outside of Ashe and when they find them they take a sizeable portion of the county's female population with them. That is why the county's population shrank more than 2,000 between 1950 and 1960, and why the population, despite the county's high birth rate and its low death rate, has gained only 187 over its population of 1900.

Dr. Dean W. Colvard, loyal son of Ashe, now president of Mississippi State University, says that the downward trend in population may be expected to continue and may even be accelerated. He has found the same situation in Mississippi, where rural populations are shrinking and urban populations are growing. He sees little hope for bettering the situation except by strenuous efforts to bring into Ashe industries that would offer attractive employment for both men and women. As Dr. Colvard points out Ashe has many attractive assets on which it is getting no satisfactory returns, and which might prove immensely helpful in solving this problem. Backing up the words of Dr. Colvard, the United States Soil Conservation Service, interested in rural development, has come up with the suggestion that cattle, sheep, hogs, poultry, tobacco, wheat, corn, fruit, and vegetables are not the only farm crops that are marketable. The farmer is neglecting his best crop, which is recreation.

It may seem a trifle odd to speak of recreation as a farm crop, but very definitely there are in every part of Ashe County what the Soil Conservation Service calls "recreational potentials" which have real cash values and may be developed by individual farmers, a group of farmers, or a community. These include sports centers, riding stables, natural trails, picnicking and camping grounds, fishing waters, beaches, tennis courts, vacation cottages, vacation farms and selling recreation land or recreation use leases. If the individual, group or community lacks the funds to get such projects under way and cannot get the necessary money from local banks, the law under which the Soil Conservation Service operates makes it possible to get low cost federal loans in amounts up to a $60,000 maximum for any one project.

The Soil Conservation Service is enthusiastic about this new farm product. Its study and research have established the fact that Americans are traditionally outdoor people. They are ready and willing to pay liberally for the privilege of hunting, fishing, swimming, boating, and picnicking. The Soil Conservation Service says that they are presently spending in excess of twenty billion dollars per year for these things and that by 1980, which is not so far away, there will be a crying need for twenty-three million more acres for such uses. Already, in many parts of North Carolina farmers are finding recreation a new and profitable sideline and the idea is beginning to take hold in Ashe.

It is reasonable to expect the idea to grow in Ashe because of its unmatched summer temperatures, its scenic beauty and the abundance of sparkling clear water in its springs, creeks, and rivers. The county has close to 4,000 farms but its tillable acres per farm, while highly productive, are not impressive. Much of its acreage is rough and rugged and unfit for any crop except grass, but the "recreational potentials" that the Soil Conservation Service is writing about are everywhere in Ashe.

Mr. R. M. Dailey, state conservationist of the Soil Conservation Service, finds that "every day more and more families are turning to the countryside for the recreation they cannot find in the big metropolitan areas."

In a recent story in the Raleigh *News and Observer*, Mr. Dailey predicted that this ever growing demand will provide new jobs for rural people and new sources of income, while providing for both rural and urban people opportunities for relaxation and enjoyment.

There is plenty of evidence that Ashe is waking up to the importance of this new "farm crop" and is moving intelligently to fill its part of this need.

II

Mount Jefferson State Park

As the preceding chapters have disclosed, the records show that the citizens of Ashe have always been road conscious and road hungry. They have known that there was beauty all around them but that this beauty was lost to the rest of the world and would so continue without the setting aside of suitable areas for public parks and the building of good roads to make them accessible. It is worth telling here, in such detail as is available, how Ashe got its first state park.

Many an Ashe County citizen and many a visitor to Ashe, dating back to the beginning of the county and before, had been awed by the grandeur of Negro Mountain, now Mount Jefferson, and had dreamed of the day when the mountain would be easy of access to the very top. In 1827 Dr. Elisha Mitchell of the University of North Carolina climbed to the top of the mountain and in his diary recorded that he had never seen anything more beautiful than the view from the big rock near the top. For more than a hundred years after Dr. Mitchell's visit, the summit remained inaccessible, except by difficult footpaths and dim trails.

With the coming of the federal agency known as the W.P.A.,

whose various activities in Ashe are recorded elsewhere, a group of forward-looking citizens, nearly all of them from West Jefferson, set up a project for the construction of a road with W.P.A. funds to the top of the mountain. When the matter was presented to the W.P.A. it was turned down because it was adjudged to be illegal to spend public funds on roads leading to privately owned property.

The group did not quit. They saw in the project an undertaking that would bring many visitors to Ashe and contribute much to public welfare. H. C. Tucker, pioneer businessman and many times mayor of West Jefferson, and J. B. Hash, one of the county's leading school men, who owned considerable land on the top of the mountain, came forward with a donation of twenty-six acres to the town of West Jefferson for a public park. (See *Book of Deeds*, U2, p. 269, Office of the Register of Deeds of Ashe County.)

With this deed in hand the group went back to W.P.A. officials and this time the project was approved. It provided for a scenic highway to be built by hand labor. The road built was adequate for a time but in the hard days of the thirties there was no money for maintenance and it quickly became impassable for motor vehicles.

In the General Assembly of 1941 the group asked the State to accept the acreage at the top of the mountain as a state park. The effort failed but again the group did not quit. By great good fortune, William B. Austin, who had been active in the project from the beginning, became a member of the North Carolina Department of Conservation and Development. They resurrected their plan to have the State accept the acreage as a state park. This time they were successful. The State Forestry Service, which had a fire tower on a ten-acre tract, the State Highway Commission, and the State Park Service of the Department of Conservation and Development, all joined in the undertaking. The State Highway Commission appropriated $10,000 to repair the road, the town of West Jefferson deeded its acreage to the State and the State Park Service moved in to set up picnic tables and other conveniences. The new park seemed to be on its way. It was officially designated as a "recreation area," but not yet a park.

There was consternation among the backers of the park when on January 26, 1955, the Department of Conservation and Development adopted new standards for state parks, by the terms of which 400 acres was set as the minimum acreage for a state supported park. At the time the park had the twenty-six acres donated by Tucker, Hash, and others and ten acres around the fire tower, a total of thirty-six acres. This was a long way from the 400 acre minimum and the situation looked hopeless. In the first place, there were no funds available to purchase additional land and no certainty that the acreage that could be bought would fit in with the thirty-six acres already state owned.

The State Park Service was asked to send its engineers to survey the area and determine if the total acreage suitable for a park was available. They came, made their surveys, found that there was suitable land available and departed, leaving to the local group the matter of securing title to the property needed. Under the law, the State could not provide funds for the purchase of land for parks.

Very quickly a campaign was gotten under way to secure donations of land and money to provide the 400 acres of land required.

The landowners were contacted first and results were highly pleasing. The following landowners made donations:

John McFerrin, Jr., Allen Martin, Trustee, 14.00 acres; John M. Hudson, Barbara O. and Charles C. Burrus, 11.75 acres; Wade E. Vannoy, 35.00 acres; G. W. Taylor, 5.80 acres; Town of West Jefferson, 131.00 acres; Ashe County Memorial Hospital, 10.40 acres; Fred N. Colvard, 66.20 acres; providing a total of 274.15 acres.

Negotiations with other landowners in the area brought offers from the following:

H. C. Tucker (or Frances Tucker), tract, sixty-two acres for $700; the Cam Shaw tract, seventy-eight acres for $600; the J. B. Hash tract, twenty-four acres for $600.

The prices were agreed upon, after negotiations, and the group was faced with the task of raising cash to pay for the 164 acres plus cost of survey and other expenses. That they succeeded beyond their expectations was indicated by this statement from one of the leaders in the movement, who said, "This is one of the most satisfying experiences we have ever had. Every person we called on for a donation, save one, responded for the full amount requested."

The names of those who contributed cash to this fund are as follows:

J. Ivan Miller, Mr. and Mrs. Earl Davidson, Miss Ruth McNeill, Shirley Ham, Melvin Campbell, Northwestern Bank, First National Bank, Worth Gentry, J. Gwyn Gambill, Mr. and Mrs. R. H. Koontz, Mrs. C. A. Segraves, Tom Duncan, J. B. Hash, J. A. and A. R. Little, Mrs. Elizabeth Miller and Billie M. Parsons, R. L. Parrish, Dr. R. E. Ray, Phillip Eckman, C. B. Graybeal, Parker Tie Company, G. F. P. Chevrolet Company, Ashe Motor Company, Ashe Hardware Company, Bare-Little Company, Barr Insurance Agency, Burgess Furniture Company, Dr. Pepper Bottling Company, W. G. Little, Robert McNeill, B. E. Ray and E. A. Ray, Jr., Lloyd Witherspoon, W. J. Hardware Company, Rhodes Furniture Company, G. B. and W. D. McMillan.

Out of the negotiations with the State Park Service came a new name for the park and for the mountain on which it is located. Not a member of the State Park Service, or of the full Conservation and Development Department, favored the old name, Negro Mountain State Park, nor did they favor the retention of the old name for the mountain. They envisaged hosts of tourists in the future who might get the idea that the park was segregated and would stay away, thinking it was for Negroes only. They wanted it clearly understood that it was a public park, open to everybody.

Eventually someone came up with the suggestion that it be named Mount Jefferson State Park and that Negro Mountain thereafter be named Mount Jefferson, honoring the two towns at its base and Thomas Jefferson, the great President for whom they were named. This met with general approval. Changing the name of a mountain after a century or more is not accomplished overnight, but there is evidence that the new name is gaining in favor and will eventually meet with general acceptance. Already an attractive motel has been named the Mount Jefferson Motel, and the two Presbyterian churches at Jefferson and West Jefferson, and the one at Obids, have united in a single church, the Mount Jefferson Presbyterian Church.

III

Conference and Recreational Camps

There is abundant evidence that the boundless opportunities for the establishment of summer camps for church groups, Boy Scouts, Girl Scouts, and other organizations, are being generally recognized and these organizations are beginning to move forward along lines suggested by Dr. Dean Colvard and others.

Of these undertakings the oldest and first to come was the Blackburn Memorial Summer Camp, at Todd, established by members of the Holiness Church, but open to the whole world. Yearly it grows in usefulness.

The most ambitious venture is the mountain camp and conference grounds of the great Moravian Church in the southern edge of Ashe, just off State Highway No. 18. The camp is unique, in that it is located on a high mountain, where it looks down upon many miles of the Blue Ridge Parkway and has a lake, tennis courts, baseball diamonds, and other facilities, including cabins, conference halls, and other structures. At last accounts more than $350,000 had been spent on the project and plans of the church called for expansion that would bring the total cost above $500,000.

It is related that the Moravians spent seven years searching for the ideal location for their summer camp and conference site. They might have spared themselves time and trouble if they had read the diary of the famous Bishop Spangenberg who passed that way in 1753 and who pronounced the area as attractive scenically, its water the best and purest, and all conditions conducive to good health. All that information, and more, was available to them in the records of the Moravian Church at Winston-Salem.

The Moravians began holding summer conferences and camps for their young people in 1931. They quickly outgrew rented camps at Winston-Salem and at Brevard and by 1953 they had decided to build their own. It was not until September, 1955, that they found what they wanted. It was situated near Laurel Springs. The original tract of 110 acres, owned by the Woodie family, was purchased for $12,000. Adjoining tracts were purchased, bringing the total acreage to 260 and the total cost of land to $49,000.

The Moravians are looking forward to great growth and they have space for expansion. The State has completed a hard surfaced road from Highway 18 to the camp site.

Another venture that promises to be eventually as attractive as the Moravian undertaking is the Elk Shoals Camp of the Methodist Church four miles from West Jefferson. It is a venture of the North Wilkesboro District of the Western North Carolina Conference of the Methodist Church. The property was purchased from Mr. and Mrs. J. T. McLaurin of Jefferson. It comprises 235 acres and is known as the "Old Bart Marsh Place" at Boggs. It came into the possession of North Wilkesboro District by deed dated May 15, 1958. It is situated on the banks of the South Fork of New River and is almost surrounded by the river. It is in the area where the bends and turns of the river confounded Bishop Spangenberg in 1753 when he was seeking to find a way out of the mountains by following the course of the river. He gave up, declaring in his diary that the river "ran now east, now west, now north, now south, in fact to every point of the compass."

Planning for expansion sure to come, Mr. Bernard B. Graybeal and his associates acquired seventy-five acres of land adjoining the camp acreage, to be available when needed. This acreage has already been added to the original tract, making a total of 310 acres, with three miles of river front.

The Ashe County Methodists who started the movement for the camp did not go in for wide publicity. They selected the site for the camp and got developments under way. Wisely they let the camp site sell itself to leaders of the Methodist Church in the North Wilkesboro District and outside. They made it clear from the beginning that the camp would not be available to the North Wilkesboro District alone, but, to quote Rev. Garland F. Stafford, superintendent of the North Wilkesboro District, "the grounds will be open to serve Christian people of all denominations, to the limit of its facilities."

Among the Methodist leaders who accepted the invitation to come and see the camp site and its surroundings, was Dr. Nolan B. Harmon, bishop of the Charlotte Area of the Methodist Church, who pronounced it "beautiful for situation" and called for "church support for this church ministry in God's great outdoors. It is a project of which we may well be proud."

Dr. Lee F. Tuttle, superintendent of the Winston-Salem District, described the camp as "located in one of the most beautiful settings I have ever seen—ideal for Christian camping purposes."

Dr. Walter J. Miller, superintendent of the Charlotte District of the Methodist Church, pronounced it a camp site of unusual beauty. He said: "Truly it is one of the most beautiful spots in Western North Carolina—the most suitable place for a camp I have seen anywhere."

Interest in the camp grew faster than anyone had anticipated and only recently the big Winston-Salem District of the Methodist Church came into the picture. By agreement the North Wilkesboro and Winston-Salem Districts have formed what they call a "Bi-District Committee" to take charge of the matter. This committee is composed of leading members of the two districts, with the following officers:

Dr. Taylor Dodson, Winston-Salem, chairman; Win Edwards, West Jefferson, vice-chairman; Rev. John Christy, Jefferson, secretary; Bernard B. Graybeal, West Jefferson, treasurer; Rev. Herman F. Duncan, North Wilkesboro, superintendent of the North Wilkesboro District; Rev. Frank Jordan, Winston-Salem, superintendent of the Winston-Salem District.

Other members of the Bi-District Committee serving on important sub-committees, include Earl Graybeal and Win Edwards of West Jefferson on the Development Committee; Wayne Shepherd of West Jefferson, chairman of the Finance Committee; Dr. J. K. Hunter, West Jefferson, on the Publicity Committee.

Every section of the two big districts is represented and there appears to be vast enthusiasm for the undertaking everywhere. The Bi-District Committee has studied the situation and has set up a fifteen-year plan of development for the camp in five stages. Eventually there will be a central building, housing for the staff, infirmary, recreation hall, winterized cabins, shower baths, picnic shelters, caretaker's home, pump house, small group lodges, family and outpost camping areas and other conveniences.

Work on the project is being rushed so that some of its facilities may be available in 1963. Two picnic shelters have been completed by the West Jefferson and Bethany Churches and other facilities will be added. Two six-day camping sessions were set up for July of 1963 and other activities may be scheduled. By the end of the fifteen-year period, or before, it is expected that the camp will be fully equipped for year-round use, with housing, recreation grounds, and equipment adequate for the two districts and other districts that may desire to come in on the project.

There is now under way a movement to build one or more dams on New River. There are admirable dam sites on both North Fork and South Fork, not to mention the possibilities on the creeks and branches flowing into New River.

A shining example of the possibilities along this line is the recreation area owned by the Ashe County Fish and Game Club, and open to the public in season. Sixty acres were donated to the club by R. G. Lassiter in 1951 and the club has constructed a three-acre pond. The acreage is on the Ore Knob mine property which was owned at the time by Mr. Lassiter. The pond was stocked with trout by the State Wildlife Resources Commission which looks after it and restocks it every year.

What has been done here can be done throughout Ashe and establish the county as a fisherman's paradise. The possibilities of what would follow the installation of one or more big dams on New River, either North or South Fork, or both, stagger the imagination.

Many will remember the proposal several years ago to build a dam on South Fork and divert part of its flow to the Yadkin River by way of a tunnel through the Blue Ridge. The plan called for the establishment of hydro-electric facilities on the Wilkes County side of the mountain. The proposal met with opposition from Virginians and West Virginians, all the way from the Virginia line to the Ohio River, and the project was abandoned. Present plans call for no diversion of waters—only for their temporary use. Such dams would provide for fishing, boating, and other sports and bring thousands of summer visitors to Ashe.

It is worth noting that on the mountains around the Moravian Camp and the Methodist Elk Shoals Camp, the building of summer homes is under way. Business and professional men, educators and ministers of all faiths, are building summer homes. Many are planning for future development along the line, among them being many Ashe County men and women who went away in their youth and are coming home again.

IV

Tourists and Summer Visitors

A crying need of the present day and one that will increase with the development under way and in prospect, is for hotels, motels, and tourist facilities.

A great loss to the county recently has been the destruction by fire of the quaint and beautiful Healing Springs Hotel at Crumpler. It was built in the early 1870's and for years its fine mineral waters and its many surrounding attractions kept its rooms full every summer. At the time of its destruction it was owned by Dr. and Mrs. R. L. Dickson. Only the cabins which were built along the creek to take care of the hotel's overflow, remain. It is not expected that the hotel will be rebuilt, but it is hoped that a motel may take its place, utilizing the cabins remaining.

Other facilities for taking care of the tourist business of the county are the following:

Shatley Springs, Crumpler. This resort has a large number of comfortable cabins and a dining hall. Its waters, like the waters at Healing Springs, are said to have medicinal value. It is owned by Frank McMillan.

Little Phoenix Lodge, two miles north of Jefferson, owned by Mrs. Frances Thomas McMeekin-Kerr. It has a rebuilt and reconditioned log house, more than 100 years old, as the central unit, with cabins for guests along Phoenix Creek.

Mount Jefferson Motel, at Jefferson, beautifully furnished, swimming pool and other facilities. Owned by Mr. and Mrs. Roland H. Koontz.

Highlander Motel, Jefferson, owned by Mrs. Elizabeth V. Miller.

Cherry Hill Coffee Shop, Glendale Springs, just off the Blue Ridge Parkway, owned by Mr. and Mrs. Louis J. Yelanjian.

Rancho Restaurant, Jefferson, owned by Mr. and Mrs. Dallas Williams.

Bo-Jo Restaurant, between Jefferson and West Jefferson, owned by Bobby Walker and Johnny Payne.

Colvard Hotel, West Jefferson. Owned by Mr. and Mrs. R. W. Colvard.

General Adams Inn, Glendale Springs. Owned by Thomas C. Bowie, Jr.

There is reason to believe that other facilities will be needed and that they will be provided.

There is an abundance of skilled woodworkers and handicraft workers, male and female, to provide stock-in-trade for many projects, such as the very attractvie Ashe County Trading Post on the edge of the Blue Ridge Parkway at Glendale Springs. Its stock of needlework, handmade toys, wood carvings, and home-canned fruits, vegetables, and meats, draws much trade during the tourist season. There is room for other establishments of this type at Jefferson, West Jefferson, and elsewhere in the county.

With intelligent advertising, the great flow of tourist traffic may be tapped at other points on the Blue Ridge Parkway and some may be induced to explore other parts of the county. With its twenty-eight miles of Blue Ridge Parkway, Ashe is in favorable position to share in the flood of tourist dollars that flows up and down the Parkway and is increasing every year. Eventually the tourists and the casual travelers will learn that there is more to Ashe County than magnificent scenery and they will do more than just speed through. They will seek motels, inns, and hotels for extending their visits and many will seek places to establish summer homes in what Ashe County natives reverently call "God's Country."

In Conclusion

Thus endeth the effort of the writer to tell the story of the beginning, growth and present status of Ashe County. There are those who may criticize the allocation of so much space to recent developments and future prospects and projects not yet fully realized but definitely on the way. Recently a friend, reading a chapter of the manuscript, objected to part of it on the ground that it was too recent. Said he: "This is not history."

To him the writer stated that as he saw it, everything that had happened prior to the moment of their conference was history, and, as a matter of fact, all worthwhile movements under way, whether to be completed today, or tomorrow, or any day thereafter, were part of the history of Ashe County. They had their beginnings in the minds and hearts of Ashe County men and women yesterday, the day before, or some day more distant, and as this writer sees them, they very definitely constitute Ashe County history.

His only regret is that under the circumstances, he could not have done a better job and one worthy of Ashe and its people. He hopes that some day someone will do it.

APPENDIX

APPENDIX I

The lists of Confederate soldiers from Ashe, and the regiments to which they were assigned, is taken from the *Roster of North Carolina Troops in the War Between the States,* by Major John Wheeler Moore (Volumes 1, 2, 3, and 4).

Company A—Ninth Regiment (Cavalry)

The first Colonel of the 9th Regiment of Cavalry, C.S.A., of which Ashe County's Company A was a part, was Robert Ransom, later to become a major general. He was succeeded by Colonel Lawrence S. Baker, later promoted to brigadier general. He was succeeded by Colonel John B. Gordon of Wilkes, who was to become one of the South's greatest cavalry officers. He was promoted to brigadier general and later killed in action. He was succeeded by Colonel W. H. Cheek.

Company A officers were:

Captain T. N. Crumpler, able lawyer and good officer, who was quickly promoted to major and was killed in action, July 18, 1862. He was succeeded by Lt. W. H. H. Cowles of Yadkin county. He in turn was succeeded by Lt. John L. Smith of Alleghany, both of them having served as lieutenants under Capt. Crumpler. Other officers serving the company at various times were D. T. Armfield, of Mecklenburg, first lieutenant; and as second lieutenants, Herman Baker, John H. Ray, D. W. Eller, and N. G. Turner, of Ashe; John H. Forrester, of Alleghany; and D. C. Parks, of Wilkes.

The non-commissioned officers of Company A, at various times, were:

First Sergeant, Henry Hardin; 2nd Sgt., Hugh Smith; 3rd Sgt., Frank Hardin; 4th Sgt., John W. Burkett (killed at Brandy Station); 5th Sgt., George M. Burkett; First Corporal, J. B. Colvard; 2nd Corporal, J. M. Dixon; 3rd Corporal, E. R. Barker; 4th Corporal, H. L. Burgess; bugler, W. P. Parks; saddler, R. P. Livitzer; farrier, David L. Hall of Guilford County. Except where noted, all of the above were from Ashe County.

The privates were: J. A. Anderson, J. D. Arnold, Daniel Arnold,

Jacob Arnold (the three Arnold boys, from east Tennessee, enlisted on the same day and Jacob, the last named, was killed at Brandy Station), John H. Ball, John Brown, E. G. Blackburn, William Blackburn, W. P. Beeman, Solomon Brooks, C. C. Benham (captured at Gettysburg), William Blevins, P. F. Boggs, C. Burkett, John Burkett, Shade Baker, Henry H. Burkett, C. H. Campbell, P. W. Colvard, T. F. Colvard, J. U. Crumpler, A. F. Calloway, J. W. Colvard, Peyton M. Colvard, J. A. Colvard, Alexander Dixon, J. D. Dixon, Alphonso Dickerson, D. D. Dancy, W. H. Dixon, N. C. Dixon, Noah Dancey, D. W. Eller, Jesse Eller, John H. Eller, W. Edmonds, W. H. Edwards, W. J. Gambill, W. A. Graham, L. E. Greer, Isham Goss, J. J. Garvey, John Gilliam, H. Goodman, R. C. Goss, Nelson Gurley, Shubal Gardner, W. H. Grant.

W. H. Hamilton, Martin Hardin, L. M. Hodges, Elbert Hodges, Thomas Hollemon, David D. Hale, J. F. Horton, Nathan Horton, Jacob Ham, Frank B. Halsey, Thomas Johnson, Wm. H. H. Jacks, W. J. John, D. E. Kistler, David Latham, Jacob Latham, T. J. Laston, J. G. Lawrence, J. A. Martin, W. H. Martin, Lewis Merryman, W. C. Merryman, E. C. R. McEwen, J. T. L. McEwen, T. M. R. McEwen, W. H. Mendenhall, A. J. McMillan, James McMillan, George Miller, A. J. Miller, David Miller, James Miller, John Miller, William Miller, David Miller, Henry Miller, George Osborne, L. C. Osborn, Wiley Pasley, James H. Pasley, Solomon C. Parsons, Calloway Parsons, L. C. Parsons, W. G. Parsons, W. R. Parsons, J. S. Parsons.

J. C. Plummer, J. R. Plummer, G. W. Plummer, W. H. Phifer, M. D. Phifer, Eli Phillips, E. E. Phillips, John Phillips, John Paten, Nathaniel Price, John Price, Samuel Ray, J. F. Ray, Henry H. Ray, John H. Ray, Lot Riggs, James Ray, Jesse Ray, John M. Ray, Wm. Ray, Geo. W. Ray, Thos. Riggs, W. B. Roork, Willis Russell, Cicero Reeves, Charles Reeves, Thomas Royal, Harrow Ray, J. W. Roberson, Jno. A. Ray, J. B. Sharpe, Peter Saunders, Henry Severt, Geo. Sturgill, James Sturgill, J. G. Smith, A. Southerland, Joseph Southerland, Hugh C. Turner, Tolbert Triplett, H. G. Turner, N. G. Turner, W. W. Wood.

Company A—26th Regiment (Infantry)

The first Colonel of the 26th Regiment was Zebulon Baird Vance, who left the regiment to become North Carolina's war Governor in 1862. He was succeeded by Colonel Henry K. Burgwin, who was killed at Gettysburg. He was succeeded by Colonel John R. Lane. No regiment in the armies of the Confederacy, according to Major John W. Moore, suffered more battle casualties than the 26th Regiment. The records show that 1,898 men, from first to last, served in its ranks.

The first commanding officer of A Company was Captain Amos B. Cox, of Virginia. He was succeeded by A. N. McMillian of Ashe. Captain McMillan was succeeded by Samuel P. Wagg of Ashe, who in turn was succeeded by A. B. Duval, also of Ashe. First Lieutenants to serve the company were George R. Reeves of Virginia, and J. B. Houck and Jesse A. Reeves of Ashe. Second Lieutenants were John C. Plummer, James Porter, and Colton Blevins, all of Ashe. In the list of non-commissioned officers of long service in the company were First Sergeant, A. N. McMillan and Second Sergeant, Samuel P. Wagg, both of whom saw service as captains of the company; Third Sergeant, Samuel Rhea (of Tennessee); Fourth Sergeant, G. A. P. Nye; Fifth Sergeant, T. S. Doughton (Alleghany); First Corporal, W. B. Reeves; Second Corporal, F. M. Woody; Third Corporal, James M. Lane; Fourth Corporal, W. M. Moody (Wilkes).

Privates from Ashe were:

Josiah Ashley, S. B. Akers, J. P. Ashley, James Ashley, Wm. Ashley, Creed Adams, Shadrach Baker, Ambrose Baker, James Baker, J. C. Baker, Lee Bear, Thomas Burgess, Jere Blackman, Wilborn Blevins, Colton Blevins (promoted to Second Lieutenant), Felix Blevins, Horton Blevins, Albert Blevins, Bartlett Blevins, Tobias Blevins, Stephen Blevins, Alfred Bear, Christian Burkett, Edward Benken, Jackson Benken, Hugh Ballou, Lee Ballou, John Billings, George Bowen, Randolph Bear, Joseph Bear, James Bear, Eli Bowen, Joseph Baldwin, W. E. Burke, Michael Black, Benjamin Ball, Jesse Bass, A. F. Calloway, Hiram Calloway, Isaac M. Carter, T. J. Coster, A. Clark, H. H. Campbell, James M. Duval, Weston Duval (promoted to Sgt.), James Duval, Maston Duval, John Duval, Uriah Damry, Walter Denny, A. B. Duval (promoted to Sgt., 1st Lt., and Capt.), James Davis, William E. Davis, Joseph Doughton (Alleghany), James Dickson, V. Dillard.

John Esteridge, Abram Edmonston, John G. Fields (Alleghany), Joe E. Foster, E. F. Foster, Noah Furman, Calloway Furman, G. R. Fisher, Joseph R. Gentry, John F. Greer, Lowrey Grimsley, Drury Grimsby, Nichols Gentry, Hiram Grimsley, J. F. Gambrell, John Graybeal, A. C. Hawthorne, George Harless, Shadrach Harless, John E. Hash, James Hash, J. C. Houck (promoted to Sgt.), Washington Houck, J. B. Houck (promoted to Sgt. and 2nd and 1st Lt.), John Hardy, Marshall Hurley, N. P. Hurley, Jno. C. Ingram, Lewis S. Jones, J. W. Ketchum, George Ketchum, John Lewis, Geo. Little, Naaman Logan, James W. Long, J. W. Landreth, Isaac Landreth, Joseph Miller, Wm. McMillan, Hanson Miller, Jonathan Miller, J. H. Miller, S. Miller, Isham Miller, T. Mitchell, G. R. Brink, Marshall Mahab.

Joseph Osborne, Lee Osborne (promoted to 1st Lt. in Cavalry), Zach Osborne, Granville Osborne, C. A. Osborne, Wm. Pennington, Samuel Plummer, John Price, J. R. Plummer, James Porter (promoted to 2nd Lt.), Wm. R. Porter, Wm. Porter, Benjamin Phipps, Nathan Phipps, —— Pendergrass, Joshua Pendergrass, Calvin Penny, M. M. Plummer, Ambrose Perkins, W. H. Perkins, Riley Perkins, Timothy Perkins, C. N. Reedy, C. Richardson, Elbert Richardson, Jackson Reid, Ashley Roten, Jonathan Roten, Soloman Roten, J. Richardson, Thomas Rutherford, A. M. Reeves (promoted to 1st. Lt. in Cavalry), James H. Robertson, William Reeves, James A. Riley, John Stamper, Ira Stamper, M. D. Stamper, J. C. Senter, Cameron Stringer, Joseph Sheets, Troy Sheets, David Sheets, James Sheets, A. Sheets, Elijah F. Smith, Ambrose Sullen, A. B. Smith, Alexander Sanders, John Senter, Samuel Stedhorn, Lewis Stedham, Abram Stoud, Joseph Sullen, T. M. Testament, J. H. Turner, Cline Taylor, Wm. H. Taylor, William Taylor, Calloway Taylor, J. R. Taylor, W. H. Taylor, W. W. Treadway, John Vanover, Samuel Wagoner, H. D. Wagoner, R. M. Weiss, Reid Wyatt (promoted to Lt. in Cavalary), A. W. Wagg, P. M. Walton, H. Z. Walker, E. S. Young, S. S. Yates.

Approximately 150 officers and men served in Company A from the beginning of the war to the end and the records disclose that 84 of them died in battle, or of wounds or disease, or were disabled by wounds, or captured or otherwise put out of action. Many of the 84 returned to action after recovering from wounds. The record shows that the company suffered its heaviest losses in the Battle of Gettysburg. It saw action also on the battlefields at Bristol Station, Cold Harbor, Chancellorsville, Malvern Hill, Roles' Mill, and Ox Hill.

Company A—34th Regiment (Infantry)

The 34th Regiment had Collett Leventhorpe as its first Colonel. He was from Rutherford County. He was succeeded by Colonel Richard H. Riddick of Gates; Colonel William L. J. Lawrence of Iredell was next. The Lieutenant Colonels for various periods were William A. Houck of Ashe, Charles J. Hammarskold of Lincoln, H. W. Abernathy of Lincoln, and George T. Gordon of Lincoln.

Serving as company commanders in order were Stephen N. Wilson, Nelson C. Wood, and Hiram W. Abernathy. First Lieutenants were Nelson C. Wood and Bartlett Y. Martin. Second Lieutenants were Eli Chandler, Hiram Cox, and Bryan Woody. The non-commissioned officers were First Sergeant, Edwin Austin; Second Sergeant, James Woody; Third Sergeant, Jesse B. Sheets; Fourth Sergeant, Franklin

Long; First Corporal, Harrison W. Long; Second Corporal, George W. Woody; Third Corporal, Hiram T. Stamper; Fourth Corporal, Hugh Caudle; buglers, John H. Wagoner and Troy Miller.

The privates in the company were: Henry Atwood, John L. Absher, William H. Absher, Thomas J. Andrews, Meredith T. Andrews, George Baker, John Black, Wiley Bare, Jacob Bare, Sr., John Bare, Sr., John Bare, Jr., Matthew Brown, Hamilton Bare, Gray J. Brown, William D. Bailey, John S. Barnwell, Thomas Blackburn, Wesley W. Brown, Levi Cox, David Cox, John Cox, William Clay, Thomas Clay, John Clary, George W. Dunn, Franklin Eads, Alfred Eads, Robert Elliott, Sol C. Fisher, John A. Gantts, John Halloway, Martin Holloway, Joseph Hatley, Elisha Johnson, Elijah Jennings, John A. Johnson, David Johnson, John A. Jones, Hamilton Koontz, George W. Koontz, Alfred Liles, William Liles, Eli C. Long, Levi Long, Martin Long, Wilborn Long, Hiram W. Long, Hiram H. Long, Michael D. Miller, Jonathan B. Miller, James C. Miller, James Miller, Calvin Osborne, Ephraim Osborne, Zacok Osborne, Jonathan Osborne.

John W. Prevette, George Poe, James M. Poe, Mathias Poe, Henry R. Percy, Linville Price, Pinkney Parrish, William Perry, William Patrick, Andrew Pennington, John Petty, John Paschal, Allen Richardson, James Richardson, Sr., James Richardson, Jr., John Richardson, Joshua Richardson, John Rupe, Richard Richardson, John Stephens, Calvin Shepherd, Calvin Shoemaker, David Sheets, Calvin Sheets, Harden Swelivan, John F. Shepherd, William Sturgill, John W. Shepherd, James F. South, Harvey Sheets, Henry Sheets, George W. Shepherd, John W. Sharp, William Tyal, Alex Taylor, Calvin Thompson, Sanders Thompson, Wesley Taylor, Wiley Taylor, Alexander Taylor, Amos F. Viers, Calvin Woody, Loggins Woody, Bryan Woody, David C. Williams, John B. Williams, Elbert Wiles, Henry Woods.

Company L—58th Regiment (Infantry)

The 58th Infantry Regiment, of which Company L from Ashe was a part, had John B. Palmer as its first Colonel. Captain Calvin Eller was the commanding officer of Company L. Poindexter Blevins and Leander Henly were his First Lieutenants and Elisha Henly was Second Lieutenant.

The non-commissioned officers were:

First Sergeant, William Waddle; Second Sergeant, Edward Blevins; Third Sergeant, James M. Calloway; Fourth Sergeant, Jesse Spira; Fifth Sergeant, W. H. Blevins; First Corporal, J. A. Fowler; Second Corporal, F. M. Handy; Third Corporal, J. F. Hurley.

The privates were:

W. P. Barker, E. C. Barker, T. C. Barker, John Blevins, G. W. Blevins, Morris Blevins, Douglas Blevins, John J. Brown, Jesse Black, B. F. Brookshire, G. W. Bumgardner, M. B. Calloway, J. A. Calloway, James N. Calloway, Meredith Combs, L. D. Cole, Wilburn Cole, F. D. Cole, Joseph Cole, William Cornett, Felix Dodur, Arn Dallas, W. H. Dollar, J. D. Dickson, James H. Denny, John Estridge, Barrabas Estridge, Calvin Eller, Jr., Wm. Eller, J. Elliott, Stephen Elliott, Rufus Elliott, M. M. Faircloth, J. W. Faircloth, S. M. Fowler, Mumford Farrington.

Jessie Green, Isaac S. Green, Alfred Ham, George Harrell, J. W. Howell, Thomas Hanes, J. F. Houck, Thomas Hurley, Moses Harville, Harvey Hurley, D. D. Hurley, Jasper Hurley, W. H. Hartzog, Solomon Howell, Jackson Howell, A. J. Howell, H. Jolley, Adkins Jefferson, Jesse F. Jones, E. Jacob, Jason Jones, Wm. W. Knight, Landreth Wagoner, Andrew Lovelace, John May, Abraham May, Geo. W. McGuire, H. S. McLain, Barker Montgomery, Wm. Nelson, Alexander Osbokye, W. H. Parsons, Geo. W. Parsons, D. Pennington, Wm. Roark, Solomon Roark, Wyatt Ross, D. N. Shaw, L. W. D. Sheets, Joseph Stike, James Shoemaker, Hugh Testerman, Henry Treadaway, William Ward, Rufus Ward.

Company A—37th Regiment (Infantry)

Colonel Charles C. Lee of Mecklenburg was the first commanding officer of the 37th. He was killed at Frazier's Farm, Virginia, on June 30, 1862. Lieutenant-Colonel William Barbour of Wilkes, who succeeded him, was gravely wounded at Gettysburg, was captured and died of his wounds, October 3, 1864.

Company A, from Ashe, was commanded by Captain John Hartzog from August 1, 1861, to July 1, 1862, when he was succeeded by Captain Walter M. Lenoir of Caldwell County. Badly wounded in action, Captain Lenoir resigned in 1862 and was succeeded by Captain W. J. Alexander, who had previously served as a 2nd Lieutenant in the company.

First Lieutenants to serve in Company A were J. J. Goodman, William Stuart, Thomas L. Norwood, Richard Goodman; Second Lieutenants, Willis Whitaker, Elijah Carter (a sergeant, he was wounded at Chancellorsville and promoted), C. A. Greer (wounded and promoted from the ranks).

The non-commissioned officers were: First Sergeant, Isham Hartzog (promoted from the ranks; killed at Cold Harbor June 29, 1862);

Second Sergeant, Alexander B. Hawthorne; Third Sergeant, William Cox; Fourth Sergeant, William Hurley; Fifth Sergeant, John B. Young; Sergeant James H. Vannoy; First Corporal, Andrew J. Stuart; Second Corporal, Peter C. Goodman; Third Corporal, Peyton Cox; Fourth Corporal, Isaac F. Sherwood.

The privates were:

Abraham Adams, Charles Adams, Floy S. Andrew, F. B. Anderson, James M. Baker, Abraham Barker, Farrow Bare, Hamilton Bare, John M. Black, George Black, Joseph Black, Andrew Black, Geo. W. Blackburn, Jeremiah M. Blackburn, Andrew Burgess, Geo. H. Bryant, Absalom Bard, Alexander Burleyson, Eli Calloway, James W. Carpenter, E. A. Carter, Clarence Carter, Columbus R. Carter, Frank M. Capehart, Benj. C. Coldiron, George Craven, Calvin Childers, J. Franklin Childers, Jackson Church, John Cooke, Wm. Cox, Leander Cox, John Childers, Harrison Cooke, Wm. Davis, Wm. J. Davis, E. Duborde, John Eldrich, Jacob Eldrich, Elijah F. Faw, Mathis Farrington, John P. Fisher, Levi R. Gentry, Andrew Gentry (killed at Fredericksburg, 1862), Andrew Gentry (killed at Hanover Courthouse, 1862), Robert Gentry, W. Harrison Goodman, Wm. J. Goss, Levi Griffin, W. H. H. Griffin, Jesse W. Green, Aaron L. Garvey, C. A. Geer.

Andrew Hurley, Wm. Ham, Thomas Ham, Levi Ham, Jackson Ham, Isaac Ham, John A. Hudson, Joel Huff, Solomon Houck, George Houck, L. Houck, Rufus M. Holdaway, Henry Hines, Henry Hendrick, James Holloway, W. R. Jones, Wilson Jones, George Jonisee, Samuel C. Johnisee, John Johnson, Samuel A. Johnson, Wm. Kay, James H. Logans, Robert M. Lane, Ambrose Lines, Matthias M. Light, Ambrose Loyal, Walter W. Lenoir, James Marsh, Thomas Marsh, George Marsh, John Marsh, John Miller, Jasper Miller, L. Miller, W. H. Miller, Jacob Miller, Richard Miller, Hiram Tomlinson, Shadrach Miller, Thomas Matherly, Edmond Marlow, Marshall C. May, Elias M. May, George W. May, James A. McNeill, Eli H. McNeill, Madison Mullis, William McGuire, Van Buren Mullis, Robert McCormick, Enoch Osborne, Ephraim Osborne, Elijah Osborne, Benjamin Owens, Zachariah Owens.

George P. Parsons, Stephen Perry, Hiram Perry, Jonathan Perry, Basil Perry, William Perry, Richard M. Perry, Andrew Pennington, Robert L. Parish, Welborn Patrick, John Price, Ephraim Roark, —— Roten, William Roten, Josiah G. Roten, Wm. Royall, John Severt, Enoch Severt, Wiley Severt, Silas Severt, Marion Sexton, Thornton Sexton, Reuben Sexton, Joseph Sexton, John Simmons, M. B. Stringer, Absalom Strink, John Shepherd, Wiley Sheets, Abel W. Swine, Joshua Stamper, Calvin W. Taylor, John Taylor, Harrison Taylor, Jacob

Taylor, George Taylor, George Teague, James J. Testerman, Calvin Testerman, Johnston Testerman, Thomas Trivett, Sterling Vanzant, L. Dow Ward, John Ward, Absalom Wood, Jno. Wyatt, Wm. A. Walker, Benj. J. Walter, Jno. O. Walter, Wm. Weaver, John Weaver, Wm. E. Welsh, Porter Welch, Nelson F. Williford, James C. Yates, John Younts.

This company, along with the other units of the 37th, saw plenty of action. Historian Moore reports deaths in battle, deaths from wounds, deaths from disease in prison in large numbers. The company saw bloody fighting at Manassas, Cold Harbor, Hanover Courthouse, Chancellorsville, Ox Hill, Second Manassas, and Gettysburg.

Company B—37th Regiment (Infantry)

Company B of the 37th regiment had many Ashe County soldiers, among them the following:

Abram Barlow, James Burgess, Daniel Blevins, Charles H. Burke, Wilson H. Campbell, William F. Campbell, F. A. Calhoun, Calvin Davis, Levi H. DuBorde, Robert Francis, Thalbert Faircloth, Richard L. Gentry, Francis G. Gwaltney, Calvin Howell, David Hudler, William Hudler, Robert Hudler, Wm. R. Heath, J. W. Hughes, Isaiah Long, Alfred Miller, William Massey, John D. Osborne, Thomas M. Phipps, Sampson Privett, Thomas Robbins, Robert Richardson.

This company was captained at first by Jonathan Horton, who resigned in July, 1862. He was succeeded by Captain Jordan Cook, who resigned after being wounded at Gaines Mill. Captain Andrew J. Critcher followed Captain Cook.

Company K—37th Regiment (Infantry)

Many Ashe County men served in Company K, 37th Regiment, including: James M. Grimsley, Amos Anderson, Walter Bowers, Alvis Blevins, Francis M. Blevins, Isham Blevins, Robert Blevins, Wesley Blevins, Ephraim Blevins, Granville H. Blevins, Elijah Blevins, Sgt. Alfred Blevins, Meredith Blevins, Jackson Brown, Eli Blevins, Hugh Blevins, Corp. Wells Blevins, Sgt. S. V. Cox, Sgt. M. C. Cox, Benjamin DeBorde, Corp. Madison Hart, Isaac Jones, Samuel Landreth, Jonathan Lee, Wm. R. Lewis, Morris Laxton, John Miles, Thos. Martin, Jno. G. Marshall, Jacob McGrady, Jonathan Osborne, James Murkey, Ransom Phillips, Jesse B. Plummer, Isaac M. Privett, Wm. Perry, Andrew Rutherford, Samuel South, Wm. Shelton, Isaiah Speeks, Wm. Smithdeal, Harrison Smith, Wm. Sanders, Joseph Tilley, James M. Tilly, James Tilley, John Tilley, Leander Vanzant.

This company was first captained by John Ross of Alleghany County. He was succeeded by Captain Wm. Fetter of Orange County and from November, 1863, on, Captain Thomas J. Armstrong of Iredell was the commanding officer.

The remainder of the company was mainly from Alleghany County.

Company L—65th Regiment (Cavalry)

The 65th was commanded by Colonel George N. Folk of Buncombe County. Company L, from Ashe, had W. B. Councill as its Captain and H. H. Ray as First Lieutenant. John McMillan and Amos Howell were Second Lieutenants. The non-commissioned officers were: First Sergeant, G. H. Phillips; Second Sergeant, H. Hardin; Third Sergeant, John Goodman; Fourth Sergeant, Leander Baker; Fifth Sergeant, C. M. Graybeal; First Corporal, J. M. Gambill; Second Corporal, E. C. Faw; Third Corporal, Hansford Eller; Fourth Corporal, James Greer.

The privates were: Creed Ashley, C. A. Burkett, John Barlow, Hamilton Banlin, W. A. Bird, W. A. Campbell, John Church, W. F. Church, W. B. Call, J. F. Dickson, W. R. Dicks, Washington Dishman, H. P. Eller, Amos Faw, Jacob Faw, B. F. Faw, J. S. Fouts, George Faucett, G. W. Foster, G. W. Grubbs, Wm. Graybeal, D. H. Graybeal, Simon Graybeal, David Graybeal, Isaac Goodman, P. P. Goodman, G. A. Gilley, Zachariah Glasgow, James Graves, Alexander Greer, David Howell, Wm. Howell, James Howell, D. S. Hartzog, C. E. Hartzog, J. F. Hartzog, J. W. Houston, Henry Hardin, Martin Hardin, Mark Hardin, David Hines, Abraham Jones, Mathias Little, John Little, James Latham, David Latham, Peter McNeill, T. M. McGuire, G. L. Price, James Powers, J. H. Powers, J. W. Ray, J. J. Ray, J. M. Ray, J. A. Ray, G. W. Ray, William M. Rowland, J. A. Scott, L. R. Scott, B. P. Snitzer, D. F. Shepherd, J. A. Shepherd, A. L. Shepherd, W. L. Thomas, L. W. Vannoy, Cotton Watt, Ransom Williams, Colton Wyatt.

69th Regiment (Infantry)

The 69th Regiment did not have enough men from Ashe in its ranks to make up an Ashe County company, but a goodly number served under Captain William B. Love of Ashe, commanding Company D. Colonel William H. Thomas of Jackson County, commanded the regiment. Serving under Captain Love were First Lieutenant G. C. McBea and Second Lieutenants Henry Needham, Adam C. Peck, Thomas R. Smart, and W. W. Jones, all of Ashe. Non-commissioned officers from Ashe were Second Sergeant, Alexander Carmack; Third Sergeant,

James V. Walker; Fourth Sergeant, —— Wilgrove; Fifth Sergeant, Joseph C. H. Hodges; Sergeant, W. M. Walker; First Corporal, John W. Morgan; Second Corporal, J. R. Franklin; Third Corporal, William Walker, Jr.; Corporal, James W. Bailey; bugler, Campbell Stansberry.

The privates were: Thomas Alexander, Edward Arms, P. E. Bettes, J. E. Bettes, Martin Byerly, John Bates, James Bates, James Cozart, Calvin Estep, William Hatcher, William C. Hayes, John W. Hays, C. B. C. Hodges, W. W. Jones, William Kendrick, Lee C. Jasper, William C. Lee, John C. Lee, Joseph C. Lee, Wiley B. Large, Joseph Large, David Lawrence, Calvin Lawrence, William H. Pearson, John T. Pearson, Robert Sellers, Thomas T. Simmons, William Walker, Sr., John Wilson, William H. Watkins, William M. Waters, William Weedon.

APPENDIX II

Ashe County in World War I

The list below contains the names of the Ashe County men who were registered and inducted into the armed forces of the United States in World War I as they appear on the registration cards presently on file in the Department of Archives and History, Raleigh.

Elsewhere will be found casualty lists and other information concerning Ashe County's participation in World War I.

A

Finley F. Absher, Mack Absher, John Thomas Adams, Charlie S. Ashley, Robert Ashley, Walter C. Ashley, Robert Lee Austin, William B. Austin, Walter O. Ayers.

B

Guy T. Badger, John M. Baker, Edward Baldwin, Estill Baldwin, Gaither N. Baldwin, John Baldwin, Lester Baldwin, Nelson Baldwin, Wiley Baldwin, Lester Ball, Cecil Bare, Darius Bare, Goodman Bare, Iron Bare, Wagoner Bare, Gaither Barker, Wiley Barker, Home C. Barlow, Basil D. Barr, Edward D. Barr, Roger Felix Barr, Frank Barton, William P. Bell, William M. Benge, Letcher R. Bingham, Edward E. Blackburn, Joe Blackburn, Vester V. Blackburn, Wiley W. Blackburn, Grover Bledsoe, Horton Bledsoe,

Banner Blevins, Carl L. Blevins, Claude L. Blevins, Eli Walter Blevins, Elisher Blevins, Ezekiel M. Blevins, Filloing Blevins, Fred Wood Blevins, Henry F. Blevins, James E. Blevins, James J. Blevins, Lillard C. Blevins, Orange Talmage Blevins, Randolph Blevins, Ransom W. Blevins, Russell Blevins, Russell G. Blevins, Samuel M. Blevins, Upton Blevins, Vay Blevins, Walter M. Blevins, William A. Blevins, John R. Bower, Corelais F. Bowers, Jake W. Boyden, Ben Brewer, Charles G. Brooks, Chester A. Brook, Cicero S. Brooks, Edward Brooks, Edward Wiliam Brooks, Fielden F. Brooks, John W. Brooks, Robert T. Brooks, Thomas Daniel Brooks, Billie Brown, Charles Walter Brown, Floyd Oscar Brown, Robie F. Brown, Roscoe C. Brown, Walter M. Burkett, John M. Burkett, William J. Burkett.

C

Guy Coldiron, Grover C. Calloway, Charles J. Calloway, Grover O. Calloway, James G. B. Calloway, John McKay Calloway, Levi Morton Calloway, George M. Campbell, Thomas A. Campbell, Walter Lee Campbell, John Art Carson, James B. Carter, John Carter, John R. Carter, Elihu G. Caudell, Felix B. Caudell, Robert L. Caudell, Authur Childers, Ellis M. Church, George I. Church, Turner Church, Arthur Clark, Russell Alger Clark, Wells Clark, William Clark, Doughton Cockerham, Marcus W. Cockerham, Levi Coldiron, Estle E. Colvard, Fred Neal Colvard, George Todd Colvard, Larry P. Colvard, Harlie Cook, Clinton Cornett, Roy Cornett, Albert L. Cox, Bob G. Cox, Bronson Cox, Doughton Cox, Franklin Cox, Garland E. Cox, George C. Cox, Plateau Rex Cox, Robert Johnson Cox, Thomas Cox, Lee Crysel.

D

Alvin Dancy, Jesse Darnell, Quincy Davis, Edmand Deboard, Hoyt DeBoard, Quincy N. Dickson, Benjamin C. Dixon, Frank T. Dixon, Mason H. Dollar, Bower H. Duncan, Flake E. Duncan, Quincy A. Duncan, Eugene B. Duvall, Fields Duvall.

E

Erwin Eastridge, Edwin G. Eller, Floyd O. Eller, Lester Eller, William Eller, William W. Eller, Joseph E. Elliott, Oscar E. Elliott, Thomas W. Elliott.

F

Clifford A. Faw, Arthur L. Fletcher, Charles W. Foley, Edwin N. Foster, William Friesland.

G

Wiley F. Gambill, John Henry Garris, Fred K. Garvey, Clarence R. Gentry, Clyde Gentry, Joseph H. Gentry, Walter F. Gentry, David C. Gilley, Halford B. Gilley, Walter F. Gilley, William A. Gilley, Thomas Goss, Charles B. Grace, Charles C. Graham, Jacob K. Graham, John H. C. Graham, Bernard Burkett Graybeal, Carl B. Graybeal, Glenn Burkett Graybeal, Martin Luther Graybeal, Wiley H. Graybeal, Joe S. Greene, Alphonso Greer, Charles S. Greer, Gay Greer, E. Greer, Fred H. Greer, Hubert Greer, James S. Greer, John A. Greer, Joseph Blain Greer, Larkin Greer, Leonard Greer, Lillard Greer, Marshall Raymond Greer, Max B. Greer, Oren Greer, Ralph Graden Greer, Walter T. Greer, Millard Grogan, McKinley Grubb, William R. Grubb.

H

John Bartlett Hagaman, George W. Hall, Elizie Ham, Lester Ham, Wells Ham, Bower Hamby, Edward Hamilton, James W. Hampton,

Samuel C. Hardin, Allen Harless, Arthur Harless, Ballard Harless, David Harless, Fields Harless, Worth Harless, John Hartsog, Charles B. R. Hartzog, Lester Hartzog, Watson F. Hartzog, William Fields Hartzog, Walter Hash, Jamie Hilliard, Coy Hinson, Ronda B. Hodge, Piper Hodgson, Johnson Hollifield, Floyd Hopper, Calvin B. Houck, Charles E. Houck, David Harper Houck, Elbert Price Houck, George Houck, Heggie R. Houck, William David Houck, Charles C. Howell, George A. Howell, Walter L. Howell, Walter M. Howell, Walter Hudler, William Cicero Hudler, William B. Hudson, Avery E. Hurley, Cicero C. Hurley, Fitzhugh Lee Hurley, Thomas Hurley, Thomas L. Hurley.

J

Ed Jenkins, Everett Jenkins, Charles R. Johnson, Charlie Johnson, Cicero Johnson, Roy T. Johnson, Silas Johnson, Ira Thomas Johnston, Walter C. Johnston, Ambrose Jones, Avery O. Jones, Edgar D. Jones, Frank E. Jones, Garvey C. Jones, Glen Jones, Jacob A. Jones, James F. Jones, James Marvin Jones, Lester H. Jones, Rex Perry Jones, Robert Dewey Jones, Roby Q. Jones, Thomas S. Jones, William E. Jones, William H. Jones, William W. Jones.

K

Mack Killen, Marion Knotts, Dick Krider.

L

Walter Lambert, Charles Latham, Itful Gentry Lemly, Richard V. Lenly, Arthur Lewis, Earl Ross Lewis, Edgar C. Lewis, Varney C. Lindsey, Fields Macks Little, Fred Little, Robert L. Little, Willie Little, Lee Azer Loggins, Carl Long, Ola Long, William T. Luther, John Gordon Lyall, William Carbet Lyall.

Mc

William Haig McGuire, Add C. McMillan, Claude L. McMillan, Joseph A. McMillan, Willis McMillan, Wecham G. McMillan, Charles G. McNeill, Grover W. McNeill, Lee McNeil.

M

Cicero Mahala, Joll K. Mahala, Oscar D. Mahala, President L. Mahala, Hoy C. Marsh, Bert Mash, Vonley Mash, Arthur C. Massey, Thomas Maxwell, John May, Robert Todd May, John Mayberry, Edward B. Medley, Poindexter Medley, Daniel Miller, Ernest F. Miller, Edward Miller, Gordon Miller, Harrison H. Miller, James B. Miller, James M. Miller, Jesse Hampton Miller, Kirby Miller, Lloyd N. Miller, Thurman G. Miller, Vance Miller, William T. Miller, Cicero Miller, Bruce Mink, Edward Mock, David O. Montgomery, Horace G. Moretz, Walter S. Moretz, John E. Mullis, Quincy Mullis, Turner Mullis, Tossie Munday.

N

Audie Nichols, Joseph Norris.

O

Sherman Oliver, Ambrose Osborne, Brack Osborne, James L. Osborne, Joel Osborne, John Osborne, John M. Osborne, Joseph Osborne, Quincey E. Osborne, Raleigh Osborne.

P

James Pappas, Greer Parsons, Harry E. Parsons, Henry Blaine Parsons, Loyd Parsons, Robert G. Parsons, Tom Parsons, Arthur F. Pasley, Geter Pasley, Mack I. Payne, Carl Pennington, Davie Pennington, Dent Pennington, Kirby S. Pennington, Smith Pennington, Sol Pennington, Will Pennington, George Olney Perkins, Glenn Perry, Clint Phillips, Kirby O. Phillips, Walter A. Phillips, William Phillips, Alonzo Fred Phipps, Harding H. A. Phipps, John B. Phipps, Lester P. Phipps, Joseph B. Pierce, David N. Pless, John G. Poe, Winfield Poe, Amon Pope, Frank C. Porter, Thaddeus D. Porter, Warner Porter, John O. Potter, John Powell, McKinley Powers, Solomon E. Powers, Walter Powers, Albert Price, Ernest Price, Stauffer S. Price, Wiley M. Price, Jesse C. Pugh.

R

Ronda Ragan, Amos P. Rash, John E. Rash, Earl A. Ray, Ritz Clyde Ray, John Redmond, Clint Reed, Bower C. Reeves, Curtis E. Reeves, William E. Reeves, Jack Rhodes, Boyd C. Richardson, George C. Richardson, Guy Richardson, James L. Richardson, Ralph Richardson, William R. Richardson, Linney Ring, Dewey R. Roark, Glenn Roark, Hedrick Roark, Moton Roark, Olney B. Roark, Walter Lee Roark, William Roark, Emery Roberts, Roan Roberts, Claude T. Roland, James Scott Roland, Lee Roland, Andrew Rose, Troy William Roten, Bill Roup, John L. Roup.

S

Charles A. Sapp, Earl Saults, John Sawyers, Will E. Sawyers, Earl Scott, Grady M. Scott, Bradford Segraves, James L. Segraves, Granville Curtis Sexton, Ira Levi Sexton, James D. Sexton, Avery Shatley, Donald Shatley, Fields Lonzo Sheets, Hillary W. Sheets, Willey G. Sheets, William E. Sheets, William L. Sheets, Marion A. Shepherd, David F. Shoemake, Edgar W. Sluder, Paul Smith, Robert L. Speaks, Humphrey K. Spencer, Victor F. Spencer, Winton M. Spence, Edgar C. Sproles, Dump Stanley, Oscar L. Stanley, Wade F. Stansberry, Gaither Stansberry, Howard S. Steelman, Noah T. Stevens, John Stuart, James Lester Stump, Joe S. Stump, Walter S. Sturgill, Arthur Sturgill, Roy Sturgill, Winfield Scott Sturgill, Harvey Sullins, Thomas L. Sullins, James Sutherland, Jolly Sweat.

T

Colonel Edward Taylor, Charles William Taylor, David S. Taylor, Everett Lester Taylor, Ferchus Taylor, Floyd Ulmant Taylor, Horton B. Taylor, Robert H. Taylor, James Ira Teague, Avery Testerman, Charley Testerman, Felix W. Testerman, Cornett J. Thomas, Edison M. Thomas, Carson Thompson, Roscoe Isham Thompson, Wesley Thompson, Greek Todd, Troy Tredway, Conley Tredway, Joseph Oren Tucker, Quincy C. Tucker, Henry E. Turner.

V

Wade E. Vannoy, Mack R. Vannoy, Wiley Vannoy, Earl Vaught.

W

Alsan P. Waddell, Leo B. Waddell, John C. Walker, Reece Walker, Robie Alexander Walker, Robert B. Wall, Thomas J. Wall, William McWallace, Ben J. Walters, David J. Walton, Charlie C. Watson, Otis W. Watson, Delmer M. Waugh, Walter C. Waugh, Arthur W. Weaver, David W. Weaver, Hubert Orris Weaver, Walter E. Weaver, Walter R. Weaver, Wayne A. Weaver, Edgar F. Weiss, Charles Edward Welch, Walter F. Welch, John G. Wellington, Arthur J. West, Samuel Wilcox, Arthur F. Williams, John R. Williams, Quincy Williams, William A. Wilson, Jr., Arthur L. Winebarger, John L. Winebarger, Glenn McKinley Wolfe, Ambrose Wood, Charlie Wood, Ed H. Woodie, William L. Woodie, Mack E. Woodruff, Irvin E. Woods, Square L. Woody, Samuel I. Worley, James Wyatt.

Y

Allen Yates, Claude Yates, Conrad Yates, James F. Yates, John E. Yates, Archie L. Young.

APPENDIX III

Ashe County in World War II

The list below was compiled from the official World War II records of the Adjutant General of North Carolina. Individual records of those Ashe county men who were registered and inducted into the armed forces were set up on cards and the list below is the result of a careful examination of every card in the Ashe County section of the files, now in the keeping of the State Department of Archives and History in Raleigh.

Elsewhere in this book will be found casualty lists and other information concerning Ashe County's participation in World War II.

A

Harold L. Absher, John E. Absher, John Thomas Absher, Robert Mack Absher, Sidney Samuel Absher, Walter Worth Adams, Auther Emmet Allen, Conley Allen, Francis C. Allen, James Allen, Jr., James H. Allen, Lloyd E. Allen, Earley B. Allen, John I. Anderson, Jr., Theodore R. Anderson, Joseph G. Arnold, Lester V. Arnold, Quincy A. Arnold, R. C. Arnold, Roy V. Arnold, Clarence J. Ashby, Carl F. Ashley, Claude W. Ashley, Elden Ashley, Gale J. Ashley, Joseph H. Ashley, Luther A. Ashley, Robt. R. Ashley, Carl C. Atwood, Dale N. Atwood, Glenn B. Atwood, Robt. B. Austin, Grant R. Austin, Sr.

B

Guy T. Badger, James A. Badger, Roy C. Badger, Alexander J. Baker, Hal E. Baker, J. C. Baker, Robt. E. L. Baker, Wm. B. Baker, Wm. E. Baker, Hugh H. Baker, James W. Baldwin, Jessie R. Baldwin, Wiley J. Baldwin, Wm. G. Baldwin, Elton V. Ball, Wm. C. Ballou, Chester R. Banks, Blair K. Bard, Edwin R. Bard, Everett B. Bard, Fred D. Bard, Russell B. Bard, Albert S. Bare, Arnold O. Bare, Bertie Bare, Bruce C. Bare, Burmont P. Bare, Burrell S. Bare, Carl D. Bare, Cecil O. Bare, Charles B. Bare, Clell C. Bare, Clifton E. Bare, Donald Roy Bare, Edwin D. Bare, Ernest E. Bare, Foye D. Bare, Freel E. Bare, Freelin L. Bare, Gale F. Bare, Glenn J. Bare, Governor G. Bare, Grover C. Bare, Guy D. Bare, Guy T. Bare, Harry G. Bare, Robt. L. Bare,

Howard W. Bare, Jack E. Bare, John R. Bare, Kenneth A. Bare.

Lawrence H. Bare, Leonard R. Bare, Maynor F. Bare, Paul B. Bare, Paul E. Bare, Sr., Paul H. Bare, Pell C. Bare, Roy Bare, Roger B. Bare, Roland F. Bare, Roy H. Bare, Thos. R. Bare, Vestal McC. Bare, Wade A. Bare, Wm. F. Bare, Willie W. Bare, Wiemer C. Bare, Arthur B. Barker, Carl G. Barker, Earl C. Barker, Elmer L. Barker, Gilbert R. Barker, Hester P. Barker, Howard A. Barker, James G. Barker, John R. Barker, Millard W. Barker, Paul T. Barker, Ralph Barker, Raymond L. Barker, Wm. H. Barker, Arlyne J. Barlow, Dean E. Barlow, Donald W. Barlow, Owen Barlow, Quayle Barlow, Quinton T. Barlow, Robt. W. Barlow, James E. Barnes, Clifford Barr, Fred M. Barr, James A. Barr, John C. Barr, Paul J. Barr, Franklin B. Barton, Zeb D. Barton, U. S. Grant Bauguess, Freeman E. Bauguess, Ira T. Belcher, James L. Benge, Blane C. Bennett, Archie L. Black, Carl Black, George E. Block, Julius C. Block, Marshall W. Black, Ralph G. Black, Robert G. Black, Warren G. Black.

Blaine R. Blackburn, Earl E. Blackburn, Elmer Blackburn, Ivan S. Blackburn, Joe Henry Blackburn, Joseph Herbert Blackburn, Leslie W. Blackburn, Mackajune Blackburn, Byne G. Bledsoe, Claude R. Bledsoe, Gilmer L. Bledsoe, Joseph R. Bledsoe, William E. Bledsoe, Ambrose E. Blevins, Carl W. Blevins, Charles C. Blevins, Clarence F. Blevins, Claude M. Blevins, Clayborne W. Blevins, Dale J. Blevins, David A. Blevins, Edward R. Blevins, Ernest G. Blevins, George W. Blevins, Henry F. Blevins, Herbert D. Blevins, Hyte J. Blevins, J. C. Lannis Blevins, Jackson Blevins, James C. Blevins, Joseph Blevins, Jesse W. Blevins, Jethro Blevins, John F. Blevins, Junior E. Blevins, Kenneth B. Blevins, Libert H. Blevins, Linda D. Blevins, Lannie A. Blevins, Manley J. Blevins, Marvin E. Blevins, Odes L. Blevins, Orville J. Blevins, Oscar R. Blevins, Otho B. Blevins, Paul C. Blevins, Purvey L. Blevins, Roy J. Blevins, Robert F. Blevins, Robert W. Blevins, Russell J. Blevins, Thelmus R. Blevins, Thos. W. Blevins, Ulas G. Blevins, Vieland C. Blevins, Wm. B. Blevins, Wm. C. Blevins, Wm. R. Blevins.

Charles H. Bowen, Geo. P. Bower, Joseph S. Bowers, Robt. C. Bowers, Thomas C. Bowie, Jr., Albert W. Bowlin, Lester G. Boyden, Carl R. Brinegar, Dewey T. Brinegar, Wm. V. Brinegar, Billy D. Brooks, Garney H. Brooks, Leonard R. Brooks, Millard A. Brooks, Paul S. Brooks, Winford G. Brooks, Albert G. Brown, Bobbie J. Brown, Chas. S. Brown, Chas. W. Brown, David R. Brown, Glenn E. Brown, James I. Brown, James M. Brown, Jesse C. Brown, John H. H. Brown, Joseph B. Brown, Lester O. Brown, Lida A. Brown, Loren E. Brown, Mayor F. Brown, Rodney L. Brown, Roscoe C. Brown, Roy C. J. Brown, Wm. G. Brown, Wm. T. Bumgarner, Wm. E. Burchett,

George A. Burgess, Heggie Burgess, Otto R. Burgess, Clyde R. Burkett, Lawrence P. Burchett, Paul J. Buttrey, Fred J. Buland, Roy D. Byrd, Sr.

C

Joseph W. Caldwell, Raymond R. Caldwell, Rober C. Caldwell, Albert Caldwell, Gaythe E. Caldwell, Ira J. Calhoun, Jno. L. Calloway, Walter H. Calloway, Wm. A. Calloway, Archie D. Campbell, Dewey B. Campbell, Elmer C. Campbell, Ezekiel S. Campbell, Gerald C. Campbell, Grant W. Campbell, Mack D. Campbell, Paul G. Campbell, Panel L. Campbell, Paul S. Campbell, Raymond B. Campbell, Wm. R. Campbell, James T. Capps, Jr., Cyril G. Carpenter, James L. Carpenter, John H. Carpenter, Shelton S. Carpenter, Ralph F. Carter, Gwyn Caudill, Herbert G. Caudill, Herman Caudill, James C. Caudill, Larry T. Caudill, Lee G. Caudill, Roy Caudill, Russell D. Caudill, Wade B. Caudill, Paul J. Cearley, Robert B. Cearley, Jr., Chas. D. Cheek, Conley B. Cheek, Denver L. Cheek, Henry F. Cheek, John E. Cheek, Lesley W. Cheek, Robt. E. Cheek, Robt. M. Childress, Delmas W. Childress, Tom J. Childress, Walter W. Childress, Bowie Church, Cecil A. Church, Claude H. Church, Edward J. Church, Fields H. Church, Franklin H. Church, Guy Church, James H. Church, James M. Church, John Church, Lester W. Church, Ralph H. Church, Robt. L. Church, Roy L. Church, Walter E. Church, Wm. W. Church, Arley O. Clark, Armpo Clark, Erskine Clark, Vaughn Clark, William S. Clark.

Chas. H. Cockerham, Ivan T. Cockerham, Jno. L. Cockerham, Clarence W. Coldiron, Joe E. Coldiron, Lucius W. Coldiron, Onnie M. Cole, Charles D. Colvard, Harold B. Colvard, Neal D. Colvard, Wm. P. Colvard, Wm. R. Colvard, Frank L. Combs, George Combs, Graves F. Combs, Russell A. Combs, Wm. G. Combs, James F. Cook, Albert L. Cooper, Henry F. Cooper, Marion E. Cooper, Walter M. Cooper, Wint Cooper, Albert R. Cope, Clyde J. Cornett, Grey D. Cornett, Milton C. Corvette, William J. Council, Glenn S. Cox, Harry R. Cox, Howard B. Cox, Joe H. Cox, John A. Cox, Jr., John D. Cox, Johnnie R. Cox, Joseph W. Cox, Lee G. Cox, Robt. C. Cox, Robt. E. Cox, Robt. L. Cox, Wilford G. Cox, Robt. T. Crawford, Russell C. Crawford, Francis H. Crapps, Jno. W. Crowson.

D

Dale R. Dancey, Vester C. Dancey, Wm. C. Dancy, Boyd R. Dougherty, James R. Dougherty, Bill V. Davis, Carl Davis, Chas. H. Davis, Chas. P. Davis, Dennis E. Davis, Ford L. Davis, Gaither F. Davis, Gale M. Davis, John H. Davis, Paul H. Davis, Paul W. Davis, Robert Davis, Samuel L. Davis, Solomon B. Davis, Walter E. Davis, William G. Davis, Chester A. Day, Herbert G. Day, Conley D. Debord, Frank M. Debord, Geo. S. Denny, Alvin H. Denny, Jr., Ezra D. Denny, John T. Dent,

Earl H. Dickson, Glen G. Dickson, Kent G. Dickson, Carl F. Dillard, Frank M. Dillard, Ira A. Dillard, Jesse L. Dillard, John J. Dillard, Thomas G. Dillard, Carl V. Dishman, Glenn Dishman, Mont Dishman.

Blan D. Dixon, French G. Dixon, John T. Dixon, Leslie V. Dixon, Charlie C. Dolinger, Dean W. Dolinger, Dent E. Dolinger, Clint D. Dollar, Thos. J. Dollar, Walter H. Dollar, Wm. G. Dollar, Deronda W. Donnelly, Bernard H. Dougherty, Paul S. Douglas, Roy O. Douglas, Ray Dula, Branard C. Duncan, Lee V. Duvall, Eugene R. Duvall, Jr., Everett W. Duvall.

E

Chas. L. Estridge, James H. Eastridge, John T. Eastridge, Joseph B. Eastridge, Walter E. Eastridge, Charles C. Edwards, Ernest K. Edwards, Eugene G. Edwards, Howard W. Edwards, Jimmy J. Edwards, Lee S. Edwards, Ward B. Edwards, Wm. F. Eggers, Avery R. Eldreth, Claude E. Eldreth, Edgar E. Eldreth, Elmer C. Eldreth, Fred S. Eldreth, James S. Eldreth, Verna E. Eldreth, Walter H. Eldreth, Wayne Eldreth, Wiley W. Eldreth, Wm. L. Eldreth, Windred Eldreth, Worth Eldreth, Avery D. Eller, Blanco Eller, Bland Eller, Clifford R. O. Eller, Donald Eller, Edwin C. Eller, Ervin Eller, George T. Eller, James B. Eller, John C. Eller, John S. Eller, Kay L. Eller, Jr., Lane Eller, Morris E. Eller, Robt. G. Eller, Robert L. Eller, Todd S. Eller, Wade E. Eller, Jr., Walter Eller, Wm. L. Eller, Wm. M. Eller, Elmer Elliott, Henry H. Elliott, James H. Elliott, Raymond V. Elliott, Walter M. Elliott, Carl C. Ellis, Grover C. Ellis, Ray D. Ellis, Thos. G. Ellis.

F

Junior Farmer, Vernon Farmer, Charlie L. Farmington, Floyd C. Farmington, John M. Farningham, Robert Farmington, Bryan T. Faw, Earl C. Faw, Elmer J. Faw, Wade V. Faw, Fred Fender, Jno. W. Fender, Robt. A. Fender, Robert W. Fleetwood, Cecil E. Fletcher, Grady H. Fletcher, A. L. Fletcher, Loyd B. Forester, Carl W. Fowler, Thos. B. Fowler, Clarence L. Francis, Hoke A. Francis, Joseph C. Francis, Milburn C. Francis, Osborne E. Francis, W. S. Francis, Wm. E. Francis, Roy O. Freeman, Cecil G. Friesland, Robt. D. Friesland, Robert E. Furches.

G

James C. Gambill, Jr., John W. Gorney, Joseph H. Garvey, Thomas L. Garvey, Basil H. Gaultney, Baston G. Gentry, Billie F. McC. Gentry, Homer S. Gentry, Jesse E. Gentry, Jr., John R. Gentry, Ray A. Gentry, Thomas P. Gentry, Tine H. Gentry, Vonley D. Gentry, Wayne M. Gentry, Wm. P. Gentry, Conley V. Gilley, Earn Gilley, Elmer L. Gilley, Ray E. Gilley, Ray V. Gilley, Vaughn G. Gilley, Howard G. Girtman, Ronald Girtman, Alonzo T. Goodman, Clifford

W. Goodman, Clyde Goodman, Don B. Goodman, Jno. W. Goodman, Joseph C. Goodman, Joseph E. Goodman, Kenny H. Goodman, Lloyd T. Goodman, Neal T. Goodman, Newland R. Goodman, Paul H. Goodman, Raymond E. Goodman, Reece A. Goodman, Jr., Roy A. Goodman, Warren G. Goodman, Sr., Wayne C. Goodman, Wesley W. Goodman, Albert W. Goss, Gwyn L. Goss, Jesse W. Goss, Robert W. Goss, Andrew J. Graham, Carl C. Graham, Gilles W. Graham, Howard E. Graham, Jesse P. Graham, L. D. Graham, Lawrence J. Graham.

Alvin L. Graybeal, David E. Graybeal, James V. Graybeal, Joseph H. Graybeal, Robt. T. Graybeal, Robert T. Graybeal, Walbert R. Graybeal, Wm. S. Graybeal, James C. Greene, Earl R. Greer, Earl W. Greer, Edwin A. Greer, Everett J. Greer, Ford E. Greer, Harris J. Greer, Howard F. Greer, James E. Greer, Jay S. Greer, Jefferson F. Greer, Joseph L. Greer, Lawson R. Greer, Mack W. Greer, Marvin W. Greer, O. C. Greer, Oscar H. Greer, Paul C. Greer, Raleigh S. Greer, Ralph O. Greer, Ralph V. Greer, Ray A. Greer, Ronda D. Greer, Roy D. Greer, Odell B. Griffin, Reggie M. Griffitts, Bernard S. Grimes, Edd A. Grimes, Ellis D. Grogan, Elmer P. Grogan, James G. Grogan, John D. Grogan, John I. Grogan, Mick T. Grogan, Pete H. Grogan, Quary H. Grogan, Wm. R. Grogan, Burl M. Grubb, Ervin W. Grubb, Glenn V. Grubb, Lloyd W. Grubb.

H

James Haire, Jr., Roland C. Haire, Delmar P. Hale, Sr., Armond H. Halsey, Barnie B. Ham, Claude E. Ham, Dale Ham, Dean Ham, Edgar Ham, Elmer L. Ham, Fairlie F. Ham, Freeman Ham, Glenn R. Ham, Herman C. Ham, James A. Ham, James E. Ham, James G. Ham, Ray R. Ham, Roger Ham, James G. Ham, Ray R. Ham, Roger Ham, Thos. E. Ham, Walter B. Ham, Wiley V. Ham, James L. Hamby, Jones B. Hamby, Leonard A. Hamby, Walter L. Hamilton, Garland Hamm, Russell M. Hamm, Exelin J. Hampton, Robt. A. Hanks, Fred H. Hardin, John E. Hardin, Richard H. Hardin, Wm. H. Hardin, Wm. T. Hardin, Donald R. Harless, Earl K. Harless, Harold B. Harless, Hursel F. R. Harless, McDaniel Harless, Moses G. Harless, Albert D. Harrald, Floyd D. Harris, Kyle R. Harris, Benjamin A. Harris, Fred Hart, Jr., Jewel C. Hart, Joe Hart, Lester P. Hart, Paul O. Hart, Quinton R. Hart, Sherman Hart, Vaughn L. Hart, Wells R. Hart, Winfred L. Hart, Worth Hart, Arvel W. Hartsoe, Ben E. Hartsoe, Earl D. Hartsoe, Miles G. Hartsoe, Robt. D. Hartsoe, Warren G. H. Hartzog, Burl W. Hartzog, Gwyn E. Hartzog, John D. Hartzog, Willard C. Hartzog.

Fitzbugh L. Hash, James L. Hash, Norman K. Hege, Jr., Elmer O. Herron, Cloyd E. Hodges, James E. Holscomb, George C. Holmon,

J. C. Holmon, Jack Holmon, John J. Holmon, Thos. G. Hobson, Wade L. Hobson, Gilmer H. Holton, Jr., Clifford H. Hoosier, Howard W. Hosier, Marion S. Hosier, Robert A. Hosier, Wm. D. Hosier, Worth A. Hosier, James G. Hopkins, Joseph E. Hopkins, Paul A. Hopkins, Charles M. Horton, Church H. Houck, Claude T. Houck, Dean McK. Houck, Dent D. Houck, Dent W. Houck, Dwight L. Houck, J. C. Houck, Joseph D. Houck, Lee J. Houck, Lowell E. Houck, Noel C. Houck, Norvel F. Houck, Oscar D. Houck, Phil S. Houck, Robt. M. Houck, Ross D. Houck, Jr., Roy F. Houck, Wallace G. Houck, Wm. H. Houck.

Arthur F. Houser, Ashley W. Howell, Clifford Howell, Clyde H. Howell, David L. Howell, Edison G. Howell, Fritz A. Howell, G. B. Howell, Gus Howell, James C. Howell, James M. Howell, James R. Howell, John V. Howell, Leonard R. Howell, Robert L. R. Howell, Roger D. Howell, Vonley L. Howell, Webb W. Howell, William E. Howell, Wm. H. Howell, Worth E. Howell, James B. Huddler, William B. Huddler, Harold Huddler, Earl T. Huff, Jno. B. Huffman, Roy C. Huffman, Wm. C. Huffman, Jos. J. Humphrey, Richard D. Humphries, Loyd R. Hunt, Wm. C. Hunt, Bryant C. Hunter, James E. Hunter, Bracket D. Hurley, Robert D. Hurley, Thurman E. Hurley, Wm. E. Hurley, Joe K. Hunt, Robt. C. Hunt.

J

Carl R. Jackson, John G. Jackson, Robt. B. Jackson, Frank M. James, Ray H. James, Vance James, Conley Jenkins, Jack Jenkins, James H. Jenkins, Dewey Johnson, Edgar A. Johnson, Edward B. Johnson, Elbert D. Johnson, James W. Johnson, John G. Johnson, Robert T. Johnson, Thomas W. Johnson, Vance Johnson, Jr., Worth L. Johnson, Charles M. Johnston, Thomas S. Johnston, Wm. R. Johnston, Robert E. Jones, Andrew M. Jones, Jr., Billie Jones, Breece Jones, Clyde T. Jones, Douglas Jones, Edwin H. Jones, Emmett F. Jones, Frielden B. Jones, Garnie W. Jones, Henry A. Jones, Hebert J. Jones, Howard E. Jones, Howard T. Jones, Hoyt E. Jones, Ivory P. Jones, James C. Jones, James E. Jones, Jesse W. Jones, John A. Jones, John B. Jones, Marvin B. Jones, Percie P. Jones, Robert F. Jones, Ronda Jones, Ryland F. Jones, Shirley T. Jones, Verner L. Jones, Victor W. Jones, Walter B. C. Jones, Walter F. Jones, Walter G. Jones, Warren N. Jones, Wayne F. Jones, William L. Jones.

K

James V. Kearney, Chas. B. Keller, Robt. T. Keller, George B. Kelley, Claude A. Key, Carson M. Keys, John W. Keys, Robt. H. Keys, Delmer T. Kilby, Lionel C. Killen, Gerald W. Kimberlin, James E. Kimberlin, James Robert Kimberlin, Joseph W. Kimberlin, William R. Kimberlin, James W. King, Bryan Kirby, Jr., Ray Knight, Clifford S. Koontz, Chas. G. Krider, Thos. K. Krider.

L

Avery M. Lambert, Oscar B. Lambert, Ottis J. Lambert, Roy J. Lambert, Wm. Lambert, William C. Lambert, Ernis P. Latham, Clifford A. Lawrence, Gladstone Lawrence, Warren D. Lawrence, Joseph B. Lawson, Gale G. Lemly, Ithel C. Lemly, Carl H. Lewis, Charles D. Lewis, Dennis S. Lewis, Don C. Lewis, Emmett H. Lewis, Emory G. Lewis, Ernest P. Lewis, Jack H. Lewis, John P. Lewis, Robt. N. Lewis, Roby P. Lewis, Jr., Roy R. Lewis, Wade McK. Lewis, Willard G. Lewis, Wm. P. Lewis, William W. Lewis, Willie A. Lefuers, Everett W. Liddle, Robert C. Little, Arnold R. Little, Billie T. Little, Broadus P. Little, Bruce J. Little, Charlie Little, Herman F. Little, James C. Little, James L. Little, John C. Little, Joseph G. Little, Leroy L. Little, Quinsen R. Little, Ralph W. Little, Raymond H. Little, Robert Blan Little, Robert Bruce Little, Thomas B. Little, Edgar W. Long, Elmer D. Long, James R. Long, Joseph H. Long, Sanford N. Lyall, Sidney E. Lyall, Vernon R. Lyall, Guy Lyle, Ralph C. Lyle, Tom C. Lyle, Thomas C. Lyle, Wm. E. Lyle, Jr., Guy W. Lyon.

Mc

Worth McClure, Jasper McCormick, Matthew McCormic, Walter T. McCoy, Raymond A. McCullough, Thos. J. McGinnis, John C. McGrady, Cledford McGuire, Howard B. McGuire, Julian S. McGuire, Walter S. McGuire, Andrew McMillan, John T. McMillan, Odell McMillan, Reeves C. McMillan, Russell C. McMillan, Thos. D. McMillan, Jr., Burl R. McNeill, Claude A. McNeill, Claude H. McNeill, Dean P. McNeill, Dempsie G. McNeill, Iron McNeill, James G. McNeill, Jones W. McNeill, Peter T. McNeill, Peter T. McNeill, Jr., Ralph R. McNeill, Robert D. McNeill, Robert F. McNeill, Robert G. McNeill (Obids), Robert G. McNeill (West Jefferson), Thos. McNeill, Thos. E. McNeill, Wm. Dean McNeill, William Doughton McNeill, Willard H. McNeill.

M

Robert G. Mahaffey, Russel Mahaffey, Charlie C. Mahala, Joseph W. Mahala, Leonard S. Mahala, Owen Mahala, John D. Maines, Ballard G. Marsh, Fred R. Marsh, Guy C. Marsh, Herbert W. Marsh, Ralph D. Marsh, Albert L. Martin, Joseph S. Martin, Delvert C. Marsh, Fred N. Marsh, Benjamin F. May, Geo. L. May, James B. May, Willard J. May, Gwyn H. Mayberry, Clifford Medley, Willard W. Medley, Winford T. Medley, Edwin A. Meeks, Leighton A. Meeks, Coy B. Mileal, Enoch R. Mileal, Jr., Jno. W. Mileal, Eugene Milam, Albert W. Miller, Alfred E. Miller, Allan Miller, Ardin G. Miller, Arlin Miller, Arnold

B. Miller, Avery H. Miller, Avery W. Miller, Benjamin D. Miller, Bill Miller, Bower B. Miller, Bryant F. Miller, Burl L. Miller, Burton R. Miller, Cameron E. Miller, Cameron M. Miller, Casie J. Miller, Cecil M. Miller, Charles S. Miller, Clarence D. Miller, Daniel C. Miller, Dean J. Miller, Don C. Miller, Earl F. Miller, Elmer G. Miller, Ford K. Miller, George R. Miller, George N. Miller, Gilbert A. Miller, Glenn Miller, Harry L. Miller, Howard D. Miller, Hunter W. Miller, Jack D. Miller, Jacob Miller, James R. Miller, Jesse W. Miller, Joe G. Miller, Joe H. Miller, Sr., John C. Miller, John D. Miller, John H. Miller (Othello), John H. Miller (Glendale Springs), John H. Miller (Warrensville).

John J. Miller, Joseph G. Miller, Joseph W. Miller, Kenneth B. Miller, Kilce Miller, Lawrence W. Miller, Leo G. Miller, Lee O. Miller, Leonard G. Miller, Lester Miller, Lonford R. Miller, Luther E. Miller, Max G. Miller, Milt H. Miller, Milt J. Miller, Monroe B. Miller, Odell Miller, Patton Miller, Paul A. Miller, Paul E. Miller, Paul F. Miller, Powell Miller, R. C. Miller, Ralph E. Miller, Rash Miller, Ray Miller, Ressel K. Miller, Robert C. Miller, Robert P. Miller, Roger F. Miller, Roy F. Miller, Russell Miller, Russell E. Miller, Robert D. Miller, Thurman G. Miller, Jr., Tom Miller, Walker B. Miller, Walter C. Miller, Walter T. Miller, Wayne Miller, Wm. D. Miller, William G. Miller, Wm. S. Miller, Samuel C. Misher, James L. Mitchell, Jesse J. Moretz, Lee J. Moretz, Lester Moretz, Bruce D. Mullis, Davis W. Mullis, Ernest D. Mullis, Edward Mullis, Robert H. Mullis, Roby B. Mullis, Starrett W. Mullis, Wm. C. Mullis, Sr., Wm. F. Mullis, Winford A. Mullis, Chas. E. Munday, Dan B. Munday, Jno. R. Munday, Noah J. Myers, Robt. F. Myers, Sherman W. Myers, Wm. E. Myers.

N

Quincy R. Neal, Joseph Gwyn Neal, Albert L. Neaves, Fred H. Neaves, Jones A. Neaves, Arlin J. Nelson, Carroll C. Nelson, James W. Nichols, Vaugh J. Nichols, Claude H. Norris, Edgar F. Norris, Guavin T. Norris, Robert G. Norris, Walter A. Nye.

O

Bower R. Oliver, Carl E. Oliver, Dave L. Oliver, Earl Oliver, Isaac G. Oliver, Lester W. Oliver, Robert S. Oliver, Ambrose J. Osborne, Arthur J. Osborne, Boyd D. Oliver, Charles F. Osborne, Dwight Osborne, Eula Osborne, Fred B. Osborne, Fred J. Osborne, Golden Osborne, Graves C. Osborne, Hamp V. Osborne, Harlie Osborne, Henry W. Osborne, Herman E. Osborne, Hugh W. Osborne, James H. Osborne, James W. Osborne, John H. Osborne, John R. Osborne, Joseph G. Osborne, Junior A. Osborne, Marvin E. Osborne, Norman J. Osborne, Oscar O. Osborne, Ray A. Osborne, Ray W. Osborne,

Raymond B. Osborne, Reggie R. Osborne, Robert Osborne, Robert H. Osborne, Robert T. Osborne, Spencer C. Osborne, Tivis S. Osborne, Victor W. Osborne, Walter H. Osborne, Wm. C. Osborne, Gilbert G. Owen, Glen R. Owen, Pozy L. Owen, Glenn R. Owens, Joseph E. Owens, Sr., Lance Owens.

P

Lida W. Paisley, Ben F. Parker, Clive W. Parker, Dennis Parker, Charles E. Parsons, Jr., Clyde E. Parsons, Fred H. Parsons, Henry F. Parsons, Irvin M. Parsons, James F. Parsons, John L. Parsons, James W. Parsons, Paul B. Parsons, Wiley B. Parsons, Wm. B. Parsons, Arthur F. Pasley, Jr., Gilmer W. Pasley, Harold D. Pasley, Isaac W. Pasley, Arthur F. Patrick, Charles E. Patrick, Wm. A. Patton, Buford W. Pendry, Clifford F. Pendry, Charles B. Pennington, Dayton G. Pennington, Gentry Pennington, Geo. W. Pennington, Jesse H. Pennington, John M. Pennington, Paul W. Pennington, Preston W. Pennington, Robert B. Pennington, Willie F. Pennington, Woodrow G. Pennington, Dan T. Perkins, Marshall V. Perkins, Monroe C. Perkins, Raymond C. Perkins, Roscoe C. Perkins, Thomas F. Perkins, Clarence H. Perry, Claude M. Perry, Lassie E. Perry, Ralph L. Perry, Willard E. Perry, Fielden D. Petty, Donald F. Pierce, John C. Pierce, Jr., Maness L. Pharr, Alfred Phillips, Arley Phillips, Cleveland W. Phillips, Dewey S. Phillips, Foster A. Phillips, Grady R. Phillips, Henry F. Phillips, Ray Phillips, Richard B. Phillips, Stanford S. Phillips, Thomas T. Phillips, Walter E. Phillips, Willard G. Phillips, Wm. H. Phillips, W. J. Bryan Phillips, Charles E. Phipps, Ronda Powers, Thos. J. Powers, Jr., Warren G. Powers, Audie L. Presnell, Jr., Cecil B. Price, Clalley C. Price, Elmer Price, Fearey V. Price, Fred R. Price, James E. Price, Joe Price, Joe G. Price, Thomas G. Price, Hansel H. Pruitt, Andrew J. Pugh, Cecil D. Pugh, Robt. L. Pugh, Roger Pugh, Wm. O. Pugh.

Q

Horatio D. Quessenberry.

R

Jennings B. Rader, Dennis W. Rash, Fred L. Rash, Henry F. Rash, James O. Rash, John R. Rash, Paul W. Rash, Thos. E. Rash, Jesse R. Ray, Thos. B. Ray, Blane F. Reese, Thos. W. Reed, Thos. L. Reedy, Glen Reeves, George H. Reeves, Wilber W. Reeves, James E. Rhodes, James W. Rhodes, Bert Richardson, Cecil W. Richardson, Edward B. Richardson, Everett Richardson, Ferd T. Richardson, Fred W. Richardson, James W. Richardson, James N. Richardson, Joseph C. Richardson, Marvin M. Richardson, Wm. A. Richardson, Glenn S. Riddle, John R. Riddle, Charles R. Riley, Howard R. Riley, Jno. W. Riley, Edsill Ring, Loyd N. Ring, Bruce W. Roark, Clarence L. Roark, Clyburn E. Roark, Delmer H. Roark, Emerson Z. Roark, Estel L. Roark, Ferry R. Roark, Ford A. Roark, French T. Roark, Harold P. Roark, Hildred J. Roark, Howard D. Roark, Kenneth E. Roark, Ralph J. Roark, Raymond J. Roark, Roger Roark, Sylvester R. Roark, Herman C. Roberts, James H. Roberts, Clarence O. Roberson, Denver D. Robinson, Arthur C. Roland, Edwin F. Roland, Kenneth A. Roland, Millard F. Roland, Roy E. Roland, Warren Roup, Harley H. Ross, Braner B. Roten, Beauford Roten, Buel E. Roten, Charlie T. Roten, David G. Roten, Henry Roten, James C. Roten, Johnie F. Roten, Lester H. Roten, Lilliard H. Roten, Millard W. Roten, Montgomery Roten, Roy L. Roten, Vance Roten, Wm. E. Roten, Claude S. Roupe, Jack R. Roupe, Victor A. Roupe, Victor A. Royal, Wm. T. Rupard, James G. Russ, Clifford C. Rutherford, Marion S. Rutherford, Walter R. Rutherford.

S

Gene L. Salsbery, Vernon Sanders, Howard J. Scott, James E. Scott, Glenn E. Sills, Albert Severt, Archie F. Severt, Avery E. Severt, Bland B. Severt, Bower K. Severt, Branson D. Severt, Charlie H. Severt, Charlie Severt, Charles R. Severt, Earl D. Severt, Earl W. Severt, George Severt, George A. Severt, Jesse L. Severt, Leonard J. Severt, Lonie C. Severt, Robt. L. Severt, Robert W. Severt, Thomas H. Severt, Earl Seton, Howard S. Sexton, James G. Sexton, Kermit T. Sexton, Richard W. Sexton, Thomas D. Sexton, Worth A. Sexton, Charles B. G. Sharpe, Athur R. Shatley, Carroll D. Shatley, Clarence M. Shatley, Guy T. Shatley, Henry M. Shatley, Ovid O. Shatley, Walter C. Shatley, Bryes F. Sheets, Carl D. Sheets, Charles N. Sheets, Claude A. Sheets, Edward E. Sheets, Garfield H. Sheets, Gordon D. Sheets, Herbert T. Sheets, James C. Sheets, John W. Sheets, Larry Sheets, Milton Sheets, Oscar C. Sheets, Paul G. Sheets, Richard F. Sheets, Rudd Q. Sheets, Urcle M. Sheets, Wade G. Sheets.

Bonney G. Shepherd, Darrel G. Shepherd, Elmer E. Shepherd, Elmer L. Shepherd, Everett L. Shepherd, Glenn H. Shepherd, James W. Shepherd, Leonard H. Shepherd, Mont F. Shepherd, Norman Shepherd, Roger A. Shephard, Roscoe R. Shepherd, Verna R. Shepherd, Wm. D. Shepherd, John T. Shoaf, Robert C. Shoaf, Franklin S. Shoemake, Leonard K. Shoemaker, Lloyd A. Shoemaker, Robert B. Shoemaker, Bower Shumate, Ethern Shumate, Lawson Shumate, Mack Shumate, Ralph G. Sluder, Geo. C. Smith, Ray M. Smith, James L. Smithey, Cecil W. Snyder, Wm. H. South, Robt. H. Spaulding, Gaither A. Speaks, Jno. Speaks, Wm. B. Speaks, Austin O. Spencer, Clarence W. Spencer, Fred L. Spencer, Joe B. Spencer, John T. Spencer, Joseph C. Spencer, Kyle E. Spencer, Reeves I. Spencer, Robert Spencer, Roy W.

Spencer, Russell V. Spencer, Joseph C. Spieer, Sr., Samuel L. Staley, John W. Stamper, Wm. B. Stamper, Worth T. Stamper, Donald E. Stanley, Howard G. Stanley, Thomas B. Stanley, Thomas W. Stanley, Emmett J. Stansberry, Gwyn H. Stansberry, Howard E. Stansberry, Hunter Stansberry, John S. Stansberry, Langdon R. Stansberry, Wm. L. Stansberry, Carl H. Stark, Jr., Odell Starnes, Don N. Stevens, Veemer G. Stewart, John H. Stewart, Phil A. Stewart, Verna W. Stiddam, Worth E. Stike, Conley L. Stout, Stanley B. Stout, Grover W. Stringer, Harold Stringer, Walter H. Stringer, James M. Stump, Robert L. Stump, Reid Sturdivant, Ezra B. Sturgill, Joe Sturgill, John Sturgill, Dee C. Sullivan, Ora A. Sullivan, John D. Sutherland.

T

Breakfield Taylor, J. C. Taylor, Ray C. Taylor, Robert G. Taylor, Wiley B. Taylor, Wm. M. Taylor, Leonard Teaster, Wm. H. Teaster, Orlie L. Tedder, David Testerman, Earl W. Testerman, Edison C. Testerman, Elwood R. Testerman, Harding W. Testerman, Henry F. Testerman, Jesse K. Testerman, Joseph T. Testerman, Ralph E. Testerman, Wayne Testerman, Ray Thomas, Alvah B. Thompson, James L. Thompson, Joseph R. Thompson, Ralph L. Thompson, Calvin E. Toliver, Jr., Charles A. Toliver, Jr., Lessel L. Toliver, Carl E. Toliver, Harry W. Tribble, Archie R. Tripplett, Clemon Trivett, Fred O. Trivett, Leonard Trivett, Riley Trivett, Willard R. Trivett, Mack A. Trivette, Melvin Trivette, Wm. H. Tucker, Aldon J. Turner, Quincy T. Turner, Van J. Turner, Walter J. Turner.

V

James L. Vannoy, James R. Vannoy, Raymond K. Vannoy, Wm. F. Vannoy, Winfred L. Vannoy, Elmer A. Vanover, Fred E. Vanover, Thomas E. Vaught, Eugene Viero, Rex Viero, Willard Viero, Paul A. Vineyard, Richard H. Vineyard.

W

Burl G. Waddell, Dale C. Waddell, Doras C. Waddell, Norman W. Waddell, Roger B. Waddell, Charles L. Wagg, Clabon Wagoner, Wm. I. Wagoner, Arthur B. Walker, Darwin H. Walker, Edwin Walker, Jasper C. Walker, Stanley R. Walker, Dale Wallace, Wayne J. Wallace, Charles H. Walters, Sr., Herbert O. Walters, James B. Walters, James D. Walters, Wm. E. Walters, Henry M. Walton, Joe A. Warren, Jones O. Watson, David K. Waugh, Fred L. Waugh, Joe T. Waugh, Ambrose R. Weaver, Boyd B. Weaver, Charles B. Weaver, Charles F. Weaver, Clarence E. Weaver, Clayton D. Weaver, George C. Weaver, James E. Weaver, James O. Weaver, John Weaver, John A. Weaver, Jr., Joseph E. Weaver, Lester S. Weaver, Montie M. Weaver, Ned Weaver, Reave D. Weaver, Reggie E. Weaver, Richard J. Weaver,

Roby J. Weaver, Roy R. Weaver, Thomas R. Weaver, Wayne D. Weaver, Robert C. Webster, Charles E. Welch, Jr., Joseph F. Welch, Wm. H. Welch, George F. Welch, Quincy M. West, Earl R. Wheatley, Gordon C. Whitener, Benny H. Wilcox, Charles S. Wilcox, Steward J. Wilcox, Wm. C. Wilcox,Wm. L. Wilcox, Clifford W. Wilder.

Albert K. Williams, Doctor J. Williams, Fred E. Williams, Glen W. Williams, James U. Williams, Joe H. Williams, Thomas B. Williams, Wade J. Williams, Wayne H. Williams, Wm. B. Williams, Wallace Willien, Ernest G. Wilson, John C. Wilson, Paul L. Wilson, Thomas W. Wilson, Earl W. Winebarger, Evans B. Winebarger, Worth J. Winebarger, Edison Wingler, Monroe Wingler, John C. Wetherspoon, Larken L. Wetherspoon, Lucius C. Witherspoon, Wade H. Witherspoon, William W. Witherspoon, John H. Wolfe, Ray McK. Wolfe, Robert S. Wolfe, Cecil E. Wood, Charles T. Wood, George H. Wood, Herman B. Wood, Hoyt H. Wood, James W. Wood, Marion W. Wood, Norman L. Wood, Richard R. Wood, Ulysses S. Woodard, Bower J. Woodie, Bryce L. Woodie, Carl L. Woodie, Clarence C. Woodie, Demma J. Woodie, Edward H. Woodie, Frank G. Woodie, Richard E. Woodie, Rixie B. Woodie, Walter R. Woodie, Worth G. Woodie, John T. Woodruff, Eugene Woods, Alfred L. Worley, General G. Worley, James R. Worley, Samuel T. Worley, Sr., Theodore A. Worley, Allen Worth, Joseph P. Worth, Will A. Worth, Banner Wyatt, Donald S. Wyatt, Lester Wyatt, Martin L. Wyatt, Paul Wyatt, Roy H. Wyatt, Thomas E. Wyatt, Thomas N. Wyatt, Von R. Wyatt, Walter R. Wyatt, Clarence Wyrick, Clifford A. Wyrick, Daniel W. Wyrick, Wm. J. Wyrick

Y

Phillip H. Yarborough, Con Yates, James V. Yates, Rufus G. Yates, Wm. S. Yates, Howard B. Yearick, John H. Yearick, Walter W. Younce, Armond D. Young, Edwin B. Young, Stanley I. Young.

APPENDIX IV

LAND ENTRIES IN ASHE COUNTY BEGINNING MARCH 4, 1778.

Hon. Johnson J. Hayes, famous Federal Judge, born and reared in Wilkes County, upon his recent semi-retirement from the Federal bench, at the request of many citizens of his native county undertook the writing of a history of Wilkes County. It was published recently under the title, *The Land of Wilkes*, and a splendid piece of work it is. The book comprises 577 pages and is profusely illustrated. It should be interesting reading to citizens of Ashe because Wilkes was Ashe's mother county. Wilkes was formed from Surry County and Washington District in 1772 and it took in the northwestern corner of the State of North Carolina and on west indefinitely. Ashe was the first slice off of Wilkes and embraced all of Wilkes west of the crest of the Blue Ridge Mountains.

Judge Hayes thought it worthwhile to check the land entry records of Wilkes to secure accurate locations of the early settlers of Wilkes and in Appendix A of his book will be found the "Land Entries in Wilkes County, beginning March 4, 1778." Judge Hayes has authorized the publication here of those parts of the Appendix connected with Ashe County of today. For that kindness the writer is duly grateful.

The record of grants and entries does not go back before 1778 because prior to 1778 title to the lands in question was in the Earl of Granville. In 1778 the lands of British subjects were confiscated and became the property of the State and there was a great rush on the part of property-holders to secure grants from the State and list them under the state law.

Says Judge Hayes:

"For convenience, I present these entries by counties as they exist in 1958, although all of it was Wilkes at that time (1778). After each name, in parentheses, will be the number of his entry. If you want the details of the entry you can give the number to the Register of Deeds of Wilkes County and get a copy of the entire entry."

Judge Hayes then proceeds to list the entries for Alleghany County, later to be cut off from Ashe (1859); for Watauga County, cut off from Ashe in 1849; and for present-day Ashe as follows:

Alleghany County

On the waters of Little River: Chas. Morgan (52 and 53); Martin Gambill (117) (866 and 867); Moses Woodruff (288); William Gambill (398) on no headed branch; William Hardin (518) on Crab Fork and (803); William Lenoir (697) and (837); Jonathan Hughes (717); John Allen Woodruff (780) on east end of Bullhead Mountain; Clesby Cobb (827) (839) and (926); Jonathan Haines (835); Jacob Mainard (849); Young Edwards (850); Benjamin Herndon (852) where Ambrose Hammon had a claim and (924); Wm. Connelly (856); Ambrose Hammon (859) on a ridge near Mades Knob where the said Ambrose Hammon now lives; Thomas Endicott (860); Micajah Pennington (899); Moses Woodruff (1164); Richardson Owens (1441); James Fletcher (1469); Francis Bryan (1613); Andrew Canady (1614) and (1655); Charles Cate (1709); Bradshaw Harden (1736); Thomas Ayers (Yairs) (1741); Daniel Sutherland (1742); Benjamin Rose (1771); Benj. Morgan (1866); James Hampton (1912); Daniel Hoppers (1921).

On Elk Creek and Prathers Creek: Beverly Watkins (708); Enoch Osborne (367) (903) (1726 and 1728); Barnabas Evans (921); William Maxwell (1785); Theophilas Evans (1787); James Mulkey (943); George Morris (938 and 939) on Prathers Creek.

On New River: Moses Tolliver (966); George Gibson (967); William Sturdie (1496) and (1744) on south side of the enchanted ridge near Prathers Creek, a branch of New River; Daniel Richardson (1748).

On Bledsoe Creek: Hanry Gambill (399).

On Peach Bottom Mountain or at foot of it: Jonathan Haines (864) and William Nall (865); John Carrol (1654); Benj. Morgan (1936) and (1937) Peach Bottom and Cranberry.

Watauga County

South Fork of New River—including three forks: Christopher Mainard (60), at lower end of a great glade called Three Forks; John Ayers (80) on Flannery Fork; Daniel Yarnell (81) on Barton's Fork; John Green (89) at mouth of Howard's Creek; James Tompkins (90) at Buckeye Island; Benj. Cuthberth (216) at mouth of Flannery's Creek and (1525) on Deep Gap Creek; Jesse Council (539), (699), (1073); Andrew Baird (794); Rowland Judd (1123) near the fire spring and including good land on each side the path that leads from Tim Perkins' (near mouth of Gap Creek) to Cuthberth Cabin on top of the mountain at head of Lewis Fork; Garret Hendrick (1270) top of Blue Ridge including head waters of New River and (1271) on Chestnut Knob; William McLain and Andrew Baker (1314) head waters of Beaver Dam of New River.

Howard's Creek: Zebulon Beard (227) at the head of Howard's Creek. Zebulon Baird sold to James Brown, Feb. 9, 1793, 300 acres on the head of Howard's Creek (Watauga) recorded in Book B-1 292. Ebeneezer Fairchilds (541); James Brown (1042) between head of Howard's Creek and Meat Camp Creek; James Brown Sr. sold to Ebeneezer Fairchild on July 26, 1796, 300 acres on Howard's Creek Book D pg. 5. Robert Ayers (1045) in same area. Memucan Hunt (1532) on the path that goes from Camp Creek to the head of a fork of Cove Creek, and Samuel Simpson (1773) including a small clearing made by Chas. William.

Deep Gap and Pine Swamp creeks: Thos. Gilbert (1877) on Pine Swamp Creek (1876) on Deep Gap Creek.

On Blue Ridge: Thomas Cotrell (375) at head of Buffalo; Daniel Eggers (229) between the head of Elk and New River.

Meat Camp Creek: William Snoddy (792) including an old camp and forks of said creek, and William Miller (1093) beginning at John Brown's line; (959) lying on ridge north side of Elk Path that leads to Three Forks.

Ashe County

On south fork of New River: George Morris (2) beginning at the mouth of a branch on the north side of the New River below Wm. Ray's mill, and (160) adjoining above entry; William Ray (5) at fork of Dog Creek; William Humphries (9) at fork of Naked Creek joining south side of George Morris', being the land he now lives on; Timothy Perkins (55) which includes the mouth of Gap Creek, the Old Fields and improvements whereon Timothy Perkins and Royal Porter then lived and the one bought of Samuel McQueen; John Johnson (105) near mouth of Roans Creek; Samuel Wilcoxen (126) three miles above the Old Fields; William Sperry (127) adjoining (126); William Nall (146) at the "bent" of the river above the mouth of Peak Creek; Matthew Sparks (163) on little Naked Creek; Isiah Cass near the head of Pine Swamp on the path that leads from Spaneyards to the Old Fields; William McLane McLane (McLain) (187) head of Crab Creek of Beaver Creek and was formerly Samuel Ray's claim; Benj. Cleveland (248) at Nathaniel Judd's Camp on Beaver Creek (701) around mouth of Cranberry, including improvements where Micajah Bunch and

Jonathan Smith now live; James Hampton (249) above mouth of Old Fields; Aaron Mash (250) on Deep Gap Creek 3 miles above its mouth; also (258) on main ridge on headwaters of Roan's Creek and Reddies River; William Fletcher (281) on Old Fields Creek; Benj. Herndon (287) on Cranberry near lower end of Elk Hill; Samuel McQueen (335) near mouth of Mill Creek, including old Baker Camp; William McNeill (337) including Nall's improvement; David Smith (376) above mouth of Nathan's Creek; John Cox (377) known by the name of Roundabout on south side of Cranberry, also (1272) and (1495); Andrew Baker (476) on both sides of Naked Creek; Nathaniel Vannoy (492) on Beaver Creek adjoining Wm. Colvard's; George Reaves (517) (613); Christian Birkhead (565) on Beaver Creek; William Colvard (575) beginning near mouth of Sugar Tree branch that empties into Beaver Creek; Morris Baker (616) where he now lives, (937) between Peak Creek and Cranberry Creek; George Morris (634) at mouth of Dog Creek; Jonathan Courtney (658) adjoining George Morris'; Benjamin Right (Wright) (686) including Joseph and Benjamin Taylor improvements; Martin Gambill (702) and (1081) including improvements where Vincent Jones lives; Henry Harden (703) including improvements made by Reubin Stringer and Samuel Collins; James Mulkey (706) adjoining Daniel Richardson, where said Mulkey now lives; Thomas Payne (711) and (713) on Obids Creek (907) Peak Creek; John Johnston (720) in and about the fork of Naked Creek, adjoining Matthew Sparks, including the great Crab orchard; Benjamin Cleveland (729) on both sides of Bakers Road on waters of Cranberry Creek, including improvements where Thomas Little and Joseph Massey formerly lived; John Church (731) and (783) on little fork of Pine Swamp, waters of New River where he now lives; Benjamin Herndon (737) on Dog Creek, beginning near the Rattlesnake Den, including the old cabins that formerly belonged to George Collins and William Howell; Henry Chambers (738) below three forks adjoining Benj. Cleveland's survey at the horse ford; Spillsbery Tribble (759) on Obids Creek; Joseph Ayers (760) above mouth of Howard's Creek; Samuel McQueen (784) near mouth of Pine Swamp branch; Samuel Simpson (819) and (1130) top of Blue Ridge down Peak Creek; John Dick (942) on waters of Beaver Creek; Conrad Dick (868) on south side of Roans Creek adjoining Robert Baker's; John Baker (886) on Roan's Creek (1458) on Peak Creek; (1700) opposite Hugh Smith plantation; James Baker (936) head waters of Naked Creek; also (1283) between Peak Creek and Cranberry; and (1366) on Cranberry; Daniel Johnson (961); John Johston (1096) at mouth of Roan's Creek; Francis Vannoy (1019 and 1020) on Sugar Tree branch above Wm. Colvard's and (1020) on South Beaver Creek beginning at the Path that goes from Wm. Colvard's to Old Fields; Christopher Shan or Shown (1059) at head of Naked Creek, including rich cove at the northern end of Negro Mountain; John Vickers (1085) above mouth of Beaver Creek; Thomas Calloway (1155) including the rich bottom; George Morris, Jr. (1158); Daniel Vannoy (1248) on south Beaver Creek; William Nall (1281) and (1282) Cranberry and New River, and (1668) on Peak Creek including the Mill Seat; John Younce (1284) near mouth of Peak Creek; Barnet Owens (1296) on Obids Creek; Daniel Yarnel (1382) bought of Abner Smalley; Robert Nall on Obids Creek lying near the main road and down both sides of the branch that "Owens Camp is at."

James Fletcher (1434) near the road from Squire Morris' to Pennington's mill, including some headwaters of Silas Branch and Dog Creek; Christian Burkett (1459) including Slippery Shore bottom; Justice Bolin (1467) below Elk Shoals island.

All the foregoing entries were made before January 1, 1780. The following are from January 1, 1780:

Thomas Terry (1468) on Beaver Creek; John Johnson (1521 and 1522) Obids Creek adjoining John Brown; Peter Whitaker (1653) on road from mouth of Cranberry to Cox's settlement on Fighting Creek; Andrew Baker (1702), (1701) and (1707) on path from Naked Creek to Geo. Morris' at head of Three Forks and last tract on Roan's Creek, and (1068) on Buffalo; Peter Eller (1703) on Roan's Creek; William Wright (1743) above mouth of Beaver Creek; Thomas Gibson (1858) on Obids Creek waters; Closs Thompson Jr. (1859) on Beaver Creek; Devalt Pouts (1896) on Muddy Branch that empties into Beaver Creek below John Baker's Pounding Mill; Rowland Judd (1923) on Naked Creek; William Chapman (1924) on Naked Creek.

On North Fork of New River and its tributaries: Abel Pennington (3) where he lived but transferred by order of court to Enoch Osborne and by him to Gideon Lewis; William McLain (29) at lower end of Rich Bent of North Fork; William McLain (30) at mouth of Three Top where he now lives; William McLain (273 and 274) at Sycamore Ford and where the Path North Fork to Roan's Creek crosses North Fork; William McLain (900) on Helton; Joshua Neaves (31) including Hickory bottom; James Ward (148) above mouth of Fennick Creek; Isaac Weaver (222) beginning at the Ford below the mouth of Skeggs Creek, also (275) at Sycamore Ford, also (1896) on Helton Creek; Paul Henson (331) just above Horse Creek including plantation where Richard Smith lived; Zachariah Wells (368) at mouth of Boundary Branch between his and Micajah Pennington's land; Micajah Pennington (370) on both sides of New River below mouth of a branch, also (1152) above Zack Wells, beginning on his line and runs up the

River, also (1157) at mouth of Silas Creek, also (1661) at mouth of Old Fields Creek.

Benajah Pennington (371) on Grassy Creek at the Ground Hog den below *his mill*, and running up said creek on both sides, (1086) on Martin's Branch where William Spencer lives, and (1088) above Mr. Weaver's; George Baker (395) on Buffalo and Paddy Knob and Three Top Mountain including Baker's Camp; William Adkins (695) on both sides of the river below the improvement on which James Ward lives; Stephen Reed (696) beginning on Gideon Lewis' line and including the improvements where Edward King and Charles Little live, and (833) at mouth of Laurel Fork; William Lenoir (698) on Grassy Creek, including improvement where Joshua Yates and Benajah Pennington, Jr. now live, (1056) on both sides of Buffalo Creek and on the Path from Baker's settlement to Three Top Mountain; William Huff (707) on both sides of Helton below improvement where Benjamin Pennington formerly lived; Thomas Payne (714) on Helton, including where Mark Foster lives; Aaron Mash (728) on Buffalo; John Henson (747) at the mouth of Buffalo, including the improvement where he lives, also (1088) lying between old William Henson and his sons; Jiles (Giles) Parmely (935) on Buffalo, including Paul Patrick's improvement; John Brown (982) on head waters of North Fork on top of Rich Mountain on south side of the road that leads from New River to Roan's Creek, also (983) beginning at Washington County line; J. P. Fletcher (1087) on Grassy Creek below old William Pennington's mill seat, but including it; Charles Rowland (1135) on branches of Grassy Creek, including improvements by Martin Mains and Joshua Yates; Elijah Vickers (1218) on Pond Mountain; James Sparks (1295) on ridge between Beaver Creek and Buffalo; James Tompkins (1299) on Rich Mountain and partly between Green Bald and the Pinacle mountain; Elisha Baldwin (1352) on Helton Creek; James Ward (1398) on Beaver dam of Horse Creek; James Ward (1399) on Silas Creek above the forks; James Ward (1400) on North Fork; Joseph Herndon (1405) on Horse Creek known by the name of Old Fields, including where William Smith now lives; Richard Allen (1406) on North Fork joining my line at Cow Camp; Solomon Baker (1410) head waters of Horse Creek and on Pond Mountain; Reuben Wood (1429) on head waters of Horse Creek, Dec. 23, 1779, on the dividing ridge between the head of Little Horse Creek and some of Laurel Fork and known as Nall's Elk Garden, including said garden.

Enoch Osborne (1657) adjoining George Reaves below Rock Creek, also (1658) beginning at Micajah Pennington's line on Elk Creek (This is probably over in the northwestern end of what is now

Alleghany County); Levey Pennington (1660); George Morris (1670) on Grassy Creek; Abraham May (1682) beginning at the horse ford below the mouth of Horse Creek; Gideon Lewis (1682) on Horse Creek, beginning at Capt. Osborn's line.

David and John Witherspoon conveyed to William Brown Esq. (July 25, 1794) (B-1 471) 300 acres on the south fork of New River on Lynch's mill creek; Ezekiel England conveyed to William Brown (Sept. 23, 1794) (D 81) 150 acres on the north side of New River; William Brown had a grant (D 703) for 50 acres on the waters of New River; there was a grant to John Brown, Richard Allen and Francis Reynolds (D 803) for 450 acres on the north fork of New River.

About the Author

(See the photograph of Colonel Fletcher facing page 33)

Arthur Lloyd Fletcher, eldest of the nine children of the Rev. James Floyd Fletcher and Mrs. Louisa (Barker) Fletcher, was born July 7, 1881, on the banks of New River, near the mouth of Phoenix Creek, in Ashe County. He began his working life as a public school teacher, but in 1901 entered Wake Forest College to prepare for the legal profession. Graduating in 1907 (his attendance was intermittent because he had to work his way) with an A.B. degree awarded *magna cum laude*, he gained admittance to the Bar that same year.

His career in the practice of law was brief, however; he gave it up in 1908 to become city editor of the *Raleigh Evening Times* and for the next twelve years held editorial and reportorial posts on half a dozen North Carolina newspapers.

A second attempt to enter the private practice of law, this time at Raleigh in association with his brother, A. J. Fletcher, was interrupted almost immediately when he was called to duty with the North Carolina National Guard in 1916 for service on the Mexican border and, later, as a captain of field artillery, A.E.F., in World War I. Following the war, he continued in the National Guard in various capacities and was promoted to major and finally lieutenant colonel.

Colonel Fletcher did not return to the legal profession after 1916, except in the field of administrative law. He became attorney for the income tax division of the North Carolina Department of Revenue, later moved up to chief of the division, and then served for twelve years as chief deputy of the North Carolina Insurance Department.

In 1932 he won election as North Carolina Commissioner of Labor, and was re-elected in 1936. In 1938 he resigned to accept a presidential appointment as Assistant Administrator, Wage and Hour Division, U.S. Department of Labor. He built the division from himself and one secretary into an organization of more than 1,800 people, covering every state in the Union, Hawaii and Alaska (at that time territories), and Puerto Rico. He left the Department of Labor when recalled by the Army for service in World War II.

Upon appointment by Governor J. Melville Broughton, Colonel Fletcher became chairman of the North Carolina Employment Security Commission after World War II and held that position until he reached retirement age. Then he moved over to the U.S. Veterans Administration and served five years as Readjustment Allowance Agent, a capacity in which he supervised the payment of some $96,500,000 to North Carolina veterans and their dependents.

In addition to his professional duties, Colonel Fletcher served as Commander of Raleigh Post No. 1, American Legion; Chef de Gare of the 40 & 8; charter member and president, Raleigh Lions Club; and director and president, Raleigh Y.M.C.A.

He was also the author of *History of the 113th Field Artillery, 30th Division* and a three-volume *History of the N.C. Department of the American Legion, 1919–1959*. He lived in Raleigh with his wife, the former Miss Mae Pitzer of Kernersville, whom he married November 1, 1905. They had no children. Colonel Fletcher died in January of 1966, a few years after this book was first published.

Index